Dictionary of Psychological Testing, Assessment and Treatment

Second Edition

Ian Stuart-Hamilton

Jessica Kingsley Publishers
London and Philadelphia

First edition published in 1995
Paperback edition published in 1996

This edition published in 2007
by Jessica Kingsley Publishers
116 Pentonville Road
London N1 9JB, UK
and
400 Market Street, Suite 400
Philadelphia, PA 19106, USA

www.jkp.com

Library of Congress Cataloging in Publication Data
Stuart-Hamilton, Ian.
    Dictionary of psychological testing, assessment, and treatment / Ian Stuart-Hamilton. -- 2nd ed.
    p. cm.
    ISBN-13: 978-1-84310-494-0 (pb : alk. paper) 1. Psychological tests--Dictionaries.
    2. Psychometrics--Dictionaries. 3. Psychotherapy--Dictionaries. I. Title.
    BF176.S78 2007
    150.28'7--dc22
                                                            2007004935

British Library Cataloguing in Publication Data
A CIP catalogue record for this book is available from the British Library

ISBN 978 1 84310 494 0

Printed and bound in Great Britain by
Athenaeum Press, Gateshead, Tyne and Wear

Dictionary of Psychological Testing, Assessment and Treatment

by the same author

The Psychology of Ageing
An Introduction
4th edition
ISBN 978 1 8431 0426 1

An Asperger Dictionary of Everyday Expressions
2nd edition
ISBN 978 1 84310 518 3

Dictionary of Cognitive Psychology
ISBN 978 1 85302 148 0

Dictionary of Developmental Psychology
ISBN 978 1 85302 146 6

Key Ideas in Psychology
ISBN 978 1 85302 359 0

To the present and future members of the

*Sunley Appreciation Society**

* Well, some of them, anyway…

Introduction to the First Edition

This dictionary is intended as a guide to the basic tools of the trade of psychology – namely, the commonly-used (and some of the less commonly-used) tests, experimental methods and analyses, and therapies. A quick glance through the book will show that some definitions get much lengthier definitions than others. I have intentionally pitched definitions at the likely readership. Thus, in writing the fairly basic definitions (e.g. of some statistical tests), I have assumed that the reader is a newcomer to the subject, and hence I have provided a greater depth of information. For definitions of more complex matters, the immediate definition is aimed at a reader with some background knowledge (although use of the cross-referencing allows a less experienced reader to retrace his or her steps for greater levels of explanation).

I have intentionally not included every test (statistical or psychological) known to humankind, because there simply wasn't room (unless there is genuinely a demand for compact dictionaries the size of the London A-Z telephone directory). When one considers that approximately 20,000 new tests are devised each year (most to be reported in one journal article and then never seen again), the reader will appreciate why I have chosen only those which appear to be most frequently mentioned in the literature. If I have inadvertently omitted a test which a reader feels I should have included, then if they write to me, I will be happy to consider it for inclusion in any future edition of this dictionary.

Many of the dictionary entries are cross-referenced. This has the advantage, that by judiciously using this facility, the reader should be able to gain at least an overview of the appropriate subject area. However, a caveat to this is needed. Dictionary definitions, no matter how lengthy, are intended solely as guides and primers – they are *not* a substitute for reading a textbook or journal article, which can provide a deeper, if less immediately accessible level of understanding than a dictionary can ever hope to do.

I finish with the traditional plea to dictionary readers to send me details of omitted definitions.

Dr Ian Stuart-Hamilton,
Principal Lecturer in Psychology,
Worcester College of Higher Education
1995

Introduction to the Paperback Edition

This new paperback edition gives me an opportunity to spruce up a few of the existing definitions and to add a few entries which slipped through the net. It also gives me the chance to respond to a couple of enquiries I received about the hardback edition of this text. First, it will not have escaped the reader's notice that there is no Bibliography in this book. Why is this so? This can be best explained in the following way: Q: why will someone be looking up a term or the name of a test in a dictionary? A: because they have read about the term or test in a book or article – *which will have a bibliography.* Not only would a list of references be superfluous, but it would also at least double the length of the book. The second point is that descriptions of some of the tests in this book are very brief. There are two reasons for this. The first is that usually all the information someone wants is what the test is assessing – details can be burdensome and will militate against understanding. The second reason is that this dictionary and its companion volumes are textbooks which are going to be readily available, inter alia, to the general public and undergraduates – in other words, not fully trained psychologists. Without being pompous about this, I feel a certain moral responsibility not to divulge lots of details of tests to the occasional reader who may be looking up a definition to see what sort of test they are about to be given or have been given during, for example, a clinical examination or selection procedure. Where tests are described in greater depth, it is because the details are already widely available in textbooks. If people want to know lots of details of tests, then they are welcome to consult the *Mental Measurements Yearbooks* – that is their purpose. However, if people want to understand the terms used in books such as the MMYs, then they may well need a dictionary such as this one – that is *its* purpose.

I would like to take this opportunity once again to thank the staff of Jessica Kingsley Publishers for their invaluable support in the preparation of these dictionaries, and to my wife for putting up with my behaviour whilst writing them.

Dr Ian Stuart-Hamilton,
Principal Lecturer in Psychology,
Worcester College of Higher Education
1996

Introduction to the Second Edition

Ten years have passed since the first edition of this dictionary appeared (though in the interim there has been a revised edition). For the new edition I have taken the opportunity to revise some of the existing definitions and add new ones. In total, about 10 per cent of the book is new.

As with the previous edition, I have intentionally only given the briefest of descriptions of tests. To quote from the introduction to the revised edition:

> if people want to know lots of details of tests, then they are welcome to consult the *Mental Measurements Yearbooks* – that is their purpose. However, if people want to understand the terms used in books such as the MMYs, then they may well need a dictionary such as this one – that is its purpose.

The intention of this book has always been to provide a reader stuck on a technical phrase in a book or journal paper with just enough information to allow them to carry on with their reading. No dictionary (unless it offers several paragraphs of information on each entry, in which case it's no longer a dictionary of course) can realistically hope to do more. For many readers (e.g. professionals and students from outside psychology) this may in any case be all they require or need to know. I have only tended to provide lengthier definitions when some technical background information is required to make any sense at all of the term in question. I have also intentionally restricted the number of entries on types of test in use. As noted in the introduction to the first edition, some 20,000 new tests are created each year, and there is no realistic chance of covering all of them in a compact space. All I can say is that I hope I have covered the frequently used tests.

In a similar vein, I have attempted to place pragmatic limits on entries on other topics. Thus, statistical terms used in typical university syllabuses are included, as are tests commonly available in computer packages and cited in psychology journals and similar publications. Measures rarely used in psychological research have tended to get rather shorter shrift. The same applies to therapies.

As usual, I shall be delighted to hear from readers. I must however offer an apology to several people who were kind enough to write in with suggestions for new definitions and amendments after the first edition was published. I faithfully kept a copy of this correspondence with the intention of incorporating it into the next edition. However, over the last decade I have moved houses twice and indeed changed not only offices but universities. Somewhere along the line, the correspondence was lost. All I can do is to say sorry – an author never willingly tries to antagonize their readers!

Professor Ian Stuart-Hamilton,
Faculty Head of Research and External Activity,
University of Glamorgan
2007

Guide to Use

Cross-references are in italics. Four caveats are required, arising from a desire to avoid unnecessary repetition or superfluous entries and definitions.

(1) Very occasionally, italicized words' entries are in a slightly different grammatical inflexion (e.g. *feral children* may actually be entered as **feral child**). In addition, I have deliberately not included every spelling variant or semantic permutation (e.g. 'water therapy' would not be included if 'water treatment' already had an entry) unless there is a danger of misunderstanding.

(2) Within a definition, an italicized word in bold type (e.g. ***definition*** rather than definition) indicates that the term is fully defined within the entry being read. The word's own entry will simply refer the reader back to this definition.

(3) An entry followed only by a word or phrase in italics indicates a synonym, which should be consulted for the full definition. It should not be supposed that the main entry necessarily denotes the best phrase – in many instances, use of terms is a matter of personal taste.

(4) Words linked by a hyphen are treated as if there is a space between them, and numbers are entered as if they were given their full spelling.

There are relatively few inverted headings – entries are usually given the word order they have in normal text. Therefore, if the reader looks up 'deep play', he or she finds **deep play**, not an irritating note to see *play, deep*. If the reader should be aware of related terms, then a cross-reference is provided. Where an inverted heading has been used, it is for clear logical reasons. On rare occasions, the reader may be sent on a trip through two or three definitions before gaining the information he or she wants. I apologize in advance, but assure the reader that using other methods, these occasions would be more frequent.

A

A *agreeableness.*

a- As a prefix in descriptions of disability see *dys-*.

a posteriori test *post hoc test.*

a priori test Any method of assessing a *planned comparison*. See *post hoc test*.

a priori validity Whether, by the 'laws' of common sense, a test will measure what it claims.

A scale A measure of ability to accept ambiguity.

A-state *state anxiety.*

A-trait *trait anxiety.*

A-S scale A measure of strength of anti-Semitic opinions.

A-type personality *Type A personality.*

AA *Alcoholics Anonymous.*

AAD *Academic Achievement Discrepancy.*

AAI *acute alcoholic intoxication.*

AAMD *American Association for Mental Deficiency.*

AAMD Adaptive Behaviour Scale Adaptive Behaviour Scale.

AAMI *age associated memory impairment.*

AAT *Achievement Anxiety Test.*

AATP *Alcohol Assessment and Treatment Profile.*

AB design Shorthand for the stages in an experimental design. 'AB' denotes that there are two separate phases. The shorthand can of course be applied to other designs. E.g. 'ABC' indicates 3 separate stages.

ABA design Experimental design in which the first stage of the experiment is followed by a second stage before the first stage is repeated. The method is often used to assess the effect of a treatment. E.g. A=measure of behaviour (e.g. biting nurses); B=therapeutic intervention (e.g. course of therapy).

abasia A *somatoform disorder* in which the patient is unable to walk.

Abbe criterion Measure of level of randomness in a series of events occurring over time.

ABC *Movement Assessment Battery for Children.*

ABC approach The study of a behaviour (B) in terms of its antecedents (A) and its effects (C). The model is particularly used in *rational-emotive therapy* and *behaviour therapy*.

abducens cranial nerve *cranial nerve* number VI. Concerned with the eye muscles. Compare with *trochlear cranial nerve* and *oculomotor cranial nerve*.

abduction Explaining what is known.

ability grouping Group of subjects united by having a similar level of ability on a particular measure.

ability test The term is a confusing one – some researchers use it synonymously with *achievement test*, others with *aptitude test*. Since the everyday use of the word 'ability' is similarly ambiguous, it is a term best avoided.

ablation surgical removal.

abreaction A release of emotion. Usually the term denotes such a release during a therapeutic session which has tapped the root of an underlying problem. A feeling of *catharsis* may accompany it.

ABS *Adaptive Behaviour Scale.*

ABS-SE *Adaptive Behaviour Scale – School Edition.*

abscissa *X axis.*

absolute deviation The size of the difference (ignoring the plus or minus sign) between a particular value and a value being used as a point of reference.

absolute difference The size of the difference (ignoring the plus or minus sign) between two variables.

absolute error See *true scores theory.*

absolute frequency The number of times an event actually occurs (as opposed to e.g. the proportion of times on which it occurs relative to other events).

absolute rating Rating made without comparison with other stimuli.

absolute risk The probability of having a particular disease within a stated time period. Compare this with *relative risk,* the differences in probability of having a particular disease across different groups (e.g. risk of a heart attack in smokers and non-smokers).

absolute threshold See *threshold.*

absolute value The value of a number regardless of whether it is positive or negative (e.g. the absolute values of 2 and -2 are identical). Usually denoted by vertical lines around the number in question (i.e. $|x|$).

absolute zero *true zero* (see *ratio scale*).

absorbing barrier (1) See *random walk.* (2) *absorbing state.*

absorbing state A state in some types of *stochastic sequences* which once reached cannot be escaped.

abstinence syndrome *withdrawal.*

abstract intelligence (1) The ability to process abstract concepts. This is contrasted with *concrete intelligence* – the ability to deal with practical problems and 'real-life' situations. (2) In some theories of psychological development, particularly those of, or influenced by, Jean Piaget, the term 'abstract intelligence' has much the same meaning as above. However, 'concrete intelligence' means a rather inferior method of thinking, in which the subject (an as yet undeveloped young child) is restricted only to being able to think about what s/he can see – genuine abstraction of thought is held to be beyond him/her.

absurdity test Test (usually of intelligence) in which the subject must identify what is wrong with an illogical statement or picture.

abulia profound indecisiveness.

abuse The misuse of a position of power and/or responsibility in order to cause suffering. Typically divided into three types: physical (suffering and/or injury by means of e.g. blows or poisoning); sexual (forcing an unwilling partner to engage in sexual activity or to persuade or command a partner to participate when they are incapable of making an informed decision); and emotional (use of behavioural measures to inflict suffering whether through action or neglect). The terms are often applied to cases of child abuse, but can denote abuse in any situation where the abused is in a position of weakness (e.g. elderly frail patients).

ABX design Experimental design in which the subject is presented with three stimuli and must decide if one of them ('X') is the same as 'A' or 'B'.

AC *assessment centre.*

ac- The prefix is often used interchangeably with *ak-*. A sought-for word may be entered with an ak- prefix.

Academic Achievement Discrepancy (AAD) A measure of level of scholastic *underachievement.*

acalculia A profound failure of arithmetic skills.

acanthaesthesia A *hallucination* in which the patient has the sensation of suffering pin pricks.

acarophobia A *phobia* of small animals or objects.

acatamathaesia A profound failure of comprehension.

acataphasia A profound inability to construct grammatical and/or meaningful statements.

acathisia A profound and uncontrollable restlessness and agitation.

accelerated test Test that exaggerates and/or speeds up conditions so that the long-term effects of a process can be seen within a practicable length of time. Calculating how a process will perform in normal conditions from such data can be problematic.

acceptance error *Type II error.*

accidental sample Sample in which the items and/or participants are gathered on an ad hoc basis, or at least with no clear rationale (i.e. there is no attempt to ensure that they are truly randomly selected). See *opportunistic sampling.*

account analysis Analysis of subjects' verbal accounts of their thoughts, behaviours, etc.

accuracy test Any test in which the accuracy of the answers, rather than time taken to answer, is of prime importance.

ACE test *American Council on Education test.*

acenaesthesia An absence of feeling of existing.

ACER Tests Set of tests of basic skills pertinent to engineering.

acerophobia A *phobia* of sourness.

acetylcholine Form of *neurotransmitter.*

ACF *Microcog – Assessment of Cognitive Functioning.*

Ach *acetylcholine.*

achievement age The age at which the average subject (usually a child) scores at a particular level on an *achievement test.* E.g., if the child's scores have an appreciably higher achievement age than the child's actual age, then s/he is considered to be bright for his/her years.

Achievement Anxiety Test (AAT) Measure assessing the degree to which anxiety enhances an individual's performance (the 'facilitation scale') and hinders it (the 'debilitating scale').

achievement motivation level of ambition.

achievement need *need for achievement.*

achievement quotient Calculated as for an *intelligence quotient*, except using *achievement age* rather than *mental age.*

achievement test A measure of what the subject is currently capable of (e.g. a child's scholastic attainment). Compare with *aptitude test*, and see *achievement age.*

achluophobia A *phobia* of the dark.

achromatopsia A disorder of visual perception, in which everything is seen in shades of grey (or more rarely, a single colour).

ACL *Adjective Checklist.*

acmaesthesia An abnormal perception of what would normally be considered painful stimulation purely in terms of the stimulation, and without any feeling of pain. E.g. being squeezed very hard would feel like strong pressure, with no pain.

acoasm A *hallucination* of a formless noise.

acoria gluttony.

acousma *acoasm.*

acousticophobia A *phobia* of noise.

acquiescence *acquiescent responding.*

acquiescent responding Habitually agreeing with the semantic direction of questions, regardless of what the statement is arguing. E.g. in answer to the questions 'do you agree with hanging?' and 'is capital punishment a bad idea?', the subject would answer 'yes' on both occasions.

acquiescent response set *acquiescent responding.*

acquired aphasia See *aphasia.*

acquired dysgraphia A profound difficulty in spelling resulting from brain damage.

acquired dyslexia A profound difficulty in reading resulting from brain damage. This takes various forms, some of which resemble *developmental dyslexics* or children learning to read (see *phonological dyslexia* and *surface dyslexia),* and one form *(demented dyslexia)* is usually associated with *dementia.* See *attentional dyslexia, deep dyslexia, direct dyslexia, phonological dyslexia, surface dyslexia* and contrast with *alexia.*

acrasia A profound absence of self-discipline.

acroaesthesia Heightened sensation in the extremities of the body.

acroanaesthesia Reduction in sensation in the extremities of the body. Complete loss of sensation is *acroparaesthesia.*

acrocinesia excessive movement.

acroparaesthesia See *acroanaesthesia.*

acrophobia See *phobia.*

ACS *Analysis of Coping Style.*

act psychology School of psychological thought active in the late nineteenth century, which concentrated on the totality of the mental experience and the act of thinking, rather than on the subprocesses of thought.

ACTH *adrenocorticotrophic hormone.*

acting out (1) A characteristic of a patient's behaviour which reveals a key aspect of his/her problem but which may not be a direct manifestation of the problem (e.g. being hostile to a particular therapist because s/he reminds the patient of his/her parents). (2) A sudden outburst of virtually uncontrollable behaviour.

action research (1) The evaluation of a situation (usually connected with the workplace), the introduction of a change (hoped to be an improving one), and the evaluation of the effects of the change. The process can be repeated – i.e. having seen the effects of the change, further changes may be introduced, and their effects evaluated (these changes can lead to further changes, etc.). (2) Research in which the experimenter is also one of the subjects (typically, in a study of social behaviour). (3) Research on an active process.

action tremor Trembling during an intended movement.

activating event An event which can be identified as the trigger for a particular behaviour.

active therapy General term for any therapeutic technique in which the therapist directly offers advice, rather than guiding the patient's own thoughts. In contrast, *passive therapy* seeks to give as few overt instructions as possible.

activities of daily living *assessment of daily living.*

activity dimension See *semantic differential technique.*

activity inventory A catalogue of actions performed in a particular task.

activity scheduling The division of time into a series of activities, so that the person is aware of what s/he should be doing at particular points of the day, week, etc.

actor-observer bias The tendency for an observer to exaggerate the role of the actor's own personality in causing a particular sequence of events, and for the actor to exaggerate the importance of the particular situation.

actual illness A mental illness which has a physical cause.

actualizing tendency The drive towards *self-actualization.*

actualizing therapy Therapeutic process which emphasizes *self-actualization* as the primary goal, rather than dealing with specific problems of which the patient may complain.

acuity (vision) The ability to focus on distant objects/fine detail.

aculalia garbled speech.

acute (1) Lasting a short time and/or sudden: contrast with *chronic.* (2) Very severe/debilitating.

acute alcoholic intoxication (AAI) Short-lived but severe mental and physical incapacitation resulting from over-consumption of alcoholic beverages.

acute confusional state *delirium.*

acute post-traumatic stress disorder See *post-traumatic stress disorder (PTSD).*

acute stress disorder See *post-traumatic stress disorder (PTSD).*

acute tolerance *tachyphylaxis.*

AD *Alzheimer's Disease.*

AD-MID A dementia in which the patient displays symptoms of *dementia of the Alzheimer type* and *multi-infarct dementia* simultaneously.

adaptation (1) Adjustment to stimulation and/or the environment. (2) Hence, the ability of long-stay patients to adjust to the 'real world' upon release.

adaptation syndrome Physical reaction (principally hormonal) to extreme *stress.*

adapted child See *transactional analysis.*

adaptive behaviour The degree to which an individual copes with society. Important in judging degree of *mental retardation* when conventional *IQ* tests might be inappropriate (e.g. in some mentally retarded members of an ethnic minority with poor command of the majority language).

Adaptive Behaviour Scale (ABS) Rating scale, devised by the *AAMD,* for assessing the degree to which a *mentally retarded person* can adapt into the community. Can be divided into three sub-scales – measuring how far the subject is self-sufficient in looking after him/herself, how well s/he fits into the community, and how firmly s/he understands the concept of social norms and responsibility.

Adaptive Behaviour Scale – School Edition (ABS-SE) Version of the *Adaptive Behaviour Scale specifically* designed for *mentally retarded* participants of school age.

adaptive test Test whose structure is based upon the answers given to earlier questions.

ADC *AIDS dementia complex.*

ADD *attentional deficit disorder.*

ADD-H *attentional deficit disorder with hyperactivity.*

addiction Psychological and/or physiological dependency on a drug or other (usually pleasure-giving) substance or event. Common addictions include illegal drugs (***drug addiction***), alcohol, tobacco, and gambling. If the addiction is purely governed by a psychological drive, then it is known as a *psychological addiction*, or *psychological dependency*. If the patient's bodily mechanisms require the drug (i.e. if s/he feels physically ill if the drug is withdrawn), then the phenomenon is called *physiological addiction* or *substance dependence* (note that there may be a psychological drive as well).

Addison's disease *Organic affective syndrome* caused by a deficiency of cortisone, and characterized by tiredness and depression. See *Cushing's syndrome*.

additive interaction See *interaction*.

additive scale *interval scale*.

ADEPT *Adult Development and Enrichment Programme*.

ADHD Attention deficit hyperactivity disorder, a.k.a. *ADD-H*.

adiadochokinesis An inability to execute repetitive actions, usually caused by damage to the *cerebellum*. Impaired ability to execute repetitive actions is known as *dysdiadocbokinesis*.

adipsia A profoundly low drive to drink (any fluids).

Adjective Checklist (ACL) List of 300 adjectives, out of which the subject selects those which s/he feels most apply to him/herself. Yields an impressive (if unwieldy) 37 scales of personality measurement.

adjunctive behaviour Inappropriate behaviour reinforced by events resulting from that behaviour.

adjusted correlation (r_{adj}) Mathematically adjusted value of the *correlation coefficient* that controls for potential biasing in small samples.

adjusted mean *mean* adjusted in value to account for the effects of a *covariate*.

adjusted R^2 Mathematically adjusted value of R^2 designed to compensate for measurement errors when the data set being analysed is small.

adjustment disorder A profound distress resulting from a failure to cope with a stressful event or drastic change in circumstances.

adjustment inventory Name for any measures of how well the subject has adjusted to (i.e. is in harmony with) his/her environment.

adjuvent therapy Supporting therapeutic techniques given in addition to the principal form of therapy.

ADL *assessment of daily living.*

Adlerian theory/therapy *individual psychology.*

AD-MID A *dementia* in which the patient displays symptoms of *dementia of the Alzheimer type* and *multi-infarct dementia* simultaneously.

adrenaline Chemical which can act as both a hormone and a *neurotransmitter*, and which is involved in 'fright, flight and fight' – namely, it raises metabolic, heart and breathing rates and generally prepares the body for more energetic action.

adrenocorticotrophic hormone (ACTH) Hormone which stimulates the release of *adrenaline*.

adrenogenital syndrome Premature sexual development caused by an over-active adrenal gland.

adult children Grown up sons and daughters; usually the term more specifically refers to adults who experience problems as a result of events which occurred during their childhood (e.g. 'adult children of abusing parents').

Adult Development and Enrichment Programme (ADEPT) A training programme for older people.

adult ego state See *transactional analysis*.

adult offspring *adult children.*

adult survivors *survivors* (definition 2) who are adults, who suffered a traumatic event (e.g. sexual abuse) as children.

Advanced Progressive Matrices (APM) See *Raven's Progressive Matrices*.

adventitious resulting from injury.

adventitious deafness Deafness resulting from injury.

advocacy group Group representing the case for a particular cause. In the context of this dictionary, advocacy groups commonly encountered are those representing the interests of patients with a particular condition.

aeroacrophobia A *phobia* of flying.

aerophagia 'gulping' in air.

aerophobia A *phobia* of wind and draughts.

aetiological validity The concept that a patient possessing a particular set of symptoms must be suffering from a particular disease, because other patients known to suffer from the same disease possess the same set of symptoms. See *validity*.

aetiology (1) The study of causes (e.g. of disease). (2) cause(s) (e.g. of disease).

AFF *auditory flutter fusion.*

affect emotion.

affectionless psychopathy Disorder characterized by an absence of emotional responses and disregard for other people's emotions.

affective bridge A link made between emotional states on different occasions.

affective disorders General term for a group of illnesses whose principal symptom is a severe disturbance in emotional state. Principal examples are *depression* and *mania*.

affective flattening *flat affect.*

affective psychosis *psychosis* in which a major symptom is a gross disturbance of *affect.*

afferent (neurons) Carrying signals from the *peripheral nervous system* to the *central nervous system*. See *efferent.*

affiliation motivation A drive to belong to a group, form friendships, etc.

affiliation need (nAff) The need to belong to a group, family, etc.

affirming the consequent Error of logic in which it is assumed that because event y can be caused by event x, then the existence or truth of y proves the existence or truth of x.

AG age group.

age associated memory impairment (AAMI) Normal memory decline associated with old age.

age cohort A group of people born and raised in the same period of time/history. Generally, the age range of such a group increases the older its average age. E.g. an acceptable grouping of newborn babies would not include a three-month-old; a group of year-old babies would not include a 5- year-old, but a group of 'old' subjects could have a 20-year age range of 60–80-year-olds.

age-equivalent scale Test scores expressed in terms of the proportions of an age group who typically possess them, enabling the assessment of whether a person is advanced or retarded for their age.

age-grade scale Test scores expressed in terms of the school year/grade in which they are usually found.

age norm The mean score for a given age group, and hence the score one would expect an average person of that age group to possess.

age normative effect A factor which influences the majority of people at the same point in their lives.

age scale *age-equivalent scale.*

age score *mental age.*

AGECAT A computerized package for assessing the mental state of elderly patients.

ageusia loss of taste.

aggregate data Data about a group of items, people or events which have something in common (e.g. all aardvarks called Kevin, sandwiches with vegan fillings).

aggression An intent to cause harm, aggressive socialized conduct disorder *antisocial personality disorder* in which the patient is also capable of caring behaviour.

agitated depression *depression* accompanied by extreme levels of physical agitation.

agitated melancholia (Now outmoded) term for *depression* coupled with *anxiety.*

agitation Term covering a set of symptoms indicative of restlessness and dissatisfaction, including acts of physical aggression, grabbing, complaining, shouting, verbal abuse, etc. Often used to describe a range of problematic behaviours found in institutionalized older adults, particularly those who are intellectually compromised or suffering from *dementia.*

agitolalia Rapid speech, in which it seems that the words cannot be pronounced quickly enough.

agnosia A profound failure of recognition. The failure can be restricted to one sense – e.g. *auditory agnosia, visual agnosia*, etc.

agnosic alexia An inability to read, although other linguistic skills (including writing) are intact.

agoraphobia See *phobia.*

agrammatism A profound failure of grammar.

agraphia A complete failure to write/ spell. See *dysgraphia.*

agreeableness (A) Personality *trait* (one of the '*Big Five*') measuring the degree to which the subject is prepared to 'go along with' a situation. Accordingly, the trait has extremes of gullibility and cynicism.

agreement coefficient *item reliability.*

agricultural psychology Study of psychological aspects of farming and the rural lifestyle.

agrypnia *insomnia.*

agyiophobia A *phobia* of streets.

AH intelligence tests A collection of *fluid intelligence* tests devised by Alice Heim (hence the name). The tests are available in several versions, from AH1 (the easiest) to AH6 (the hardest), which are intended for different subject groups. E.g., by giving the AH6 test to a group of bright subjects, one avoids the problem of *ceiling effects*, which would be encountered if one gave them a test designed for the general population. Similarly, a group of dull subjects might benefit from taking the AH2, because a more demanding test would create *floor effects.*

ahedonia *anhedonia.*

ahistorical therapy Therapy which takes no or relatively little account of the patient's past.

ahypnia *insomnia.*

aichmophobia A *phobia* of pointed objects.

AIDS dementia complex (ADC) *dementia* caused by the onset of AIDS.

ailurophobia A *phobia* of cats.

air encephalograph *pneumoencephalograph.*

Ai3Q *personality inventory* assessing *obsessional personality.*

ak- The prefix is often used interchangeably with *ac-*. A sought-for word may be entered with an ac- prefix.

akathisia extreme restlessness.

akinaesthesia Loss of sensitivity to signals from muscles and tendons.

akinesia Inability to initiate movements.

akinetic apraxia Inability to perform spontaneous movements.

alalia A profound absence of speech.

Alcohol Assessment and Treatment Profile (AATP) *structured interview* package eliciting details of a patient's drinking habits and attitudes.

alcohol dependence *alcoholism.*

alcohol withdrawal delirium *delirium tremens.*

alcoholic dementia Old (and misleading) synonym for *Korsakoff's syndrome.*

alcoholic psychosis General term for intellectual impairment caused by *alcoholism.*

Alcoholics Anonymous (AA) Self-help group for people suffering from *alcoholism.*

alcoholism *substance abuse* where the substance in question is alcohol. Although most alcoholics are heavy drinkers, the condition is determined less by the quantity consumed than by the alcoholic's abnormal need for it (either constantly or in binges), and the fact that the alcohol consumption is having negative effects on the patient's well-being and on those close to him/her. As the illness progresses, alcoholics tend to require ever-increasing amounts of drink in order to attain the same effects. With heavy drinkers, withdrawal can result in *delirium tremens.*

aleatory Pertaining to chance.

alethia Inability to suppress a memory.

Alexander technique A therapeutic technique, whose principal point of interest lies in its emphasis on bodily posture. It is claimed to help alleviate negative symptoms and create a feeling of greater well-being.

alexia A complete failure to read or to recognize words or letters (in *dyslexia* there is a partial ability). Only usually seen in brain-damaged individuals.

alexia without agraphia *agnosic alexia.*

alexithymia Inability to monitor one's own emotional state.

algebraic transformation *square root transformation.*

algesia (1) Sense of pain. (2) Heightened sense of pain.

algolagnia General term for receiving sexual pleasure from pain, whether through *masochism or sadism.*

algophilia *masochism.*

alienation An actual state and/or perceived feeling that one is separate and detached from others.

alienation coefficient The opposite of the *correlation coefficient* – a measure assessing how unrelated two *variables* are.

all or nothing thought Erroneous belief that anything less than absolute success in seeking a particular goal is to be regarded as abject failure.

allachaesthesia *allaesthesia.*

allaesthesia A misperception of the location of a sensation in the body – often that it is on the opposite side of the body (when it is more properly called **allochiria**).

allele One possible form a gene may take at a particular position on a chromosome.

allesthesia *allaesthesia.*

allocentrism Attributing an event to environmental factors (as opposed to the self).

allochiria See *allaesthesia.*

allopsychosis Any mental illness in which the patient's principal problem is directed towards the outside world. This contrasts with *autopsychosis*, where the perceived problems lie within the patient.

allotriophagia Consumption of unusual foods or food combinations.

Allport-Vernon-Lindzey Scale *Study of Values.*

Allport's theory of personality development Gordon Allport argued that children do not possess personalities as much as a collection of behaviours, which vary according to the needs of the moment (e.g. children behave radically differently with their friends and their parents). The behaviours eventually coalesce into *selves*, which are sets of behaviours consistently used in different settings (e.g. the child has a 'home self', a 'school self', etc.). An individual reaches maturity when the selves in turn coalesce into a *proprium*, which is a personality or self relatively stable across situations. In addition, Allport saw maturity as involving shifting the motivation for actions from simply earning reward, avoiding punishment, obeying orders, etc., to motivation to do something for its own sake and virtues (*functional autonomy*). This shift in motivation is called the *lack of emotional continuity*.

alogia Lack of, or very limited, speech.

alpha coefficient *coefficient alpha.*

alpha error *Type I error.*

alpha level *significance level.*

Alpha Test Test of verbal intelligence used by the American Army during World War I for personnel selection (the **Beta Test** was visuo-spatial). The test was one of the first wide-scale uses of *psychometrics*, and has been heavily criticized for *cultural bias*.

alpha waves A pattern of electrical activity in the brain detected by electroencephalograph (*EEG*) with a frequency between 8 and 12 Hz.

alternate form reliability See *reliability.*

alternating personality See *multiple personality.*

alternating psychosis *bipolar disorder.*

alternative hypothesis (H^i) The reverse of the *null hypothesis* – the prediction that the experiment will demonstrate a statistically *significant* event of the type predicted by the researcher.

altruistic suicide See *Durkheim's taxonomy of suicide.*

aluminium theory of dementia of the Alzheimer type The (unproven) theory that an abnormally large intake of aluminium (through environmental factors and/or faulty 'body filters') is the cause of *dementia of the Alzheimer type.*

Alzheimer's disease *dementia of the Alzheimer type.*

amaurotic idiocy Inherited *mental retardation*, accompanied by blindness.

amaxophobia A *phobia* of motor vehicles.

ambiguous figure A visual stimulus which can be perceived as possessing two or more distinct identities.

ambiguous loss Phenomenon usually encountered in severely *demented* patients, whereby the afflicted individual exists only physically – there is no sign of a sentient being occupying the body.

ambivalence The simultaneous holding of positive and negative feelings about something or someone.

ambiversion See *extroversion.*

amblyopia Defective vision with no discernible physical cause.

ambulatory schizophrenia *schizotypal personality disorder.*

amenorrhoea An abnormal absence of menstrual bleeding. In *primary amenorrhoea* there is no onset of periods at puberty whilst in *secondary amenorrhoea*, periods cease during adulthood for reasons not commensurate with the onset of the menopause.

amentia *mental retardation.*

American Association for Mental Deficiency (AAMD) American group promoting the rights and needs of *mentally retarded* people.

American Council on Education (ACE) Test Intelligence test primarily designed for (American) students.

amimia A profound inability to use gestures.

amitriptyline An *antidepressant.*

amnesia A failure of memory usually abnormally severe, arising from e.g. *stroke*, head injury, illness (e.g. *dementia*), or poisoning. The term is occasionally used for memory loss which is normal or not unduly serious in its effects (e.g. *childhood amnesia*). *Anterograde amnesia* is amnesia for events which took place after the brain damage occurred (see *amnestic syndrome*). *Retrograde amnesia* is amnesia for events preceding the brain damage (usually this is confined to memory failure for a brief period before the damage occurred, not the patient's entire past life – see *psychogenic amnesia.*

The term, strictly speaking, means total memory loss, although it is rarely used as such – see *dysmnesia.*

amnesic aphasia *anomic aphasia.*

amnesic apraxia Inability to remember sequences of movements.

amnesic syndrome *amnestic syndrome.*

amnestic apraxia *amnesic apraxia.*

amnestic dysgraphia A profound writing disability – the patient can write individual letters, but writing is otherwise incomprehensible.

amnestic syndrome *Amnesia* resulting from brain damage (either injury or damage from toxins, alcohol, etc.) where there is no other severe intellectual impairment. Some commentators treat the syndrome as synonymous with *anterograde amnesia*, although the DSM includes *retrograde amnesia* as well.

amniocentesis A sampling of amniotic fluid (the fluid surrounding the baby in the womb) during early pregnancy, which can reveal chromosomal defects (particularly *trisomy 21*) in the *foetus.*

amok A *culture-bound disorder* (found chiefly in Asia) characterized by a period of extreme listlessness followed by a very energetic and violent outburst.

amphetamine sulphate Type of *amphetamine.*

amphetamines Group of drugs whose principal effect is an increased level of energy and euphoria (in large doses, they can induce *delusions*). They have accordingly found popularity as an illegal drug. They are still used for legitimate medical purposes, and until the 1960s, were available in the UK without prescription (principally as a slimming aid – the drugs also reduce appetite).

amusia A profound failure in musical perception (i.e. tone and rhythm deaf).

amyl nitrate A drug with a legitimate use as a heart stimulant, but more often used illegally – induces a burst of energy and feelings of euphoria.

amyloid precursor protein (APP) Gene located on chromosome 21 linked to some cases of *dementia of the Alzheimer type*.

Amytal A type of *barbiturate*. The drug lowers inhibitions, and accordingly, has been dubbed the 'truth drug', much beloved of spy films (in which its efficacy has been grossly exaggerated).

anaclisis Extreme dependence on others.

anaclitic depression *Depression* experienced by a child upon prolonged separation from its parent(s); more generally, depression upon the death of a parent.

anal expulsive personality See *anal retentive personality*.

anal retentive personality Derived from the *anal stage* of *Freud's psychoanalytic theory*, a personality type characterized by miserliness and an obsessional need for detail, rules and procedures. Held to be due to retaining faeces rather than expelling them when the need is felt as an infant. The reverse behaviour leads, it is argued, to the *anal expulsive personality*, which is overamenable and over-relaxed.

anal stage See *Freud's psychoanalytic theory*.

analeptic drug Any drug designed to stimulate.

analogue study Study in which a naturalistic situation is replicated in a laboratory. Often the situation cannot be precisely replicated, so an analogous situation is devised (e.g. taking ability at video games as an indication of ability to fly fighter planes).

analogy test Intelligence measure in which subjects must identify the logic of an analogy in an example, and then provide a similar analogy (usually from a multiple choice). E.g. 'kippers are to marmalade as soup is to: (a) washing powder (b) mashed potatoes (c) hot chocolate (d) penguins'.

analysand The patient in *psychoanalysis*.

Analysis of Coping Style (ACS) Measure of social skills in subjects aged 5–18 years.

analysis of covariance (ANCOVA) *analysis of variance* in which a difference is examined after the coincidental effects of a *covariate* have been statistically controlled for. This means that any differences found cannot be attributed to the coincidental effects of the covariate. It logically follows that the ANCOVA can also be used to demonstrate that a difference is attributable to the effects of the covariate if controlling for it removes the group difference. E.g. one can show that in 5–10-year-olds, children with big feet have higher maths scores than small-footed children. This may indicate advantages of big-footedness, but it is also the case that the big-footed children are usually older (i.e. the difference between the groups may simply be due to their different average ages). By using age as a covariate in an ANCOVA, the effects of age can be removed from the equation, and the difference between the scores of big and small-footed children can be re-examined.

analysis of covariant structures Form of *LISREL* measuring causal relationships.

analysis of variance (ANOVA) A *parametric* measure of the differences between two or more groups' scores on one or more measures or between one group's performance on two or more measures. *Significance* is assessed using the *F ratio*. Essentially, the ANOVA can be employed to measure three things: differences between two or more groups on the same measure (***between groups measure***); differences in the same group's performance on two or more different measures (***within groups measure***); and differences in the pattern of responses made by two or more different groups on two or more different measures (the *interaction* measure). Analyses of quantitative differences (i.e. everything but the interactions) are also known as ***main effects***. The format of the ANOVA remains basically the same when the number of *variables* being assessed is increased or decreased, although the interactions become more complex (see *interaction*). It should be noted that when two groups are being compared on one variable with one level, then this is a *t test*, which can thus be regarded as a form of ANOVA. The ANOVA is labelled according to the number of between and within groups measures used, and whether the measures are all within, all between, or a mixture. Hence, a two way *between ANOVA* analyses two between groups measures; a four way *within ANOVA* analyses four within groups measures; and a three way *mixed ANOVA* analyses three measures, of which at least one and no more than two is between groups. The ANOVA is one of the commonest measures of group differences employed by psychologists. It assumes *normally distributed* populations. See *analysis of covariance, ANOVA table, Hoyt's analysis of variance, interaction, multivariate analysis of variance, post hoc tests, repeated measures analysis of variance* and *Type I sums of squares*.

analytic psychology *analytical psychology*.

analytical psychology Term sometimes applied to *Jung's psychoanalytic theory*.

anamnesis Medical history of a patient before treatment. Often the term is restricted to the patient's own account. The medical history post-treatment is known as *catamnesis*.

anancasm *compulsion*.

anancastia A state of feeling compelled to perform an action against one's will.

anancastic disorder Disorder characterized by an unrealistic level of perfectionism and/or pedantry and/or an expectation that others should obey similar unfeasibly exacting standards.

anaphia A profound absence of the sensation of touch.

anaphylaxis The recurrence of symptoms which had been triggered by an earlier upsetting event, when experiencing a similar event.

anarithmia *acalculia*.

anarithria A profound absence of speech.

anatomically correct dolls *anatomically detailed dolls*.

anatomically detailed dolls Dolls possessing genitalia, used by therapists in e.g. cases of child abuse, to enable the children to describe the nature of the abuse.

anchor point A point of reference on a scale against which a participant makes his/her judgements.

ANCOVA *analysis of covariance*.

androgen General term for hormones determining male sexual characteristics.

androgynous personality A personality combining the 'better' attributes of stereotypical 'masculine' and 'feminine' behaviours (e.g. being gentle but independent, tough-minded but succouring, etc.). Compare with *undifferentiated sex role identity*.

andromania *nymphomania*.

androphobia A *phobia* of men.

anecdotal evidence Evidence accrued from hearsay or witness reports, which has not been systematically examined for its veracity. A more specific form of testing is implied by *anecdotal testing*.

anecdotal testing Measurements of a participant's behaviour gathered from observers who have seen the subject in question (e.g. of a mentally ill patient's behaviour in the time before referral – the reports of relatives, friends, etc., may be more reliable than the patient's self-report). See *anecdotal evidence*.

anemophobia *aerophobia*.

anencephalia Absence of brain.

anergasia Loss of function, usually with the implication that there is a known physical cause.

anergia Loss of energy.

anergic Pertaining to *anergia*.

anergy *anergia*.

anginophobia A *phobia* of choking or of suffocation.

anhedonia Loss of pleasure or the ability to seek and feel pleasure.

aniconia A profound inability to produce mental images.

anima See *Jung's psychoanalytic theory*.

animal assisted therapy Using interaction with animals (typically, providing the patient with a pet – more precisely known as *pet therapy*) as a therapeutic measure.

animal model Using the findings from observations and experiments on animals as an analogue of human performance.

animus See *Jung's psychoanalytic theory*.

ankle clonus See *clonus*.

Anna O See *hypnosis*.

anniversary reaction Negative feelings engendered by it being the anniversary (or general time of year) of an event distressing to a subject (e.g. death of a close friend or relative). The term can also refer to positive feelings associated with the anniversary of a more cheerful event.

Annual Review of Psychology Annual collection of critical essays on recent developments in key areas of psychology.

anodyne drug Any drug with pain-killing or soothing properties.

Anomalous Sentences Repetition Test (ASRT) Measure designed to distinguish patients in early stages of *dementia* from those with *pseudodementia*. Participants are required to repeat sentences spoken by the tester which are grammatically correct but have no meaning.

anomia (1) Inability to name. (2) *anomie* (rare usage).

anomic aphasia *Aphasia* characterized by an inability to find specific words. The term is largely interchangeable with *anomia*.

anomic suicide See *Durkheim's taxonomy of suicide*.

anomie Loss of a value system, caused by extreme *stress*.

anomie scale A measure of moral values or, more usually, lack of them.

anorexia Undereating, for reasons other than a conventional reduction diet. The disorder can have many causes: the commonest are some forms of cancer and *anorexia nervosa*.

anorexia nervosa A mental disorder in which the patient wilfully starves/seriously undereats, in the erroneous belief that s/he is overweight and has an unattractive body shape. The illness is largely (but not solely) confined to females, usually in adolescence. Compare with *bulimia* and *bulimia nervosa*. See *anorexia*.

anorexigenic appetite-suppressing.

anorgasmia Inability to orgasm.

anosmia Inability to smell.

anosognosia Denial of illness. The term is usually employed specifically to describe denial of a very 'obvious' debilitating problem such as paralysis or blindness.

ANOVA *analysis of variance.*

ANOVA table The 'correct form' for presenting the results of an *analysis of variance*. The table varies in complexity with the size of the *ANOVA*, but all contain the following headings: Source, S.S., d.f., M.S., F. 'Source' refers to the source of the *variance*. This includes all the empirically observed measures (the *between groups measures* and *within groups measures*), plus any *interactions*. In addition, it also lists headings of BETWEEN GROUPS, WITHIN GROUPS, and TOTAL VARIANCE. These refer to all between group variance, all within group variance, and the total variance of the whole analysis. They are essential in calculating the *F ratios* and *eta squared*. *S.S.* refers to the **sum of squares**, which is the sum of all the squared deviations from the *mean*. *D.f.* refers to the *degrees of freedom* for the section of the analysis in question. *M.S.* is the **mean square**, which is the mathematically-adjusted mean of the sum of squares. *F* refers to the F ratio, calculated as the ratio of the mean squares.

anoxia A lack of oxygen; if this occurs at birth, then *mental retardation* can result.

ANS *autonomic nervous system.*

answer until correct (AUC) score Marking system for a multiple choice test, in which a subject makes as many attempts as is necessary until s/he obtains the right answer; the more attempts made, the fewer points scored. See *inferred number right (INR) score*.

Antabuse Trade name of *disulfiram*.

antecedent In expressing a ratio (e.g. 'x:y'), the first number in the expression (i.e. 'x'). The second number (i.e. 'y') is the *consequent*.

antecedent variable A *variable* preceding another one, and often inferred to be the cause of the latter.

anterior Anatomical term denoting the 'head end' or front section in a quadruped, and the front or 'face end' in a bipedal animal (e.g. human). See *cranial*.

anterograde amnesia See *amnesia*.

anthropomorphism Attributing human qualities, thought processes, etc., to non-human animals. The most extreme reaction against it is *behaviourism*.

anthropomorphizing *anthropomorphism*.

anthroposophy Therapeutic method devised by Rudolf Steiner (1861–1925), aimed at 'liberating' spiritual aspects of the mind and behaviour.

anticathexis Expressing the opposite emotion from the one actually felt.

anticipatory grief Preparing for the death of a loved one.

antidepressant A drug to counteract the effects of depression.

antimode The least frequently occurring value in a sample.

antipsychiatry movement Movement which began in the 1960s which criticizes mainstream psychiatric methods for their alleged degrading of mentally ill patients (e.g. by stereotyping patients according to their perceived 'disease', over-using tranquillizing drugs, etc.).

antipsychotic drug Drug designed to counteract the effects of *psychotic* illnesses.

antisocial personality disorder (psychopathy) *personality disorder* characterized by a profound lack of moral sense, often resulting in illegal and/or violent behaviour. Sufferers may also engage in sports and other activities with a high level of risk.

antonym test Test in which the subject must supply the opposite of a word supplied by the experimenter.

anxiety The term is usually used in the lay sense of the word. Namely, a feeling of profound agitation and of an imminent unpleasant experience, often with accompanying physical symptoms of racing pulse, sweating, breathlessness, etc. Normally, the sensation is experienced as a reaction to anxiety-provoking events (e.g. a trip to the dentist, 'exam nerves', etc.), and is relatively quickly dissipated. If the feeling of anxiety is unusually severe or protracted, or arises without apparent reason, then it is usually classified as one of the *anxiety disorders*.

anxiety disorders General term for a group of illnesses whose principal symptom is a high level of (unrealistic) *anxiety*. Principally, these are the *anxiety states*, and the *phobias*.

anxiety hierarchy Therapeutic technique in which an over-anxious patient arranges a series of events in order of how anxious they make him/her feel. This forms the basis of developing strategies to cope with the problem. See *desensitization*.

anxiety hysteria *phobia*.

anxiety neurosis (1) Old term for *generalized anxiety*. (2) *anxiety disorder*.

anxiety object An object inducing a feeling of anxiety (including *phobic objects*).

anxiety-relief response *Behaviour therapy* technique. The patient learns to associate a word or act with a feeling of calmness. Accordingly, repeating the act or word in moments of *anxiety* should help reduce the negative feelings.

anxiety states Group term for *generalized anxiety, obsessive-compulsive disorder and panic disorder*.

anxiety tolerance The maximum level of anxiety an individual can experience without suffering psychological and/or physical damage.

anxiolytic drug *minor tranquillizer*.

anxyolytic *anxiolytic*.

AOA *age of acquisition*.

APA (1) American Psychiatric Association. (2) American Psychological Association.

APA guidelines Any set of guidelines (usually on codes of professional conduct and publication protocol) issued by the American Psychological Association.

apeirophobia A *phobia* of infinity.

Apgar score Named after its inventor Apgar. A scaled measure of a newborn baby's physical condition. Takes five criteria – heart rate; respiratory effort (i.e. how well s/he is breathing); muscle tone; reflex irritability (i.e. how well baby responds to an irritating stimulus); and colour (for Caucasians, the pinker the better). Each measure is scored on a three point scale, and provides a quick indicator of the baby's health.

aphagia A profoundly low drive to eat.

aphasia Failure of language. Strictly speaking, the term refers to an entire loss of language (a partial failure is *dysphasia*), but it is generally used for any language failure. Also, usually refers to *acquired aphasia* – i.e. the patient has acquired it through accident or illness, and prior to this s/he had normal linguistic abilities. Aphasia can be broadly divided into three categories – *receptive aphasia* is a specific failure to understand language, *expressive aphasia* a failure to produce it, and *global aphasia* a failure of both comprehension and production. For more specific categories, see: *anomic aphasia., ataxic aphasia, audio-verbal aphasia, auditory aphasia, Broca's aphasia, conduction aphasia, developmental aphasia, mixed transcortical aphasia, transcortical aphasia, transcortical motor aphasia, transcortical sensory aphasia*, and *Wernicke's aphasia*. Also see *jargon aphasia*.

aphephobia A *phobia* of being touched.

aphonia Inability to speak (the patient may, however, be able to whisper or croak).

APM *Advanced Progressive Matrices.*

apoE *apoliproprotein E.*

apoliproprotein E (apoE) A gene found on chromosome 19 believed to be linked to *dementia of the Alzheimer type* (and also *vascular dementia*). The gene comes in several forms, the commonest being e2, e3 and e4. It is e4 that is believed to be associated with a higher possibility of developing late-onset DAT. Interestingly, the e2 variant seems to carry a lower risk of developing DAT.

apoplexy *stroke.*

APP *amyloid precursor protein.*

applicant *client.*

application blank American term for application form.

applied psychology Any method of applying psychological theory and techniques to 'real life' problems. The term principally covers *clinical psychology, educational psychology and occupational psychology.*

applied research Research with a solution to a practical problem as its goal. This contrasts with *basic research*, whose principal interest is in a theoretical concept, but not necessarily its practical utility.

approach-approach conflict The conflict a participant feels when s/he equally desires to perform two acts.

approach-avoidance conflict (1) The conflict a participant feels when s/he desires to perform an act, which s/he knows has previously been punished. (2) In young children, the simultaneous desire to approach and to avoid a stranger.

Approaches to Study Inventory (ASI) Questionnaire of study habits. Divided into 16 sub-scales, it assesses a range of study skills (e.g. over-reliance on details, ability to comprehend broad issues, etc.).

approximate visual access Misreading a word as one which looks similar (e.g. 'house' for 'horse'). Found especially in beginning readers and *surface dyslexics*.

approximation error Inaccuracy introduced by using approximate rather than stringently accurate measurements (e.g. in calculating the circumference of a circle, estimating the value of pi to be $21/7$). The seriousness of the error is usually dependent upon demands of the particular situation (e.g. using the $22/7$ value may be adequate for planning a garden pond, but may be seriously inaccurate when planning a space voyage).

apraxia Inability to perform intentional movements.

aprosexia A profound failure of attention.

aprosodia Failure of speech intonation.

apsychognosia Absence of understanding of the effects of one's actions.

aptitude test A measure of what the participant is potentially capable of, even although s/he may not currently attain such heights (e.g. an IQ test might show that a child's teaching is not stretching him/her sufficiently). Compare with *achievement test*.

aqua-energetics Therapeutic technique which, through emphasis on posture and breathing whilst floating in water, attempts to release tensions, repressed feelings, etc. A central feature of some forms of the therapy is the use of nude *group therapy* sessions in swimming pools.

aquaphobia A *phobia* of expanses of water and/or bathing.

arachnophobia See *phobia*.

arbitrary inference The drawing of a wildly incorrect conclusion about an event by a patient, which conforms to his/her dysfunctional views (e.g. interpreting anything less than an effusive greeting as 'evidence' that nobody likes him/her).

archetype See *Jung's psychoanalytic theory*.

area sampling *cluster sampling*.

arena The situation in which a therapy takes place (e.g. one-to-one, group sessions, etc.).

arhythmia A profound absence of sense of rhythm.

ARIMA *autoregressive integrated moving average*.

arithmetic mean *mean*.

arithmomania (1) An unnatural preoccupation with the mathematical properties of events. (2) An obsessive desire to count.

Arlin Test of Formal Reasoning Measure of a child's reasoning abilities. Based around Piaget's concepts of formal and *concrete intelligence*.

array (1) Set of data or stimuli (often arranged in order of size). (2) The set of variables associated with another variable.

arrested development A failure to develop beyond a particular stage of development (particularly with reference to *social age*).

arrows (in correlation/regression illustrations) A line with an arrow head at one end indicates a causal relationship, with the arrow indicating the direction of causation. A line with arrow heads at both ends indicates the items are related, but there is not a causal relationship. In *structural equation modelling*, a two-headed arrow indicates variance shared by the connected items that is not explained by the equation.

art therapy Therapeutic method in which the patient, through making an artistic object (e.g. painting, sculpture), explores his/her feelings, motives, etc.

arteriosclerotic dementia *multi-infarct dementia*.

articulated thoughts during simulated situations Therapeutic technique in which the patient hears or sees a situation acted out and paused at regular intervals, to allow him/her to comment on what s/he thinks about the enacted scene. The scenes could be e.g. situations which the patient finds hard to deal with.

artifact An incidental by-product of an experimental method, which may colour the results.

artificial dichotomy See *dichotomous variable.*

artistic morphology The study of the use of shape in art.

Arthur Scale A non-verbal intelligence test for children.

ascending pathways *nerves* conducting impulses along the *spinal cord* to the brain. Compare with *descending pathways.*

ascriptive responsibility Acknowledgement of responsibility for an illegal or morally wrong act, which will be punished.

ASD *autistic spectrum disorder.*

ASDS *Asperger Syndrome Diagnostic Scale.*

asemia A failure to recognize and/or use symbols and gestures. Sometimes used more loosely to denote a failure to understand language.

ASH *Automated Social History.*

ASI *Approaches to Study Inventory.*

ASI-S Shortened version of *Approaches to Study Inventory.*

asitia A profound aversion to food. Loosely used as a synonym for *anorexia nervosa.*

asociality Inability to form social relationships.

asonia Inability to discriminate between sound frequencies.

Asperger's syndrome Named after its discoverer, H. Asperger. A condition quite similar to, and currently classified by many authorities as, a form of *autism* (sometimes the two illnesses are found in the same family, indicating a genetic component). The principal differences between the conditions are that the Asperger patient possesses near-normal language, and usually has a higher degree of social skills. Sufferers are often perceived as normal, if eccentric.

Asperger Syndrome Diagnostic Scale (ASDS) Test for assessing presence or absence of symptoms associated with *Asperger's syndrome.*

ASQ *Attributional Style Questionnaire.*

ASRT *Anomalous Sentences Repetition Test.*

Assertion Inventory Measure of the degree to which a person feels comfortable about asserting him or herself in particular situations.

assertion training (AT) Form of *behaviour therapy,* training people to express themselves and their wishes more easily and forcefully (but not aggressively, as is often erroneously supposed).

assertiveness training *assertion training.*

Assessing Reading Difficulties Reading skills test for subjects aged 5–8 years. Subjects are given an *odd man out test,* in which all but one of a list of words have the same sound in common – the subjects have to name the 'odd one out' (e.g. 'cat, hat, rat, man'). The test claims to assess phonemic awareness skills, and performance is correlated with reading ability.

assessment centre (AC) A detailed *personnel screening,* using a variety of techniques.

Assessment for Training and Employment (ATE) Set of tests assessing basic intellectual and social abilities and aptitudes in the context of suitability for employment. The *Differential Aptitude Tests* form a sub-section of the battery.

assessment of daily living (ADL) Any method of measuring daily activities, usually with the purpose of identifying memory slips, etc.

asset search Therapeutic technique in which the patient lists all his/her attributes. Sometimes the search is confined to looking for positive attributes (positive asset search) e.g. to increase the confidence of patients with low *self-esteem, depression*, etc.

assets-liabilities technique Technique used in some therapies, in which the patient lists everything which is good and bad in his/her life. This list is used to decide what the therapy should try to remove, what should be enhanced, etc.

assignment therapy *group therapy*.

association The degree to which two or more *variables* are related to each other.

association area *association cortex*.

association cortex See *primary cortex*.

association test Any test in which the participant must produce a word associated with a given example. See *controlled association test* and *free association*.

associational fluency Fluency in producing similes or synonyms. Often tested by giving a participant a list of words and asking for their synonyms.

associative visual agnosia A less severe form of *visual agnosia*. The participant may be able accurately to copy an object, and/or use it as part of a routine learnt before the illness. In other respects, however, his/her behaviour is as that of a patient with full visual agnosia.

astasia A psychological inability to stand.

astasia-abasia A *somatoform disorder*, in which the patient is unable to stand or walk, although the legs otherwise function normally.

astereognosis A failure to recognize by touch.

asthenia A feeling of profound weakness.

asthenic personality Abnormally pronounced inability to experience pleasure and enthusiasm, coupled with increased sensitivity to *stress*.

asthenophobia A *phobia* of weakness.

Aston Index Reading skills *test battery* for subjects aged 5–14 years. Includes picture recognition, a vocabulary test, the *Goodenough Draw-a-Man Test*, the *Schonell Graded Word Reading Test*, various tests of phonological skills and memory. Primarily designed to assess poor readers with suspected *dyslexia*.

astraphobia A *phobia* of thunder and lightning.

asymbolia A failure to recognize symbolic information.

asymbolia for pain A failure to recognize that pain signals indicate pain.

asymmetric correlation See *symmetric correlation*.

asymmetric distribution Distribution with *skew*.

asymptote The uppermost value, of e.g. performance (may be actual or a theoretical perfect upper limit).

asymptotic Approaching (but never actually reaching) the *asymptote*.

asynergia A form of *ataxia* characterized by a profound lack of coordination between different muscle groups.

AT *assertion training*.

At Ease Collection of computerized *relaxation therapy* techniques.

at-risk children/infants Children/ infants with a heightened risk of suffering a deleterious change. Although a popular media shorthand for 'at risk from parental abuse', the term also refers to threats from disease, environmental factors, etc.

at-risk subjects Subjects who stand a higher than average chance of developing an illness, being abused spouses, children, etc.

ataractic drug Any drug which tranquillizes or otherwise calms.

ataraxia calmness.

ataxia Absence of muscular coordination.

ataxic (1) Pertaining to *ataxia*. (2) Muddled, uncoordinated.

ataxic aphasia *Aphasia* due to an inability to articulate.

ataxic speech Speech with no intonation or stress.

ATE *Assessment for Training and Employment.*

athetosis Slow repetitive movements (often twisting) of the limbs, fingers and toes, resulting from brain damage.

atonia Absence of normal muscle tone.

ATQ *Automatic Thoughts Questionnaire.*

atrophy Loss or severe wastage.

attainment test *achievement test.*

attention The ability to concentrate on a target item(s) or task at hand despite distracting stimuli. See *distractibility, divided attention, selective attention,* and *sustained attention.* The term is also used in the everyday sense.

attention seeking behaviour Behaviour, often unpleasant (e.g. very late night or otherwise inconvenient telephone calls), used to attract the attention of others. Usually an expression of a need for help.

attentional deficit disorder (ADD) A disorder first found in childhood, characterized by an extreme inability to attend. The condition of *attentional deficit disorder with hyperactivity (ADD-H)* indicates that the patient cannot attend, and also exhibits *hyperactivity.*

attentional deficit disorder with hyperactivity See *attentional deficit disorder.*

attentional dyslexia An *acquired dyslexia* in which the patient reads segments of separate words as a whole (e.g. 'kill' and 'sock' read as 'kick').

attenuation Reduction in the size of a *correlation,* due to measurement error.

attenuation, correction for *correction for attenuation.*

attitude measure *attitude scale.*

attitude scale Any method of assessing the strength of a person's attitudes, thoughts or feelings about a topic. Commonest examples are the *Guttman scale,* the *Likert scale* and the *Thurstone scale.*

attitudinizing See *catatonic state.*

Attributional Style Questionnaire (ASQ) A measure of level of *causal attribution.*

attrition *subject attrition.*

atypical In diagnosis, a prefix denoting that the patient's symptoms are most like those of the disease forming the suffix (e.g. 'atypical schizophrenia'), but that other uncommon symptoms are also present.

atypical paraphilia Term for a group of *paraphilias* not adequately covered by the other sub-categories. They include *coprophilia, frotteurism, necrophilia,* and *telephone scatologia.*

audile *auditory type.*

audio-oculogyric reflex Turning the eyes in the direction of a sound.

audio-verbal aphasia An inability to comprehend phrases (although comprehension of single words may be intact).

audiogenic seizure A fit induced by high frequency sound.

audiometry The study of hearing.

auditory agnosia An inability to recognize an item or an event by its sound.

auditory aphasia An inability to comprehend spoken language.

auditory cortex Collective term for areas of the *cortex* responsible for collating and interpreting auditory information. Principally located in the *temporal lobe* (see *primary auditory cortex*).

auditory evoked potential *evoked potential* created by administering a sound to the subject.

auditory flutter fusion (AFF) The rate at which a pulsing sound must repeat itself for it just to be heard as a continuous sound.

auditory projection area *primary auditory cortex.*

auditory type Participant whose mental imagery is primarily auditory. The phrase is sometimes applied to readers who have a tendency to read words by mentally 'sounding them out'. This contrasts with the *visual type*, whose imagery (and reading) is predominantly visual.

auditory-vestibular cranial nerve *cranial nerve* number VIII. Concerned with hearing and balance.

aura (1) An 'unreal' and practically indefinable sensation (often a feeling akin to dizziness, or that one is losing full contact with one's surroundings), which may precede the onset of an *epi-leptic* attack or a *migraine*. (2) In some versions of *parapsychology*, the psychic field which supposedly surrounds the body.

authoritarian personality *trait* measuring strength of belief in a disciplined society, in blindly accepting orders from higher authority figures, in conforming to societal norms, etc.

authoritarianism *authoritarian personality.*

autia Cattell's term for a personality *trait* corresponding to 'imagination'.

autism (1) An obsessional interest in the self to the exclusion of others. (2) Rare (approx. 4 per 10,000 live births) but serious disturbance of thought processes arising in infancy. First identified by L. Kanner, although an independent paper by H. Asperger also identifies the condition. The autistic child usually avoids social contact, and may have lacked 'cuddliness' as a baby. S/he often seeks a monotony of environment and action (resulting in repetitive stereotyped movements) which appear to provide some comfort. There is usually a strong linguistic handicap, and social skills are poor. Media coverage of autistic children with remarkably good (by any standards) artistic or arithmetical talents can create the impression that the disease always has compensations. However, most autistic children appear to have poor abilities, and are frequently diagnosed as *mentally handicapped*. Autism is usually *inherited*, but cases resulting from brain damage have been reported. A case has been made for it being the product of faulty parenting methods (see *refrigerator parent*), but this has been largely discounted. The disease is four times more common in males. In earlier terminology, 'autism' referred to schizophrenia, and later the term was used synonymously with schizophrenia (the degree of division between the two diseases is still debated). The immediate explanation of what is wrong with autistic patients is still not fully resolved, but an ingenious recent theory is that they cannot create representations of how other people think see *mind, theory of.* See *Asperger's syndrome and triad of impairments.*

autistic Pertaining to *autism.*

autistic continuum The argument that autistic spectrum disorders is a continuum of dysfunction, ranging from extremely dysfunctional behaviour through to apparently 'normal' individuals with traces of ASD-like behaviour that are explained away as eccentricities.

autistic spectrum disorder (ASD) Group term for *autism, Asperger's syndrome* and (by some but not all commentators) *pervasive developmental disorder not otherwise specified.*

autochthonous From within.

autocorrelation *correlation* between events or items in a sequence of events or items.

autoeroticism masturbation.

autogenic From within the self.

autogenic training A therapy in which the patient trains him/herself to relax, using a series of exercises which induce progressively deeper levels of relaxation/meditation.

automated reporting General term for any computerized method of scoring tests and reporting an interpretation of the findings.

Automated Social History Computerized questionnaire eliciting personal, medical, and familial details.

automatic speaking Speaking without any conscious control.

automatic thought A thought which appears unbidden. A preponderance of these (particularly if negative) can be indicative of mental illness.

Automatic Thoughts Questionnaire (ATQ) A standardized measure of the degree of *automatic thoughts* a participant/patient experiences.

autonomic nervous system Carrying signals to and from the *central nervous system* to bodily systems over which there is little conscious control (e.g. glands, smooth and cardiac muscle).

autonomy versus shame and doubt See *Erikson's theory of development.*

autophobia A *phobia*, of being alone and/or of oneself. (Not a fear of cars – see *amaxophobia*).

autopsy, psychological *psychological autopsy.*

autopsychosis See *allopsychosis.*

autoregressive Dependent upon preceding events.

autoregressive integrated moving average (ARIMA) Statistical method of discerning trends in sequences of *autoregressive* events and/or measures.

autosomal Any aspect of chromosomes other than the sex chromosomes.

autosomal dominant Describes genetic inheritance where the genetic material responsible is on one non-sex chromosome. In the case of *autosomal recessive* the genetic material must be on both of a pair of non-sex chromosomes for the inheritance to manifest itself. It follows from this that autosomal recessive traits are easier to pass on.

autosomal recessive See *autosomal dominant.*

autotelic Pertaining to the defence of one's own interests.

autotopagnosia An inability to name parts of the body.

availability heuristic The phenomenon that the more often one thinks about something, the more likely one is to identify it as occurring in real life, regardless of the probability of it actually occurring.

average deviation The *mean* of all *raw score deviations* in a sample.

aversion relief therapy Therapeutic technique in which it is the cessation of the aversive stimulus which is rewarding (rather than using the threat of punishment as in *aversive therapy*).

aversion therapy Therapeutic technique using *counterconditioning*.

aversive therapy *aversion therapy*.

avoidance Any method of avoiding confronting an aversive issue. This can range in severity from avoiding answering an awkward question to *avoidant personality disorder*.

avoidance conditioning *conditioning* technique in which the participant learns to prevent an aversive stimulus occurring. This contrasts with *escape conditioning*, in which the subject is trained to stop an aversive stimulus once it has started.

avoidant disorder of childhood An abnormal aversion to approaching strangers.

avoidant personality disorder *personality disorder* characterized by an abnormally poor *self-image*, and an avoidance of social contacts.

avolition A profound lack of willingness to do anything 'off one's own bat', lack of drive, etc.

B

B-type personality *type B personality*.

Babinski reflex A type of *primitive reflex*. If a baby's foot is tickled the toes fan out and then curl. The reflex usually disappears at 8–12 months of age. Its retention after this time probably indicates neurological damage.

'baby blues' *post-natal depression*.

Baby Talk Register (BTR) Non-sexist (but less memorable) synonym for *motherese*.

BAC British Association for Counselling.

bacillophobia A *phobia of* germs and/or infection.

backward child Largely outdated term for a child whose abilities fall appreciably below his/her *age norm*.

backward elimination Method of *multiple regression* in which all the *predictor variables* are entered and then those that do not significantly add to the predictive power of the equation are removed.

backward reader Individual whose reading abilities fall appreciably below his/her *age norm*. No cause for this state of affairs is inferred (i.e. the term is not synonymous with *developmental dyslexia*).

backward speller Individual whose spelling abilities fall appreciably below his/her *age norm*. No cause for this state of affairs is inferred (i.e. the term is not synonymous with *developmental dysgraphia*).

BAI *Beck Anxiety Inventory*.

balanced Latin square See *Latin square design*.

Balthazar Scales of Adaptive Behaviour Rating scales assessing the degree to which a *mentally retarded* child/teenager can adapt into the community.

Bandura's theory of social learning Albert Bandura (1925–) observes that in many situations, people (especially children) learn skills simply by observing others performing them, and then copying (an example of *modelling*). Often the very first attempt at imitation is very accomplished – an example of *no-trial learning*. Bandura identifies various factors which influence the success of *social learning*. The person must attend to the to-be-copied activity, and be physically capable of replicating it (e.g. it is no use an infant watching someone toss the caber in the hope of being able to copy the action). The person must also be able to retain a memory of the task. Bandura argues that this is often done with a verbal code (e.g. 'right hand hold sprocket, then left hand turn screw') which is more flexible than a visual image. Children under 5 years lack this code, and so are more restricted in what they can learn. The motivation for learning and, more important, performing the task, depends largely upon whether it is perceived as rewarding. This can be learnt by *vicarious reinforcement* (observing if others are rewarded or punished for performing the same actions). In one study, children were shown a film in which aggression was either rewarded, punished, or ignored. Left to play afterwards, children who had seen aggression rewarded were significantly more likely to behave violently to toys than were children in the other two conditions. There is a considerable debate over the range of learning situations for which Bandura's methods are applicable. See *reciprocal determinism*.

Bangor Dyslexia Test (BDT) *test battery* of *dyslexic* symptoms, for subjects aged 7 years and above. Little direct emphasis on reading. Subjects are tested for e.g. knowledge of which is the left or right side of their bodies; they have to repeat polysyllabic words, perform various arithmetical tasks, recite the list of months forwards and backwards, etc.

Bannatyne-WISC categories Regrouping by Bannatyne of *WISC* sub-test scores into three categories – Spatial, Conceptual and Sequential (essentially maths skills).

bar chart *bar graph*.

bar graph Graph for *discrete variables*, in which the name of each *variable* is shown on the X *axis*, and the values on the Y *axis*. The data entries are represented as solid bars, separated by equally-sized spaces. This is not synonymous with a *histogram* (which is for *frequency distribution* data), although the two terms are often used interchangeably (erroneously).

barbiturates Group of *minor tranquillizers*, now rarely used therapeutically because they are addictive.

Barnum effect The erroneous belief that a general description of personality is an exact description of an individual. This can apply to (a) credulous souls who believe that e.g. newspaper horoscopes exactly describe them, or (b) clinicians who decide that a patient's symptoms and personality fit the too general profile created by a test.

Barron-Welsh test A measure of preference for simple or complex designs.

BARS *behaviourally anchored rating scale*.

Bartlett's method See *factor analysis*.

BAS *British Ability Scales*.

basal age In a *standardized test*, the average age of participants who pass all the items passed by an individual participant.

basal ganglia Section of *diencephalon*. Involved in planning and execution of movement.

basal measure *baseline measure*.

basal metabolism The minimum metabolic rate of the participant's body at rest necessary for the participant to remain awake.

BASC *Behavior Assessment System for Children*.

baseline measure (1) The level of performance before the onset of treatment. (2) The standard of performance against which assessment will be made.

Basic Achievement Skills Individual Screener (BASIS) Measure of scholastic attainment for subjects aged 5–13 years.

Basic Number Diagnostic Test (BNDT) See *Basic Number Screening Test*.

Basic Number Screening Test (BNST) Group test of numerical skills for children aged 7–12 years. A related test – the **Basic Number Diagnostic Test (BNDT)** is for individual testing to identify older children with numeracy problems (or to identify normal numeracy skills in children aged 5–7 years).

basic research See *applied research*.

basic skills Education's equivalent of *primary mental abilities* – the educational skills which must be present if the education process is to succeed (i.e. basic literacy, numeracy, etc.).

Basic Skills Test (BST) Measure of basic literacy and numeracy skills. Intended for assessment of unskilled or lowly skilled staff.

basic trust versus mistrust See *Erikson's theory of development*.

basiphobia *basophobia*.

BASIS *Basic Achievement Skills Individual Screener*.

basophobia A *phobia* of standing or walking.

bathophobia A *phobia* of depths.

Battelle Developmental Inventory (BDI) A *test battery*, assessing development from 0–8 years, in five principal areas: adaptation to the environment, *cognitive* skills, communication skills, motor skills and social skills.

battered child syndrome Pattern of behaviour which may result from being a victim of physical *child abuse* (includes inability to form adequate relationships, poor *self-image*).

Baye's formula *Baye's theorem*.

Baye's theorem Formula expressing the probability that an event will occur because of a particular *mutually exclusive event*. E.g. suppose we know that disease X causes a certain type of rash in 90% of patients, but the same rash occurs in 20% of patients with disease Y and 7% of patients with disease Z. Baye's theorem can calculate the probability that a patient with this rash has each of the three diseases.

Bayley Scales of Infant Development (BSID) Test battery of mental, motor and behavioural skills/attributes of infants and young children (up to 42 months) used particularly to identify abnormal development. A revised version (Bayley Scales II) was published in 1993.

BBCS *Bracken Basic Concept Scale*.

BCDP *Bracken Concept Development Programme*.

BDAE *Boston Diagnostic Aphasia Examination*.

BDI (1) *Beck Depression Inventory*. (2) *Battelle Developmental Inventory*.

BDS *Blessed Dementia Scale*.

BDT *Bangor Dyslexia Test*.

Beck Anxiety Inventory (BAI) Self-report questionnaire, measuring level of *anxiety*.

Beck Depression Inventory (BDI) Widely-used self-report questionnaire, measuring *depression*.

Beck Hopelessness Scale (BHS) Self-report questionnaire, measuring the degree to which the patient feels hopeful about his/her long-term expectations.

Beck Scale for Suicide Ideation (BSI) Self-report questionnaire, measuring the degree to which a patient has intentions to commit suicide.

befriending Activity in which (usually professionally unqualified) volunteers visit sick, lonely or otherwise disadvantaged individuals to chat, do odd jobs, etc. The effect can be therapeutic (for both parties).

behaviour The term is used in a variety of ways in psychology. Often it is used in the lay manner (i.e. meaning overt actions), but it can refer to emotional states and thought processes.

Behavior Assessment System for Children (BASC) *test battery* assessing behavioural and emotional development in people aged from early childhood to young adult.

behaviour checklist Set of descriptions of aspects of behaviour, against each of which the respondent indicates if the description applies to the subject in question.

behaviour contracting Agreement between therapist and patient regarding the structure and course of the treatment.

behaviour disorder A maladaptive behaviour which is not simply a direct manifestation of an underlying mental illness.

Behaviour Evaluation Scale Measurement of emotional and social development for 5–16-year-olds.

behaviour modification *behaviour therapy*.

Behaviour Rating Scale (BRS) See *Clifton Assessment Procedure for the Elderly*.

behaviour therapy (1) The treatment of a mental illness or maladaptive behaviour by attempting to modify the patient's behaviour, rather than discussing the underlying mental state which caused it. The technique is derived from *behaviourism* (this excludes introspection, inter alia). (2) More generally, any therapeutic method which draws upon experimental psychological research on the acquisition of traits, and general learning. Examples of behaviour therapies include *desensitization* and *flooding*.

behavioural assessment (1) A measure of a subject's behaviour in a 'real life' situation. (2) *behaviour therapy*.

behavioural checklist *behaviour checklist*.

behavioural competence The ability to use appropriate behaviour.

behavioural contagion The acquisition of a new behaviour by members of a group copying each other.

behavioural contract See *contingency contracting*.

behavioural disorder *functional mental disorder*.

Behavioural Event Recording Package (BERP) Timing and recording device for measuring several different events simultaneously.

behavioural expectation scale (BES) Form of *behaviourally anchored rating scale*.

behavioural genetics The study of genetic factors fully or partly determining behaviour.

behavioural interviewing In *behaviour therapy*, helping a patient recognize his/ her problem behaviour, how it arises and what its effects are.

behavioural medicine (1) A combination of *behaviour therapy* and medical treatment, primarily used to treat *psychophysiological disease*. The treatment of children with this technique is called *behavioural paediatrics*. (2) More generally, the study of the relationship between behaviour and issues pertaining to medicine.

behavioural observation scale (BOS) A measure (often used in *occupational psychology*) in which the observer records how often the subject performs a particular key act.

behavioural paediatrics See *behavioural medicine*.

behavioural therapy *behaviour therapy*.

behavioural toxicology The study of the effects of toxins (e.g. poisons, pollution) on behaviour.

behaviourally anchored rating scale (BARS) A rating scale in which a description of typical features associated with the behaviour in question is provided to help the scorer make his/ her choice, and thus improve the *reliability* and *validity* of the measure. E.g. in a (hypothetical) scale of trustworthiness from 1 ('completely untrustworthy') to 5 ('completely trustworthy'), against the score of 1 might be written 'cannot be left alone for a minute – has often been suspected of, or has actually been caught, stealing').

behaviourism In its rigid form, the belief that psychologists should only study what can be objectively measured. All voluntary acts can be seen as a response to some form of stimulation. Of the various stages in this process, the stimulus can be measured, as can the strength and/or appropriateness of the response, but the thought processes used to do this cannot. Hence, behaviourism concentrated on the stimulus and response, and rigorously excluded discussion of mental processes. The theory had a very strong hold on psychology from the 1920s to the late 1950s, but was eventually recognized as being too limited in its scope, and researchers began to create models of mental processing. With its emphasis on stimulus and response and *operant conditioning*, behaviourism gave rise to a number of therapies which essentially worked by more or less explicitly *conditioning* the patient (see *learning theory* and *stimulus-response* learning). Critics have argued that the methods were too harsh and mechanistic – in part, objections may stem from the fact that symbolically identical conditioning techniques can be used to train laboratory animals. However, for certain conditions, the treatment is effective (e.g. see *token economy*). See *behaviour therapy* and *neobehaviourism*.

Belbin test A measure of self-perception of one's principal abilities in managerial tasks.

Bell Adjustment Scale *Adjustment inventory*, for participants aged 12 years and over.

bell-shaped curve Shape of curve of a *normal distribution*.

bell-shaped distribution *normal distribution*.

belle indifférence, la See *conversion disorder*.

Bellevue Scale *Wechsler-Bellevue Scale*.

benchmark measure A test or measure which is commonly used in a particular situation, and hence likely to be used as a *common measure*. The term usually implies that the test or measure is widely recognized as being of good quality.

Bender-Gestalt Test A test of visuo-spatial skills. The subject is required to copy geometrical shapes of increasing complexity. Test is suitable for participants aged 8 years and over. Part of the *Bender Visual Motor Gestalt Test* battery.

Bender Report A computerized assessment of performance on the *Bender-Gestalt Test*.

Bender Visual Motor Gestalt Test (BVMGT) Battery of visual and motor skills, including the *Bender-Gestalt Test*.

benign senescent forgetfulness *age associated memory impairment*.

Bennett Differential Aptitude Test *Aptitude test for* basic scholastic and clerical skills.

Bennett Test of Mechanical Comprehension *Aptitude test* of basic engineering skills.

Benton Revised Visual Retention Test Measure of visual skills. The participant has to remember a series of increasingly complex shapes. For participants aged 8 years and over.

benzedrine Type of *amphetamine*.

benzodiazapines Group of *minor tranquillizers*.

Bern Sex Role Inventory (BSRI) Measure of the degree to which a participant conforms to a 'traditional' gender role.

Bernoulli distribution *binomial distribution*.

Bernreuter Personal Adjustment Inventory Personality measure yielding six scores, representing personality *traits*.

BERP *Behavioural Event Recording Package*.

BES *behavioural expectation scale*.

Beta (ß) (1) The symbol for the probability that a *Type II error* (*beta error*) will be made. See power (*of a statistical test*). (2) See *signal detection analysis*. (3) *standardised coefficient*.

beta blockers General term for a range of drugs that block or reduce stimulation of a component of the *autonomic nervous system* (more specifically, the beta-adrenergic receptors). Beta blockers are used in the treatment of a number of heart conditions and blood pressure problems, and can also reduce levels of *anxiety*.

beta error *Type II error*.

Beta Test See *Alpha Test*.

beta waves A pattern of electrical activity in the brain detected by *EEG* with a frequency below 12 Hz.

beta weight (1) A measure of how well a test score predicts a *criterion*. (2) See *multiple regression*.

between-group variance The degree to which the scores of groups differ on the same measure. Contrast with *between- subject variance*.

between groups ANOVA *Analysis of variance* in which all the measures are between groups measures.

between groups measure See *analysis of variance*.

between-subject variance The degree to which the scores of subjects within the same group differ. Contrast with *within-group variance*.

between-subjects design See *within-subjects design*.

between-subjects measure (1) *between groups measure* (2) *between-subject variance*.

Bexley-Maudsley Test A *test battery* assessing psychological dysfunction following brain damage.

BHS *Beck Hopelessness Scale.*

bias *test bias.*

biased sample A sample of items or subjects which, either deliberately or accidentally is not representative of the *population* (e.g. assuming that political opinions collected from a fascist rally represent the views of the entire electorate).

BIB *biographic information blank.*

bibliotherapy The use of reading materials for therapeutic purposes (e.g. self-help guides, exercises, etc).

Big Five *five factor model of personality.*

bilateral Involving both sides. Hence, in discussing brain damage, a' bilateral loss' means that the structure has been lost from both sides of the brain.

bimodal distribution *Frequency distribution* with two *modes*. In graphical form, appears as a distribution with two peaks. Not to be confused with *binomial distribution.*

binaural Of both ears.

Binet/Binet-Simon Scale Original (French) version of the *Stanford-Binet Scale/Test.*

binge drinking Drinking excessively large amounts of alcoholic drink in sporadic sessions to the point of (often severe) intoxication.

binge eating Eating excessively large amounts of food in sporadic sessions, well beyond the needs of satisfying hunger. The sessions may be followed by self-induced vomiting. Most commonly found in *bulimia nervosa.*

bingeing binge eating or binge drinking.

binomial distribution *Frequency distribution* of the probability of a particular *mutually exclusive event* occurring at each possible number of occasions in a set of trials (e.g. if a coin is tossed six times, the probability of heads coming up on 0,1,2,3,4,5 and 6 occasions). The larger the number of trials, the more the binomial distribution resembles the *normal distribution.* See *bimodal distribution* and *Poisson distribution.*

binomial test A test of probability of a particular series of *mutually exclusive events* (e.g. of throwing 4365123 on a die of TTHHHTT in a series of coin tosses). The *sampling distribution* is the *binomial distribution.* Different formulae are used for series above and below 25 in length.

Binswanger's disease *Dementia* whose origins are disputed, but whose symptoms are akin to those of *lacunar dementia.*

bioavailability The speed with which a drug becomes active in the body.

biodynamic therapy (1) General term for a range of therapies exploring links between mind and body through physical exercises, massage, etc., the principal aim being to reach the 'inner self' beneath the socialized exterior. (2) The original therapeutic technique devised by Boyesen using the general principles of (1).

bioenergetics Therapeutic technique devised by Lowen out of the work of Reich (see *orgone therapy*, though note that bioenergetics is shorn of the excesses of Reich's theories). The technique concentrates on bodily exercises, and, akin to *biodynamic therapy*, stresses the need to concentrate on the 'inner self' rather than outward appearance and attitudes that have been created by socializing forces.

biofeedback Providing information on the state of a bodily function. The technique can be used for therapeutic purposes – e.g. a patient might be given information on his/her brain wave patterns enabling him/her to judge how well a relaxation technique is working (an example of *biofeedback training*).

biofeedback training See *biofeedback*.

biogenic Of biological origin.

biographic information blank (BIB) (1) Sheet requesting biographical details which the participant fills in. (2) A (computerized) system for extracting biographical details in which the participant's early answers determine the questions he or she is subsequently asked.

biographical approach The analysis of the lives of people. The term is often specifically applied to the analysis of lives of unusual individuals (e.g. those pre-eminent in their fields) to find common factors explaining their unusualness.

biographical inventory List of personal details about a person.

biological age The body's state of physical development/degeneration. This is gauged against the state of an average person of the same *chronological age*.

bionomic *exogenous*.

biopsychosocial research Research combining biological, psychological and sociological perspectives.

biosocial theory Theory that discusses the interaction between the body (including its psychological processes) and social forces.

bipolar depression *bipolar disorder*.

bipolar dimension See *dimension*.

bipolar disorder See *depression*.

bipolar I disorder *bipolar disorder*.

bipolar scale Scale on which participants make their evaluations on a scale finishing at either end with opposite values (e.g. good-bad, light-dark etc.).

bipolar II disorder See *depression*.

birth cohort A group of people born in the same period of time. See *cohort*.

birth order Siblings arranged in order of age.

birth trauma In some *psychoanalytic* theories, the distress surrounding birth, which is argued to lie at the root of future psychological problems.

biserial correlation coefficient (rbis) See *point biserial correlation coefficient*.

bivariate With two *variables*.

bivariate correlation *correlation* between two *variables*.

bivariate method Any method using two *variables* (although typically refers to the procedure of changing the *independent variable* and observing the changes in the *dependent variable*).

Blacky Pictures test *projective personality test*, based on *Freud's psychoanalytic theory* (i.e. examines how well the participant has 'resolved' the various stages of development). The pictures used are of a family of dogs.

blank American term for a form (either a test sheet or a form requesting biographical information).

blank experiment An experiment or task administered to participants which in itself is of no interest, but is necessary in order to distract the participants from another task whose performance is of interest.

BLAT *Blind Learning Aptitude Test*.

Blessed Dementia Scale (BDS) A simple test of intellectual impairment and functioning, usually employed in the assessment of *demented* patients. The test requires the patient to answer some simple memory questions (e.g. 'what is your name?', 'who is the current Prime Minister?') and to perform some simple intellectual tasks (e.g. 'count backwards in steps of three'). Details of how capable the patient is of looking after him- or herself are collected from a *caregiver*. The test provides a useful 'ready reckoner' of how intellectually impaired a patient is, and how much professional nursing care and assistance is required. The Blessed Dementia Scale (named after its author, Dr Blessed) is a British test. An American equivalent is the *Mental Status Questionnaire*, which has a very similar format.

Blind Learning Aptitude Test (BLAT) Non-verbal intelligence test for visually handicapped children, using only tactile skills. Participants must distinguish between shapes by touch, and identify the 'odd one out'. The shapes increase in complexity as the test progresses.

blind study Study in which the participant is unaware of the group to which s/he has been assigned whilst the study is conducted (although usually s/he is informed after it is over). E.g. participants may be divided into two groups and receive two different drug treatments. Knowing which drug they are receiving might influence motivation and hence performance; this is an undesirable extra variable, and accordingly, participants are kept unaware of the nature of their treatment. A special form of the blind study is the *placebo study*. In conventional blind studies, the experimenters recording the participants' performance are aware of which participants belong to which groups (the studies are sometimes called *single blind studies*). However, in certain circumstances, this knowledge could (consciously or unconsciously) sway the experimenters' judgements where measures are essentially subjective. E.g. if the drugs are being compared for their effect on mood change, then the experimenters may exaggerate differences in effects in support of the drug they favour. This is an example of *observer bias*. In these instances, a **double blind study** is used, where neither the participants nor the observers know the groupings (the information is kept by a third party until testing is complete). See *Clever Hans*.

blindsight Phenomenon whereby a patient, although supposedly blind from brain damage, can respond to some visual stimulation (e.g. pointing to the source of a light). The patient is unaware that s/he can 'see' the stimulus. The phenomenon is due to intact connections to parts of the brain involved in relatively minor aspects of visual perception.

block (1) Group of participants assigned together because of something they have in common. (2) Group of tests or other items, whose link is either that they are all given to the same participant, or that they are given in the same time period (the latter definition applies particularly to repetitious measures such as *reaction times*). For either definition, the source of the similarity is called the **blocking factor**. (3) In therapy, the inability (either voluntary or involuntary) to progress along a particular line of thought.

block design test Sub-test of the *Wechsler* intelligence tests. The participant is required to replicate patterns using a set of blocks. As the test progresses, the designs become harder to replicate.

block randomization (-isation) (1) Experimental procedure in which subjects are presented with the same *block* of items on more than one occasion, but on each new presentation, the items are presented in a different order. (2) Presenting blocks of items in a random order.

block sampling Taking samples of subgroups in proportion to their incidence in the total population.

blocking factor See *block*.

blood–brain barrier A physiological mechanism which prevents many chemicals carried in the blood from entering the brain. This protects brain tissue from damage, but it can also filter out potentially beneficial drugs.

blood pressure The pressure of blood against the walls of the arteries. Is measured in two components – *systolic pressure* is the pressure when the heart contracts, and *diastolic pressure* is the pressure when the heart relaxes. The pressure is measured in terms of millimetres of mercury moved in the measuring apparatus (a *sphygmomanometer*) and is expressed as a ratio of systolic/diastolic (e.g. '120/80', which is a typical reading for a young, reasonably healthy adult). High blood pressure (*hypertension*) is in itself without symptoms, but can be a precursor of serious illness, particularly cardiovascular problems, including *stroke*. There are many causes of high blood pressure, including disease, but the culprits also include an over-rich diet, smoking and stress. The condition can also arise for no apparent reason (*essential hypertension*).

BLUE best linear unbiased estimator.

blueprint *test specifications*.

blunting Responding to a stressful situation by trying not to think about it. This contrasts with *monitoring*, in which the stressful situation is deliberately concentrated on.

BMDP Bio-Medical Data Package – a commonly-used computerized statistical analysis package.

BNDT *Basic Number Diagnostic Test*.

BNST *Basic Number Screening Test*.

Boder Test of Reading-Spelling Patterns Measure of types of reading handicap, including a separation of *developmental dyslexia* from motivational or perceptual problems.

body dysmorphic disorder A dysfunctional and illusory belief that one's body is severely distorted or abnormal in appearance.

body image The subjective impression one has of one's own body. An inaccurate image – a *body image disturbance* – can lead to problems such as *anorexia nervosa*, in which the patient is convinced that s/he is too fat.

body image disturbance See *body image*.

body language The behavioural state of an individual as indicated by his/her posture and/or physical movements. The study of body language can be a useful research and therapeutic tool (e.g. in estimating the emotional state of an individual when a direct question is impossible). However, several studies have shown that the method is not infallible. See *non-verbal communication*.

Body Shape Questionnaire (BSQ) Measure of the degree of satisfaction a patient finds in his/her body shape. Used in e.g. assessment of *anorexia nervosa*.

bodywork General term for any therapeutic method which emphasizes or is wholly based on bodily movements and exercises.

Boehm-PV *Boehm Test of Basic Concepts – Preschool Version*.

Boehm-R *Boehm Test of Basic Concepts – Revised.*

Boehm Resource Guide for Basic Concept Teaching A collection of teaching aids for developing certain concepts in young (3 years and over) and retarded children.

Boehm Test of Basic Concepts – Preschool Version (Boehm-PV) Test of 3–5-year-old children's comprehension of 26 basic concepts. See *Boehm Test of Basic Concepts – Revised.*

Boehm Test of Basic Concepts – Revised (Boehm-R) Test of 4–7- year-old children's grasp of basic concepts. See *Boehm Test of Basic Concepts – Preschool Version.*

Bogardus scale A measure of the distance (physical and/or social) which a participant likes to keep between him/herself and members of other social or ethnic groups.

Bogen cage A measure of visuo-spatial intelligence. The participant propels a ball around a maze using a prodder.

bogus pipeline A technique for eliciting truthful rather than socially acceptable answers. The experimenter convinces (i.e. deceives) the subject into believing that s/he is being assessed using a very accurate lie detector. This supposedly acts as an incentive for the subject to tell the absolute truth in answering potentially embarrassing questions.

BOLD-fMRI (Blood Oxygen Level Dependent fMRI) Commonly used *fMRI* technique.

bond (1) Emotional attachment – in lay terms, a 'relationship', with a set of societal expectations on how it should be conducted (e.g. mother–child bond). (2) The verb for the same process.

bonding The formation of a *bond.*

Bonferroni correction Mathematical procedure applied when a group of comparisons are being made on the same data to control for the *familywise error rate.*

Bonferroni inequality Measure of probability of committing a *Type I error* when employing a *t test* to compare several pairings of groups drawn from the same larger set of groups (e.g. if there are groups A, B, C and D, using the t test to compare A and B, A and C, A and D, B and C, etc).

booster session In therapy, a session arranged some time after the main body of treatment has ceased, to check on progress, reinforce the original therapy, etc.

bootstrap statistics General term for a range of tests in which there are repeated random samplings from a group of data to determine the data's statistical characteristics, rather than making reference to the hypothesized *population* from which the group was drawn.

borderline intelligence *IQ* level which places a subject on the border of being classified as *mentally retarded.*

borderline personality disorder *personality disorder* characterized by sudden and unpredictable swings in mood, and a chronic need for companionship. There may also be thought disorders.

borderline significance See *significance.*

borderline state The state of an individual who displays symptoms of a mental illness, but who retains sufficient vestiges of 'normality' to be considered sane (although only just). Note that the term often carries an implicit value judgement.

Borke Interpersonal Awareness Test Two-part measure of children's awareness of others' emotions. Part I:

emotion-inducing situations are described to the participant, who must decide which emotion would be elicited. Part II: the participant hears stories in which s/he is described as behaving in various ways towards another child. The participant must judge how the child would feel.

BOS *behavioural observation scale.*

Boston Diagnostic Aphasia Examination (BDAE) Test battery used in the assessment and classification of *aphasia.*

BOT *Bruininks-Oseretsky Test of Motor Proficiency.*

bottom up data mining See *data mining.*

bovine spongiform encephalopathy (BSE) Degenerative disease of the nervous system in cattle, colloquially known as *mad cow disease*. The disease probably originated from eating animal feed contaminated with *scrapie* (or possibly infected human remains) and was (at least in the early stages) principally confined to the United Kingdom. A new human disease – *variant Creutzfeldt–Jakob Disease (vCJD)*, first identified in 1995, is believed to have been caused by eating BSE-infected beef products. At the time of writing, this is largely confined to the UK. Early predictions were of tens or hundreds of thousands of deaths, but at the time of writing, vCJD has killed circa 150 people (mostly young adults), with predictions of all future deaths being circa 70 (though some more pessimistic predictions have a higher figure). The symptoms of vCJD are akin to *Creutzfeldt–Jakob Disease* but typically early symptoms are *anxiety* and *depression* before movement and/or cognitive impairment, and brain cell damage has a different appearance.

Bowman Test of Reading Competence Reading test for 7–10-year-olds. Uses *cloze procedure.*

box and whisker plot Method of summarizing data in which the typical values are presented as a box plotted on the graph, with more extreme values shown as vertical lines (often T-shaped) projecting from either end of the box. Typically, the bottom of the box represents the 25th *percentile*, the top of the box the 75th percentile, and a horizontal line within the box represents the 50th percentile. The ends of the lines represent the highest and lowest scores. The length of the box thus represents the *interquartile range* and whiskers that are appreciably longer than the box indicate *outliers*. Although this is the normal usage, on occasion authors use the box and whiskers to denote different values, so caution is advised.

BPS (1) British Psychological Society. (2) Bricklin Perceptual Scales.

BPS guidelines Any set of guidelines (usually on codes of professional conduct) issued by the British Psychological Society.

BPVS *British Picture Vocabulary Scale.*

brachycephalic wide-skulled.

Bracken Basic Concept Scale (BBCS) Measure of concept acquisition in children aged 2 years 6 months–8 years. Consists of a group screening test and a more searching diagnostic test done on a one-to-one basis. See *Bracken Concept Development Programme.*

Bracken Concept Development Programme (BCDP) Teaching programme for developing concept acquisition. Related to *Bracken Basic Concept Scale.*

bracketing *collapsing.*

brady- As a prefix: slow and/or halting.

bradyarthria Slow and/or halting speech, caused by brain damage.

bradyglossia Slow and/or halting speech, caused by damage to the mouth.

bradykinesis Abnormally slow movements.

bradylalia Slow and/or halting speech.

bradylexia Slow and/or halting reading, not simply attributable to low intelligence.

bradylogia Slow and/or halting speech.

bradyphasia *bradylalia.*

bradyphrenia Abnormally slow thought.

bradypraxia Abnormally slow actions and reactions.

brain death Cessation of function in the brain, particularly the brain stem and other areas controlling basic reflexes, such as pupillary contraction in bright light.

brain stem Section of the brain which is the meeting place between the spinal cord and the brain. Besides acting as a relay station between the spinal cord and other areas of the brain, the brain stem controls many 'life support' mechanisms (e.g. blood pressure, respiration).

brain stimulation Physical stimulation of the brain by chemical or electronic means.

brainstorming Session in which a group of people is encouraged to generate ideas, however inappropriate, in the hope of creating fresh approaches to a problem. The method has been used therapeutically to encourage patients to consider ways of solving their problems.

brainwashing Rather nebulous term for a variety of methods of attempting to coerce individuals or groups to change their opinions, attitudes or beliefs. The term has been overused by the media and is probably best avoided.

Brazelton Scale Measure of newborn infant's mental state, by measuring reactions to a variety of stimuli (light, rattle, etc.), reflexes, etc. Used to identify possible brain damage, *mental retardation*, etc. An amended version – the *Neonatal Behavioural Assessment Scale with Kansas Supplements (NBAS-K)* is also in wide use.

brick test Semi-serious term for a *creativity test* in which the subject must think of novel uses for an everyday object (often a house brick, hence the name).

Bricklin Perceptual Scales (BPS) Measure of children's perceptions of their parents.

brief psychotherapy *short-term psychotherapy.*

brief psychotic disorder In DSM-IV, the preferred term for *brief reactive psychosis.*

brief reactive psychosis *Psychosis* in which the patient possesses some of the symptoms of schizophrenia, which is a reaction to a highly stressful event, and which lasts under a fortnight. See *schizophreniform disorder.*

brief therapy Any therapeutic method which is intentionally limited to a small number of sessions. The definition of small varies between therapists (e.g. two or three to 20 or more). See *short-term psychotherapy.*

Brinley plot A graph of the average response times of older people plotted against those of young people performing the same task.

Briquet's syndrome A *somatoform disorder,* characterized by the patient constantly seeking medical treatment for non-existent physical complaints.

Bristol Social Adjustment Guides (BSAG) Measure of the degree to which school age children are able to adjust to social situations.

British Ability Scales (BAS) *test battery* to assess 2–17-year-old children's intellectual abilities. The test can be used as a straightforward measure of overall intelligence, and can also provide a profile of abilities.

British Picture Vocabulary Scale (BPVS) Updated version of the *English Picture Vocabulary Test (EPVT)*. Test of vocabulary in young children. Participants are shown four pictures and are asked which best represents a word provided by the experimenter. The words increase in difficulty as the test progresses. The original (American) version of the test is known as the *Peabody Picture Vocabulary Scale*.

broad categorizing *cognitive style* in which the participant uses a small number of categories, each containing a large number of items. This contrasts with *narrow categorizing*, in which the participant has a larger number of categories, each with fewer items.

Broca's aphasia *Aphasia* whose principal symptom is an inability to speak. Contrast with *Wernicke's aphasia*.

Broca's area *Area of temporal lobe* (in most people, the left lobe) controlling various aspects of speech production. Damage to it causes *Broca's aphasia*.

Brodmann's Areas Division of *cerebral cortex* into 47 areas, based on differences in tissue structure.

brontophobia A *phobia* of thunder.

Brook Reaction Test *psychoanalytic* measure, in which participants produce free associations to a list of words.

Brown–Peterson task Named after its inventors, the task presents participants with a list of to-be-remembered items,

then gives them a distracting task (usually counting backwards in units of two or three), before asking participants to recall the items. The task thus assesses the fragility of *short-term memory*.

BRS *Behaviour Rating Scale.*

Bruininks-Oseretsky Test Test of children's (4–14 years) motor skills.

Bruininks-Oseretsky Test of Motor Proficiency (BOT) Measure of gross and fine motor skills for age range young child to young adult.

BSAG *Bristol Social Adjustment Guides.*

BSE *bovine spongiform encephalopathy.*

BSI *Beck Scale for Suicide Ideation.*

BSID *Bayley Scales of Infant Development.*

BSQ *Body Shape Questionnaire.*

BSRI *Bern Sex Role Inventory.*

BST *Basic Skills Test.*

BTR *Baby Talk Register.*

buddying *befriending.* The term has recently been used particularly for the befriending of AIDS patients.

buffering hypothesis Belief that social support systems act as a protection against developing illness.

buggery (1) Anal intercourse. (2) Old term for *bestiality*.

bulimia Gross over-eating. The cause may be due to organic changes in the brain (e.g. a tumour) but the most common reason is *bulimia nervosa*, where the over-eating may take the form of *binge eating*, rather than a constant over-eating.

bulimia nervosa The urge to eat unnaturally large quantities of food (usually *binge eating*, followed by self-induced vomiting). Patients are usually teenage and young adult women. An appreciable proportion (some studies record circa

50%) of patients have previously suffered from *anorexia nervosa*. See *bulimia*.

burnout A loss of *affect*, feelings of *depression*, and generally negative feelings and poor *self-image*, resulting from excessive pressures of work.

Burt Word Reading Test Reading test for 6–12-year-olds. Requires subjects to read out loud single words, which increase in difficulty as the test progresses.

BVMGT *Bender Visual Motor Gestalt Test.*

Bzoch-League Receptive-Expressive Emergent Language (REEL) test Measure of language development from birth to 3 years.

C

C (1) *contingency coefficient.* (2) (In some models of intelligence) speed of thought. (3) *conscientiousness.*

CA *chronological age.*

CAAS *Children's Attention and Adjustment Survey.*

CAB (1) *Comprehensive Ability Battery.* (2) *Cognitive Ability Battery.*

CAC *Compulsive Activity Checklist.*

cachexia Weakness resulting from malnutrition.

cachexis *cachexia.*

cachinnation Laughter – the term often applies specifically to inappropriate laughter.

cacodaemonomania The *delusion* that one is possessed or controlled by the Devil, or some other evil force.

cacoguesia Disorder of taste in which normal food has an unpleasant taste.

cacosmia Disorder of smell in which non-aversively smelling substances are perceived as malodorous.

CAD *cortical atherosclerotic dementia.*

cafeteria feeding Any study in which the participant is given a range of foods to choose from, rather than being presented with a fixed menu.

caffeinism Addiction to substances which contain caffeine (principally coffee).

CAG *creative aggression therapy.*

California F Scale A measure of *authoritarian personality.*

California Infant Scales Forerunner of *Bayley Scales of Infant Development.*

California Personality Inventory (CPI) Personality measure derived from the *Minnesota Multiphasic Personality Inventory*, but intended for normal subjects, rather than clinical populations.

callosum *corpus callosum.*

Cambridge Research Mood Survey (CRMS) Measure of wide variety (23) of moods in the 'normal' population.

CAMDEX Cambridge Mental Disorders of the Elderly Examination. A *test battery* of measures for assessing older people for *dementia* and other aspects of mental health and psychological well-being.

Campbell and Fiske multitrait multimethod Method of measuring *construct validity.*

Camphill Movement Worldwide therapeutic movement for training and treating mentally handicapped people (children and adults). A particular feature are 'Camphill Villages', therapeutic working communities for adults.

campimetry The measure of the size of a participant's visual field (i.e. how big an area can a person's sight 'take in').

cannabis A variety of *hemp*, from which is derived **marijuana**. In low doses, it produces feelings of relaxation, heightened perception, and mild euphoria. In larger doses, some intellectual impairment and (rarely) *hallucinations* are observed. The drug is rarely addictive, but it has carcinogenic properties.

canonical correlation *canonical regression*.

canonical regression *multiple regression* technique in which there are two or more *criterion variables*.

CANTAB Battery of tests of neurological and psychological impairment.

CAO *computer assisted observation*.

CAPE *Clifton Assessment Procedure for the Elderly*.

Capgras's syndrome *paranoid disorder* characterized by an irrational suspicion that one's friends and close associates have been replaced by imposters.

Captain's Log Set of exercises designed to improve basic intellectual functioning. The exercises are specifically aimed at subjects with *mental retardation*.

CAQD *Clinical Analysis Questionnaire*.

card sorting task Any task in which the participant must sort a set of cards (conventional playing cards or cards specially devised for the test in question) into particular sub-groups.

cardinal trait *general trait*.

cardiophobia *A phobia* of heart disease.

'care in the community' *community care*.

caregiver A person who looks after a patient or child.

caregiver burden The psychological and material demands and *stress* placed on a *caregiver*.

Caregiver Strain Index (CSI) Measure of *stress* and strain in *caregivers* (usually caregivers of older patients).

caretaker (1) *caregiver*. (2) For the benefit of American readers – 'caretaker' is more commonly used in British English to denote a janitor, particularly of a school.

carryover effect (1) See *test wise subjects*. (2) The influence of performing in the early part of an experiment on later parts of the experiment (e.g. confusing memories of items encountered in early and later parts of the experiment).

CARS *Childhood Autism Rating Scale*.

Carver Word Recognition Test Reading test for participants aged 4–8 years. Participants must choose the printed representation of a word spoken by the experimenter from a list of alternatives.

CAS (1) *Cognitive Assessment Scale*. (2) *Clinical Anxiety Scale*.

case The patient, or group of patients regarded as a single entity being treated (as in e.g. *family therapy*).

case study A detailed investigation of a single participant or small group of participants, who exhibit a particularly unusual or even unique characteristic (e.g. a particularly exotic type of brain damage).

caseload The number of cases for which a therapist is responsible.

CASL *Comprehensive Assessment of Spoken Language*.

CAT (1) *Children's Apperception Test*. (2) *Cognitive Abilities Test*. (3) *cognitive-analytic therapy*. (4) *computerized adaptive test*.

CAT scan *computerized axial tomography*.

catagelophobia *A phobia* of criticism.

catalepsy The maintainance of a bodily posture for an abnormally long period. Many commentators use the term interchangeably with *catatonic state*.

catalexia (1) The inappropriate repetition of a word or phrase when reading. (2) A form of *dyslexia* in which this occurs to an abnormal degree.

catalogia Persistent and illogical repetition of a nonsense word or phrase.

catalytic In therapeutic settings, the effect created by a question, event or person which creates a fresh insight or action in the patient.

catamnesis See *anamnesis*.

cataplexy Sudden and temporary collapse (resulting from loss of muscle tone) whilst in a state of extreme *anxiety* or strong emotion.

catatonia *catatonic state*.

catatonic schizophrenia See *schizophrenia*.

catatonic state State of extreme immobility, without unconsciousness. In some instances, it is possible to move the patient's limbs into new postures (without apparent reaction from the patient) which are maintained (the effect is rather like posing a doll). This is known as *waxy flexibility*. The catatonic state is a principal feature of *catatonic schizophrenia*. The postures formed during a catatonic state are sometimes called *attitudinizing*.

catchment area The geographical area served by a school, hospital, social services group, etc.

categorical variable *variable* which defines membership of a category (definition 1).

categorization (-isation) test Any test in which participants must place items into groups or categories. The measure can gauge intelligence, or may be used simply to examine a specific disability at categorization (e.g. after brain damage).

categorized list List of items which all belong to the same category or small group of categories. Sometimes used in memory experiments.

category (1) A grouping of participants or items on the basis of a unique feature which distinguishes them from members of other categories (e.g. male and female, university students and school pupils, etc.). A *natural category* is one which is 'innately' perceived as valid (e.g. basic perceptions of colour, etc.). (2) In some more exacting (and rarely used) definitions, the set of all groups to which individuals can be assigned.

category scaling Assigning participants or events to *categories*. If the categories are suitable, the resulting 'scores' can be treated as a *nominal scale* or *ordinal scale*.

Category Test Computerized version of the *Halstead-Reitan test battery*.

catharsis A feeling of immense relief from tension and release of emotion. See *cathartic therapy* and *abreaction*.

cathartic therapy Any therapeutic method which enables the patient to release a suppressed emotion or memory, e.g. through an outburst of emotion or *hypnosis*.

cathexis (1) *Freudian* concept of the 'mental energy' which people place in thoughts of objects or of other people. (2) In *transactional analysis*, the energy required to move between *ego states*.

CATI *computer assisted telephone interview*.

catotrophobia A *phobia* of mirrors/of breaking mirrors.

Cattell Culture-Fair Test (CCFT) Intelligence test. By avoiding measures of linguistic skills and general knowledge, it supposedly measures intellectual skills equally accessible to people of all cultural/linguistic backgrounds.

Cattell Infant Intelligence Scale Companion to the *Stanford-Binet Scale*, for infants aged 3–30 months.

Cattell scree test *scree analysis*.

Cattell Sixteen Personality Factor Questionnaire (16PF) Personality test assessing 16 aspects of personality identified by the test's author, Raymond Cattell. The scores can be compressed into a more manageable four item scale, for which population norms (including details of how prevalent the particular type is in common occupational groups) are available.

caudal Anatomical term referring to the 'lower' part of the body or the section of an organ which is closest to the tail end.

causal analysis The analysis of causes.

causal attribution theory A revision of the *learned helplessness* model, in which the patient attributes causes of his/her problem to three factors – (a) the degree to which s/he feels that it is due to personal factors, rather than the workings of the outside world (*internal-external scale*); (b) the degree to which the problem is specific to the situation, as opposed to being a general feature of the patient's life (*specific-global scale*); and (c) the degree to which the situation is perceived to be a permanent or temporary feature (*stable-unstable scale*).

causal-comparative research Studies which assess the causes of a phenomenon by comparing two or more groups which possess the said phenomenon in differing strengths (e.g. do children with good and poor attendance records [the phenomenon] vary because they have different levels of neuroticism [the hypothesized cause]?).

CBF *cerebral blood flow.*

CBRSC *Comprehensive Behaviour Rating Scale For Children.*

CBQ *Cognitive Bias Questionnaire.*

CBS *chronic brain syndrome.*

CCEI *Crown-Crisp Experiential Index.*

CCFT *Cattell Culture-Fair Test.*

CD *conduct disorder.*

CDAP *Chemical Dependency Assessment Profile.*

CDD *childhood disintegrative disorder.*

c.d.f. *cumulative density function.*

CDI *Child Development Inventory.*

CDM *Harrington–O'Shea Career Decision-Making System.*

CDR *Clinical Dementia Rating.*

CDS *Children's Depression Scale.*

ceiling effect Effect achieved by giving a group a test which is too easy – an undesirably large proportion of group members score full or nearly full marks, making discrimination between them impossible. See *floor effect*.

cell In statistics, an intersection of a row and column in a data table. If the rows and columns represent different treatments or conditions, a cell thus represents a specific combination of treatments/conditions.

censored observations Those observations that do not record what is being looked for over the period of the study. E.g. in measuring new cases of mental illness in a random sample of the population over ten years, at the end of the decade of observations, a high proportion of the sample will not have contracted any mental illness, and they are said to be censored observations. Note that there is an implication that what is being looked for may occur outside the range of the study (e.g. one year later, a proportion of the 'sane' members of the sample may have developed mental illness). See *left censoring, single censoring* and *type I censoring.*

centile *percentile.*

central aphasia *conduction aphasia.*

central deafness Deafness resulting from damage to the inner ear and/or brain.

central limit theorem See *sampling distribution.*

central nervous system The collective term for neurons which form the brain and the *spinal cord.*

central sulcus The *sulcus* which marks the divide between the *frontal lobe* and the *parietal lobe.*

central tendency, error of See *error of central tendency.*

central tendency, measures of See *measures of central tendency.*

central tendency error *central tendency set.*

central tendency set See *evaluative set.*

central trait *trait* which influences a significant proportion of behaviour, although not as much as a *general trait.*

centrencephalic epilepsy See *epilepsy.*

centroid In mathematics, the overall 'direction' in which several vectors are 'moving'. The concept is used in, inter alia, *factor analysis* and *multivariate analysis of variance* to determine the strength and nature of certain group trends compared with others.

cephalo-caudal growth Growth progressing from the head to the tail.

cerebellar speech A speech disorder attributable to damage to the *cerebellum,* and characterized by poor pronunciation and lack of a controlled 'tempo'.

cerebellum Area of the brain, primarily responsible for balance and coordinating movement.

cerebral arteriography Method of assessing the state of the blood supply to the brain – a tracer dye is injected into the *cerebral blood flow,* which is then observed by X-rays or a similar device.

cerebral blood flow (CBF) Blood supply to the brain.

cerebral contusion Bruising/bleeding in brain tissue.

cerebral cortex Usually known by its abbreviated name of *cortex.* The cerebral cortex is the characteristic wrinkled surface of the brain. It is divided into two linked *hemispheres* (left and right) and can be divided into four regions or lobes (see *frontal, parietal, occipital* and *temporal lobes*) which have different functions. The cerebral cortex is responsible for the majority of higher intellectual functions.

cerebral dominance The control of other brain functions by the *cerebral cortex.*

cerebral haemorrhage See *stroke.*

cerebral localization (-isation) *localization.*

cerebral palsy General term for any defect in motor skills (movement) resulting from brain damage.

cerebral thrombosis See *stroke.*

cerebral ventricles Chambers within the brain containing *cerebrospinal fluid.*

cerebrospinal fluid Fluid which cushions the brain and in part supplies it with nutrients.

cerebrotonic personality See *Sheldon's personality types.*

cerebrovascular accident (CVA) *stroke.*

cerebrum Largest and outermost section of the brain, whose 'surface' is the *cerebral cortex*. Concerned with most higher intellectual functions.

cervical level (of spinal cord) Topmost section of the *spinal cord*. Consists of eight segments, labelled C1 (the topmost) to C8.

CFF *critical flicker fusion*.

CFQ *Cognitive Failures Questionnaire*.

C-GAF Version of *Global Assessment of Functioning* for use with children.

Chambless Scale *Mobility Inventory for Agoraphobia*.

chance error Error due to chance factors – any curious deviation in performance which cannot be attributed to known factors.

chance-half correlation *split-half correlation*.

chance level result A result which fails to reach statistical *significance*.

change agent A participant who plans and/or initiates change (the term usually applies to studies of the workplace).

character disorder A rather nebulous term for a maladaptive behaviour or personality (e.g. a gross lack of self-confidence), which, whilst not necessarily indicating mental illness, may be sufficiently unusual to merit treatment.

character neurosis *character disorder*.

characteristic root *eigenvalue*.

Charteris Reading Test Reading test for 10–13-year-olds.

CHD coronary heart disease.

chemical dependency substance abuse.

Chemical Dependency Assessment Profile (CDAP) *structured interview* package eliciting details of a patient's *substance abuse*.

chi squared distribution *sampling distribution* for the *chi squared* statistic.

chi squared goodness of fit test See *chi squared* (x^2) *test*.

chi squared one sample test *chi squared goodness of fit test*.

chi squared (x^2) test A *non-parametric* test of the frequency of occurrence of one or more *discrete variables*. The **chi squared goodness of fit test** measures the frequencies with which each of a single *discrete variable's* categories occurs – i.e. do all categories occur with the same frequency, or are some categories *significantly* over- or under-represented? E.g., given five ice cream flavours to choose from, are all selected with equal likelihood? Chi squared is also employed to measure whether two or more groups fall into two or more categories with equal likelihood. E.g. the ice cream problem can be converted into a two group problem by considering if men and women have different preferences for the flavours. The test analyses the differences between the observed number of occurrences and the numbers which would be expected from a random set of data. The bigger the discrepancy between the observed and the expected, the greater the probability that the result is significant. There are two important caveats to the chi squared analysis. The first is that if an expected value is < 5, then the test should not be run. The second is that when there are only two groups and two categories, 0.5 should be deducted from the calculated value of chi squared. This is known as **Yate's correction**. See *chi squared test of independence*.

chi squared test of independence A use of the *chi squared test* to calculate whether responses to one test influence responses to another, subsequent test.

child abuse Deliberate psychological or physical mistreatment of a child, usually by his/her parents and/or other caregivers. Compare with *child neglect*.

Child Development Inventory (CDI) Measure of young children's behavioural and intellectual development.

child ego state See *transactional analysis*.

child neglect Psychological or physical damage befalling a child resulting from lack of care, usually by his/her parents and/or *caregivers*. Compare with *child abuse*.

childhood amnesia The loss of memories about early childhood which is disproportionately greater than would be predicted from simple forgetfulness. Originally thought (e.g. by Freud) to be due to suppression of emotionally fraught memories, more recent explanations have taken a cognitive approach (e.g. young children are intellectually incapable of storing memories efficiently, so they are forgotten).

Childhood Autism Rating Scale (CARS) Test assessing the level of *autism* a child with the condition has.

childhood disintegrative disorder (CDD) A type of *pervasive developmental disorder* characterized by normal development in the first 2 years, then regression and loss of language, social skills, bowel and bladder control, play and/or motor skills. There are often repetitive stereotyped patterns of behaviour and/or interests.

childhood neurosis Rather nebulous term denoting a *neurosis*-like, illness occurring in childhood.

childhood onset pervasive developmental disorder Disorder which begins in childhood, and whose symptoms appear to be a mixture of autism and *schizophrenia*. Amongst the symptoms are: an abnormally low desire for normal social contacts, distress at changes in surroundings, sudden temper tantrums, and a *flattened affect*.

childhood psychosis *psychosis* whose onset is in childhood. The term includes *autism* and *childhood onset pervasive developmental disorder*.

childhood schizophrenia *schizophrenia* whose onset is in childhood. The term is now largely outmoded. In some older texts, the term is used fairly interchangeably with *autism*.

Children's Apperception Test (CAT) *projective personality test* of children's beliefs and motivations. The participant is shown a series of pictures and is asked to make up a story about each one.

Children's Attention and Adjustment Survey (CAAS) Measure of behaviour problems in children with *attention deficit disorder* and/or *hyperactivity*.

Children's Depression Scale (CDS) Measure of symptoms of *depression* and related ideas and behaviours (e.g. guilt, lowered *self-esteem*, etc.) in children aged 9–16 years.

Children's Self-Report and Projective Inventory Set of *projective tests* for children aged 5–12 years.

Children's State-Trait Anxiety Inventory (CSTAI) Junior version of the *State-Trait Anxiety Inventory*.

chlorpromazine Type of *major tranquillizer*.

choice reaction time (CRT) See *reaction time*.

cholinergic hypothesis Theory that much of the memory loss in *dementia of the Alzheimer type* can be attributed to depletion of the *cholinergic system*. See *ganglioside, ondansetron*, and *tacrine*.

cholinergic system Shorthand for the network of *neurons* which use *acetylcholine*. About 90% of neurons in the brain are cholinergic.

chorea Uncontrollable jerky movements (as seen in e.g. *Huntington's chorea, senile chorea*, and *Sydenham's chorea*). The adjective is **choreiform**.

choreiform See *chorea*.

chromophobia A *phobia* of colour.

chronic Long-lasting/long-standing. See *acute*.

chronic brain disorder Any long-lasting (although not *congenital*) disorder of mental efficiency, usually resulting from a long-standing cause (e.g. malnutrition/vitamin deficiency from a poor diet). Can produce *dementia- like* symptoms, or can 'flare up' relatively suddenly into *acute confusional state*.

chronic brain syndrome (CBS) Long-term degeneration of brain tissue, resulting in severe impairment of personality and/or intellectual functioning. Largely synonymous with *dementia*.

Chronic Pain Battery (CPB) Questionnaire assessing the subjective discomfort of patients suffering from chronic pain, their medical history, and their general background. Formed in part from the *Pain Assessment Questionnaire*.

chronic post-traumatic stress disorder See *post-traumatic stress disorder (PTSD)*.

chronically accessible construct A *self-concept* which is very readily available.

chronological age (CA) The length of time a person has been alive.

CI *confidence interval*.

circular behaviour A behaviour which causes others to react similarly (e.g. yawning).

circular reaction (1) *circular behaviour*. (2) A term used by the child psychologist Piaget, denoting certain repetitive acts in children, which are held to be critical features of intellectual development.

circumlocution Talking around the topic in question because the appropriate word cannot be recalled (found to spectacular effect in some *demented* patients).

CIT *critical incident technique*.

civil commitment (American) The committal of a patient for treatment, regardless of the patient's wishes.

CJD *Creutzfeldt-Jakob Disease*.

clang association Language disorder in which the patient produces sequences of words which sound similar – usually the statements are nonsensical. Most often encountered in patients suffering from *schizophrenia*.

Class A drugs Drugs, whose possession, under UK law, carry the severest penalties (i.e. long jail sentence, unlimited fine, etc.). They include the *opiates, Ecstasy*, and *psychedelic drugs*. *Class B drugs (amphetamines, barbiturates*, and *cannabis)* carry a lesser fine, and *Class C drugs* (some of the milder stimulants) carry a smaller penalty.

Class B drugs See *Class A drugs*.

class boundaries The upper and lower limits of a *class interval*. Synonymous with the concept of apparent and real limits (see *class interval*).

Class C drugs See *Class A drugs*.

class interval width (i) See *class intervals*.

class intervals Groups of scores for which any recorded score uniquely belongs to one group. E.g. suppose that a test has a maximum score of 30 and a minimum of 0, and scores are always in whole numbers. If we define 'high' scores as between 21 and 30, 'medium' as between 10 and 20, and 'low' as between 0 and 9, then it can be seen that a score can only fall into one of these three categories, which can thus be defined as class intervals. Such a definition would not be possible if the category boundaries overlapped (e.g. High =19–30, Medium = 9–21, Low = 0–11). The lowest score necessary to be within a particular class interval is called the *lower apparent limit*, whilst the highest score to merit inclusion in the same class interval is called the *upper apparent limit*. The *upper real limit (URL)* is half the smallest unit of measurement being used, above the upper apparent limit (e.g. if the smallest unit of measurement is whole numbers of degrees fahrenheit and the upper apparent limit is 90 degrees, then the upper real limit is 90.5 degrees). Similarly, the *lower real limit (LRL)* is half the smallest unit of measurement below the lower apparent limit (e.g. lower apparent limit = 80 degrees, lower real limit = 79.5 degrees). This is to allow for the presumed inaccuracies in the measuring instruments (e.g. if the measure is only accurate to the nearest degree, there there is a good chance that any individual measure will be inaccurate by up to half a degree) – see *real limits. Class interval width (i)* is the difference between the upper real limit and the lower real limit. The middle value of a class interval is called the *midpoint* (e.g. in a class interval of 1–7, the midpoint is 4). See *grouped frequency distribution*.

classical conditioning A method of training subjects to make a response to a stimulus which in itself would not normally elicit the response, because the stimulus is associated with another stimulus which normally elicits the response. The technique was first objectively studied by the Russian physiologist Ivan Pavlov, in the early years of the twentieth century. Dogs salivate when presented with food; Pavlov discovered that if a bell was rung (or in other experiments, a light was flashed) just before the presentation of the food, then after several days, the dogs began to salivate simply on hearing the bell, presumably because they expected food to follow. The technique is used in certain forms of *behaviour therapy* – the therapist trains the patient to associate a behaviour which is to be encouraged with a rewarding stimulus, and, conversely, to associate an undesirable behaviour with an aversive stimulus. For an extreme case of this see *Little Albert*. See *operant conditioning*.

classical migraine See *migraine*.

classical probability Theory of *probability* which assumes that each possible outcome can occur with equal likelihood (e.g. a card drawn from a pack, the outcome of tossing a coin, etc.).

classical psychoanalysis *psychoanalysis* which follows fairly rigidly the precepts of *Freud's psychoanalytic theory*.

classificatory scale *nominal scale*.

claustrophobia A *phobia* of enclosed spaces.

clerical aptitude test *aptitude test* of skills associated with clerical work.

Clever Hans An example of the *experimenter effect*. Clever Hans was a nineteenth century circus horse who, given a simple addition problem, could tap out the correct answer with his hoof. This was taken as evidence for equine arithmetic, until it was noted that the animal was responding to a slight relaxation in the features of the humans watching him when he had tapped the correct number of times.

client Term used by some therapists as a synonym for 'patient'.

client-centred therapy Therapeutic technique (principally derived from *Roger's self theory of personality*) in which it is assumed that the best person to resolve a patient's internal conflict is the patient him/herself. Accordingly, the therapy principally consists of the patient talking to the therapist, with the therapist making minimal interjections (e.g. to amplify discreetly a key point by asking the patient to go into greater detail). The therapist holds the client in *unconditional positive regard* – i.e. the client is always right – his/her beliefs and emotions are uncritically accepted by the therapist. The technique can be mimicked by a computer programme, the best known example of which is *Eliza*. See *humanistic psychology*.

client group (1) A group of patients with the same problem. (2) The group of patients being treated by the same therapist or group of therapists.

Clifton Assessment Procedure for the Elderly (CAPE) *test battery* consisting of two 'sub-batteries' – the *Cognitive Assessment Scale (CAS)* and the *Behaviour Rating Scale (BRS)*, measuring intellectual skills and personality respectively in older subjects (particularly hospital patients and the institutionalized elderly).

climacteric *menopause.*

Clinical Analysis Questionnaire (CAQ) Measure of personality, intended primarily for clinical populations. Identifies personality features akin to those of the *16PF*, and also a further 12 features characteristic of particular types of mental illness.

Clinical Anxiety Scale (CAS) Measure of level of *anxiety* and associated behaviours.

Clinical Dementia Rating (CDR) A checklist for assessing the level of functioning of which a patient suspected of *dementia* is capable on various tasks. From this, his/her level of impairment and hence the severity of the dementia can be calculated.

clinical depression A rather nebulous term for a state of *depression* felt to be severe enough to merit professional help.

clinical interview An interview with a patient to elicit details of his/her illness. In addition to the description of the symptoms, the interviewer also usually monitors the manner in which the patient replies and his/her general mannerisms.

clinical method (1) Any method of study based upon or around the treatment of illness (compare with *clinical study*). (2) The assessment of subjects in a naturalistic setting.

clinical psychology The treatment and analysis of mental illness by purely psychological means (i.e. usually without drug therapies, unlike many branches of *psychiatry*). Clinical psychologists have an initial training in general psychology before taking a more specialized postgraduate qualification.

clinical study A study of the efficacy of a treatment. See *clinical method* (definition 1).

clinical theology Therapeutic regime with a philosophical basis drawn from Christian belief.

clinical trial A *clinical study* (often the term is particularly applied to the study of a drug treatment).

clock drawing test A *design copying test* in which the to-be-copied item is an analogue clock face. The test is most often used in assessing patients suffering from brain damage, and particularly, *demented* patients.

clonic convulsion See *convulsion*.

clonus Rapid muscular contractions and relaxations in reaction to sudden and then sustained stretching. The condition is indicative of neurological damage, and is most readily demonstrated by stretching the ankle, causing a twitching of the calf muscle (*ankle clonus*).

closed question A question for which there is a specific answer being looked for and where any extra information provided is treated as irrelevant. Common examples include requests for basic factual information such as a person's name, their date of birth, where the answer required is a simple 'yes' or 'no' etc. This is in contrast to an *open question*, in which all the information supplied in the answer may potentially be of relevance. Thus, 'do you agree with the Government's policy on immigration – yes or no?' is a closed question, but 'please will you comment on the Government's policy on immigration?' is an open question.

closed system A system unaffected by external forces.

closure In some intelligence tests, the ability to perceive a whole shape when only some of its features are visible.

cloze procedure Reading test method – participants have to insert appropriate words into blanks in a passage of text (e.g. fill in the blank in 'the cat sat on __ mat'). The term is meant to indicate a link with the gestalt concept of 'closure' (the hypothesized drive to mentally fill in missing gaps in an image).

Cloze Reading Tests Set of reading tests for 8–12-year-olds, which (predictably) use the *cloze procedure*.

cluster analysis A statistical method of grouping subjects or items according to their scores on a number of *variables*.

The results of the analysis are sometimes expressed as **dendograms**, which resemble 'family trees', and show the stages by which progressively smaller and more defined groups are created.

cluster sampling Taking a sample of subjects from a confined geographical area (e.g. school, area of a town etc.) as representative of the general *population*. In **multistage cluster sampling** only a sub-group of the initial sample is selected for analysis.

CMMS *Columbia Mental Maturity Scale (CMMS)*.

CNS *central nervous system*.

coaction The joint working of two or more items or subjects.

cocaine Drug which stimulates the nervous system producing intense euphoria and heightened sensations. It can be addictive. Like most drugs used illegally, it was originally devised for legitimate medical reasons, as a painkiller and an *antidepressant* (an early enthusiast was Freud).

coccygeal level (of spinal cord) Lowest level of the *spinal cord*. Consists of one *segment* (labelled CO1 – actually formed from several [usually three] fused segments).

Cochran Q test See *McNemar test*.

code test Measure of intellectual ability in which data must be receded according to a rule provided by the experimenter.

codeine See *opiates*.

Coding Test Sub-test of the *Wechsler* intelligence tests, which is a *digit-symbol substitution task*.

coefficient (1) Something which acts in conjunction with something else. (2) In statistics, an index of measurement. The term is sometimes used as an abbreviation of *correlation coefficient*. (3) In mathematics, a constant value by which an item in an equation must be multiplied.

coefficient a *coefficient alpha.*

coefficient alpha *coefficient of equivalence.*

coefficient of alienation *random variance.*

coefficient of concordance *Kendall's coefficient of concordance.*

coefficient of determination (R^2) The square of a correlation coefficient. See *correlation* and *multiple regression.*

coefficient of dispersion *coefficient of variation.*

coefficient of equivalence See *reliability.*

coefficient of internal consistency See *reliability.*

coefficient of reproducibility The proportion of consistent answers given by a subject on a test which has been scaled in difficulty/strength of opinion. E.g. a scholastic test beginning with 'what is 2+2?' and ending with demands for the proof of the special theory of relativity; or, a measure of opinions beginning with statements such as 'the law has not always given women equal rights' and progressing to 'a woman should always be appointed instead of a man'. If the test is accurate, then the subject should always give the 'right' answers up to the point where the test items get too hard for him/her, or express too extreme a view for his/her taste.

coefficient of stability See *reliability.*

coefficient of total determination See *multiple regression.*

coefficient of validity General term for a measure of validity.

coefficient of variability *coefficient of variation.*

coefficient of variation Calculated as the *standard deviation* of a sample, divided by its *mean* and multiplied by 100 (e.g. a sample with a mean of 1 and a standard deviation of 0.2 has a coefficient of variation of 20%). The figure can be used to compare the relative degree of *variance* in different samples whose means vary in size, and accordingly, where direct comparisons would be difficult.

coenaesthesia Awareness of one's own condition.

cognition The processing and acquisition of knowledge.

cognitive Adjective from *cognition.*

Cognitive Abilities Test (CAT) Intelligence test battery, with a chief subdivision into non-verbal and verbal measures.

Cognitive Ability Battery (CAB) *test battery* assessing 20 basic *cognitive* abilities.

cognitive-analytic therapy (CAT) Version of *cognitive therapy* drawing upon an eclectic mix of other therapeutic methods. Places a strong emphasis on the patient doing 'homework' to identify needs and problems.

Cognitive Assessment Scale (CAS) See *Clifton Assessment Procedure for the Elderly.*

cognitive behaviour assessment Any assessment method which concentrates on the expressed thoughts of the patient.

cognitive behaviour therapy Any therapeutic technique combining features of *behaviour therapy* and *cognitive therapy.*

cognitive-behavioural therapy *cognitive behaviour therapy.*

Cognitive Bias Questionnaire (CBQ) Measure of the degree to which a subject misinterprets events in a maladaptive fashion.

cognitive competence *competency* to perform *cognitive* tasks.

cognitive empiricism See *cognitive therapy*.

Cognitive Failures Questionnaire (CFQ) A test which asks subjects to report instances of memory failure in recent everyday life (e.g. forgetting to buy items when shopping, etc.). Assesses how forgetful people are in 'real life' (compared with more artificial laboratory tasks).

cognitive intervention General term for providing training in intellectual skills to people perceived as being intellectually disadvantaged.

Cognitive Participation Rating Scale (CPRS) A measure of general intellectual functioning, designed to assess the changes in brain damaged and/or *mentally retarded* subjects as they progress through therapy.

cognitive rehabilitation Therapeutic process of restoring (where possible) the intellectual skills lost as a result of brain damage.

cognitive restructuring Replacing 'faulty' ideas and concepts with new and 'better' ones (e.g. replacing *arachnophobia* with more rational ideas about spiders).

cognitive strategy A strategy used to cope with a particular situation. Can refer to a maladaptive behaviour in the onset of a stressful situation.

cognitive style A problem-solving method/method of intellectual functioning consistently used by a subject.

cognitive therapy It can be argued that many mentally ill or behaviourally maladjusted patients misinterpret events so that they 'feed' the illness (e.g. a person afraid of rejection will take the slightest negative comment as further 'proof' that they are unlovable). Cognitive therapy attempts to make patients realize, through self-analysis and various exercises, that the majority of events can be explained in a rational and non-negative manner (i.e. the therapy tries to restore common sense to the patient). The process whereby the patient and therapist examine the problems jointly is sometimes called *cognitive empiricism*.

cognitive triad Term devised by Beck (author of *Beck Depression Inventory*) to denote the threefold maladaptive thought processes of a depressed patient: that s/he is a failure, that the future can only be viewed pessimistically, and that the world is a frustrating place.

Cogrehab Computerized battery of measures and therapeutic exercises designed to identify and to help ameliorate problems resulting from mental handicap.

Cohen's d Measure of *effect size*.

Cohen's kappa Measure of *inter-rater reliability*.

cohort A group of people raised in the same environment and/or period of time. Almost invariably refers to a group of people of similar age.

cohort analysis Analysis of individuals belonging to the same *cohort*, often for the purpose of examining a unique characteristic of that cohort.

cohort effect A difference between age groups which is better attributed to differences in the ways they were raised and educated than to their ages per se. See *overlapping longitudinal study*.

cohort sequential design *overlapping longitudinal study*.

cohort study See *panel study*.

colinearity See *multiple regression*.

collapsing In statistics, combining the results of a lot of groups and/or individuals into a single larger group or smaller number of larger groups in order to simplify the analysis. This is usually only justifiable if there is a bona fide reason for putting the groups/individuals together, and it makes logical sense to treat them as a coherent unit – it cannot simply be done to make calculations easier if there are real differences being covered over by this method. E.g. it may be reasonable to look at the performance of all the schoolchildren in a particular school by classifying them into age groups. However, it would not make much sense to collapse them into two groups dependent upon whether their surnames began with A–M or N–Z, even though it would make the statistical comparison of the groups much easier.

collective unconscious See *Jung's psychoanalytic theory*.

collinearity A high level of *correlation* or relationship between *independent variables* in a *regression* calculation. This is a problem because a high level of collinearity undermines the assumptions the analysis is based on.

Colorado Childhood Temperament Inventory Battery of scales of aspects of temperament/behaviour (e.g. 'emotionality', 'reaction to foods', etc.).

colour agnosia A failure to recognize colours (although note that patients can often match up colours – i.e. they can 'see' them).

colour anomia A failure to name colours.

Coloured Progressive Matrices (CPM) See *Raven's Progressive Matrices*.

Columbia Mental Maturity Scale (CMMS) Intelligence *test battery* for children aged between 3 years 6 months and 10 years. Requires no spoken answers and little movement, and is particularly intended for children with restricted movement and/or speech impairment.

column marginal See *row marginal*.

coma State of unconsciousness from which the patient cannot be roused. Some *reflexes* may or may not be present, and the depth of the coma can be graded according to this.

combat fatigue *combat stress*.

combat stress *Post-traumatic stress disorder* specifically resulting from being caught up in military combat.

commissurotomy The surgical severing of the *corpus callosum* (usually done to treat certain forms of *epilepsy*). The patient thus has left and right *hemispheres* which have lost their principal means of communicating with each other. These **split brain patients** often complain that they simultaneously experience two different worlds.

common measure A measure used by more than one study, enabling direct comparisons to be made between studies.

common metric *common measure*.

common migraine See *migraine*.

common trait *trait* possessed by all the population.

commonality In *multiple regression*, the degree to which the *variance* of the *criterion variable* is accounted for by each of the *predictor variables* individually, and how much is due to the combined effects of two or more of the predictor variables.

communality The amount of *variance* of a measure which is accounted for by a *factor* or group of factors derived from *factor analysis*.

community care Generic phrase for any system of maintaining mentally ill people in the general community (even if in sheltered housing) rather than keeping them in hospital (and hence divorced from everyday life).

community psychiatry Psychiatry concerned with the general issue of mental health in the community and *community care.*

community psychology Nebulous term for studies and therapies which measure/treat people in their homes, workplaces, etc., rather than in a laboratory/clinic.

comorbidity The simultaneous existence of two or more illnesses in the same patient.

compensable factors Factors of a job which determine the rate of compensation (e.g. pay).

compensation (1) Compensating for a weakness in a limb, organ, etc. by greater reliance on another limb, organ, etc. (2) *defence mechanism.*

compensation therapy Any therapeutic technique which trains patients to compensate for the absence or weakness of a skill by placing greater reliance on the skills they do have.

compensatory striving See *individual psychology.*

competence *competency.*

competency (1) An ability to process information within a particular field. (2) An appropriate level of training, skill, and experience in a practitioner. (3) An appropriate degree of 'normality' in a patient (e.g. in deciding if s/he can be held legally responsible for his/her actions).

competitive aggression *aggression* directed at factors preventing the achievement of a desired goal.

completely randomized design Experimental design in which groups of entirely different subjects receive different treatments. See *randomized block design* and *repeated measures design.*

completion rate (1) The rate at which a task is completed. (2) The proportion of the total original sample which completed all the tests.

completion test Any measure in which the subject must complete an item (e.g. an incomplete sentence, a shape with a section missing, etc.).

complex Loose term for a group of *traits* which together form a guiding behaviour and/or set of beliefs (usually maladaptive).

compliance Obeying an order or request without necessarily believing in its wisdom.

component efficiency hypothesis Hypothesis that the decline in a skill is due to a decline in one or more of the 'basic' sub-skills governing it.

componential intelligence See *triarchic theory of intelligence.*

composite event In *probability* theory, a sequence of *simple events* (e.g. in coin tossing, a sequence of four successive 'heads').

composite score The overall score on a measure. Not necessarily synonymous with 'total score', because components of the measure might be given different *weightings.*

comprehension test (1) A measure of ability to understand a passage of text. (2) A *crystallized intelligence* measure of knowing the correct things to do in particular circumstances (e.g. 'what should you do if you cut your finger?').

Comprehensive Ability Battery (CAB) Intelligence *test battery* for participants aged 15 years and over. Assesses *primary mental abilities*.

Comprehensive Assessment of Spoken Language (CASL) Measure of principal aspect of spoken language skills for age range young child to young adult.

Comprehensive Behaviour Rating Scale For Children (CBRSC) Measure of behaviour of schoolchildren aged 6–14 years.

Comprehensive Test of Adaptive Behaviour (CTAB) Measure primarily of coping and housekeeping skills in subjects (5–60 years) with potential problems.

Comprehensive Test of Non-Verbal Intelligence (CTONI) Measure of *non-verbal intelligence*, with no or minimal linguistic skills required.

Comprehensive Test of Phonological Processing (CTOPP) Measure of ability of process phonological information (loosely, 'word sounds').

compulsion A drive to perform an act (often with a ritualistic element), which the patient cannot keep under control. Compulsions can be further classified into *overt compulsions* (where the acts are external to the person and can be observed by others) and *covert compulsions* (where the act is an internal, ritualized thought process).

Compulsive Activity Checklist (CAC) Measure of degree and type of *compulsive* activities performed by a patient.

compulsive personality disorder *personality disorder* characterized by a desire for perfection in everything done by the patient. Not to be confused with *obsessive-compulsive disorder*, where the tasks the patient wishes to perform perfectly are limited to a narrow range of often pointless, trivial, and ritualistic procedures.

computer assisted observation (CAO) Any system of recording behaviour in which data are directly entered into a computer database, and/or in which the computer 'prompts' the experimenter with instructions.

computer assisted telephone interview (CATI) Telephone interviewing technique in which the responses are immediately keyed into a computer. The programme automatically prompts the interviewer with the next question – this can be especially advantageous where there are a number of alternate question routes.

Computer Generated H-T-P Clinical Assessment Computerized version of the *House-Tree-Person Test*.

Computer Programmer Aptitude Battery (CRAB) *aptitude test* of ability to perform computer programming.

computerized adaptive test *adaptive test* run by a computer programme.

computerized axial tomography (CAT scan) A body scan by means of a sequence of highly sensitive X rays, which display successive cross-sections of the body.

computerized transaxial tomography (CT) *computerized axial tomography*.

Comrey Personality Scales Measure yielding eight scales of personality (e.g. 'activity versus lack of energy', 'empathy versus egocentrism' etc.).

conative pertaining to intention.

conceptual organization The ability to treat items at an abstract level in order to uncover basic rules and principles.

conceptual replication See *replication*.

concomitant variable *covariate*.

concrete intelligence See *abstract intelligence*.

concrete thought Immature or disordered mental abilities, in which the subject is incapable of abstract thought, and is constrained to thinking about the 'here and now'.

concurrent processing Any task which requires the participant to perform two or more separate tasks simultaneously.

concurrent validity See *predictive validity*.

concussion (1) A temporary confusion and/or loss of memory resulting from a blow to the head. (2) Temporary unconsciousness following a blow to the head.

condition The form or state of the *independent variable* being administered (e.g. a test would have two conditions if it was available in two formats).

condition of worth See *Roger's self theory of personality*.

conditional correlation The *correlation* between variables in a *conditional crosstabulation* table.

conditional crosstabulation See *crosstabulation*.

conditional mean The *mean* of a variable when other variables assume particular values.

conditional positive regard See *Roger's self theory of personality*.

conditional probability The situation in which the *probability* that one event will occur is dependent upon another event also occurring (e.g. for there to be a chance of a rainbow, it must first rain).

conditional relationship A relationship that is described in terms of the influence of other variables. E.g. older adults generally have lower intelligence test scores than younger adults. But if differences in level of education are accounted for the test score difference is lowered. Thus, the conditional relationship between age and intelligence test score taking into account level of education is lower than the *zero order* relationship when level of education is not accounted for.

conditioned aversion *aversion therapy*.

conditioned behaviour The behaviour produced by *conditioning*.

conditioned emotion An emotional response created by *conditioning* (e.g. *Little Albert*).

conditioned response (CR) The response to a stimulus created by *conditioning*.

conditioned response learning *classical conditioning*.

conditioning Process whereby a subject is trained to respond to a stimulus which previously did not elicit the reaction desired. Training a subject NOT to respond to a stimulus in a particular way is called **deconditioning**, and the loss of the response itself is called *extinction*. See *classical conditioning, counterconditioning, operant conditioning*, and *token economy*.

conduct disorder (CD) Nebulous term for serious misbehaviour by children. Can be divided into two sub-categories. *Socialized conduct disorder* describes breaches of social or moral codes (e.g. truancy), whilst **undersocialized conduct disorder** describes offences against other people or objects (e.g. arson). The two sub-categories can be further divided according to whether the acts performed are violent or non-violent.

conduction aphasia *Aphasia* characterized by an inability to repeat words, although other aspects of language are relatively normal.

conductive hearing loss Hearing loss resulting from damage or obstruction to the outer or middle ear. This contrasts with *sensorineural hearing loss*, which results from damage to the inner ear or nerves. *Mixed hearing loss* is attributable to a mixture of both of the above.

confabulation Condition in which the patient makes up stories or other implausible explanations to cover up gaps in his/her memory or other skills. Generally, the term is reserved for situations where there is no conscious attempt to deceive.

confidence interval (CI) A range of scores within which a certain percentage of all possible observations of the same variable is predicted to occur. For example, a 95% confidence interval describes the range of scores within which 95% of all observations are predicted to occur. The values of the upper and lower limits of the confidence interval are called the *confidence limits*. The measure is of importance in, inter alia, *significance* calculations.

confidence limits See *confidence interval*.

confirmatory factor analysis Form of *factor analysis* designed to test a hypothesis about the interrelationships within the data being analysed. In contrast, *exploratory factor analysis* attempts to find factors without prior assumptions of what they will be.

confluence A *dysfunctional* over-identification with another person, idea or situation.

conforming personality An excessive desire to behave according to the actual or perceived wishes of other people.

confounding The simultaneous change of two or more *independent variables*, so that any subsequent changes in a *dependent variable* cannot be unambiguously attributed to just one of the said independent variables. E.g. if wages are increased by 100% at the same time as the workplace temperature is raised by 3 degrees, it would be difficult to ascribe a subsequent increase in productivity purely to the change in temperature.

confounding variable A variable which may distort the finding of primary interest.

congenital Born with. Strictly speaking, the term applies to both genetically-inherited effects and effects resulting purely from changes in the womb (e.g. *foetal alcohol syndrome*). However, several commentators restrict its use to the former category.

congenital adrenal hyperplasia *inherited* (but treatable) malfunction in which female sufferers are born with genitals which look like those of a male. In rare cases this is undetected at birth, and the patient is raised as a boy, the error not being discovered until puberty. Such cases are obviously of interest to sex difference researchers.

congenital hypothyroidism *cretinism.*

congenital rubella syndrome Set of dysfunctional symptoms and behaviours induced by the mother of the individual contracting rubella (German measles) during the first 4 months of pregnancy. Symptoms vary, but in addition to numerous physical symptoms, may include intellectual dysfunction and poor sight and hearing.

congenital word blindness Old term for *developmental dyslexia.*

congruence Complete concord between *self-image* and the image projected to others. Hence, more loosely, appearing and being completely genuine in expression. See *Roger's self theory of personality.*

congruent validity The degree to which the findings of a test concur with an established test of the same phenomenon.

conjoint measure Measure of a *variable* which itself consists of two or more sub-components.

conjoint therapy Therapy administered to partners or to two or more patients simultaneously.

conjoint variables A set of *variables* which all play a role in determining an event (e.g. personality, age, wealth, and physical appearance are some of the conjoint variables most people would consider in choosing a partner).

Conners Parent Rating Scale A measure of parental assessment of emotional and social development of children aged 3–7 years.

Conners Teacher Rating Scale A 40 item measure of a teacher's assessment of a pupil's behaviour and abilities.

conscientiousness (C) Personality *trait* (one of the *'Big Five'*) measuring the *degree* to which the subject is organized and reliable.

consequent See *antecedent*.

consequent variable The results of an action, often with the implication that the results reward or punish the subject (thereby shaping future behaviour). See *SORC*.

conspecific Of the same species or group.

constant A value in an equation which can only have one value (e.g. [XX] in the equation, circumference = 2[XX]r). See *variable*.

constant error A consistent direction of error in performance.

constant variable *control variable*.

constellatory constructs See *personal construct theory*.

constitutional types *Sheldon's personality types*.

constraint seeking strategy In solving a problem (e.g. in a '20 questions' game), seeking answers which progressively reduce the set size of all possible answers.

constriction See *personal construct theory*.

construct (1) A method of interpretation. (2) A concept or set of concepts. See *personal construct theory*.

construct theory *personal construct theory*.

construct validity The degree to which a test measures or expresses a particular theoretical stance. See *validity*.

construction competence The ability to form concepts and thought processes.

constructional apraxia A profound inability to construct objects from their component parts.

constructive alternativism See *personal construct theory*.

constructivism The argument that learning is not objective and factual but is inevitably shaped and even biased by the learner's prior experience, the context in which the learning takes place, etc.

constructs See *personal construct theory*.

consumer psychology The study of consumer behaviour (e.g. in choosing particular brands of washing powder, etc.).

contagion (1) The transmission of ideas, and, by extension, changes in behaviour and attitudes resulting from this. (2) The spread of disease, particularly by physical contact.

contamination *statistical contamination*.

content analysis (1) The codification and analysis of communicative acts. (2) Analysis of a test to assess its usefulness.

content criterion The minimum mark a subject must attain on a test to be deemed to know the topic being tested in sufficient depth. See *criterion-referenced test*.

content validity The degree to which a test assesses skills encountered in 'real life' situations. Hence, it is also a measure of (a) the degree to which the test adequately covers all aspects of the skill in question, and (b) how much it does NOT rely upon extraneous skills (the commonly-given example is that a test of maths should not require an advanced knowledge of English to understand the questions). See *validity*.

contextual intelligence See *triarchic theory of intelligence*.

contingency (1) The degree to which the existence of an event or state is dependent upon the existence of another event or state. (2) The conditions necessary for *conditioning* to occur.

contingency coefficient (C) *Correlation* between two *variables*, both of which are divided into more than two categories (for analysis of correlations between two *dichotomous variables*, see *tetrachoric correlation coefficient*).

contingency contracting Therapeutic method, akin to the *token economy*, in which the patient agrees to behave in a particular way (often signing a doc-ument – a *behavioural contract*) in exchange for a series of rewards and/or avoidance of punishments administered by the therapist. In *self-management therapy*, the patient administers the rewards/punishments him/herself.

contingency management *contingency contracting*.

contingency table Presentation of data in which two or more groups' membership of two or more *mutually exclusive events* are displayed (e.g. male and female, and whether they voted for parties x, y, or z at the last election; dogs, cats, and monkeys, and their first choice of ice cream flavour from strawberry, vanilla, chocolate and kumquat, etc.). The most common method of assessment of the contingency table is the *chi squared* statistic.

continuous biserial correlation coefficient *point biserial correlation coefficient*.

continuous recording Recording all of the available information within an observation period. See *interval recording*.

continuous variable *quantitative variable* for which (given sufficiently accurate measures) a theoretically infinite number of scores is possible (e.g. height). This is in contrast with a *discrete variable*, a quantitative variable for which only a limited number of scores is possible (e.g. points in a snooker game). In reality it is impossible to measure an infinite number of different scores. Measuring instruments have a smallest measure below which they cannot 'see', and hence measures can only fall within the range provided by the smallest measure which can be taken. E.g., suppose that a rule can only accurately measure down to a thousandth of a metre, and everyone measured is between 0 and 2 metres in height. A subject can only fall into one of 2000 height categories. It thus follows that a continuous variable is always, pedantically speaking, a discrete variable. In most instances, however, this distinction is treated as a mathematical nicety, and it is assumed that to all intents and purposes, a supposed continuous variable measures with the accuracy it claims.

contra-indication to therapy A symptom which indicates that the patient's illness is better treated using another therapy.

contracting *behaviour contracting.*

contraction bias The tendency for people to rate subjects or events in the middle of the scale, when more extreme ratings might be justified. See *error of central tendency.*

contralateral On the opposite side of the *midline* from the section of the body in question. Compare with *ipsilateral.*

contrast pole See *repertory grid test.*

contrast sensitivity function (CSF) A measure of the changing ability to focus clearly on a fine pattern of dark and light parallel lines when the relative darkness and lightness of the lines is altered.

contre coup injury Injury which occurs on the opposite side of the body from where the damaging blow was received.

control group Group of subjects who do not receive a particular treatment, or possess a particular characteristic in which the experimenter is interested and who are measured as a comparison with the **experimental group**, who receive the treatment or possess a particular characteristic. E.g. a control group might be a group of healthy people being compared with a group of patients suffering from a particular disease.

control theory See *reality therapy.*

control through fear The restraint upon performing an act caused by fear of punishment. Contrast with *control through guilt.*

control through guilt The restraint upon performing an act caused by fear of the ensuing guilty feelings. Contrast with *control through fear.*

control variable An experimental *variable* which is held constant for all subjects (e.g. the same test room might be used).

controlled association test Any test in which the subject must produce a word associated with a given word in a manner specified by the experimenter (e.g. *antonym test*).

controlled drinking A therapeutic method in which alcoholics are trained to keep their alcohol consumption within prescribed limits.

controlling behaviour Behaviour which seeks to control or otherwise limit the freedom of others.

controlling for General term for any method of ensuring that a particular *variable* does not interfere with the running or interpretation of an experiment. At its simplest, this means e.g. controlling for extraneous noise (i.e. choosing a quiet test room), but can also mean more complex statistical methods, such as the *analysis of covariance.*

convergence analysis Complex statistical technique combining findings from a variety of different methods of study (e.g. of *longitudinal studies* and *cross-sectional studies*) to determine a general rule.

convergent research Different methods of inquiry addressing the same problem and arriving at the same conclusions.

convergent thinking See *divergent thinking.*

convergent validity The degree to which a test correlates highly with measures with which it is expected to correlate (e.g. a measure of mathematical ability should correlate highly with scores on a trigonometry test). See *discriminant validity.*

converging operations Different methods of enquiry/experimental methods, which all support the same conclusion/theoretical concept.

conversion disorder A *somatoform disorder*, characterized by loss of control over the muscles and/or senses. The patient seems surprisingly unconcerned about their condition (*la belle indifference*). The term *hysteria* is sometimes used synonymously – hence also *hysterical blindness*, etc.

conversion hysteria *conversion disorder.*

conversion neurosis *conversion disorder.*

convulsion An involuntary muscular contraction, which is either a prolonged contraction (a *tonic convulsion*) or a series of contractions and relaxations (a *clonic convulsion*).

convulsion therapy General term for any therapeutic technique in which the patient is deliberately given a *convulsion*. The most common version is *electroconvulsive therapy (ECT)*, although insulin overdoses (*insulin therapy*) were used in the past.

convulsive therapy *convulsion therapy.*

Cook's D *Cook's distance.*

Cook's distance (Cook's D) A measure of the extent to which an *outlier* is distorting results and hence whether the outlier should be removed from the calculations.

coping behaviour Any behaviour or act which reduces or negates the deleterious effects of a harmful situation.

coping skill *coping behaviour.*

coping skills training Training in coping behaviour.

coprolagnia The feeling of excitement induced by *coprophilia*.

coprolalia Obsessive swearing.

coprophagia Eating faeces.

coprophilia An *atypical paraphilia* in which the patient obtains sexual gratification from faeces.

coprophobia A *phobia* of excrement.

core construct See *personal construct theory.*

corneal reflection technique Method of measuring eye movements by shining an (invisible) infra-red beam onto the participant's eyeball, and by measuring the angle at which the beam is reflected back, calculating where the participant's eye is directed.

corollary discharge Adjusting to changes in posture and orientation so that the environment appears stable (e.g. if one moves one's head, what one sees remains stable – it does not also appear to have moved).

coronary prone behaviour (CPB) Any pattern of behaviour which appreciably raises the probability of suffering a *stroke*, heart attack, etc.

corpus callosum The principal anatomical link between the left and right *hemispheres* of the brain.

correction for attenuation A method of correcting for measurement error in *correlations*.

correction for chance *correction for guessing.*

correction for continuity A mathematical adjustment to discontinuously-distributed data so that they approximate to a *continuous distribution*. This enables a potentially wider range of statistical tests to be used on them.

correction for guessing In a multiple choice test, or one requiring simple 'yes-no' answers, it is possible to get a certain percentage correct by guessing. The correction for guessing formula calculates how many correct answers could have been guesses, and based on this, the subject's score is adjusted.

correction for range restriction A method of correcting *correlations* where the range of scores on one or both of the *variables* is stunted (the limited range distorts the size of the correlation).

correlated subjects design *repeated measures design.*

correlation Technically speaking, a measure of how much of the *variance* in one *variable* can be predicted by variance in another. In layperson's terms, a correlation describes the strength of the relationship between two variables, and the extent to which a change in one is met by a change in the other. The symbol for a correlation is *r*, often suffixed with a letter or symbol, depending upon the formula used to calculate it. Correlations can be positive (i.e. as one variable increases, so does the other) or negative (i.e. as one variable increases, the other decreases). Correlations also vary in strength – a value of 0 means that no relationship exists between the variables, a value of 1 indicates a perfect *positive correlation* (i.e. for every increase in one variable, there is proportionately the same increase in the other) and a value of -1 indicates a perfect *negative correlation* (i.e. every rise in one variable is met with proportionately the same fall in the other). In 'real life', correlations fall somewhere between these extremes. The closer the figure is to 1 or -1 (known as the *perfect correlation*), the stronger the correlation (typically, a value of 0.3 or better is taken to be a good indicator). 'Correlation' is not synonmous with 'causation'. There is no method of deciding from the statistic alone whether one variable is causing the other to alter; in any case, both might be controlled by a third party (see *partial correlation*). For the mathematically minded: the percentage of the variance in one variable which the other predicts can be easily calculated by squaring r and multiplying the result by 100 (e.g. variables A and B correlate at 0.6; A predicts 36% of B's

variance). The value r^2 is also known as the *coefficient of determination*. Correlations can be measured in several ways, depending upon the nature of the data. The most common is the correlation between two *continuous variables*. This is called the **product-moment correlation coefficient**, and when 'correlation' is discussed without a further qualifying statement, it should be assumed that the product-moment correlation is being referred to. Also see e.g. *alienation coefficient, contingency coefficient, correlation matrix, Fisher's z test, Kendall partial rank correlation coefficient, Kendall rank correlation coefficient, linear correlation, Pearson correlation coefficient, point biserial correlation coefficient, semi-partial correlation, Spearman rank order correlation coefficient,* and *tetrachoric correlation coefficient.*

correlation coefficient The mathematical expression of a *correlation* (i.e. the value of r).

correlation matrix Analysis of *correlations* between three or more *variables*. Usually displayed as a table (hence its name) with the variables listed along the top horizontal axis and also along the left vertical axis – the correlations between them are listed at the intersections.

correlation ratio (N) A measure of *correlation* for a *non-linear relationship* between two *variables*.

correlational research Any research method whose basic measure is *correlation*. There is usually the implication that no experimental manipulation of the subjects or test materials has taken place.

Corsi blocks task A test of visuo-spatial memory. Subjects are shown an array of blocks positioned on a table. The experimenter taps on some of these blocks in a sequence which the subject is asked to copy. The experimenter gradually increases the length of sequence until the subject's *memory span* is discovered.

cortex *cerebral cortex.*

cortical Pertaining to the *cerebral cortex.*

cortical atherosclerotic dementia (CAD) *vascular dementia* whose primary damage occurs in the *cortex.*

cortical dementias *dementias* in which the principal damage occurs in the *cortex* (e.g. *dementia of the Alzheimer type, multi-infarct dementia*). Compare with *sub-cortical dementias.*

cortical evoked potential *evoked potential.*

cortices Plural of *cortex.*

cosmetic psychopharmacology The use of drug treatments to enhance a personality or mood, when the patient is not mentally ill.

cotherapy *conjoint therapy.*

counselling Nebulous term – it traditionally means 'formally giving advice'. Within psychology and related disciplines, the term refers more specifically to any method using a treatment regime whose principal component is the provision of advice, be it tacit or explicit. The term can be misleading because, in addition to trained counsellors, the media have tended to apply the phrase to relatively untrained individuals who are described as offering 'counselling', although their services are more properly described as simply offering advice without a systematic rationale (although this does not mean that their services are necessarily poor). The term is often prefixed with a description of the area in which counselling is offered – 'careers counselling', 'feminist counselling', etc. The term *therapy* is perhaps preferable, because its general usage is largely confined to trained (usually full-time)

practitioners, and implies that the treatment follows a systematic course. However, 'therapy' can also cover physical treatments with relatively little provision of advice and with no psychological content (e.g. chemotherapy). Another difference between the terms is that 'therapy' usually refers specifically to the treatment of an illness, whilst 'counselling' can also include the enhancement of a behaviour which is not necessarily causing debilitating problems (e.g. *leisure counselling*). Generally, within specialist texts, the terms 'counselling' and 'therapy' are used interchangeably, and different individuals may call themselves 'counsellors' or 'therapists' whilst being identically qualified and offering identical services. However, the reader is advised to check for him/herself.

counselling psychology The study and practice of *counselling* within a psychological framework.

counter-transference See *transference.*

counterbalancing Presenting different subjects with the same set of treatments, tests, etc. in different orders, so that any observed effects cannot be attributed to one particular order of presentation. Also, the order of presentation by design is such that each treatment appears equally often in each place in the presentation order (e.g. if there are three treatments, the subject has an equal chance of receiving one of these first, second, or third). See *fixed order presentation, Latin square,* and *randomization.*

countercathexis *anticathexis.*

counterconditioning Removing an undesirable behaviour by associating it with aversive stimuli, and perhaps in addition *conditioning* the patient to adopt a new one in response to the same conditions. E.g. a patient with a *fetish* for women's shoes might be presented with pictures of shoes and simultaneously administered electric shocks. This makes the fetishistic object no longer desirable.

counterphobic Condition of a patient who deliberately encounters a *phobia*-producing event or item to 'prove' that s/he can cope with it (although the anxiety caused by the phobia is undiminished and may even be increased).

couple counselling/therapy General term for any therapeutic method treating both partners in a relationship.

covariance (1) The degree to which change in one *variable* is met by changes in another. (2) The term is also used by some commentators to denote the degree to which two or more variables share *variance* in common because of a shared relationship with a third variable (see the 'foot and maths example' in *analysis of covariance*).

covariance matrix A matrix of *covariances* between variables arranged akin to a *correlation matrix*.

covariate *variable* causing *covariance*.

covert compulsion See *compulsion*.

covert modelling See *modelling*.

covert sensitization *covert therapy*.

covert speech *inner speech*.

covert therapy Any therapeutic technique in which a situation, stimulus, etc., is imagined and dealt with in the mind, rather than in reality. The technique can be more efficacious than this description at first appears to imply.

CP *cumulative proportion*.

CPAB *Computer Programmer Aptitude Battery*.

CPB (1) *Chronic Pain Battery*. (2) *coronary prone behaviour*.

CPI *California Personality Inventory*.

CPM *Coloured Progressive Matrices*.

CPP *Wonderlic Comprehensive Personality Profile*.

CPRS *Cognitive Participation Rating Scale*.

CR *conditioned response*.

Cramer's V Measure of *correlation* between *nominal variables*.

cranial Anatomical term denoting the 'head end' or front section in a quadruped. However, in a bipedal animal (e.g. human) the term denotes the 'top' of the head. See *anterior, dorsal* and *superior*.

cranial nerves *nerves* which enter and leave the brain without the intermediary of the *spinal cord*. The nerves are numbered (traditionally in Roman numerals) from 1 to 12: I *Olfactory*, II *Optic*, III *Oculomotor*, IV *Trochlear*, V *Trigeminal*; VI *Abducens*; VII *Facial*; VIII *Auditory-vestibular*, IX *Glossopharyngeal*; X *Vagus*, XI *Spinal Accessory*, and XII *Hypoglossal*. Often the nerves are referred to by their number (e.g. the facial cranial nerve is the 'seventh nerve'). Compare with *spinal nerves*.

Crawford Small Parts Dexterity Test Test of manual dexterity, involving tasks similar to those of *pegboard test*, using tweezers or a screwdriver to insert pegs into holes.

creative aggression therapy (CAG) Therapeutic technique in which patients are encouraged and trained to channel aggressive thoughts and feelings into more constructive acts.

creative arts therapy *creative therapy*.

creative therapy General term for any therapeutic method using artistic expression and appreciation as a significant part of the process (e.g. *art therapy, music therapy*).

creativity Largely synonymous with *divergent thinking*. The term generally refers to any ability to produce novel ideas. Note that the term has a less 'dramatic' meaning than the layperson's use – i.e. it is not confined to great artists, writers, etc.

creativity test Any measure of ability to produce original ideas. Usually there are caveats that the ideas should be plentiful and feasible. Frequently used measures include the *brick test, word fluency test*, ability to create narratives on a given theme, etc. See *divergent thinking*.

cretinism A *congenital* form of *mental retardation* caused by an underactive thyroid gland. If identified early (before 3 months of age) the illness can be largely successfully treated.

Creutzfeldt–Jakob Disease (CJD) A very rare *dementia* (affecting circa 1 person per million per year), possibly contracted through contact with infected nervous tissue. In addition to archetypal *demented* symptoms of intellectual and mnemonic impairment, there are severe disturbances of gait and movement. CJD can strike at any age in adulthood, but is typically found in middle aged and older people, probably because in most cases there is a long incubation period (e.g. decades). In recent times, CJD has been associated with *bovine spongiformence-phalopathy (BSE)*.

cri du chat *inherited* condition with physical and psychological handicaps, and characterized by the strange cat-like sounds made by patients as babies.

Crichton Vocabulary Scale (CVS) A measure of vocabulary and *crystallized intelligence* measure.

criminal responsibility The degree to which an individual can be held mentally responsible for a criminal act.

crisis clinic A clinic or other therapeutic group for the administration of *crisis intervention*.

crisis intervention Nebulous term for treatment of a patient's reaction to a sudden catastrophic event, which the patient cannot adequately deal with on his/her own.

criterion (1) Level of ability. (2) The standard against which others must be judged.

criterion deficiency See *criterion relevance*.

criterion group Group whose members possess a characteristic, or set of characteristics, which separates them from the rest of the population (e.g. patients suffering from a particular illness, Nobel prizewinners, etc.). Other participants' performance may be compared with that of the members of this group.

criterion-keyed test Test which can identify members and non-members of a *criterion group*.

criterion prediction *expectancy table*.

criterion-referenced tests *attainment tests* in which subjects' scores can be compared to a particular standard or *criterion*. The nature of this criterion is an absolute value, independent of considerations of e.g. *age norms*.

criterion-related validity See *predictive validity*.

criterion relevance The degree to which the criteria for judging a person's competence at their job are actually appropriate (e.g. judging a typist by his/her manual dexterity is a reasonably good indicator, whilst judging them by his/her knowledge of algebra is not). The degree to which the criteria fall short of ideal is called *criterion deficiency*.

criterion score The minimum score necessary to pass a test.

criterion validity *criterion-related validity.*

criterion variable (1) The variable the value of which is to be predicted. (2) See *multiple regression*.

critical flicker fusion (CFF) The slowest rate at which a flickering light is perceived as a 'continuous' light. The rate decreases in old age (i.e. an older person cannot perceive as fast a rate of flicker).

critical incident measurement Evaluating a subject by how well they perform during a key incident in which certain skills are demanded, stretched or called into question.

critical incident technique (CIT) *critical incident measurement.*

critical loss Pertaining to the *terminal drop model* the theory that in old age, declines in some intellectual abilities can be endured, but falls in others constitute a 'critical loss' which heralds death.

Critical Reasoning Tests (CRT) Measure of verbal and numerical skills, for assessing managerial level staff. Uses a mock-up of (fictional) company documents as test materials.

critical region The area of the *sampling distribution* within which a result must fall if it is to be *significant*.

critical value (CV) The value of a statistic which marks the borderline between a *significant* and a non-significant result.

CRMS *Cambridge Research Mood Survey.*

Cronbach's a *Cronbach's Alpha.*

Cronbach's Alpha See *reliability.*

cross-cultural research Comparing the characteristics of people of more than one race/culture.

cross-cultural treatment Any treatment in which the patient and those giving the treatment are from different cultures.

cross-dressing transvestism.

cross-over interaction See *interaction (ANOVA).*

cross partition Creating a sub-group of a sub-group (e.g. divide the sample into men and women, and then divide the men into those named 'Brian' and those not).

cross-sectional research/samples/ study The experimental method of testing different groups (usually different age groups) in the same test period. Contrast with longitudinal research/samples/study. See *overlapping longitudinal study.*

cross-sequential design *overlapping longitudinal study.*

cross-tolerance Being more resistant than average to the effects of a drug, because of prior exposure to a related substance.

cross-validation Checking that a test performs in an identical manner with separate samples of the same *population.*

crossed design *factorial design* in which the *levels* of one *independent variable* are the same for every level of the another independent variable. E.g. an *analysis of variance* in which the subjects are given temperature-controlling drug treatments A and B (the independent variables) and their effect on body temperature (the *dependent variable*) is observed. Treatment A has three dosage levels (1, 2 and 3) and treatment B has 2. Hence, the subjects are assigned to six groups – those receiving treatment A at dosage level 1 and treatment B at dosage level 1 (A1 and B1); those receiving treatment A at dosage level 1 and treatment B at dosage level 2 (A1 and B1); A2 and

B1, A2 and B2, A3 and B1, and A3 and B2. The alternative method – the **nested design** – gives a different level of one variable for every level of the other variable. Hence, if there are three levels of treatment A, each will receive a different level of treatment B (e.g. A1B1, A2B2, A3B3 or A1B1, A1B2, A2B3, A2B4, A3B5, A3B6 – further permutations are possible).

crosstabulation Method of showing in a table how the same group of people, divided according to two independent categorization methods behave. E.g. the same group of people might be divided into males and females in one categorization and into whether they voted for candidate A or B in an election. The crosstabulation would reveal how many females voted for A or B and how many males voted for A or B. In a *conditional crosstabulation*, the figures show the relationship between categories after a *conditional relationship* has been accounted for (e.g. males tend to have higher incomes than females – the data when examined in terms of income level may reveal that high income earners, whether male or female, tend to prefer one candidate, and the gender difference is largely coincidental).

Crown-Crisp Experiential Index (CCEI) Measure of general *neurotic* state, including sub-scales on level and types of *depression, anxiety* etc.

CRT (1) *choice reaction time.* (2) *Critical Reasoning Tests.*

crucial experiment Experiment which determines which of two or more equally plausible theories is correct.

crying cat syndrome *cri du chat.*

crystallized intelligence The amount of factual (as opposed to autobiographical) knowledge a person has acquired during a lifetime – roughly corresponds to the lay term 'general knowledge'.

CSA child sexual abuse.

CSF(1) *contrast sensitivity function.* (2) *cerebrospinal fluid.*

CSI *Caregiver Strain Index.*

CSRPI *Children's Self-Report and Projective Inventory.*

CSTAI *Children's State-Trait Anxiety Inventory.*

CT *computerized transaxial tomography.*

CTAB *Comprehensive Test of Adaptive Behaviour.*

CTONI *Comprehensive Test of Non-Verbal Intelligence.*

CTOPP *Comprehensive Test of Phonological Processing.*

cuddliness The degree to which a baby positively responds to being cuddled by its mother/caregiver – some babies repel cuddles, which may indicate mental illness (e.g. *autism*).

cued recall task See *recall task.*

cultural bias (1) A bias against subjects from certain sections of the population. (2) Using tests which presuppose a knowledge of a particular culture (typically, white middle class). Subjects from groups unfamiliar with this culture might perform badly on such tests, simply because they do not have the appropriate social background to understand the questions (see example for *picture completion task*). See *cultural test bias.*

cultural drift Changes in societal values over time (usually decades at least).

cultural norm That which is acceptable or conventional within a particular culture. The issue becomes an issue in treatment of some dysfunctional people when their 'condition' is considered normal in some cultures but not others. E.g. homosexuality is considered a disease in some cultures (and in the past by many more – e.g. the DSM used to classify it as an illness) but not others. The *antipsychiatry movement* argues that many types of mental 'illness' are nothing of the sort and are the product of imposing outmoded cultural norms on different but valid behaviours.

cultural relativism The argument that behaviour (and by extension, research findings) must be judged against the society in which they are produced and judged relative to the requirements and mores of that society.

cultural test bias The degree to which a test fails to be a *culture-fair test*.

culture-bound disorder Disorder (e.g. *koro*) restricted to members of a particular culture.

culture-fair test Test which is equally fair to all subjects, no matter what their cultural background (e.g. *Cattell Culture-Fair Test*). See *culture-specific test*.

Culture Free Self-Esteem Inventory Measure of *self-esteem*, claiming to be a *culture-fair test*. It exists in two formats: Form AD for adults, and Form A for children.

culture-free test *culture-fair test*.

culture-specific test Test which is specifically targeted at individuals from one (usually minority) culture. See *culture-fair test*.

cumulative density function (c.d.f.) *cumulative frequency distribution*.

cumulative frequency distribution *frequency distribution* in which each observation is given a 'score' indicating the number of observations which have values equal to or below the observation in question. See *percentage cumulative frequency distribution*.

cumulative proportion (CP) *cumulative frequency distribution*.

cumulative scaling *Guttman scaling*.

curvilinear correlation A *non-linear correlation* in which the line assumes a curved shape.

curvilinear regression A *non-linear regression* in which the line assumes a curved shape.

curvilinear relationship Relationship between two *variables* such that if a line graph is plotted to express it, the line is curved.

Cushing's syndrome *organic affective syndrome* caused by an excess of cortisone, and characterized by a bloating of the body and severe mood swings. The disease is more common in women. See *Addison's disease*.

cut-off score The minimum score which must be attained to qualify for inclusion in the group in question (usually used in connection with job and other selection tests).

CV (1) *critical value*. (2) cardiovascular (i.e. pertaining to the heart and blood vessels).

CVA *cerebrovascular accident*.

CVS *Crichton Vocabulary Scale*.

cyclothymia Personality type characterized by pronounced swings of mood, although not necessarily severe enough to merit treatment.

cyclothymic disorder (1) See *depression*. (2) *cyclothymia*.

cyclothymic personality *cyclothymic disorder*.

cyclozine A *heroin antagonist*.

cynophobia A *phobia* of dogs.

cypridophoia A *phobia* of sex and/or venereal disease.

D

d *difficulty index.*

D (1) *deductive reasoning.* (2) *drive.* (3) Measure of the number of *standard deviations* by which the *mean* of one group exceeds (or is less than) another if all their scores are pooled together and an overall mean and standard deviation are calculated (in effect, a kind of *z score* for groups).

d-lysergic acid diethylamide (LSD) A *psychedelic drug.*

d prime The pronunciation of *d.*

D scale See *Minnesota Multiphasic Personality Inventory.*

d' See *signal detection analysis.*

DAF *Draw a Family Test.*

DAI *Dissertation Abstracts International.*

Dale Word list See *Teachers' Word Book of 30,000 Words.*

dance therapy *Disjunctive therapy* technique in which the patients are encouraged to use the postures and movements of dance to explore expressions and sensations, feelings and thoughts.

Daniels and Diack reading tests *Standard Reading Tests.*

DAP test *draw-a-person test.*

DARD *Durrell Analysis of Reading Difficulty.*

DAS (1) *Differential Ability Scales.* (2) *Dysfunctional Attitudes Scale.*

DAT (1) *dementia of the Alzheimer type.* (2) *Differential Aptitude Tests.*

data contamination technique Method of eliciting group data on potentially embarrassing topics (e.g. we might want data on how many people have committed undetected crimes, performed strange sexual acts, hold socially embarrassing opinions, etc.). Respondents are told to answer truthfully, but to roll a die (or select a number or value in a similarly random manner) before answering. The respondents are told that if they roll a certain number (e.g. '3'), then they must tell a lie to the question asked. The experimenter does not know what the subject has rolled, and hence cannot be certain if the subject's answer is true or false. Data on individual subjects is accordingly rather unreliable. However, if the average responses for a large number of people are considered, then the experimenter can calculate fairly accurately the proportion of false answers (in the above example, one sixth will be lies), and hence the number of people within a group who have committed the various acts or hold the particular beliefs in question. See *direct pipeline technique.*

data dredging (1) *data mining.* (2) More specifically, a contemptuous term for a method of last resort when an experiment has failed to prove the looked-for outcome. Namely, looking through the data for anything that might be of interest (and publishable).

data mining Searching through a set of data for a meaningful pattern. The term is often applied to very large data sets where statistical analysis is the only possible means of extracting information. The term is often used in a derogatory sense to denote searching blindly in the hope of finding at least something meaningful. *Top down data mining* involves examining the data with a preset idea of what is being looked for, whilst *bottom up data mining* involves analysing the data using statistical measures with no preconceived idea of what the pattern will look like. See *data dredging.*

data point *datum.*

datum A single piece of data.

DDST *Denver Developmental Screening Test.*

de Clerembaut's syndrome A persistent *delusion* that a completely unattainable and famous person is in love with the patient. The slightest actions by the famous person may be construed as a secret signal, but the patient may also eventually experience violent feelings against the object of their affections for his/her 'failure' to return their love.

de novo mutation A mutation in genetic structure that occurs in the sperm or egg (i.e. it is not a mutation already present in the parents' genes).

death instinct In some versions of *Freudian* theory (particularly Freud's own later work), a drive towards self-destructiveness.

death preparation Preparing for the psychological and practical impact of the death of oneself or of a loved one. Usually helps to lessen the negative effects of the event. To some extent, 'passive' death preparation increases with age, as the probability of dying increases.

death wish *death instinct.*

DEBQ *Dutch Eating Behaviour Questionnaire.*

debriefing (research) Informing test subjects of the purpose of the study in which they have participated.

decatastrophizing The process of persuading a patient that a situation s/he is experiencing, although terrible, can be coped with, and that ultimately, a normal life is possible.

deception study Study in which subjects are deliberately misled by the experimenter in order to examine a hypothesis. In such circumstances, *dehoaxing* (telling the subjects how and why they were misled) after the experiment is usually a moral necessity.

decile A *percentile* for multiples of 10 (e.g. 10th percentile, 60th percentile, etc.).

decision rule See *significance.*

decision threshold *response criterion.*

descision tree A graphical or visual representation of a descision-making process, in which the total range of options available is represented as akin to a branching tree with the initial stage of the process as its root.

Decisionbase A computerized psychiatric diagnosis programme.

decompensation A failure of *coping behaviour.*

deconditioning See *conditioning.*

decortication The removal or decay of all or part of the *cerebral cortex* or the outer layer of any organ.

deductive reasoning Using a rule or principle to explain a specific example. In contrast, **inductive reasoning** derives a rule or principle based upon interpretation of a set of examples.

deep dysgraphia A profound writing difficulty akin to *deep dyslexia* – patients have great difficulty in spelling new or *nonsense words*, and tend to write down words which are synonyms of the words they are supposed to be writing.

deep dyslexia An *acquired dyslexia* in which patients cannot read new or *nonsense words* (see *phonological dyslexia*) and also misread words for words of similar meaning.

deep reflex See *reflex.*

defence mechanisms (1) See *Freud's psychoanalytic theory.* (2) Generally, patterns of behaviour exhibited in times of stress/perceived danger.

Defence Mechanism Test (DMT)
Measure of strength of *defence mechanisms*. The subject is shown a *tachistoscopic presentation* of a threatening image, and is asked to draw it. The length of exposure is progressively increased on successive trials, and the drawings produced are examined.

defensive style The characteristic pattern of *defence mechanisms* exhibited by a patient.

deferred gratification *delay of gratification*.

Defining Issues Test Measure of moral reasoning based on Kohlberg's theory of moral development.

degrees of freedom (d.f.) At a general level, degrees of freedom refers to the number of events which are free to vary without the requirement that they assume particular values. For example, suppose that there is a requirement that a group of 5 numbers must always add up to 100. We can choose any values we want for the first 4 numbers, but the value of the 5th one is constrained – it must make the series add up to 100. For example, we might choose the numbers 1,5,78, and 24. The 5th number must take the value of -8 for all 5 numbers to add up to 100. Similarly, if we had chosen 5,1,1, and 2, then the 5th number would have to be 91. In this instance, the value of only one number is constrained – the remainder are free to assume any values. Therefore, there are said to be (5 – 1), or 4 degrees of freedom. It logically follows that we could take differently sized groups, and the same constraint would apply. If we insist that a group must add up to a fixed value, then all but one of the group can assume any value. Therefore, we can generate the rule that for any group of numbers which must add up to a fixed value, the degrees of freedom = n - 1. It follows from this that if

instead of being added, the numbers had to be multiplied or divided to create a desired number, the same rule would apply – all but one of the numbers in the group can have any value at all – only one of them must assume a particular value. If more sophisticated demands are made (e.g. the final sum must equal a set target, and one of the numbers must be a prime number), then this means that fewer numbers can have any value at all (e.g. 2 numbers might have to assume particular values in order to make the sum 'work'). Therefore, the degrees of freedom might have to be lowered to n - 2, n - 3, etc. The degrees of freedom thus represent the total number of observations made, minus the number of observations which must assume certain values if the requirements of the mathematical operations being used are to be fulfilled. In statistics, this is a very important concept, which underpins many of the subject's key formulae.

dehoaxing See *deception study*.

deindividuation Loss of personal identity.

deinstitutionalization (-isation) (1)The intellectual and emotional 'recovery' upon release from institutionalized care (see *institutionalization*). (2) The recent/official policy of many countries of allowing many patients, who would once have been institutionalized, to live in the general community.

delay of gratification Restraining oneself from performing particular behaviour until the appropriate time (e.g. when it is socially appropriate).

delayed echolalia See *echolalia*.

delimiting observations Deciding which phenomena are to be observed and which are to be ignored in a study.

delinquent (Usually) under-age breaker of the law. See *hebesphalmology*.

delirium A major disturbance (usually temporary) in intellect and perception resulting from a general deleterious change in the central nervous system's metabolism (e.g. through fever, intoxication, drug overdose). Can be confused with *dementia*, but its very rapid onset is in itself a sufficiently distinguishing feature. Occurs in three basic forms: *hyperactive delirium* is characterized by an agitated level of behaviour; *hypoactive delirium* by an unusually subdued level of behaviour; and *mixed delirium* by a mixture of hyperactive and hypoactive symptoms. Delirium may also occur without any 'obvious' behavioural symptoms.

Delirium, Dementia, Amnesia and other Cognitive Disorders See *organic mental disorders.*

Delirium Rating Scale (DRS) A test assessing the likelihood that a patient's symptoms indicate *delirium (acute confusional state)* rather than an illness with which it can be easily confused (e.g. *dementia*).

delirium tremens (DTs) See *withdrawal.*

delta waves A pattern of electrical activity in the brain detected by *EEC* with a frequency between 0 and 4 Hz.

delusion A persistent misinterpretation of information, which need not necessarily be a misperception of a real stimulus (as in an *illusion*). Also not to be confused with *hallucination*. Often the delusion is identified by a suffix (e.g. 'delusion of grandeur' has entered everyday speech). Most are self-evident. However, note that *delusion of control* refers to the patient's misinterpretation that s/he is being controlled, not that s/he is controlling.

delusion of control See *delusion.*

delusion of influence *delusion of control.*

delusion of reference The *delusion* that (perfectly innocuous) statements and events are directed against oneself.

delusional jealousy A *delusion* that one's partner is being unfaithful.

Delusions-Symptoms-States Inventory (DSSI) Measure of a wide range of psychiatric symptoms. Produces three sub-scales: *anxiety* and *depression; neurotic symptoms;* and *personality disorders.*

demand characteristics The (usually) implicit demands which the experiment places on the subject. Hence, the attributes, goals, etc., which the subject thinks the experimenter is measuring in an experiment, but which may not concur with what the experimenter intended.

demented The adjective from *dementia.*

demented dyslexia A condition found in some *demented* patients, who can read aloud perfectly normally, and yet have no understanding of what they are reading.

dementia A global deterioration of intellectual function, resulting from *atrophy* of the central nervous system. In some (older) textbooks, 'dementia' applies purely to *pre-senile dementia and senile dementia* to the over-60s. This distinction is now largely disregarded. The illness takes many forms (the most common are *dementia of the Alzheimer type* and *multi-infarct dementia*), but in all cases it kills the person before the body (see *ambiguous loss*). Patients in the later stages of the disease lack any sign of memory (and hence recognition of friends and relatives), intellect, personality, and often language. Diagnosis of the types of dementia is difficult, and post-mortem studies of patients have found that up to 70% of them have been misdiagnosed during life (this is currently only of academic interest, because there are no cures for dementia although recent drug trials look promising). See *acute confusional state, Blessed Dementia Scale, bovine spongiform encephalopathy (BSE), chronic brain disorder, chronic brain syndrome (CBS), cortical dementias, Creutzfeldt-Jakob Disease (CJD), Pick's Disease, pseudodementia, pre-senile dementia, pugilistic dementia, senile dementia, sub-cortical dementias, and Wernicke's dementia.*

dementia of the Alzheimer type (DAT) The most common form of *dementia*, first described by Alois Alzheimer in the nineteenth century. Typically, the first symptom is *amnesia*, followed by *aphasia*, and a general loss of intellectual functioning. Disturbance of language and visuo-spatial skills also typically occur early in the course of the disease. *Senile dementia of the Alzheimer type* (held only to afflict patients aged over 60 years) was at one time felt to be qualitatively different from the disease contracted by younger patients, but this distinction is now largely ignored. See *aluminium theory of dementia of the Alzheimer type.*

dementia praecox Obsolete term for the illness now known as *schizophrenia*. The term literally means 'pre-senile dementia', but should not be confused with the condition now graced with that name.

dementia pugilistica *pugilistic dementia.*

Dementia Rating Scale (DRS) *test battery* of a range of basic psychological skills, assessing the severity of the impairment of a patient suffering from *dementia*. Items on the test are presented in descending order of difficulty – if the first couple of items are correctly answered, then the rest of that particular section is assumed to be correct.

dementia syndrome of depression (DSD) *pseudodementia.*

demonology The belief that a supernatural and malevolent spirit has invaded a person's mind, causing him/her to become mentally ill. A commonly held belief in many 'primitive' societies (e.g. eighteenth century Britain).

demonomania The *delusion* of being controlled or even possessed by the Devil or other evil forces.

demophobia A *phobia* of crowds/large groups.

dendograms See *cluster analysis.*

denial A *defence mechanism* for denying the existence of an anxiety-producing or otherwise painful truth about oneself or an event.

denominator See *numerator.*

Denver Developmental Screening Test (DDST) *test battery* for detecting delayed development in infants. Based on the *Gessell Developmental Schedules.*

dependence addiction.

dependent measures Measures of a *dependent variable* obtained by experimental observation (e.g. if the dependent variable is weight of newborn babies, then typical dependent measures might be 7 lbs, 9 lbs, 8.5 lbs, etc.).

dependent personality *personality type* I found in some older people – possessors have some life satisfaction, but rely on others to help them. Not to be confused with *dependent personality disorder*, which is a much more severe condition.

dependent personality disorder *personality disorder* characterized by an extreme and illogical willingness to let other people make decisions on the patient's behalf.

dependent sample Sample, the selection of whose members is determined by who or what has been allocated to other groups (e.g. in a comparison of two groups trying different dieting methods, it would be a sound idea to ensure that people of roughly equal weight were assigned to the two groups). Compare with *independent sample.*

dependent samples t test *paired t test.*

dependent variable (DV) *variable* which is expected to alter because of its treatment (e.g. skin rash after application of ointment, reaction time after dosage of alcohol). This is contrasted with the ***independent variable***, which is the means by which the treatment of the dependent variable takes place (e.g. in the above examples, the independent variables are the ointment and the alcohol). More loosely, a variable measured in an experiment or study. See *dependent measure.*

depersonalization (-isation) A loss of feeling of personal identity (usually temporary).

depressant General term for any drug or substance that decreases activity, particularly activity in all or part of the nervous system. The psychological effect is typically to induce a feeling of relaxation (typically pleasant) and often (some or total) relief from feelings of pain. Uses of depressants range from medically legitimate (e.g. some painkillers) through socially-acceptable drugs (e.g. alcohol) through to socially-proscribed drugs (e.g. heroin).

depression *affective disorder* characterized by a profound feeling of sadness, usually accompanied by other symptoms. The commonest of these are disorders of sleep, loss of energy, perseverance, and/or enthusiasm, poor self-image, and changes in appetite and weight. Also, the condition must not be transitory (i.e. someone having one 'off day' is not depressed in the clinical

sense). In ***unipolar disorder***, the patient solely exhibits depression, which is long-lasting (e.g. a minimum of two months), and severe enough to interfere with normal functioning. ***Dysthymic disorder*** resembles unipolar disorder, except that the episodes of depression last a relatively short time period (a couple of months at maximum), or last for a few days, but recur at regular intervals. In ***bipolar disorder***, the patient swings between episodes of depression and *mania*, often with periods of relative normality in between (the episodes can vary in length from days to months). In ***bipolar II disorder***, the patient swings between depression and *hypomania*. ***Cyclothymic disorder*** resembles bipolar disorder, in that there are swings between depressed and manic states, but they are relatively mild in their impact. Some commentators distinguish between ***reactive depression*** (depression arising after a distressing event) and ***endogenous depression*** (depression which arises for no apparent reason), but this distinction is not now universally accepted.

deprivation Removal of something or someone – this contrasts with ***privation***, which denotes never having had contact with the thing or person. The terms are not often used accurately, and caution is therefore advised.

depth psychology General term for areas of psychology or psychology related topics which emphasise the role of the unconscious (e.g. Freudian theories).

derealization (-isation) The misperception that the world is unreal.

derived score See *raw score.*

Derogatis Psychiatric Rating Scale (DPRS) Measure of the symptoms, and in particular level of distress of a

Drs. Sid E. & Nell K. Williams
Library - Life University
770-426-2688

User ID: 0196989

Title: Student handbook to
psychology
Item ID: 00001121094
Date charged: 8/22/2013,13:25

Date due: 9/19/2013,23:59

Title: Dictionary of psychological
testing, assessment, a
Item ID: 00001120053

Date charged: 8/22/2013,13:29

Date due: 9/19/2013,23:59

Title: New psychological tests and
testing research
Item ID: 00001121176
Date charged: 8/22/2013,13:29

Date due: 9/19/2013,23:59

Fines $.10 per day per item
Reserve item fine $1.00 p/hr
Renewal available online w/PIN
No renewals by phone
***
***

patient. The test may be given in conjunction with a self-report questionnaire to see the degree to which the patient's perceptions of their own symptoms tally with those of a clinician.

Derogatis Sexual Functioning Index (DSFI) Measure *of sexual dysfunction.*

descending pathways *nerves* conducting impulses along the *spinal cord* from the brain. Compare with *ascending pathways.*

descriptive research Studies which seek simply to catalogue the features of an item or event, without necessarily placing an evaluative judgement or linking the findings to a theoretical stance.

descriptive statistics Calculations summarizing and describing data (e.g. *mean, standard deviation,* etc.), rather than describing relationships between them. See *inferential statistics.*

desensitization (-isation) The process of *conditioning patients* to become unafraid of a situation or object which previously gave cause for anxiety. Because this is usually done gradually, the process is often called *systematic desensitization.* The therapy presents the patient with very mild examples of the threatening stimulus (e.g., in the case of an *arachnophobic* patient, a drawing of a spider in a case at the other end of a room), and gradually exposes the patient to more 'threatening' examples of the *phobic object* (an *anxiety hierarchy*). At each stage, the patient practises relaxing responses, so that s/he comes to associate the situation with neutral or even positive feelings. In this manner, the subject gradually gains the confidence to approach the feared item, until s/he can handle it (often literally). Some commentators distinguish between desensitization in which the majority

of the encounters are treated as an imaginary exercise (for which they reserve the term 'systematic desensitization') and treatment in which the patient is presented with the real phobic object or situation from the start (*in vivo desensitization*). Contrast with *flooding.*

design copying test A test of whether a participant can accurately copy a picture. The test is most often given to brain damaged patients, to test the extent of their visuo-spatial skills. See *clock drawing test.*

Design Copying Test Commercial version of a *design copying test.*

design matrix Generally, a matrix representing an experimental design. However, note that individual authors use this term with variations, so caution in interpretation is advised.

desipramine A *tricydic* drug used in the treatment of *depression.*

detection theory *signal detection theory.*

deterioration index Any measure of declining ability (through ageing, illness, etc.) – e.g. *deterioration quotient.*

deterioration quotient (DQ) Measure of rate of intellectual decline associated with ageing, first devised by Wechsler. Sections of the *WAIS* (and indeed many other intelligence *test batteries*) can be divided into those measuring *crystallized intelligence* (held to be unaffected by ageing), and those measuring *fluid intelligence* (held to decline with ageing). These can also be referred to as **hold tests** and **don't hold tests** respectively. The DQ is calculated as {[(score on hold tests) – (score on don't hold tests)]/ (score on hold tests)} x 100. A phenomenon of the WAIS is that hold and don't hold scores are equal in early adulthood. Hence, the bigger the gap in an older person's hold and don't hold test scores, the greater the deterioration. The DQ expresses this change as a percentage. The term may also refer to other forms of deterioration (e.g. through illness). See *efficiency quotient*.

determinism Philosophical argument that everything has a cause, and that if all causes of a type of event are known, then the nature of future events can be precisely predicted. Taken to the extreme, this argues against free will, since if everything is caused by something else, then one can never have a genuinely spontaneous thought or action.

detoxification The removal of toxins from the body. These include alcohol and drugs.

Detroit Tests of Learning Aptitude (DTLA) Measure of general intellectual abilities in children through to late teenagers. The DTLA can also produce measures of more specific abilities. A 'primary' version for younger children is also available.

developmental age Age at which a particular set of characteristics normally first appears. Strictly speaking, *mental age* is a facet of this, but usually developmental age refers to changes other than those of the intellect.

developmental aphasia A *congenital* failure of language. In its 'pure' form, it refers to a condition in which the child suffers delayed speech and linguistic skills in general, which cannot be attributed to e.g. hearing impairment, damaged vocal cords, *mental retardation*, *autism*, or environmental factors (e.g. having suffered extreme parental neglect). However, the term is often used to denote congenital language failure, regardless of whether other symptoms are present or not.

developmental disorder Any disorder present at birth or which first appears in infancy, childhood or adolescence.

developmental dysgraphia A profound difficulty in spelling and in learning to spell, with which the person appears to have been born.

developmental dyslexia A profound difficulty in reading and in learning to read, with which the person appears to have been born. *Developmental dysgraphia* almost always appears in conjunction with it. See *dyseidetic dyslexia*, *dysphonetic dyslexia*, and *developmental phonological dyslexia*. Contrast with *acquired dyslexia*.

developmental dysphasia A profound language difficulty, with which the person appears to have been born.

developmental history The 'biography' of a patient or subject, usually paying special attention to facets of his/her life which are pertinent to the situation – e.g. in studying a person suffering from *dyslexia*, his/her experiences of education will be of central interest.

developmental phonological dyslexia *developmental dyslexia* in which the participant has unusually limited phonological skills.

developmental quotient (DQ) Calculated as for *intelligence quotient*, except that general physical and mental development, rather than purely intellectual development, is calculated.

developmental reading disorder *developmental dyslexia*.

Developmental Test of Visual-Motor Integration (VMI test) Measure of visual perceptual abilities in 3–13-year-olds.

Devereaux Elementary School Behaviour Rating Scale Measure of social and emotional development in 5–12-year-olds.

deviant case analysis The examination of similar cases or studies which have yielded radically different findings, in an attempt to find the source of the discrepancy.

deviation The degree to which an score differs from the *mean*.

deviation IQ The degree to which a person's intelligence test score deviates from the norm. See *intelligence quotient*.

Dexedrine Type of *amphetamine*.

d.f. *degrees of freedom.*

DGS *DiGeorge syndrome.*

diachronic Over a long period of time. This contrasts with *synchronic*, which refers to a single instant in time.

diagnosis Evaluation of the current state (e.g. of the patient, what diseases s/he is suffering from, etc.). Contrast with *prognosis*.

Diagnostic and Statistical Manual (DSM) A system of classification of mental illness, devised by the American Psychiatric Association. The first DSM (DSM-I) appeared in 1952, followed by DSM-II in 1968, and DSM-III in 1980, later revised (DSM-III-R 1987). The current version, DSM-IV, appeared in 1994. The classification system is not the only one in use (see e.g. *WHO classification of diseases*) but it is the most widely accepted, particularly in the USA, and other classificatory systems are usually very similar in structure (indeed, the DSM-IV has sought to increase its compatibility with the WHO system). The current version is divided into five axes. Axes I and II describe the disease the patient is suffering from. Axis II consists of two types of mental disorder: problems in development (other than learning and and motor skills development disorders, which are on Axis I) and all *personality disorders*. Axis I consists of all other mental disorders. Axes III and IV provide information on factors which may exacerbate or ameliorate the con-

dition. Axis III describes all other physical conditions the patient may suffer from, and Axis IV rates the severity of recent events in the life of the patient on a scale of one (none) to six ('catastrophic'). Axis V describes the highest level at which the patient coped in the past year, on a scale of one (serious danger of death/hurting self or others) to 90 (practically normal coping).

Diagnostic Interview for Children and Adolescents (DICA) *structured interview* format, assessing the mental status of child and adolescent psychiatric patients.

Diagnostic Interview Schedule (DIS) *structured interview* format, assessing the current status and mental health of participants. There is also a ***Diagnostic Interview Schedule for Children (DISC)***, which divides into ***DISC-C***, which is administered to the child, and ***DISC-P***, which is administered to the child's parents.

Diagnostic Interview Schedule for Children (DISC) See *Diagnostic Interview Schedule (DIS).*

Diagnostic Language Tests (DLT) *test battery* of six language skills (including punctuation and written expression). Part of *Metropolitan Diagnostic Tests* series.

Diagnostic Mathematics *test battery* of six mathematical skills (including computation, graph skills and statistics). Part of *Metropolitan Diagnostic Tests* series.

Diagnostic Reading Tests (DRT) Reading *test battery* assessing 11 aspects of formally taught reading skills (letter recognition, comprehension, grapheme-phoneme conversion, etc.). Part of *Metropolitan Diagnostic Tests* series.

Diagnostic Screen Batteries Computerized psychiatric assessment package. Generates diagnoses based upon the DSM.

Diagnostic Spelling Test Spelling *test battery* for participants aged 7–11 years. Tests a variety of spelling skills – producing spellings, 'proof reading', dictionary use, etc.

Diagnostic Spelling Tests Spelling *test battery* for participants aged 9 and over. Consists of several 'Levels', which assess increasingly complex spelling rules.

diary study (1) Study of contents of a person's diaries, for changes in writing style, topics of interest, etc., as the person ages or otherwise changes. (2) Method of assessing autobiographical memory. Participants complete a diary, and they are subsequently asked what they can recall of particular events, days, etc., which can be checked against diary entries. (3) Method used to assess a particular aspect of a person's activity for the purposes of research and/or therapy (e.g. recording how much and what type of food is eaten, etc.).

diaschisis Alteration in psychological functioning due to secondary effects of brain damage, rather than disruption at the principal point of injury.

diastolic pressure See *blood pressure*.

diathesis innate *trait*.

diathesis-stress paradigm The argument that disease arises from an interaction between the environment and the body's predisposition to the disease.

diazepam (trade name – *valium*) A very widely prescribed *minor tranquillizer*.

DICA *Diagnostic Interview for Children and Adolescents*.

dichoptic stimulation Presenting different stimuli to the two eyes simultaneously.

dichotic listening task An experimental method in which different messages are presented (usually via stereo headphones) to the two ears. The subject may be required to follow the message to one ear only, to report what is fed to both ears, or one of several other permutations. The method is extensively used in cognition, usually to assess how well a subject can attend to one message and ignore the extraneous information in the other, or how well s/he can integrate information from two physically separate sources.

dichotomous variable An 'either/or' *variable*. I.e. it records whether something is either in one category or another (e.g. male or female, living or dead etc.). An *artificial dichotomy* is a division of scores on a *continuous variable* into two categories (typically, into those above and below the *mean*). A *natural dichotomy* is a 'natural' division (e.g. male and female).

Dictionary of Occupational Titles (DOT) A compendium of over 40,000 job descriptions classified into various types according to their features and demands.

diencephalon A collective term for a number of key segments of the brain 'sandwiched' between the *brain stem*, *cerebellum* and *cortex*. More 'important' areas include the *basal ganglia*, *thalamus*, *hypothalamus* and *hippocampus*.

difference score The difference in a person's score on the same measure on separate occasions.

difference threshold See *threshold*.

Differential Ability Scales (DAS) *test battery* of intelligence and (in appropriately aged participants) educational achievement. For children aged 2 years 6 months–18 years.

Differential Aptitude Tests (DAT) *test battery* of a variety of intellectual skills, including verbal and numerical abilities, mechanical reasoning and 'clerical perception'. The battery is primarily intended to identify the careers a pupil is best suited for.

differential deficit Phenomenon where differences between groups/subjects are bigger for some measures than for others.

differential diagnosis Distinguishing between two illnesses with the same basic symptoms.

differential preservation The theory that some intellectual skills may be preserved better than others in ageing and illness.

differential psychology *individual differences.*

differential validity The ability of a measure to predict differences in performance of two or more skills. See *validity.*

difficulty index (d) Measure of difficulty of test questions (often calculated as the proportion of subjects who correctly answer the question).

diffuse neurological disorder Disorder of the nervous system in which the damage is relatively widespread. This contrasts with a *focal neurological disorder*, where the damage is relatively localized.

DiGeorge syndrome (DGS) Congenital condition caused by a significant loss of genetic material from chromosome 22. Symptoms depend upon the size of the loss, but typically include cardiovascular and thymus gland problems, intellectual dysfunction and behavioural disturbances (there is a strong probability of developing *schizo-*

phrenia). ***velocardiofacial syndrome (VCFS)*** is a very similar condition, and commentators are undecided about the degree of difference between DGS and VCFS.

digit span See *span.*

digit-symbol substitution task A measure *of fluid intelligence.* The subject is shown letters or numbers paired with patterns or shapes. Given a sequence of letters/numbers or patterns, the subject must identify their matches as quickly and accurately as possible.

dilation See *personal construct theory.*

dimension A *trait* which is viewed as qualitatively identical for everyone – it is simply the strength with which the trait is possessed which differs. In a ***unipolar dimension***, possession ranges from simply lacking the trait to possessing the trait in its strongest form (i.e. the extremes of the continuum represent 0 and 100%). E.g. everybody is likely to be afraid of heights to some extent, but some will only feel the merest frisson when dangling by one hand from a cable car, others when on a ladder mending a loose roof tile, whilst others will be afraid if asked to stand on a house brick. In a ***bipolar dimension***, the ends of the continuum represent opposite traits, and in the middle of the continuum lies a point representing no possession. Bipolar dimensions are often named after their extremes, with a hyphen separating them. E.g. one might construct a bipolar trait with extremes of niceness and nastiness, which would be called the niceness – nastiness dimension. Adolf Hitler would score at the extreme of the nastiness dimension, St Francis of Assisi at the end of the niceness dimension, and we mere mortals somewhere between these two extremes (i.e. not very good, but not very nasty either). Contrast with *type*, and see *dimension versus type debate.*

dimension versus type debate The argument as to whether certain personality traits and illnesses are *dimensions* or *types*.

dimensional trait *dimension.*

Diogenese syndrome A condition of extreme self-neglect found in some patients with *dementia*, characterized by a very pronounced lack of personal hygiene, lack of awareness of the filthy and untidy state of their surroundings, etc.

direct correlation *positive correlation.*

direct dyslexia *demented dyslexia.*

Direct Oblimin See *factor analysis.*

direct pipeline technique Method of eliciting honest responses to questions where the subject might prefer to lie to save face, etc. The experimenter convinces subjects that they are to be tested using a very accurate lie detector, and that any prevarication will be detected. The technique relies on the gullibility of the subjects, and accordingly has limited uses. The ethics of such a technique are also open to debate. See *data contamination technique.*

direct replication See *replication.*

direct scaling A measure of ability to detect changes in the intensity of a stimulus. The subject assigns a value to each stimulus encountered. Compare with *indirect scaling.*

directional hypothesis *alternative hypothesis* in which the direction of the difference is predicted. Some commentators treat directional and alternative hypotheses as synonyms.

directional test Test that only counts results as statistically *significant* if they are in the predicted direction.

directive therapy *active therapy.*

'dirty' drug Drug which has serious or unpleasant side-effects.

DIS *Diagnostic Interview Schedule.*

disaster syndrome Adverse reaction to experiencing a major catastrophe. Principal symptoms are shock and *anxiety.*

DISC *Diagnostic Interview Schedule for Children.*

DISC-C See *Diagnostic Interview Schedule.*

DISC-P See *Diagnostic Interview Schedule.*

discourse analysis The analysis of spoken and/or written communications in terms of their underlying structure.

discrete variable See *continuous variable.*

discriminability *discriminatory power.*

discriminant analysis discriminant function analysis.

discriminant function analysis *multiple regression* technique in which the *criterion variable* is a *dichotomous variable.*

discriminant validity The degree to which a test correlates poorly with measures with which it should not be expected to correlate (e.g. a test of maths skills might be expected to correlate poorly with a test of ability at foreign languages). See *convergent validity.*

discrimination index Measure of how many subjects in different groups give the correct answer to individual questions in a test (i.e. how well the items discriminate between them).

discriminative facility The ability to adjust to changing conditions.

discriminatory power The degree to which a test can discriminate between individual subjects' abilities. E.g. if everyone scores 50 on a test with potential scores ranging from 0 to 100, and/or if the potential range of scores is in any case small (e.g. subjects can score 1, 2, 3, 4, or 5), then the test has low discriminatory power. Conversely if subjects' scores are scattered more widely, and/or there is a wide potential range of scores, then the test has high discriminatory power. See *Ferguson's delta*.

disease cohort A group of people suffering from the same disease. See *cohort, patient cohort*.

disease model of mental illness The belief that mental illness has a physiological cause, and can be identified by possession of a particular set of symptoms. The approach can be criticised, because often the only method of identifying the illness is by its symptoms – no physical cause may have been identified. This leads to the strange argument that because a person has the symptoms, s/he must have a particular disease, because people with these symptoms are always classified as having this disease. Some critics have argued that this is as sensible as arguing that because a dog has a spotted coat, it must be a dalmatian, because all dalmatians have spotted coats. In addition to the logical problem, there is the added issue that by concentrating on the taxonomy, clinicians can be accused of concentrating on the disease and not on the patient.

disguised test *objective test* (definition 2).

disillusionment (1) In some therapies, the term means persuading a patient that his/her harmful views of him/herself are unrealistic. (2) The term can also be used in its everyday meaning.

disjunctive therapy General term for therapeutic techniques which use treatment of the body (e.g. posture, relaxation etc.) as a key part of the process.

dismantling treatment procedure Comparing different aspects of a therapeutic process to discover which are the most efficacious.

disordinal interaction See *ordinal interaction*.

disorganized schizophrenia See *schizophrenia*.

dispersion, measures of See *measures of dispersion*.

displacement Performing an activity in lieu of the desired, but socially less acceptable one (e.g. the example given in practically every textbook – kicking the cat instead of hitting one's cantankerous boss). The term originated in *psychoanalysis*, to denote performing an activity which was a sublimation of an unconscious desire, but the term has assumed a wider (and often milder) meaning.

dissociation The phenomenon whereby a brain-damaged patient has impaired performance in one skill but not in another. This probably indicates that the area of the brain which has been damaged normally controls the damaged skill. However, it is possible that the skill is a difficult one, and that the brain damage has simply caused a general lowering of intellectual performance. Therefore, a more satisfactory discovery is a ***double dissociation***, in which patients with one type of brain damage are found to perform skill A but not skill B, whilst patients with a different form of damage can perform skill B but not skill A. This indicates that the damage is specifically related to a particular skill, and is not due to a general lowering of ability.

dissociative amnesia *psychogenic amnesia*. The DSM-IV prefers the term 'dissociative amnesia'.

dissociative disorder not otherwise specified (dissociative disorder NOS) In DSM-IV, a *culture specific disorder* characterized by a trance-like or listless state.

dissociative disorder NOS *dissociative disorder not otherwise specified.*

dissociative disorders General term for a group of mental illnesses whose principal symptom is a drastic (and unrealistic) change in self-perception of identity. See *fugue, multiple personality,* and *psychogenic amnesia.*

dissociative identity disorder *multiple personality.*

dissociative pattern Pattern of abnormal behaviour in which some mental functions operate independently of others.

dissociative reaction *somatoform disorder.*

distal Anatomical term. Further from a reference point on the body than another section of the body under consideration. Compare with *proximal.*

distal effects Changes attributable to relatively distant events (e.g. poor self-image in old age because of childhood bullying) or events which are only felt through intermediaries. See *proximal effects.*

distal variable *variable* whose effect is only experienced through a mediating factor.

distancing (1) Taking a decreasing amount of responsibility for, and/or involvement in, a particular situation. (2) Persuading a patient (usually a *depressed* one) to perform (1), or, more generally, persuading him/her to stop unrealistically attributing blame and faults to him or herself, and recognizing that other factors may be involved. The process of more realistically apportioning blame and recognizing the involvement of other causal factors is sometimes called *re-attribution.*

distractibility The ease with which a person is distracted from a task.

distributed practice See *massed practice.*

distribution curve A graph plotting scores against the proportion of the sample attaining each score. Can be expressed as a *histogram* or a *frequency polygon.* See *kurtosis, negatively skewed distribution, positively skewed distribution, skew (of distribution), symmetrical distribution,* and *tails (of distribution).*

distribution-free statistics *non-parametric statistics.*

disulfiram (trade name – *Antabuse*) Drug used in the treatment of *alcoholism* – it makes the patient nauseous every time s/he has an alcoholic drink.

divagation disordered speech.

divergent thinking Ability to create new ideas based upon a given topic. The term is largely interchangeable with *creativity,* and is assessed with the *creativity test.* Divergent thinking is contrasted with **convergent thinking**, which is the ability to find a single principle behind a collection of information (i.e. the former takes a single point of reference and diverges from it, whilst the latter converges several strands of thought into a single premise).

divided attention The ability to attend to and process information from more than one source simultaneously. See *attention.*

dizygotic (DZ) Of two eggs. Hence, dizygotic twins are twins from separate eggs (i.e. non-identical twins). See *monozygotic.*

DLT *Diagnostic Language Tests.*

DMT (1) *draw-a-man test.* (2) *Defence Mechanism Test.* (3) An hallucinogenic drug.

Dogmatism Scale Measure of inflexibility of beliefs.

dolorology The study of pain.

domain referenced test Test in which performance is gauged against a criterion of maximum performance on the skill being assessed. See *norm referenced test.*

don't hold tests See *deterioration quotient (DQ).*

Doors and People Test of long-term memory, divided into four sub-sections (visual and verbal *recall tasks* and visual and verbal *recognition tasks*). The tests involve remembering pictures of doors and names of people.

dopamine hypothesis (1) Hypothesis which states that *schizophrenia* is caused by a surfeit of dopamine (a *neurotransmitter*). (2) Hypothesis which states that *Parkinsonism* is caused by a deficiency of dopamine.

Doren Diagnostic Reading Test of Word Recognition Skills *test battery* of various reading-related skills, for participants aged 6–9 years. Concentrates particularly on phonological skills and word recognition.

dorsal Anatomical term for the back of the body, towards the back of the body, or the section of an organ nearest the back.

DOT *Dictionary of Occupational Titles.*

dot chart Essentially, a *bar graph* in which instead of bars, there is a thin line (or dotted line) terminating in a dot or spot.

double ABCX model An attempt to account for the stress induced in a family by a major crisis befalling one of its older members. The letters refer to variables expressing the seriousness of the crisis, the amount of available help, etc.

double bind A situation in which the subject is required to obey two opposing commands; hence, whatever s/he does, s/he will be wrong. The habitual use of the double bind situation is held to be a feature of the *schizophrenicparent.*

double blind study See *blind study.*

double dissociation See *dissociation.*

double-sided test *two-tailed test.*

double Y scatter plot A *scatter plot* in which there are two vertical axes with different scales. This enables variables with different ranges to be plotted against the same variable, aiding comparisons of trends, etc.

Down's Syndrome (DS) A *congenital* condition, named after its nineteenth century discoverer, J.L. Down. Symptoms include a characteristic flattened face, extra folds of skin on the eyelids, stubby fingers, unusual folds of skin on the soles and palms, and an overlarge tongue. Severe *mental retardation* is a frequent but not inevitable symptom. Life expectancy is poor (a maximum of 40–50 years) – in the terminal stages, the Down's Syndrome patient's intellectual state may resemble that of a *dementia of the Alzheimer type* patient (there are suggestions that the two illnesses may be genetically linked). Down's Syndrome is caused by faulty cell division soon after fertilization – about 90% of patients have an extra chromosome 21 *(trisomy 21)*. The incidence of the disease rises with the age of the mother – there is a fairly high (but by no means overwhelming) risk in mothers over 40.

doxepin A *tricyclic drug.*

DPI *Dynamic Personality Inventory.*

DPRS *Derogatis Psychiatric Rating Scale.*

DQ (1) *developmental quotient.* (2) *deterioration quotient.*

dramatherapy See *psychodrama.*

Draw a Family Test (DAF) *projective* test in which the participant draws a picture of his/her family. See *Kinetic Family Drawing*.

draw-a-man test (DMT) *Goodenough Draw-a-Man Test*. Not to be confused with the *draw-a-person test*.

draw-a-person test (DAP test) Test requiring a subject to draw a person and create a story about their creation. The test can be used to assess if unusual emphasis/lack of emphasis is placed on certain features, and may be of use in assessing some mentally ill patients. Not to be confused with the *draw-a-man test* or the *Goodenough Draw-a-Person Test*.

dream analysis Therapeutic technique in which the patient recalls his/her dreams, which are then analysed for their meanings by the therapist. The technique is virtually confined to *psychoanalysis*, which believes that dreams are a method of expressing otherwise repressed beliefs and memories in symbolic form.

dream interpretation *dream analysis*.

drinamyl Type of *amphetamine*.

drive (D) The psychological 'force' which motivates a subject to perform a particular behaviour. Sometimes further classified into **primary drive** (innate) and **secondary drive** (learnt).

DRS (1) *Dementia Rating Scale*. (2) *Delirium Rating Scale*.

DRT *Diagnostic Reading Tests*.

drug abuse *substance abuse*.

drug addiction See *addiction*.

drug induced congenital disorder created by drugs prescribed or illegal taken by the mother during pregnancy (e.g. *foetal alcohol syndrome*).

drug tolerance *pharmacodynamic tolerance*.

DS *Down's Syndrome*.

DSD *dementia Syndrome of depression*.

DSFI *Derogatis Sexual Functioning Index*.

DSM *Diagnostic and Statistical Manual*.

DSM-I See *Diagnostic and Statistical Manual*.

DSM-II See *Diagnostic and Statistical Manual*.

DSM-III/DSM-III-R See *Diagnostic and Statistical Manual*.

DSM-III-R On-Call Computerized version of the DSM-III-R.

DSM-IV See *Diagnostic and Statistical Manual*.

DSM-IV-TR The DSM-IV with a revised text, produced in 2000. Otherwise, it is essentially the same as DSM-IV.

DSSI *Delusions-Symptoms-States Inventory*.

DTLA *Detroit Tests of Learning Aptitude*.

DTLA-P *Detroit Tests of Learning Aptitude – Primary*.

DTREE Computerized version of the DSM.

DTs *delirium tremens*.

DTVP *Marianne Frostig Developmental Test of Visual Perception*.

dual diagnosis Diagnosis of two or more illnesses simultaneously.

dualism The belief that the mind and the body (including the brain) are completely distinct entities.

dummy variable A recategorization of a set of categories reducing the data to membership or non-membership of a single category within the set. Dummy variables are necessary in some types of *regression* analysis. Usually, a set of categories are reduced to a set of such 'either/or' categorzations. E.g. a group of European people may have been originally categorized according to their nationality. A set of dummy variables would be e.g. re-categorizing into 'French' or 'Not French', 'German' or 'Not German', etc.

Duncan's multiple range test A *t test for multiple comparisons* and *post hoc test* for the *analysis of variance*. It is derived from the *Newman-Keuls test*.

Dunnett t-test *Post hoc test* for the *analysis of variance*.

Durbin-Watson test Measure of *autocorrelation*.

Durkheim's taxonomy of suicide Durkheim (nineteenth century sociologist) identified three types of suicide: *altruistic suicide* – killing oneself because the results of one's death will benefit others; *anomic suicide* – killing oneself because of a considerable change in fortunes; and *egoistic suicide* – killing oneself because of a feeling of severe alienation from society. The taxonomy has been criticized.

durophet Type of *amphetamine*.

Durrell Analysis of Reading Difficulty (DARD) Reading *test battery*, designed to identify early and pre-readers' areas of difficulty/ strength.

dustbowl empiricism Derogatory term for a test which predicts or describes a phenomenon, but adds nothing to theoretical insight.

Dutch Eating Behaviour Questionnaire (DEBQ) Measure of eating habits, with three scales assessing restrained eating, eating in response to emotion and eating in response to external cues.

DV *dependent variable*.

Dvorine Colour Vision Test A measure of colour vision/colour blindness. Participants must identify numbers made up of coloured dots printed against a background of differently-coloured dots.

Dyadic Adjustment Scale Measure of the state of the relationship between a married or cohabiting couple.

dying trajectory (1) The speed with which a person is likely to die. (2) The emotional and intellectual states associated with dying.

Dynamic Personality Inventory (DPI) Measure of 33 personality attributes based on *psychoanalytic* theory. Subjects rate words and phrases into those they like and dislike.

dynamic psychology A general term which has been claimed by several psychological schools, including *psychoanalysis*. The phrase denotes a study of dynamically interacting thought processes.

dynamic traits *traits* governing degree of activation, motivation, 'personal energy', etc.

dynamic visual acuity *acuity* for moving objects.

dys- As a prefix in descriptions of disability, the term denotes an impairment of the skill in question, (e.g. *dyslexia* – an impairment in reading). In contrast, the prefix *a-* denotes a complete absence of the skill (e.g. *alexia* – the complete absence of reading). This useful distinction has been largely lost through inaccurate usage, and readers are advised to interpret terms with a- and dys- prefixes cautiously.

dysaesthesia An impaired sense of touch.

dysarthria impaired speech.

dysbasia An impaired ability to walk.

dysbulia An impaired ability to maintain a course of action and/or line of thought.

dyscalculia A profound difficulty with arithmetical skills.

dyschiria An impaired ability to judge which side of the body is being stimulated.

dyschronaxis An impaired ability to judge what time it is (i.e. to the extent of not being sure, in the absence of obvious visual clues, if it is morning, afternoon, night, etc.).

dysdiadochokinesis See *adiadochokinesis.*

dyseidetic dyslexia *developmental dyslexia* in which there is a profound failure to recognize words by their visual appearance – every word has to be laboriously 'sounded out', and irregular words (such as 'quay' and 'yacht') are consistently mispronounced. Compare with *dysphonetic dyslexia.*

dysexecutive syndrome Impairment of the ability to organize cognitive functions (e.g. into appropriate sequences of actions).

dysfunctional Pertaining to a disadvantageous method (of thought, behaviour, etc.).

Dysfunctional Attitudes Scale (DAS) Measure of the degree to which a subject has certain inappropriate attitudes held to underlie a *dysfunctional* state of mind.

dysgeusia An impaired sense of taste.

dysgraphia A profound spelling difficulty (although note that there is evidence of some spelling ability). The syndrome can be *inherited* (*developmental dysgraphia*) or can be acquired through brain damage (*acquired dysgraphia*). See *amnestic dysgraphia, deep dysgraphia, lexical dysgraphia, phonological dysgraphia, surface dysgraphia.* Compare with *aphasia* and *dyslexia.*

dyskinesia Impairment of voluntary movement.

dyslalia An impairment of speech, for reasons other than brain damage.

dyslexia A profound reading difficulty (although note that there is evidence of some reading ability). The syndrome can be *inherited* (*developmental dyslexia*) or can be acquired through brain damage (*acquired dyslexia*). A child is typically diagnosed as dyslexic if his/her reading age is appreciably below his/her *mental age* and *chronological age* (usually this means by at least two years). Lay persons often confuse the term with *dysgraphia.*

dyslogia (1) Poor spoken articulation. (2) Used (inaccurately) by some developmental psychologists as a synonym for *developmental aphasia* in general.

dysmentia Poor performance due to lack of motivation, rather than lack of ability.

dysmetria Disorder in which movements can be initiated, but are poorly controlled and executed.

dysmnesia Impairment of memory. The term should often be used in lieu of *amnesia* (which is, strictly speaking, total loss of memory).

dysmorphophobia Irrational belief that one is abnormal (particularly physically).

dysosmia Impairment of sense of smell.

dyspareunia Painful sexual intercourse.

dysphagia An impairment of eating.

dysphasia (1) A partial failure of language (see *aphasia*). (2) Used by some commentators (inaccurately – see *dysgraphia*) to denote a profound spelling difficulty (although note that there is evidence of some spelling ability).

dysphonetic dyslexia *developmental dyslexia* in which there is an almost total failure of ability to use phonological information – hence, recognizing words by their visual shape is the only feasible (if inaccurate) strategy. Compare with *dyseidetic dyslexics*.

dysphonia Disorder of voice production.

dysphoria sadness.

dyspnoea Disorder of or difficulty in breathing.

dyspraxia An impairment in the ability to perform movements.

dyssynchronous child Child with learning difficulties.

dystaxia An impairment in muscle coordination.

dysthymic disorder See *depression*.

DZ *dizygotic*.

E

early maladaptive schema See *maladaptive schema*.

early onset schizophrenia (EOS) *schizophrenia* arising before middle age.

Early School Inventory – Developmental (ESI-D) Test assessing general physical and psychological development in 4–6-year-old children.

Early School Inventory – Preliteracy (ESI-P) Test assessing the reading readiness of 4–6-year-old children.

Early Screening Inventory (ESI) Measure for administration to children aged 3–6 years to identify atypical development requiring remedial intervention.

Early Screening Profiles (ESP) *test battery* assessing general behavioural and intellectual development in young children.

EASI Temperament Survey *test battery* of aspects of temperament/behaviour. 'EASI' stands for emotionality (fear and anger), activity, sociability, and impulsiveness.

EAT *Eating Attitudes Test.*

Eating Attitudes Test (EAT) A *self-report questionnaire* assessing the eating habits of patients, particularly those suffering from *anorexia nervosa* and *bulimia*.

Eating Disorder Inventory (EDI) Self-report questionnaire of eating habits and abnormalities of eating.

echolalia Condition in which the patient only responds to verbal statements by repeating back what s/he has just heard. In *delayed echolalia*, the repetition occurs hours or even weeks later.

echolalic aphasia *transcortical motor aphasia.*

echopathy Imitating other people (verbally and posturally) to an abnormal degree.

echophrasia *echolalia.*

echopraxia Imitating other people's actions to an abnormal degree.

Eclectic Neuro Score (ENS) Computerized package which converts scores from a variety of tests of neuropsychological dysfunction into *T scores*. This enables a profile of scores to be produced.

eclectic therapy Therapeutic regime which adopts techniques from several distinct schools of therapy. No assumptions about the theoretical stance of the therapist are necessarily inferred (e.g. s/he could be an ardent *cognitive therapist* but use some *Freudian* techniques because they are efficacious regardless of his/her opinions of the theory which produced them). See *multimodal therapy*.

ecological psychology The study of psychological acts in a natural or naturalistic environment.

ecological validity Term describing a study which is a realistic simulation of a real life event, and/or which tests skills used in 'real life'. This contrasts with a *laboratory study*, in which the skills tested and the test surroundings are artificial and without a direct or 'obvious' bearing on normal psychological activity. E.g. asking subjects to remember to buy items on a trip to the supermarket might be classed as having ecological validity. Conversely, remembering a list of nonsense syllables whilst seated in a testing room might be classed as a laboratory study.

ecoutism *paraphilia* in which the patient's principal sexual satisfaction is derived from hearing the sounds of sexual activity.

Ecstasy (E) Drug inducing feelings of intense warmth towards others, and of extreme energy. Illegal, and with potentially lethal side-effects. See *MDMA*.

ECT *electro-convulsive therapy*.

ectomorph See *Sheldon's personality types*.

EDA *exploratory data analysis*.

EDI *Eating Disorder Inventory*.

Edinburgh Picture Test (EPT) Test of reasoning skills using pictorial material, for children aged 6–8 years.

Edinburgh Questionnaire Set of measures of job descriptions, satisfaction with working environment, etc.

Edinburgh Reading Test Reading test with four 'Stages' commensurate with the age group under consideration. Stage 1: 7–9 years; Stage 2: 8.5–10.5 years; Stage 3: 10–12.5 years; Stage 4: 12–16 years. Each stage is a battery of tests of different skills. These increase in difficulty across the Stages, but they also assess increasingly complex and 'mature' reading skills (e.g. there is a greater emphasis on story comprehension and interpretation, rather than simple word recognition).

educable mentally retarded (EMR) American term for persons of low *IQ* (c. 50–60) but who can benefit from some form of very simple academic education. Compare with *trainable mentally retarded (TMR)*.

education(al) age The average age at which the skills a child possesses are usually learnt (i.e. measures how much more or less a child knows than his/her peers).

educational psychology The study of the psychology of education, and of general psychological development with regard to educational needs. The profession can be loosely divided into two camps – those who study the theoretical aspects of these issues, and those who perform practical assessments of pupils to determine their most appropriate schooling. In the UK, the training for educational psychologists is (some would argue, unnecessarily) long. Practitioners must obtain a first degree in psychology, undertake a year's teacher training, have two years' teaching experience, and then a further year's specialist training, before they are qualified.

education(al) quotient Akin to *intelligence quotient*, save that *education age*, rather than intelligence test score is entered into the equation. In effect, it measures how much a child has learnt in comparison with his/her peers.

educationally subnormal (ESN) UK term for persons of low *IQ* who require a simpler than normal education if they are to benefit at all from schooling.

Edwards Personal Preference Schedule (EPPS) Personality test measuring in terms of 15 'needs' (for autonomy, etc).

Edward's syndrome Genetic disorder characterized by stunted growth, numerous physical dysfunctions and intellectual dysfunction. The severity of the symptoms appears related to the level of genetic malfunction caused by *trisomy* of chromosome 18. In the full form, all cells have an extra chromosome; in mosaic form, some cells have an extra chromosome and in partial form, some cells have an extra segment of the chromosome. Life expectancy is low varying from early childhood in the most severe cases to early adulthood in the less severe.

EE *expressed emotion.*

EEC *electroencephalograph.*

effect size (ES) (1) The difference between the mean *dependent variable scores* of a *control* and an experimental group, divided by the control group's *standard deviation.* (2) The value of the 'size' of the difference found by a test. E.g. although Group A has *significantly* higher scores than Group B, this difference may be only 5%, so although the difference is reliably found, it is perhaps not of any great importance. The effect size can be expressed as a *correlation.* (3) The level of probability of a significant result. See *power (of a statistical test).*

efferent (neurons) Carrying signals from the *central nervous system* to the *peripheral nervous system.* See *afferent.*

efficacy expectation How well a subject expects to do at a task.

efficiency quotient (EQ) Measure of an older person's intellectual abilities relative to the performance of young adults, who are assumed to be at the peak of their abilities. In basic terms, it is the IQ which the young adult would be recorded as possessing if s/he had the same *raw score* as an older subject. E.g. an older man has a raw test score of 95, which is good for his age group, and gives him an IQ of 130. However, a score of 95 would be a poor score for a young adult, and would give him/her an IQ of 70. The older person's EQ's therefore classed as 70. By comparing EQ with IQ a measure of the extent of a person's age-related decline in intelligence can be calculated. However, a more useful single measure is probably the *deterioration quotient.*

ego See *Freud's psychoanalytic theory.*

ego-alien An action or belief which the participant feels is not part of his/her 'real' self.

ego analysis *ego psychology.*

ego control The degree to which urges and compulsions are controlled.

ego-dystonic That which is anathema to the ego. See *ego-syntonic.*

ego-dystonic homosexuality *paraphilia* in which the patient has homosexual proclivities, which s/he finds distressing to the extent that s/he wishes to be 'cured'. A homosexual who is content with his/her orientation is said to exhibit *ego-syntonic homosexuality.*

ego integrity versus despair See *Erikson's theory of development.*

ego psychology See *neo-Freudian movement.*

ego resiliency The ability to adapt to different situations.

ego state (1) A characteristic pattern of behaviour. (2) See *transactional analysis.*

ego-syntonic That which is acceptable to the *ego*. See *ego-dystonic*.

ego-syntonic homosexuality See *ego-dystonic homosexuality*.

egoistic suicide See *Durkheim's taxonomy of suicide*.

eigenvalue See *factor analysis*.

eigenvector See *factor analysis*.

Eight State Questionnaire (8SQ) A measure of eight moods and aspects of personality (e.g. *anxiety, extraversion*, level of arousal).

8SQ *Eight State Questionnaire*.

ELA *expressive language age*.

elder abuse Abuse of the elderly, particularly those who are mentally enfeebled. The abuse can be physical, but also psychological or financial (e.g. extorting money).

elderspeak The use of patronizing 'baby talk' in talking to older people.

elective mutism Deliberately choosing not to speak (usually short-lived – i.e. a few weeks maximum), without any clear physiological cause (e.g. sore throat). Most often found in children, usually with another underlying psychological problem.

electro-convulsive therapy (ECT) A form of *convulsion therapy*, in which electric shocks are administered to the brain (the patient is usually sedated whilst this is done). The technique – used less in recent years than in the past – may be beneficial for some forms of mental illness, such as severe *depression*.

electrodermal response *galvanic skin response*.

electroencephalograph (EEG) A device which measures the pattern of electrical activity (the **evoked potential (EP)**) on the scalp and by extrapolation, of the *cerebral cortex* beneath. The rate of activity and where on the scalp it occurs can give some insight into how active and healthy an individual's brain is, and which parts of the cortex are most heavily used in different mental tasks.

electronarcosis The induction of relaxation or sleep through the administration of a (low) electrical charge to the skull.

electroretinograph (ERG) A device which measures eye movements from electrical activity around the eyes. Has been superseded in many instances by the *corneal reflection technique*.

electroshock therapy *electro-convulsive therapy*.

electrosleep therapy *electronarcosis*.

Eliza See *client-centred therapy*.

embedded figures test A measure of *field dependence* – subjects must find shapes hidden as part of the design of larger shapes.

embolism Caused by a blood clot becoming detached and being sent around the blood vessels until it becomes 'stuck', causing a blockage.

EMDR *eye movement desensitization and reprocessing*.

emitted behaviour Behaviour which cannot be attributed to a reaction to external stimulation.

emotional continuity, lack of See *lack of emotional continuity*.

emotional control The degree to which emotional expression is controlled.

emotional deprivation Any deprivation of emotional expressiveness towards the subject. The term is generally reserved for 'cold', emotionally constipated parenting methods or other relationships which should be emotionally 'warm'.

emotional inoculation Preparing for an anticipated stressful or otherwise emotionally unpleasant event.

emotional maturity The degree to which emotional expression is appropriate to the participant's age.

emotional stability See *five factor model of personality*.

empathic understanding See *Roger's self theory of personality*.

empathy The ability to experience and understand the feelings and needs of others (as opposed to 'sympathy' which is a feeling of sorrow but without necessarily an understanding of others).

empiricism (1) The belief that all knowledge is based upon experience gained through the senses. (2) More generally, beliefs based upon observation and experimentation (as opposed to armchair theorizing).

empowering Restoring or enhancing the behavioural or other psychological attributes of an individual.

empty chair technique Therapeutic method in which the patient is encouraged to talk to an empty chair, imagining that a particular person is sitting in it.

empty nest syndrome Feeling of severe loss experienced by some parents (usually mothers) upon their children leaving home.

EMR *educable mentally retarded*.

enabling *empowering*.

encephalitis Inflammation of the brain, caused by infection.

encephalomyelitis Inflammation of the brain and spinal cord. Caused by infection or an abnormal reaction to a mild infection or vaccination.

encephalomyelopathy General term for a widespread infection of the *central nervous system*.

encopresis Faecal incontinence. See *enuresis*.

encounter group Generic term for a range of therapeutic techniques in which a group of (usually unrelated) patients encounter each other in a variety of situations contrived by the therapist. These can be collective activities (such as touching and even fighting), *role plays*, etc. The aim of the process is to increase self-awareness, to air and solve problems, etc. Some versions of the therapy use the basic techniques described, but have more specific aims. See *human relations training group*, *personal growth group*, and *sensitivity training*.

end spurt The improvement in performance which is sometimes observed as a participant realizes that s/he is near the end of a task.

endocathection *endocathexis*.

endocathexis A psychological withdrawal within oneself. The opposite (a move to be more concerned with one's surroundings than with oneself) is *exocathexis*.

endogenous Derived from internal causes. Contrast with *exogenous*. See *intrapersonal*.

endogenous depression See *depression*.

endomorph See *Sheldon's personality types*.

endorphin An *opioid peptide*.

engineering psychology General term for the study of psychological aspects of the interaction between humans and machines.

Engineering Test Selection Battery (ETSB) Measure of skills pertinent to engineering.

English Picture Vocabulary Test (EPVT) See *British Picture Vocabulary Scale (BPVS)*.

enkephalin An *opioid peptide*.

ENS *Eclectic Neuro Score*.

ensophobia A *phobia* of sin.

entomophobia A *phobia* of insects.

enuresis Urinary incontinence. See *encopresis* and *nocturnal enuresis*.

environmental psychology The study of the effects of the environment (in all senses) on psychological states.

environmental stress *stress* induced by the environment.

EOS *early onset schizophrenia*.

EP *evoked potential*.

epidemiology The study of (strictly speaking, epidemic) diseases, particularly their causes and predisposing factors.

epilepsy Periodic uncontrollable loss or severe disturbance of consciousness. In *petit mal epilepsy* the patient simply loses consciousness, for a few seconds up to several minutes. In *grand mal epilepsy* there is a loss of consciousness accompanied by a fit, with uncontrollable thrashing of the limbs. In *masked epilepsy*, the patient may not lose consciousness but may experience a feeling of unreality. In *psychomotor epilepsy* the patient may not lose consciousness but performs motor activities (including in some instances assaulting people) and has no memory of the attack. *Jacksonian epilepsy* is characterized by muscular spasms which begin in one part of the body; the spasms then remain confined to that area, or spread. In *centrencephalic epilepsy* the abnormal electrical activity is spread across the brain, and is synchronous. It can be attributed to a disturbance in the mid-brain. *Temporal lobe epilepsy*, as the name implies, originates in the *temporal lobes*.

epileptic equivalent *masked epilepsy*.

epiloia *tuberous sclerosis*.

epinosic gain An indirect benefit from being ill (e.g. generally greater levels of sympathy). See *paranosic gain* (and note that the two terms are often confused).

epinosis *epinosic gain*.

episodic amnesia An abnormally poor ability to recall information from certain periods of one's past.

EPPS *Edwards Personal Preference Schedule*.

EPQ *Eysenck Personality Questionnaire*.

EPT *Edinburgh Picture Test*.

EPVT *English Picture Vocabulary Test*.

EQ *efficiency quotient*.

equal interval scale Scale in which the interval between any two adjacent points on the scale is the same (e.g. on a metre rule, the distance between the 1 and 2 cm marks is the same as that between the 98 and 99 cm marks).

equally weighted means In some types of *analysis of variance* where the number of items in each group is unequal, each group carries the same 'importance' in determining row and column means (used in calculating the final results) regardless of how many items there are in each group.

equamax See *factor analysis*.

equimax *equamax*.

equivalent forms Two or more versions of the same test which have the same levels of *reliability*. Measured by the *coefficient of equivalence*.

equivalent forms reliability A measure of the degree to which two or more forms of the same test are *equivalent forms*.

erectile dysfunction Failure of a man to achieve or to maintain a penile erection.

ERG *electroretinograph.*

erg (1) A unit of energy. (2) In some theories, the biological energy which drives behaviour.

ergasiophobia A *phobia* of work and/or of taking responsibility for one's actions.

ergonomics The study of the efficiency with which machines (or other inanimate objects) and their human users 'interact'. Hence, ergonomics includes e.g. design of control panels, 'time and motion' studies, design of furniture, etc. See *occupational psychology.*

ergot poisoning Ergot is a fungus found in mouldy flour and other poorly-kept cereal products. It is also a *psychedelic drug,* causing a variety of physical symptoms, such as digestive disorders, and a number of psychological sym- ptoms, including *hallucinations.*

Erikson's theory of development Erik Erikson, psychoanalyst (see *neo-Freudian movement*), and *humanistic psychologist.* A psychoanalytical theory of development, based upon *Freud's psychoanalytic theory.* Central to the model is Erikson's concept of eight 'general stages' which are conflicts between two opposing beliefs (one positive, one negative) which have to be resolved at different stages of development. These are also known as *nuclear conflicts.* The resolution is not simply a matter of the positive and beneficial belief overcoming the other, but rather of the individual coming to appreciate the uses of both; ultimately, however, the more positive belief must be dominant, giving the individual the drive to advance, with the darker, more negative value adding a degree of necessary cynicism and caution. The eight stages are: (i) *basic trust versus mistrust* (0–18

months). A baby learns that parents/ *caregivers* will reliably feed, comfort, change nappies, etc., and hence can be trusted. However, the baby also learns that sometimes his/her needs are not met, leading to mistrust. Accordingly, the baby learns trust and also recognizes that all needs are not automatically met, (ii) *autonomy versus shame and doubt* (18 months–3 years). The child wishes to acquire independence, and to do things for him/herself. This is set against the realization that these actions may look ridiculous to others, and that they might perform the same acts better, (iii) *initiative versus guilt* (3–6 years). The child begins to make plans and generally takes initiatives. However, this is offset against the awareness that some plans are doomed to failure (e.g. in boys, the famous *Oedipus complex*). Thus, the child must learn to curb his/her ambitions to take account of reality, (iv) *industry versus inferiority* (6–11 years). The child must acquire skills by dint of working hard, although this can be marred if s/he is made to feel inferior to other, brighter, children or adults, (v) *identity versus role confusion* (adolescence). Attempts to create one's own personality and behavioural standards and to identify one's aspirations are set against the knowledge that one is rejecting some of the values of one's upbringing (and hence of family/caregivers). This general process can lead some adolescents (such as Erikson himself) to take a *psychological moratorium.* This is a process of temporarily 'dropping out' of society in order to 'find' oneself. A connected issue is the fear of *identity foreclosure,* or accepting/creating an identity too soon, (vi) *intimacy versus isolation* (*early* adulthood). Assuming that marriage is the prime desirable state, intimacy is a prime consideration. However, this cannot be developed until the partners 'know themselves' –

marrying before this state is achieved means that they will be absorbed in discovering themselves rather than their partners, and this, according to Erikson, is a recipe for disaster, (vii) *generativity versus stagnation* (adulthood). There is a need for individuals to be productive – producing and successfully raising children and/or creating a better world for the next generation to live in. A failure to do this results in a feeling of stagnation, (viii) *ego integrity versus despair* (old age). The conflict between whether to come to terms with one's past, or to feel that past events cannot be amended. Erikson's theory has fallen victim to the usual criticisms of psychoanalysis, and also of the vague arguments sometimes used.

erogenous zone See *Freud's psychoanalytic theory.*

eros In later works of Freud, the concept which occupied the same slot as *libido* in earlier versions of his work.

error bars In presenting *mean* results on a graph, displaying the size of the *standard deviation* or *standard error* by thin T-shaped lines extending above and below the mean (this is in the case of a line graph; for a *frequency polygon* and *histogram*, the magnitude of the standard deviation/error is shown as a T-shaped line extending from the top of the bar). Whether a standard deviation or error is signified should be indicated in the rubric accompanying the graph.

error of central tendency *contraction bias.*

error of measurement *measurement error.*

error score Measure of *deviation.*

error variance The proportion of *variance* in a measure attributable to chance error.

erythrophobia A *phobia* of blushing and/or of red things.

ES *effect size.*

escape conditioning See *avoidance conditioning.*

escape hatch Any means by which a patient can escape from commitments (including therapy) – e.g. illness, suicide.

ESI *Early Screening Inventory.*

ESI-D *Early School Inventory – Developmental.*

ESI-P *Early School Inventory – Preliteracy.*

ESN *educationally subnormal.*

ESP (1) *extrasensory perception* (2) *Early Screening Profiles.*

essential hypertension See *blood pressure.*

eta (n) *correlation ratio.*

eta squared (n^2) A *post hoc measure* of an *analysis of variance*, which assesses the percentage of the total *variance* of a sample which can be attributed to a particular *between groups measure*. It is computed as

$$\frac{\text{S.S. for the between groups}}{\text{total S.S.}} \times 100$$

(see *ANOVA table*). E.g. suppose that an ANOVA compared two groups on a test, and the S.S. for the groups was 200, whilst the total S.S. was 400. This means that 50% of the variance is attributable to the differences between the groups.

ethnocentricity A bias (conscious or otherwise) towards adopting a viewpoint and values based on one's own cultural and ethnic background.

ethnographic research Research whose principal focus is on societal culture.

ethnospecific disorder Illness principally or solely confined to a particular cultural or geographical group.

ethogram A record of behaviour (usually of animals in their natural habitat).

ethology The study of animals in their natural habitat, as opposed to in the 'artificial' confines of a laboratory. Study may be by observation alone, or the experimenters may introduce 'artificial' stimuli (e.g. playing a tape recording of a mating call) to see how the animals react. Typically (although by no means exclusively), study has been of non-human animals.

etiological validity *aetiological validity*.

etiology *aetiology*.

ETSB *Engineering Test Selection Battery*.

eugenics The study of selective breeding to improve the health or particular characteristics of a population. The area is relatively uncontentious when concerned with animal breeding, but has raised considerable ire when humans have been the target of 'improvement'. E.g. in the first half of the twentieth century, some of the more vociferous supporters of eugenics were responsible for the passing of laws permitting the compulsory sterilization of thousands of 'mentally defective' individuals lest they 'contaminate' the population by having children (not just in Nazi Germany, but also in the USA and other western nations).

evaluation apprehension 'Exam nerves'. More generally, a layperson's nervousness about being tested and measured by a doctor, psychologist, etc. (see *subject role*).

evaluation research Assessing a system or practice to determine its efficacy and/or efficency.

evaluative dimension See *semantic differential technique*.

evaluative set A bias towards evaluating subjects or items using a band of scores which is too narrow. Using too low a range is termed a *strictness set*, too high

a range a *leniency set*, and too central a range a *central tendency set*.

'Eve White' Pseudonym of a patient in a classic account of multiple personality (made into the film 'The Three Faces of Eve').

event recording Recording the state of the person and/or situation when a particular event (e.g. a target behaviour) occurs.

evoked potential (EP) See *electroencephalograph*.

evoked response *evoked potential*.

EVT *Expressive Vocabulary Test*.

ex post facto test *post hoc test*.

exceptional children Collective term for any children who are out-of-the-ordinary (principally *gifted children* and children with *mental retardation*). As there is little in common between many of the sub-groups, the term provides only a specious unity.

excitatory (neurons) An excitatory *neuron*. (1) Causes (almost invariably in combination with other excitatory neurons) another neuron to become active and/or (2) makes a neuron which is already active send signals at a faster rate. Compare with *inhibitory (neurons)*.

executive functions General term for mental processes involved in planning and organizing behaviour and intellectual tasks.

exhibitionism *paraphilia* in which the patient's principal form of sexual gratification is exhibiting him/herself sexually in an unsolicited manner to (usually) strangers.

existential anxiety The *anxiety* felt due to the perception that one is answerable for one's actions. See *existential neurosis*.

existential neurosis Rather nebulous term indicating gross dissatisfaction and malaise created by an inability to experience free will, the realization that ultimately one has no choice but to die, etc. Contrast with *existential anxiety*.

existential psychology (1) Title bestowed on the work of some of the early experimental psychologists (Titchener *et al.*), which concentrated on introspective examination of thought processes. (2) More recently, a school of psychology loosely based on existentialism – the philosophical doctrine that, when confronted with choices, the individual is free to choose, and need not let the past determine the future (very loosely, 'life is what you make it'). It follows that therapists of this school stress the importance of treating the symptoms of mental illness (i.e. what is), and place less emphasis on what caused the problem in the first place (i.e. what was).

existential therapy General term for therapeutic methods based upon *existential psychology* (definition 2).

exocathection *exocathexis*.

exocathexis See *endocathexis*.

exogenous Derived from external causes. Contrast with *endogenous*.

exogenous depression *reactive depression*.

expectancies anticipated outcomes.

expectancy table A calculation of the probability of subjects reaching a particular *criterion* at the end of an assessment, given their current scores. The margin of error in this prediction is measured by the **standard error of the estimate of the predicted scores** (approximately 95% of actual scores will fall with 2 standard errors).

expected value (p,) See *sampling distribution*.

experiencing ego See *observing ego*.

experiential intelligence See *triarchic theory of intelligence*.

experiential therapy General term for therapeutic methods which treat the recounting and exploration of the patient's experiences as the focal point of the treatment.

experimental epilepsy *epilepsy*-like attack deliberately induced by drugs, electrical stimulation, etc.

experimental group See *control group*.

experimental neurosis (1) *neurotic state* induced by being given a series of tasks which are impossible to solve or are beyond the skill of the subject. (2) Neurosis-like symptoms deliberately induced by drugs, etc.

experimental psychosis Deliberate creation of a *psychosis*-like state by the administration of drugs or other treatment.

experimental realism Used as a loose synonym of *ecological validity*, the term also refers to efforts to ensure that a participant's performance is true to life, even if the experimental surroundings are not.

experimental research Studies which assess the effects of different treatments on the same group or on *matched* groups. Usually there is the implication that the experimenter has a high level of control over the whole of the test situation, and that the situation is fairly unrealistic. See *ecological validity* and *correlational research*.

experimenter bias *experimenter effect*.

experimenter effect A (conscious or unconscious) manipulation of participants' performance by the expectations of the experimenter. See *Clever Hans*.

experimenter expectancy effect *experimenter effect*.

experimentum crucis *crucial experiment*.

explained variance *variance* accounted for by a particular statistical technique.

explanatory research Research which seeks to explain why something occurred. This contrasts with *predictive research*, in which the researcher attempts to create a formula or other method of predicting the value of one *variable* given the value of another (or others) or to predict when a particular event is likely to occur.

exploratory data analysis (EDA) Set of methods for presenting data in visual form so that the researcher can gain insights into the data's structure (e.g. *box and whisker plot*).

exploratory factor analysis See *confirmatory factor analysis*.

explosive disorder Personality disorder in which the patient is subject to sporadic acts of intense destructiveness and violence.

explosive personality *explosive disorder*.

expressed emotion (EE) Label given to the level of criticism and statements of emotional state uttered by a person or group (often a family). A high level of expressed emotion within a family has been cited as a cause of *schizophrenia*.

expressional fluency A nebulous term for the ability to produce a lengthy, coherent argument and/or description.

expressive aphasia See *aphasia*.

expressive language age *age norm* for which the level of expressive language would be appropriate.

Expressive Vocabulary Test (EVT) Measure of expressive vocabulary in young children.

extendure A period in one's life defined by a particular fact (e.g. schooldays, time spent in a particular job).

extension of the median test See *median test*.

external control (1) The degree to which events are beyond the control of the participant. (2) The participant's perception of the same. See *internal control*.

external locus of control *external control*.

external reward *extrinsic reward*.

external speech See *inner speech*.

external validity The degree to which findings from a study can be applied to the general population.

exteroceptors Sensory receptors located in the skin.

extinction Loss of a previously learnt response because it is no longer rewarded.

extradural Pertaining to the area lying between the interior of the skull and the dura (the protective layer surrounding the brain).

extrasensory perception (ESP) The ability to perceive beyond the bounds accepted as feasible by conventional science (e.g. clairvoyance).

extraversion (E) A *trait* expressing the degree to which a person is outgoing, sociable, etc. This contrasts with *introversion*, which is the degree to which a person is shy and retiring. I.e., the terms have the same meanings as in general parlance (although not quite the same spellings). The area between the extremes is known as *ambiversion*. The terms were first used by Jung (see *Jung's psychoanalytic theory*), who conceived them as *personality types*. Subsequently, Hans Eysenck, amongst others, has argued that they are *personality dimensions* (see *Eysenck's model of personality*). See *Myers-Briggs Type Indicator*.

extraversion-introversion scale See *Eysenck's model of personality*.

extrinsic motivation See *intrinsic motivation*.

extrinsic reward In conditioning, a reward which does not relate to the behaviour being shaped (e.g. being given sweets for not wetting the bed). This contrasts with an *intrinsic reward*, which is related (e.g. feeling pleasantly dry). By extension, an extrinsic reward is a tangible gain, whilst an intrinsic reward purely creates a positive psychological response.

extrinsic test bias Discriminating between subjects on the basis of their scores on unbiased tests. See *bias*.

extroversion *extroversion*.

eye movement desensitization and reprocessing (EMDR) Therapeutic technique in which the patient is trained in eye movement exercises whilst thinking about items presented by the therapist.

Eysenck Personality Questionnaire (EPQ) Personality test, named after its inventor, Hans Eysenck. The EPQ consists of four measures: *extroversion-introversion, psychoticism, neuroticism,* and *lying (L)*. The final scale is used to identify certain pathological conditions, and to adjust over-rosy reports by subjects anxious to impress on the other three scales. The test is also available in a children's version. See *Eysenck's model of personality*.

Eysenck's model of personality Hans Eysenck (1916–), psychologist, for many years Professor of Psychology at the Maudsley Hospital (the Institute of Psychiatry), London. Eysenck argues that personality can be 'mapped out' using three *bipolar dimensions*. These are *extraversion-introversion, neuroticism-emotional stability*, and *psychoticism*. The extraversion—introversion dimen-

sion simply describes the degree to which a person is *extroverted* or *introverted*. Most people have a score around the midpoint of the scale (i.e. either mildly introverted or mildly extraverted). The *neuroticism* scale measures level of emotional stability. Scores in one direction indicate a person who is completely emotionally stable, easygoing, etc., whilst a score at the opposite end of the dimension indicates someone who is very 'touchy', easily worried, etc. (again, most people score in between). The psychoticism scale measures the degree to which a person is emotionally cold and divorced from everyday proprieties. By testing subjects on the three measures (using the *Eysenck Personality Questionnaire*), their scores on the three dimensions can be calculated and combined to form an overall profile. Dealing only with the extraversion and neuroticism scales, Eysenck has argued that combinations on these scales reproduce the ancient concept of the four 'humours' – choleric (neurotic and extraverted); melancholic (neurotic and introverted); phlegmatic (introverted and emotionally stable); and sanguine (emotionally stable and extraverted). The three dimensions are held to be underpinned by physiological factors. E.g. Eysenck has argued that differently 'tuned' nervous systems make extraverts hard and introverts easy to condition under most circumstances. The neuroticism scale measures the ease with which a person can become aroused, very neurotic people being the easiest to arouse. It was originally proposed that the three dimensions were independent of each other, but subsequent research has argued that there is some correlation between them.

F

F (1) *F ratio*. (2) *Feeling*.

F₁ See *F ratio*.

F₂ See *F ratio*.

F' See *F ratio*.

F distribution A *sampling distribution* for the *F ratio*. Used to decide if the difference in the *variance* of two measures is *significant*.

F-R *Friedman-Ranks ANOVA*.

F-R ANOVA *Friedman-Ranks ANOVA*.

F ratio (F) *parametric* measure determining if the *populations* from which two samples are drawn have the same variance. The measure plays an important role in assessing *significance* in many statistical tests (e.g. *analysis of variance*). The F_1 ratio measures *between groups*, F_2 ratio measures *within groups*, and **F'** measures *interactions*.

F scale (1) *California F Scale*. (2) A sub-scale of the *Minnesota Multiphasic Personality Inventory*.

F-to-enter test See *multiple regression*.

F-to-remove test See *multiple regression*.

face validity The degree to which a test subjectively appears to measure the skill, knowledge, attitudes, etc. it claims to assess (e.g. a test of psychotic tendencies which measured colour preferences would have a low face validity). Note that a low face validity does not automatically mean that the test does not measure what it claims. See *validity*.

facial affect therapy Therapeutic technique in which patients are trained to be aware of their facial expressions and to alter them to more appropriate ones. The therapeutic effects are in two principal domains – first, the patient sends out more appropriate signals to others, and second, s/he becomes more aware of methods of communication.

facial cranial nerve *cranial nerve number VII*. Concerned with facial muscles and taste (along with *glossopharyngeal cranial nerve*).

facility value The proportion of participants who responded to a particular item in the desired manner.

factitious disorder Feigning an illness or other problem in order to elicit sympathy. Unlike straightforward malingering, however, the desire to feign the illness is beyond the control of the patient, and may not confer an obvious advantage.

factor A *variable* directly manipulated by the experimenter.

factor analysis (i) Broad definition: general term for a set of statistical techniques for determining if the *correlations* between a large number of *variables* can be attributed to a simpler trend or small set of trends. A *correlation matrix* of the variables is created. It is then calculated whether some of the variables correlate more strongly with each other than with the other variables. Such groupings are called 'factors'. The analysis can take two major forms (known as methods of *factor rotation*). In *orthogonal factor analysis*, each factor calculated has no shared *variance* (i.e. each factor is independent of the others). In *oblique factor analysis*, the factors can have shared variance (i.e. the factors correlate with each other). Factor analysis is extensively used in studies of personality and intelligence (e.g. *g* was discovered using it). It is very complex, and although some basic 'user friendly' computing packages are available, the mathematics bar all but a few specialist psychologists from using it effectively. Some types of factor analysis can be criticized because they produce a range of equally valid solutions, and it is up to the researcher to subjectively decide which one s/he will select as the 'right' answer. (ii) Specific notes: different stages in the factor analysis can be performed in a variety of ways. The method of creating factors is called the **initial factoring procedure**, or **factor extraction method**. There are a variety of these. The most commonly used is the *principal components analysis*, which is also a statistical procedure in its own right. If this method is employed, then the procedure is sometimes called **principal component factor analysis**. This works from the original correlation matrix. Other methods manipulate the matrix before performing their analyses. These include **Bartlett's method, Direct Oblimin, Harris image analysis, iterated principal axis, Kaiser image analysis, Little Jiffy, maximum likelihood analysis, principal factor analysis**, and **Procrustes rotation**. In calculating the initial factors, **eigenvalues** (or **characteristic roots**), and **eigenvectors** are produced. These are mathematical expressions of properties of mathematical matrices which are created during the calculations. They are important in determining how many factors will be extracted from the equation. There are several ways of doing this – e.g. the experimenter determines whether factors will be extracted if their corresponding eigenvalues are less than 1 (the **Kaiser criterion**), calculations are stopped when the eigenvalues account for $> x\%$ of the variance, when the graphical plot of factor number against eigenvalues begins to show a characteristic slope (*scree analysis*), etc. The degrees to which the original test scores correlate with the factors are called *factor loadings,* and these can be shown in tabular form as a **factor matrix**. This gives an indication of what each factor represents. Many

researchers seek a *simple structure*, in which variables only correlate with one factor (the *general factor*), and always positively (i.e. each variable is 'explained' by only one factor, and that factor always has a positive influence). A factor which only correlates with one variable is known as a **specific factor**. A factor which correlates with several variables is called a **group factor**. A guide to the simplicity of the structure is the **variable complexity** measure. If a variable is only loaded on one factor, then it will have a variable complexity value of 1. The further it is from 1, the less simple the structure. Individual subjects can be given a **factor score** – that is, the level to which they 'possess' each factor. The basic factor matrix is known as the **unrotated factor matrix**, which some researchers elect as the finishing point of their analysis. Others perform an orthogonal or oblique factor analysis (known collectively as **transformation methods**) as described above (the factors at this stage are also known as **factor axes**). The factors so calculated are known as **primary factors (first-order factors)**. These in turn can be analysed, to find **secondary factors (second-order factors)**. The second-order factors are factors derived from the correlations between the primary factors (i.e. a 'factor analysis' on the factors). It is possible to find **tertiary factors (third-order factors)**, and further levels of factors by performing a similar analysis on second order factors, etc. There are a number of ways of performing the orthogonal analysis. The commonest is the **varimax** solution, with **equamax** and **quartamax** also being frequent options in computer packages. Equamax attempts to make the amount of variance 'explained' by each factor roughly equal, whilst quartamax places as much of the accountable variance as possible onto the first factor extracted (in most analyses, the first factor extracted has the biggest factor loadings). Varimax is a 'compromise' between equamax and quartamax, and whilst giving greater weight to the first factor, attempts a reasonable share of the variance between the other factors. *Kaiser's normalization* manipulates the factor loadings by normalizing them before they are further processed. This often improves the predictability of the procedure. See *Q factor* analysis.

factor axes See *factor analysis.*

factor extraction method See *factor analysis.*

factor loading See *factor analysis.*

factor matrix See *factor analysis.*

factor rotation See *factor analysis.*

factor score See *factor analysis.*

factorial *(!)* The instruction in a formula to multiply the number preceding it by every whole number down to and including 1. E.g. $5! = 5{\times}4{\times}3{\times}2{\times}1$. $0!$ is defined as equalling 1.

factorial design Experimental/statistical design in which all *levels of variable* of all *independent variables* have been examined in all possible combinations. Often the number of independent variables and their levels are denoted by a 'y x y' shorthand. Thus, a '2 x 3 factorial design' has two independent variables, one with 2 and one with 3 levels, a '2 x 3 x 5 factorial design' has three independent variables, with 2, 3, and 5 levels.

factorial validity The *correlation* between scores on different tests claiming to measure the same thing. At a more complex level, the term refers to correlations between items within tests which represent particular factors (see *factor analysis*).

FAD *familial Alzheimer's disease.*

Fake Bad Scale (FBS) Addition to the revised *Minnesota Multiphasic Personality Inventory* which detects reporting of implausible symptoms.

fallible score The score a participant obtains on a test. It is deemed to be 'fallible' because it contains a margin of measurement error which makes it deviate from his/her *true score.*

false alarm *false positive.*

false memory A 'memory' of an event which never occurred. May be symptomatic of a serious problem (such as a *delusion*) or may be an erroneous reconstruction of faint real memories taken out of context. See *false memory syndrome.*

false memory syndrome (FMS) See *recovered memory.*

false negative (1) See *true positive.* (2) Inaccurately discounting the presence of an illness.

false positive (1) See *true positive.* (2) Inaccurately diagnosing the presence of an illness.

falsifiability A concept which has gained popularity through the work of Karl Popper (twentieth century philosopher), which argues that a theory or finding cannot satisfactorily prove anything unless it can potentially be falsified. E.g. one could make the statement that the world was spontaneously created three seconds ago. This theory cannot be disproved (since any measures one might make to 'prove' it would be part of the process of spontaneous creation). Accordingly, the theory is untestable, since it can neither be proved nor disproved. On the other hand, a theory that china vases break if dropped from 100 ft buildings onto concrete pavements could potentially be falsified – if an ample proportion of the vases bounced, then the theory would be falsified.

familial Alzheimer's disease (FAD)
Relatively rare form of *dementia of the Alzheimer type* which invariably has its onset before old age, and where the patient has close older relatives who also had the condition. Children of a FAD patient usually have a 50 % chance of contracting the disease themselves. See *sporadic Alzheimer's disease.*

family-centred therapy Any therapeutic technique in which the whole of a family, or at least its key members, are treated. This can be because the problem lies within the family as a whole (e.g. members have difficulty coping with each other), or because one or a few members are experiencing problems, about which the rest of the family must be counselled.

family history See *history.*

family method Method used in *aetiology* – members of the patient's family are examined to see how many of the symptoms they share in common with him/her, and the extent to which the illness can be attributed to genetic factors.

Family Relations Test (FRT) *projective test* using a set of model figures of members of a family. The test is available in different formats for younger children (3–7 years), older children (7–15 years) and adults.

family therapy *family-centred therapy.*

familywise error rate The probability of making a *Type I error* in a set of comparisons (this contrasts with a *per-comparison error rate*, which is the probability of making a Type I error in an individual comparison). See *Bonferroni correction.*

Famous Names Test (FNT) A measure of *remote memory*. Participants are presented with a list of names of people famous for brief periods of time since the 1920s, and are asked to identify those names which they can remember being in the news at some point in the past. Included in the list are some fictitious names, to prevent participants *confabulating* and saying 'yes' to every name on the list. The test also includes a set of very famous names (Margaret Thatcher, Winston Churchill, etc.) who have been famous for appreciable periods of time. These names are always recognized by normal individuals, but may cause problems for some patients suffering from certain types of *amnesia* or *dementia.*

Fan's tables *item analysis* method.

FAS *foetal alcohol syndrome.*

FAS test A *word fluency test* – the subject is required to produce words beginning with F, A, and S in turn.

FAST model Model by Reisberg *et al.* which describes seven stages of progressively worsening intellectual deterioration found in patients suffering from *dementia of the Alzheimer type.*

faulty information processing In some therapies (particularly *cognitive therapy*), a distortion or misinterpretation of events due to faulty logical processes.

FBS *Fake Bad Scale.*

FCC *Functional Capacities Checklist.*

Fear of Negative Evaluation (FNE) Measure of the degree to which a person fears being perceived negatively by other people.

fear of success Hypothesized drive to 'explain' why people (and women in particular) shun chances to advance up the career ladder, attain further educational qualifications, etc.

Fear Survey Schedule (FSS) Measure of types and range of events which create fear in a subject. There is a version for children (FSS-C).

febriphobia *phobia* of having a fever.

feeble-minded See *mental retardation.*

Feeling (F) See *Myers-Briggs Type Indicator.*

feeling personality See *Jung's psychoanalytic theory.*

feeling therapy Therapeutic technique in which the patient is taught to recognize and fully express his/her feelings, which are motivated by true wishes, and not arising from past problems.

Feldenkrais Procedure Therapeutic technique, the principal features of which are bodily manipulation and breathing exercises.

feline spongiform encephalopathy (FSE) See *bovine spongiform encephalopathy.*

feminine identity The degree to which an individual identifies with *femininity* traits.

femininity See *masculinity.*

feminist therapy General term for any therapeutic method which is shaped and guided by principles of feminist thought.

Ferguson's delta A measure of *discriminatory power* (a score of 1 indicates maximum discriminatory power).

Ferguson's 5 *Ferguson's delta.*

fetish That which is possessed in *fetishism.*

fetishism Type of *paraphilia* in which the patient has profound difficulty in attaining sexual gratification other than from an inanimate object or specific bodily area (some patients can have sexual relations with a partner, but only provided s/he wears the fetishistic item, or it is present in the room; or, if the fetishistic item is a part of the body, grossly unnatural and prolonged attention is paid to it or to pictures of it). Typically the patient is sexually attracted to only one type of item, which can have a recognizable sexual element (e.g. lingerie, stockings, etc.), but can also be non-sexual by societal standards (e.g. prams and car exhaust pipes).

fetus *foetus.*

field dependence A measure of how far a person can analyse a visual item in isolation from its surroundings. A common measure requires a *participant* to align a rod perpendicular to the ground, the rod being surrounded by a slanted frame (the **rod and frame test**). Persons who align correctly are said to be **field independent**, those who align to match the frame are **field dependent**. Most people fall between these extremes. See also *embedded figures test* and *rotating room test.*

field dependent See *field dependence.*

field independent See *field dependence.*

field study *naturalistic research* (definition 2).

50th percentile *median.* Also, see *percentile.*

fifty minute hour The time allocated to teaching, therapy, etc., within an hour's timetabled slot. The remaining ten minutes allows for introductory conversation, time to prepare for the next class, patient, etc.

filial regression See *regression towards the mean.*

fine motor skills See *motor skills.*

finger agnosia A failure to name/identify the fingers.

finite population See *population.*

FIRO-B *Fundamental Interpersonal Relations Orientation-Behavior.*

first-order factor See *factor analysis.*

first order regression line See *polynomial regression.*

first rank symptoms Symptoms which are particularly indicative of *schizophrenia*.

FISH test *fluorescent in situ hybridization test*.

Fisher exact probability test *non-parametric* measure of whether the proportion of members of two groups who belong to two *mutually exclusive events* are significantly different. E.g. whether different proportions of men and women are for or against capital punishment. In certain calculations, the probability calculated may not reach *significance*, but more extreme variants of the same data, with the same sum totals, do reach significance. In these instances, *Tocher's modification* is employed.

Fisher's PLSD test *post hoc test* for the *analysis of variance*. 'PLSD' stands for 'Protected Least Significant Difference'.

Fisher's z test A test of *significance* for *product-moment correlation coefficients*.

Fisher's z transformation A method of transforming *product-moment correlation coefficients* into *z scores*. This in turn enables one to judge if the measure is statistically *significant*.

fishing trip research *shotgun research* – curious how researchers choose images of killing things for such terms.

fissure A fold or crease in the wrinkled surface of the *cortex*. See also *sulcus*.

five factor model of personality A model which argues that personality is composed of five traits – *openness, conscientiousness, extroversion, agreeableness* and *neuroticism*. The model is sometimes referred to by the acronym *OCEAN* (after the initial letters of the traits). Note that not all commentators agree on these label names – some describe 'extraversion' as *surgency*,

'neuroticism' as *emotional stability* and 'openness' as *intellect*.

fixation In *Freudian* theory, the 'freezing' of psychosexual development at an 'immature' stage.

fixation hysteria *somatoform disorder* in which the afflicted area has suffered genuine injury in the past.

fixed effects See *fixed factor*.

fixed effects factor *fixed factor*.

fixed effects fallacy Mistakenly assuming that the results of a narrow range of observations are applicable to the population as a whole.

fixed factor A *variable* which can only assume a limited range of values (e.g. 12 months of the year, seven days of the week, etc.). Measures of the effects of fixed factors are called *fixed effects*.

fixed order presentation Presenting different treatments, tests, etc., in the same order to every subject. This is done because the order of presentation is in itself designed to have an effect. See *counterbalancing*.

fixed role therapy Therapeutic technique in which the patient assumes the role of a person other than him/herself, to give him/her insight into other (and better) behavioural options.

FJA *functional job analysis*.

flashback Involuntary recurrence of a (usually vivid and unpleasant) memory. Encountered in *post-traumatic stress disorder* and use of *psychedelic drugs*.

flat affect Showing little or no emotion.

flexibilitas cerea *catatoma*.

flight into health The spontaneous recovery from mental illness. In psychoanalytic theory, this recovery is held to be illusory and an elaborate scheme to avoid deeper and more threatening analysis.

flight of ideas In conversation, the rapid switching between different concepts, which are often only tangentially linked at best. Can be symptomatic of *mania* and other disorders.

flooding A therapeutic technique in which the patient is exposed and immersed in exposure to a *phobic object* or other *anxiety-producing* event. The exposure continues until the anxiety is reduced (loosely, until the patient realises that the event is not harmful). This is a traumatic experience, but it can be effective in some circumstances. A variant of the technique is *implosion*, in which the patient is made to imagine the event or object. Contrast with *de-sensitization.*

floor effect Effect achieved by giving a group a test which is too difficult – an undesirably large proportion of the group members score zero or nearly zero marks, making discrimination between them impossible. See *ceiling effect.*

fluency The ease with which information can be produced. Nearly always shorthand for *verbal fluency.*

fluent aphasia Synonym for *Wernicke's aphasia*, and more generally, of any *receptive aphasia.*

fluid intelligence The ability to solve problems for which there are no solutions derivable from formal training or cultural practices. There is usually an added assumption that to have a high level of fluid intelligence, a person must solve the said problems quickly. Fluid intelligence roughly corresponds to a layperson's concept of 'wit'.

fluorescent in situ hybridization test (FISH test) Test for detecting genetic abnormalities. The test is commonly used to identify several types of genetically-inherited illnesses.

fluoxetine (brand name: Prozac) An *antidepressant* drug (member of the *selective serotonin re-uptake inhibitors* group) which has gained considerable media attention. The drug appears to be highly effective for many patients, but for a (relatively small) proportion it is alleged that the drug makes the patients feel worse.

fmri Functional *magnetic resonance imaging* – scanning technique that assesses structure and activity within the body simultaneously.

FMS *false memory syndrome.*

FNE *Fear of Negative Evaluation.*

FNT *Famous Names Test.*

focal epilepsy *Jacksonian epilepsy.*

focal neurological disorder See *diffuse neurological disorder.*

focal therapy Therapy which treats the symptoms rather than the underlying cause.

foetal alcohol syndrome (FAS) *mental retardation* (and often slight physical deformity, particularly of the face) resulting from the mother's alcohol abuse during her pregnancy.

foetus Unborn infant. Usually refers to infant 12 weeks after conception up to birth.

folie a deux Condition in which two patients hold the same *paranoia* and its attendant beliefs. Cases of more than two patients sharing the same *delusion* have been recorded (folie a trois, etc.).

follow-up session *booster session.*

FOME *Fuld Object Memory Evaluation.*

footcandle A measure of lighting intensity.

forced choice recognition task See *recognition task.*

forced choice scale Rating scale in which a series of questions require the respondent to choose between two or more answers.

forced choice test Multiple choice test with no option of a 'don't know' answer.

forced distribution ranking See *ranking*.

forced multiple regression See *multiple regression*.

forensic psychiatry Branch of *psychiatry* concerned with the study and treatment of criminal behaviour.

forensic psychology The study of psychological aspects of criminal behaviour, and, more generally, the workings of the legal system.

forensic psychotherapy Branch of *psychotherapy* concerned with the study and treatment of criminal behaviour.

formboard test General term for any test in which the participant is required to insert shapes into holes in a board with the same outline. The test assesses visuo-spatial and psychomotor skills.

formication The illusion of ants or other small insects crawling over one's skin. The sensation can be experienced as threatening in several mental illnesses and forms of drug *addiction*.

47,XXY *Klinefelter's syndrome.*

foster child fantasy The mistaken belief that one is adopted.

Foundation Skills Assessment (FSA) *test battery* for participants aged 16 years and over. Assesses basic literacy, numeracy and problem-solving skills.

fourfold-point correlation *phi correlation coefficient.*

fourth force psychology *transpersonal psychology.*

FPR *Functional Performance Record.*

Fraboni Scale of Ageism (FSA) Scale measuring attitudes to ageing, and yielding three measures: antilocution (speaking negatively about older adults), avoidance (avoiding contact with older people), and discrimination (feeling that older adults are inferior). The FSA consists of a set of 29 statements – for each one the respondent indicates his or her strength of agreement/disagreement.

fractile General term for a fraction on a scale using equally-sized divisions of measurements (e.g. *decile, percentile*).

fragile person A person who is significantly more vulnerable than a typical adult. The phrase is often used in connection with the ethical problems of testing or treating children, older people and people with intellectual and/or behavioural problems.

fragile X syndrome Genetic disorder with physical characteristics including atypically large ears and jaw. Psychological symptoms include *autistic* type behaviour and *hyperactivity*.

free association Therapeutic technique in which the patient lets his/her thoughts wander, without attempting to control them. This is believed to help the patient release thoughts and feelings which are otherwise suppressed. The technique is most often used in some forms of *psychoanalysis*.

free child See *transactional analysis*.

free entry multiple regression See *multiple regression*.

free-floating anxiety *generalized anxiety*.

free recall A memory task in which items can be recalled in any order (i.e. the order in which they were originally presented does not have to be reproduced). Compare with *ordered recall*.

free response question Question where the participant is free to provide any answer s/he wishes. See *limited response question*.

frequency The number of occasions the same score is found in the same sample.

frequency distribution A measure (usually plotted as a graph) of how often each value of a measure has occurred (e.g. how many of the sample scored 0, how many 1, how many 2, etc.). See *cumulative frequency distribution, grouped frequency distribution, percentage cumulative frequency distribution* and *relative frequency distribution*.

frequency polygon See *histogram*.

frequency table Table expressing the frequency with which something or a set of things has occurred. E.g. a table showing a list of football teams and the number of times each team has won each of several competitions.

Freudian Pertaining to *Freud's psychoanalytic theory*. The term is also often used to denote ideas arising from the *neo-Freudian movement*.

Freudian slip 'Slip of the tongue' or other unintentional action held to reveal an unconscious wish or thought which the participant was trying to conceal (deliberately or otherwise). The term is often used (not entirely accurately) in lay parlance for an unwitting double entendre.

Freud's psychoanalytic theory Sigmund Freud (1856–1939), the founder of *psychoanalysis*, created a very rich theory of human psychological behaviour, which, although not part of mainstream psychology, had a profound influence on its early development (even if only in the formation of theories opposed to it, as in *behaviour therapy*). At the heart of the theory is the belief that the human personality is empowered with *psychic energy*, which has to be released in the form of an appropriate action (e.g. if the drive is to eat, then eating is an appropriate release). The **pleasure principle** states that there will be an attempt to do this as soon as possible, but the **reality principle** attempts to ensure that the release only occurs in a socially appropriate form (e.g. a frustrated employee may have an urge to hit his/her boss, but the drive may be channelled into being nasty to an office junior – not commendable, but preferable in terms of social survival). The psychic energy drives three forces. The **id** is a primitive collection of urges with which a baby begins life. It is capable of projecting some basic thoughts of desirable goals (**primary process thought**). In order to cope more efficiently, the **ego** develops. This loosely corresponds to rational thought (**secondary process thought**); it decides on appropriate goals, and attempts to keep a check on the id and the **superego**. The latter arises in later childhood, and is a collection of (often over-harsh) ideals. It acts like an internalized set of moralistic parents. If the ego feels threatened by the id and the superego, then various **defence mechanisms** are available. E.g. the famous **repression**, where an unpleasant thought is blocked by the unconscious (in extreme cases by e.g. hysterical deafness – see also *suppression*). Freud argued that the id, ego, and superego develop as a consequence of several psychosexual stages of development. Each is centred on an **erogenous zone** – an area of the body providing sensual (and not necessarily exclusively sexual) satisfaction. **Oral stage** (0–1 year) – sensual satisfaction primarily through the mouth. **Anal stage** (1–3 years) – sensual satisfaction primarily through the retention and expulsion of faeces. **Phallic stage** (3–5 years) – according to Freud, a boy in this stage realizes that he has a penis, and desires his mother

(the **Oedipus complex**). However, he
fears that this desire will cause his
father to punish him by castration. This
leads him to cease desiring his mother,
and to identify more with his father. A
girl at this stage discovers that she lacks
a penis, but desires one (**penis envy**). She
feels that she once had one, but that it
has been cut off as a punishment. She
blames her mother for this loss, weak-
ening her identification with her, and
increasing her liking for her father.
Latency period (5 years – adolescence)
– energy is channelled into non-sexual
development of intellectual and social
skills. **Genital stage** (adolescence
onwards) – the individual now aims for
'mature' sexual satisfaction with a permanent partner of the opposite sex.
However, 'faulty' development prior to
this stage will lead an individual to
choose a particular type of partner (e.g.
the archetypal case of the man with the
unresolved Oedipus complex who
chooses a partner just like his mother).
'Faulty' development affects more than
choice of partner, however. For
example, a baby in the oral stage who
bites at the nipple will develop a
'biting' and sarcastic sense of humour
in later life. The above is a very simplis-
tic account of a very rich theory, which
has influenced a large number of
researchers as well as other fields
(notably surrealist artists and stream of
consciousness novelists). Freud's
theories have been very heavily criticized for, amongst other things, being
post hoc and untestable explanations,
as well as being sexist (e.g. women are
portrayed as having 'naturally' weaker
personalities). Freud's place in the
history of psychology is assured, but
whether he will be ultimately remembered as more than a founding father
(in the same manner as alchemists are
honoured in chemistry) is open to
doubt.

Friedman analysis of variance
Friedman-Ranks ANOVA.

**Friedman-Ranks ANOVA (F-R
ANOVA)** A *non-parametric* test of the
same group's differences on 3 or more
measures. The test bases its calculations
on the order in which the scores on the
different tests are ranked within each
subject. The test can be regarded as the
non-parametric equivalent of a *within
groups ANOVA.* See *Kruskal-Wallis one
way ANOVA by ranks.*

frigidity Outmoded (and possibly offensive) term for female *inhibited sexual
excitement.*

frontal eye field Eye movements (controlled by the *frontal lobes*) involved in
scanning.

frontal leucotomy A *leucotomy* to the
frontal lobes. A controversial *psycho-
surgical* technique, designed to alleviate
some of the more disruptive symptoms
of a number of serious mental illnesses.
It was popular in the 1940s and 1950s
(with surgeons – patients' views were
often different), but has since fallen out
of favour.

frontal lobe dementia *dementia* whose
origin and primary focus is the *frontal
lobes.* The principal form is *Pick's Disease.*

frontal lobes The front section of the
cerebral cortex extending back to the
temples. Primarily involved in
planning and controlling actions and
thoughts (e.g. by getting words in the
right order when speaking, producing
socially appropriate behaviour).

frontal lobotomy Severance of (some or
all) neural connections to the *frontal
lobes* (typically, the prefrontal section).
The surgical procedure was frequently
used in the past as a treatment for
various psychiatric conditions, with
varying degrees of success.

fronto-temporal dementia *dementia* originating in the *frontal lobes* and/or the *temporal lobes*. In practice, the term is used interchangeably with *frontal lobe dementia*.

Frostig Developmental Test of Visual Perception *Marianne Frostig Developmental Test of Visual Perception.*

frottage The act of committing *frotteurism*.

frotteurism *atypical paraphilia* in which the patient gains his/her principal sexual gratification solely from rubbing him/herself against another person (who may not even be aware of this occurring – e.g. in a packed bus).

FRT *Family Relations Test.*

FSA (1) *Foundation Skills Assessment* (2) *Fraboni Scale of Ageism.*

FSE *feline spongiform encephalopathy.*

FSS *Fear Survey Schedule.*

FSS-C See *Fear Survey Schedule.*

fugue *dissociative disorder* which, in the most extreme state, involves the patient assuming a totally new identity, even to the extent of moving to a new area of the country. In less extreme cases, the patient takes a shorter journey away from familiar surroundings, before returning, often with limited or no memory of the episode.

Fuld Object Memory Evaluation (FOME) Memory and naming test for older participants, who are given objects to recognize, first by touch, and then by sight. Participants must then recall the items several times over, interspersed with a *verbal fluency task*.

fully-loaded cost The total cost of an action, including all incidental effects.

function *variable* whose value is dependent upon that of another variable or variables, and/or a variable which can

be expressed in terms of another variable or variables.

functional analysis In *conditioning* studies, examining the relationship between the treatment regime and the corresponding changes in behaviour.

functional autonomy See *Allport's theory of personality development.*

Functional Capacities Checklist (FCC) Self-report questionnaire on how patients view their physical capacities.

functional disorder A disorder with no apparent physical cause. See *functional mental disorder.*

functional fixedness Having a limited (and usually highly conventional) perception of the uses to which an item or situation can be put (e.g. only seeing a house brick in terms of a building material, rather than e.g. as a source of rouge). The concept is of considerable importance in *creativity* research.

functional imaging See *neuroimaging.*

functional job analysis (FJA) A method of *job analysis.*

functional literacy The basic level of reading skills required for a particular occupation or lifestyle. E.g. for most unskilled jobs, a *reading age* of 11 is the maximum required. See *functional reading.*

functional mental disorder Any mental disorder for which a physical cause cannot be identified. See *organic mental disorders.*

Functional Performance Record (FPR) Wide-ranging measure of 26 different behavioural, physical and psychological skills. The test is intended for participants with mental and/or physical handicap, to determine their functional abilities.

functional reading The ability to read basic instructional materials at the barest level of proficiency expected by the society in which the participant is living. See *functional literacy.*

functional relationship Relationship between two or more *variables,* such that a change in one affects the other(s).

Fundamental Interpersonal Relations Orientation-Behavior (FIRO-B) Measure of participants' levels of behaviour in the context of belonging to a group, and the degree to which they expect the same behaviours in others.

fundamental lexical hypothesis The belief that the key facets of human behaviour have been encapsulated in single terms in language.

fundamental symptoms *primary symptoms.*

future shock Anxiety induced by living in a modern, rapidly changing industrial society.

G

g General intellectual capacity – a term devised by Charles Spearman (early twentieth century) to describe an ability he felt underpinned all intellectual skills. Today often used more loosely to denote participants' general level of intelligence. See *G g.*

G g American writers tend to use the upper case letter, British writers the lower case.

G index Specialized *correlation* measure used in some forms of *factor analysis.*

GAF *Global Assessment of Functioning.*

gain score *difference score.*

galactosaemia Genetic disorder characterized by a failure to metabolize galactose (a sugar found in milk). Failure to treat the condition results in severe intellectual dysfunction, but early intervention (principally, adopting a rigidly lactose-free diet) should avoid this.

galeophobia A *phobia* of cats.

galvanic skin response (GSR) The ease with which the skin conducts an electrical current. As people become aroused, they sweat, and this changes the GSR. This phenomenon can be used to test people's level of arousal when confronted with stimuli (it should be noted that both the degree of sweating and the electrical currents used are very slight, and unnoticed by the participant). Since people can also become aroused when they are lying, the GSR has been used (not without controversy) as a lie detector test, although usually in conjunction with other physical measures (see *polygraph*).

GAMA *General Ability Measure for Adults.*

gambler's fallacy The mistaken belief that because there has been a long string of one type of *mutually exclusive event,* another type of event 'must' occur soon. E.g. because there have been 10 'heads' tossed in a row, 'tails' must come up next. This is fallacious, because on each toss of the coin, the odds of 'heads' and 'tails' are even – the coin is not influenced by what has gone before. The debunking of the gambler's fallacy often leaves people with the equally erroneous impression that a long sequence of one type of event (e.g. tossing 'heads' 10 times in a row) is not unusual; it is unusual, in that a mixture of heads and tails is far more probable. This does not contradict the argument that 'tails' can just as easily be thrown after a sequence of TTTTTTTTTT as after HTTHTTHTHH.

game (1) In *transactional analysis*, the maladaptive situation of being in an inappropriate *ego state* and therefore acting out an encounter as if it were a game rather than expressing one's true intentions. (2) Generally, in therapies, playing a set role rather than listening to one's real wishes.

'Games People Play' See *transactional analysis*.

gamma (1) *effect size*. (2) Measure of *correlation* between *ordinal variables*.

gamophobia A *phobia* of marriage.

GAMT *Graded Arithmetic-Mathematics Test*

ganglia Plural of *ganglion*.

ganglion A group of *neurons*.

ganglioside Drug whose effects included the enhanced release of *acetylcholine* (see *cholinergic hypothesis*). Has been cited as a possible treatment for patients suffering from *dementia*. See *ondansetron* and *tacrine*.

Ganser syndrome A *factitious disorder* in which the 'illness' is a psychological one.

GAP Reading Comprehension Test Reading test for 7–12-year-olds. Uses *cloze procedure*.

GAPADOL Reading Comprehension Test Reading test for 7–16-year-olds. Uses *cloze procedure*.

GARS *Gilliam Autism Rating Scale*.

GAS *general adaptation syndrome*.

GAT *General Abilities Test*.

GATB *General Aptitude Test Battery*.

Gates-Macginitie Reading Test Reading test consisting of several 'Levels', commensurate with the age of the subjects: R: 5–7 years; A: 5–7; B: 7–8; C: 8–9; D: 9–12; E: 13–16; F: 16–18. All measure size of vocabulary and comprehension abilities, (with the exception of 'R', which also measures letter recognition and ability to recognize letter sounds).

gateway drugs 'Soft' illegal drugs (*marijuana*, etc.) which are often the first illegal substances used by drug users who subsequently 'graduate' to taking 'hard' drugs (*heroin*, etc.). The general theory of this progression is also known as the **stepping stone theory**. It should be noted that the majority of 'soft' drug users do not follow this path.

gatophobia *ailurophobia*.

Gaussian curve *bell-shaped curve*.

Gaussian distribution *normal distribution*.

gc/Gc Symbol for *crystallized intelligence*.

GCS *Glasgow Coma Scale*.

GDS (1) *Gessell Development Schedules*. (2) *Geriatric Depression Scale*.

gedanken experiment *thought experiment*.

gegenhalten An involuntary resistance by the limbs to being moved by another. Symptomatic of damage to the *motor cortex*.

gender dysphoria *transsexualism*.

gender identity disorder Group term for *psychosexual disorders* whose principal characteristic is that the patient feels that s/he is the wrong gender. See *gender identity disorder of childhood*, *gynemimesis*, and *transsexualism*. Also see *transvestism*.

gender identity disorder of childhood *gender identity disorder* exhibited in childhood, in which the patient behaves like a highly stereotypical example of the opposite gender (e.g. a girl who is very 'tomboyish'). Given that the diagnosis relies on accepting societal sex stereotypes, it is not without its limitations.

General Abilities Test (GAT) Battery of measures of verbal, non-verbal, numerical and spatial abilities, intended to evaluate and help in selection procedures of staff 'below' the level of middle management.

General Ability Measure for Adults (GAMA) Measure of general intellectual abilities in adults.

general adaptation syndrome (GAS) Hypothesized sequence of reactions to prolonged *stress*. The participant's body initially enters into a shock phase, which is counteracted by increased hormonal activity. If the stress continues too long, the protective system deteriorates, making the participant more prone to illness.

General Aptitude Test Battery (GATE) *test battery* (devised by American Employment Service) assessing basic intellectual and motor skills.

general factor See *factor analysis*.

General Health Questionnaire (GHQ) A quickly-administered checklist of recent symptoms and behaviour designed to elicit the general psychiatric state of a patient. Available in 3 forms, containing 60, 30, or 28 questions (GHQ60, GHQ30 and GHQ28 respectively).

general intelligence *g*.

general learning skill General ability to learn skills. The concept can be used to compare individuals or species. Compare with *specific learning skill*.

general linear model (GLM) Term for statistical methods such as *analysis of variance*, *correlation* and *regression*, which in essence assume that one or more *variables* can be used to predict the value of another variable.

general paralysis of the insane (GPI) *syphilitic dementia*.

general paresis See *paresis*.

general trait *trait* which occurs in many aspects of the person's life. Contrast with *specific trait*.

generality of results The degree to which the findings of a study are likely to be replicable when different subjects, situations, etc. are used.

generalizability theory Complex theory, devised by Cronbach and colleagues, exploring the relationship between *reliability* and *validity* and the application to test design and evaluation.

generalization (-isation) The degree to which a *conditioned response* to one stimulus is given to similar responses. Accordingly, a measure of the success of *transfer*.

generalized anxiety One of the *anxiety states*. A chronic state of feeling anxious for no logical reason. The patient often has physical symptoms, such as persistent minor physical ailments, the sensation of a pounding heart, tightness in the chest, etc.

generalized mental ability *g*.

generational effect *cohort effect*.

generationally biased stimuli Stimuli (or other test materials) which will only be recognized by, or be most familiar to, a particular *age cohort*.

generativity versus stagnation See *Erikson's theory of development*.

genital stage See *Freud's psychoanalytic theory*.

genuineness *congruence*.

geometric mean Calculated as the *nth* root of all the scores multiplied together (or alternatively, the *mean* of all their logarithms added together), where n = the total number of scores. The geometric mean is rarely used in psychology.

geotaxis Making a movement in response to gravitational forces.

geotropism *geotaxis*.

Geriatric Depression Scale (GDS) A 'yes/no' questionnaire measuring the level of depression in the respondent. The questions are geared to match the symptoms and lifestyles typically found in depressed older people.

Geriatric Mental State (GMS) A standardized interview package for assessing the mental state of older patients.

geriatrics Medical treatment and study of ageing. See *gerontology*.

gerontology The study of old age. The term is usually restricted to psychological and sociological aspects of ageing.

Gerstmann syndrome A simultaneous affliction of *acalculia, agraphia, finger agnosia*, and confusion of left and right. Whether the syndrome (when found) has a single root cause, is debatable.

Gerstmann-Straussler-Scheinker syndrome (GSS) (Rare) degenerative brain disease.

Gessell Development Schedules (GDS) *test battery* measuring development in infancy and early childhood – largely requires observation of child's behaviour and physical measurement, rather than more conventional psychological tests.

Gessell Preschool Schedules (GPS) *Gessell Development Schedules*.

Gestalt psychology A *humanistic psychology* which stresses the 'whole' of the patient, and encourages him/her to reclaim suppressed aspects of his/her psyche, and hence his/her suppressed creative potential.

Gf/gf Symbol for *fluid intelligence*.

GHB Gamma hydroxy butyrate – a legal sedative which, if misused, can produce feelings of euphoria. Accordingly, it has found popularity as an 'illegal drug'.

GHQ *General Health Questionnaire*.

Gibson Spiral Maze A test of psychomotor skill, in which the participant is required to trace a pencil line around a spiral shaped path as quickly as possible.

gifted children Children with exceptional talents. Often used 'merely' to denote children with high *IQs*, rather than the truly exceptionally gifted.

Gilles de la Tourette disorder *Tourette's syndrome*.

Gilliam Autism Rating Scale (GARS) Test assessing the presence of autism and its severity in children.

Gilmore Oral Reading Test Reading test for 6–14-year-olds.

GLA *Group Literacy Assessment*.

Glasgow Coma Scale (GCS) A measure of the depth of unconsciousness displayed by a patient after brain injury.

Glasgow Outcome Scale (GOS) A measure of the degree of recovery made by a patient after brain injury.

glass ceiling Metaphor to describe the unacknowledged barrier blocking the job promotion and advancement of women. The term is likely to spread to describing the blocking of minority groups in general.

glial cells Supporting cells, supplying nutrients and 'building materials' to *neurons*.

GLM *general linear model*.

global In reference to brain damage – an impairment across all aspects of the skill affected.

global aphasia See *aphasia*.

Global Assessment of Functioning (GAF) Scale from 0–100 indicating level of functioning (the higher the score, the better the function). A low score indicates a need for treatment and/or specialist care.

Global Gordon's Personal Profile-Inventory (Global GPP-I) Measure of nine aspects of personality (e.g. *self-esteem*, sociability) pertinent to the business environment.

Global GPP-I *Global Gordon's Personal Profile-Inventory.*

globus hystericus A *somatoform disorder* in which the patient is convinced there is a lump in his/her throat.

glossolalia Unintelligible or garbled speech – usually refers particularly to speech of people in a trance (e.g. religious 'speaking in tongues') and suffering from some mental disorders (e.g. *schizophrenia*).

glossopharyngeal cranial nerve *cranial nerve* number IX. Concerned with throat and taste (along with *facial cranial nerve*).

glove anaesthesia The phenomenon whereby the patient complains that his/her hands feel numb, but not his/her arms. This is anatomically impossible – the nerves concerned supply the hands and also the arms, and dysfunction in one should cause dysfunction in the other. This indicates that glove anaesthesia must be *a psychosomatic complaint*. A similar phenomenon is *stocking anaesthesia*, where the patient complains of numbness in the whole of the foot and the leg.

glue sniffing *solvent abuse.*

GMA *Graduate and Managerial Assessment.*

GMS *Geriatric Mental State.*

GMT *Group Mathematics Test.*

GNS *growth need strength.*

GNT *Graded Naming Test.*

goal The target/end result of an action, and hence, by implication, something which is desired.

goal setting Establishing behavioural or other targets for a patient undergoing therapy.

Goldman-Fristoe Test of Articulation Measure of ability in children and young adults to articulate consonants.

Goldstein-Scheerer tests Neurological measures of the degree of impairment in abstract thought and concept formation.

Gollin Incomplete Figures Test A test of memory/visuo-spatial skills. The participant is shown an incomplete line drawing of a figure, and then gradually more complete drawings of the same object, until s/he can identify it. The participant is shown the figures on subsequent occasions, and the process is repeated. With the repeated exposures, the participant should require progressively fewer complete drawings before s/he successfully identifies the object.

Golombok Rust Inventory of Marital State (GRIMS) Measure of the state of the relationship between a married/cohabiting couple.

Golombok Rust Inventory of Sexual Satisfaction (GRISS) A measure of satisfaction in sexual activity, and sexual dysfunction.

good breast-bad breast See *Kleinian theory.*

Goodenough Draw-a-Man Test Test for children aged up to 12 years. The subject is required to draw a picture of a man or woman, which is marked for detail, accuracy, etc. The measure gives a rough indication of *IQ.* See *Goodenough Draw-a-Person Test.*

Goodenough Draw-a-Person Test *Goodenough Draw-a-Man Test* with a non-sexist title. Do not confuse with the *draw-a-person test.*

Goodenough-Harris Drawing Test *Goodenough Draw-a-Man Test.*

Goodman and Kruskall's tau Meaure of *correlation* between *nominal variables.*

goodness of fit test Any test which measures how well a sample's *variance* corresponds to that of a particular *population.* Hence, the degree to which data fulfil expectations.

Gordon Musical Aptitude Profile A measure of basic musical skills (e.g. ability to spot similarities and differences in pieces of music).

Gordon Personal Inventory *self-report questionnaire* yielding measures of dynamism of thought and outlook.

Gordon Personal Profile *self-report questionnaire* yielding measures of emotional and social skills.

Gordon's Survey of Interpersonal Values (SIV) See *Gordon's Survey of Personal Values (SIV).*

Gordon's Survey of Personal Values (SPY) Measure of how the participant deals with situations. This contrasts with *Gordon's Survey of Interpersonal Values (SIV)*, which is a measure of the participant's style of interaction with other people.

Gorham test A test of knowledge of meanings of well-known proverbs.

GORT *Gray Oral Reading Test.*

GOS *Glasgow Outcome Scale.*

Gottschaldt figures Simple figures embedded in more complex figures. Used in tests of visuo-spatial ability – the subject must locate the simple figures.

GPI *general paralysis of the insane.*

GPS *Gessell Preschool Schedules.*

GRA *Group Reading Assessment.*

graceful degradation The phenomenon whereby the cell loss which accompanies ageing is reflected in a gentle loss of memories and level of skill (rather than a wholesale and absolute loss).

grade equivalent score American measure expressing the school grade level at which an average pupil can perform the task in question.

Graded Arithmetic-Mathematics Test (GAMT) Standardized test of mathematical and arithmetical skills for subjects aged 6–18 years. Has two forms – Junior (6–12) and Senior (11–18).

Graded Naming Test (GNT) Standardized test of ability to name a series of objects, which become increasingly harder to name as the test progresses. The test is used in the diagnosis of certain forms of brain damage.

graded task (1) Task which is broken down into components because it is too difficult for the person to grasp in its entirety at the first attempt. (2) *graded test.*

graded test Test which consists of several progressively more difficult levels.

Graded Word Spelling Test (GWST) Standardized spelling test for subjects aged 6–16 years.

Graduate and Managerial Assessment (GMA) Battery of tests of verbal, numerical and abstract reasoning, intended to aid the selection of managerial staff.

gramophone syndrome *stereotypy* of speech.

grand mal epilepsy See *epilepsy.*

grandiose self An unrealistic and inflated idea of one's self-worth.

grandiosity An exaggerated view of one's own worth.

granulovacuolar degenerations Malformed and usually dead *neurons* which (under a microscope) look like dense granules.

graphic rating Any method in which the participant rates an item in a diagrammatic form without recourse to a numbered scale (e.g. shading in a box to the extent with which they agree with a statement).

graphology The study of handwriting. The term has become increasingly applied to a (controversial) specialization within this general field – namely, the calculation of a person's personality from a sample of their handwriting.

graphomania An obsessive urge to write.

graphophobia A *phobia* of writing.

graphorrhea Lengthy and completely meaningless pieces of writing.

Graves' disease *hyperthyroidism.*

Gray Oral Reading Test (GORT) *achievement test,* using *oral reading measures.*

Greenhouse-Geisser correction See *sphericity test.*

grey matter The cell bodies, synapses, etc., of nerve cells of the *central nervous system,* responsible for neural processing. Contrast with **white matter**, which is principally composed of the parts of the cells responsible for transmitting the information.

Griffith Scale of Mental Development (GSMD) Invented by Griffith, this is a *test battery*, primarily of motor, social, auditory and aural abilities in infants and young children.

GRIMS *Golombok Rust Inventory of Marital State.*

GRISS *Golombok Rust Inventory of Sexual Satisfaction.*

gross motor skills See *motor skills.*

grounded theory A *qualitative research* method for the generation of a theoretical model from data. The researcher begins as a blank slate – e.g. prior expectations of how the data may fit a pre-conceived model are prohibited. A key feature of grounded theory is that the conclusions drawn should be true to the data collected (i.e. 'grounded' in the data), rather than be a general idea applied to a specific local situation. Note that grounded theory tends to arouse polarized opinions amongst researchers.

group cohesiveness The degree to which members of a group feel that they have a common bond.

group factor See *factor analysis.*

group interval *class interval.*

Group Literacy Assessment (GLA) Reading and spelling test for participants aged 7–14 years. Requires participant to identify misspellings in a prose passage and to provide the correct spelling. Also contains a *cloze procedure test,* in which the first letter of the to-be-found word is provided.

Group Mathematics Test (GMT) Test of mathematical abilities (divided into orally presented and computational sub-sections) for participants aged 6–7 years (and also for less able older children).

Group Reading Assessment (GRA) Reading test for participants aged 7–9 years (specifically, children in their first year at UK junior school). Requires participant to identify a word spoken by the tester, to find the word best suited to a given sentence, and to find homophones (same sounding but differently spelt words) of a given word.

Group Reading Test (GRT) Reading test for participants aged 6–12 years. Requires participant to choose a word from various alternatives to match a picture, and to complete sentences, given a list of alternatives.

group test Test which can be administered to a group of people simultaneously.

group therapy General name for any therapeutic method in which several patients meet together for simultaneous treatment by the same therapist. Much of the therapeutic effect is derived from the patients' interactions with each other – the therapist's role after the initial stages is often to guide rather than to order directly.

grouped frequency distribution A measure (usually plotted as a graph) of how often different ranges of values of a measure have occurred (e.g. what percentage of the sample scored between 0 and 5, how many scored between 6 and 10, how many scored between 11 and 15, etc.). This grouping of scores, such that a score can only fall within one group, is called the *class intervals* system. The number of class intervals within a grouped frequency distribution is given the symbol *k*. See *frequency distribution*.

grouping error (1) Generally, the innacurate categorization of subjects, data, etc. (2) Grouping data so that the data within an individual group are abnormally distributed given the assumptions of the analysis (typically, the data within a group are not normally distributed, and a *parametric* test is being used).

growth need strength (GNS) The level of need a person feels for growth, personal fulfilment, etc.

GRT *Group Reading Test.*

GSMD *Griffith Scale of Mental Development.*

GSR *galvanic skin response.*

GSS *Gerstmann-Straussler-Scheinker syndrome.*

guessing bias Habitually answering in a particular manner if the true answer is not known.

guidance A rather nebulous term – some commentators treat it as synonymous with *counselling*, whilst others reserve it for counselling in which the participant is presented with options for future action and advice, without the implication that the participant needs to be 'cured'.

guided discovery The process of guiding (although not leading or shaping) a patient towards discovering things about events in his/her life which have significantly influenced his/her behaviour.

guided participation *modelling* (particularly treatment of *phobias*).

guiding fiction An idealized *self-concept*, which can cause problems if it strays too far from reality.

Guilford Zimmerman Temperament Survey (GZTS) Measure of ten personality attributes (e.g. sociability, emotional stability).

Guttman scaling Method of constructing an *attitude scale*, in which statements are ranked in order of 'strength'. It is assumed that if a subject agrees with a strong statement, then weaker expressions of the same arguments would also be agreed with.

GWST *Graded Word Spelling Test.*

gynemimesis *gender identity disorder*, akin to *transsexualism* in its symptoms, but without the desire to be surgically changed to the opposite sex.

gynophobia A *phobia* of women.

GZTS *Guilford Zimmerman Temperament Survey.*

H

h *precision.* (2) *leverage statistic.*

H² *heritability ratio.*

H *heritability ratio.*

Hi *alternative hypothesis.*

Ho *null hypothesis.*

habit regression Replacing a new habit with an old one.

habitual response Response/type of behaviour which is characteristically used by a participant, and is a typical exemplar of a particular *trait*.

habituation (1) Becoming used to a form of stimulation (e.g. a drug or a signal), often with the added implication that it no longer has the power it initially had. (2) The process of becoming *addicted*.

habituation training Training a patient to bring a thought or idea to mind and to keep it there by concentrating on it. The aim is to make the patient concentrate upon thoughts of a situation which produces maladaptive or abnormal responses so that they become *habituated* to it, thereby robbing it of its potency for provoking responses.

Hachinski Ischaemic Score (IS) A diagnostic technique for distinguishing *dementias* of cardiovascular origin, and specifically, *multi-infarct dementia*. Patients are scored on the number of symptoms they display (and some more indicative symptoms are *weighted*).

HADS *Hospital Anxiety and Depression Scale.*

haematophobia A *phobia* of blood.

half-way house An institution for patients who are too mentally ill for complete integration into 'normal society', but who are not disturbed enough to merit full hospitalization. The institution attempts to replicate normal community living, whilst under professional supervision.

hallucination A severe misperception (rather than a mistaken belief, as in a *delusion*), to the extent of perceiving stimuli which cannot possibly be there (e.g. hearing entire conversations from 'voices in the head' in *schizophrenia*). See *illusion*.

hallucinogen Any drug capable of producing *hallucinations*. Largely synonymous with *psychedelic drug*.

hallucinosis Mental illness in which the patient, whilst fully conscious, suffers frequent *hallucinations*.

halo effect The tendency to allow early (and possibly inaccurate) judgements of a person or event to shape later evaluations. Alternatively, to allow one 'good' feature of a person to cloud judgement of the rest of his/her character or abilities.

halo error *halo effect.*

haloperidol Form of *antipsychotic drug*.

Halsted–Reitan Neuropsychological Battery (HRNB) A battery of neuropsychological tests, assessing abstract reasoning and linguistic, sensory, visuo-spatial and motor skills.

Hamilton Rating Scale (HRS) *observer scale* for rating the severity of depression.

Hand test *protective personality* test for participants aged 6 years and over.

Hand-Tool Dexterity Test Test of manual dexterity and tool use. Primarily designed as a *personnel screening* test for mechanical/engineering jobs.

handedness The hand which is predominantly used.

handicap An impairment sufficiently pronounced to create an atypical state. The DSM-IV grades mental dysfunction according to level of *IQ*: 0–19 (profound handicap); 20–34 (severe); 35–49 (moderate); and 50–70 (mild).

Hanfmann-Kasanin Concept Formation Test A measure of concept formation abilities (or of handicap of same). The test requires subjects to arrange blocks of different colours, shapes and sizes into categories.

haphalgesia An abnormal perception of pain on being touched.

haphephobia A *phobia* of being touched.

haptephobia *haphephobia*.

haptic Pertaining to touch.

Haptic Visual Matching Test (HVM Test) Assesses children's ability to match visual and haptic (touch) perceptions, and the degree of impulsiveness with which this is done. The child feels (but cannot see) a shape, and is then asked to pick the target by sight from a range of alternatives. The time taken to make the response, as well as accuracy, is recorded.

haptometer Any device for measuring sensitivity of touch.

hard data Data based on objective observations.

hardiness Ability to withstand *stress*.

Hare Psychopathy Test (PCL) Measure of presence and strength of *psychopathy*.

harmonic mean Calculated by converting scores into their reciprocals (i.e. divided into 1 – the reciprocal of 2 is 0.5, of 10 is 0.1, etc.), finding their *mean*, and then finding the reciprocal of this mean. The measure is rarely used in psychology.

harria Cattell's term for a personality *trait* corresponding to tough-mindedness.

Harrington-O'Shea Career Decision-Making System (CDM) Measure of interests and skills to assist school pupils in choosing a career.

Harris image analysis See *factor analysis*.

Harrison-Stroud Reading Readiness Test Test of how much a child already knows about reading (what it is, what it is used for, etc.) and hence how prepared s/he is for learning to read.

hashish See *cannabis*.

Hassles and Uplifts Scale Therapeutic questionnaire identifying sources of *stress* and their possible solutions.

hat value *leverage statistic*.

Hawthorne effect The phenomenon whereby there is likely to be an improvement in performance if there is any change in the workplace, school, or other institution, whether the change is deliberately designed to be beneficial or not.

Hd scale See *Minnesota Multiphasic Personality Inventory*.

hebephrenia *disorganized schizophrenia*.

hebephrenic schizophrenia *disorganized schizophrenia*.

hebesphalmology The study of *delinquency*.

hedonic calculus In some forms of therapy, judging the pros and cons of an action.

heliophobia A *phobia* of light or of the sun.

'Hello-Goodbye' effect Phenomenon whereby patients may exaggerate the severity of symptoms at the start of treatment and play down their extent at the end of treatment.

Help-Assert Computerized *assertiveness training* programme.

Help-Esteem Computerized programme intended to boost *self-esteem* in people lacking it.

Help-Stress Computerized programme intended to reduce *stress* levels of subjects.

helplessness *learned helplessness.*

hemi-inattention See *sensory neglect.*

hemiballismus An involuntary movement of the limbs.

hemiparesis *hemiplegia.*

hemiplegia Paralysis of one side of the body. In contrast, **paraplegia** is paralysis of the legs, and is paralysis of the legs and arms. These are produced by damage to the spinal cord (the higher 'up' the spine the damage occurs, the greater the paralysis).

hemispheres (cortex) The *cerebral cortex* is divided into two equally sized halves along a vertical axis running from the front to the back of the head. These two halves are known as the hemispheres, and are called the right hemisphere and the left hemisphere. In most individuals, the left hemisphere is principally responsible for linguistic skills and the right for visuo-spatial skills (although in some individuals, particularly left handers, this is reversed, and other, rarer, people have no simple left–right distinction). The hemispheres are linked by several pathways, of which the most important is the *corpus callosum.*

hemispheric differences Differences between the functions of the right and left *hemispheres.*

hemophobia *haematophobia.*

hemp Plant, one form of which is *cannabis.*

heritability ratio (H, h²) The proportion of *variance* in behaviour attributable to *innate* factors.

heroin See *opiates.*

heroin antagonist Drug which prevents a feeling of euphoria upon taking *heroin* (thereby reducing the drive to take it).

heroin substitute A drug used to treat *heroin* addiction. It stimulates the same *opiate receptors* as heroin (hence blocking the physical craving for it), but produces less euphoria.

heterogeneous group Group whose members have nothing in common. See *homogeneous group.*

heteroscedacity See *scedacity.*

heuristic Problem-solving method. Often applied to a method which might not be entirely accurate, but will be 'close enough' and will save mental effort (e.g. treating pi as 22/7).

Hicomp Preschool Curriculum Commercial education curriculum planner.

hidden observer Rather nebulous term for the experience of monitoring one's own behaviour and thoughts.

hierarchical multiple regression *ordered multiple regression.*

hierarchical sums of squares *Type I sums of squares.*

hierarchy of needs *Maslow's hierarchy of needs.*

high frequency words Words which occur very often in common usage.

high functioning When the term precedes the name of a condition (e.g. 'high functioning autism') it means that the patient concerned performs atypically well on psychological and/or physical tasks for someone with their condition. The term can be misleading – it may additionally imply that the patient performs well when compared with someone without the condition, or it may not. Accordingly, caution in interpretation is advised. ***Low function-***

ing indicates that the patient performs atypically badly for someone with their condition.

high risk students Students whose (mis)perception of previous academic failings may lower their motivation, and increase the probability that they will 'drop out'.

high-risk subjects *at-risk subjects*.

higher brain centres Nebulous term for areas of the brain responsible for the (also nebulously defined) *higher mental processes*.

higher functions In neurology, gait, speech and cognitive processes.

higher mental processes Nebulous term for mental operations which are regarded as 'intellectual' (i.e. which require conscious attention to operate efficiently, and which can be significantly improved through practice, learning, etc.).

higher order factor *primary factor*.

higher order interaction An *interaction* with more than two *variables*.

higher-order motive Motive whose fulfilment does not involve physiological drives.

hindsight bias In recalling a memory, exaggerating the prevalence and/or magnitude of a particular event, because it subsequently proved to be more important than it appeared at the time.

hippocampus *sub-cortical* section of the brain whose principal function is in memory, and particularly in transferring information from short- to long-term memory. Damage to the hippocampus leads to an extremely debilitating *amnesia*, with patients unable to remember practically all new information.

Hirano body A crystalline structure found in some brain cells in older people. The incidence of these increases greatly in some *demented* patients.

Hiskey-Nebraska Test of Learning Aptitude Non-verbal intelligence *test battery* designed for deaf or hard-of-hearing children.

histogram A graph for visually expressing *frequency distributions*. The X axis expresses the *class intervals* the data are divided into, and the Y axis the frequency of each category's occurrence. The data are expressed as a series of bars of equal width, with no space between adjoining bars. The height of the bar indicates the frequency with which a particular class interval has occurred. The histogram is, strictly speaking, not synonymous with the *bar graph* (which is used for *discrete variables*), although the two terms are often interchanged. The *frequency polygon* is plotted in a similar manner to the histogram, save that a continuous line is plotted instead of a series of bars. Where the class interval represents more than one number per interval, the line is plotted against the *midpoint* of the interval. The frequency polygon should not be confused with the *line graph*. See *distribution curve*.

history The factors that have led to the current state of affairs and which illustrate the nature of the problems faced. Thus, *patient history* is a collection of information about the patient's life which may be relevant to the case (e.g. previous symptoms, behavioural problems, etc). *Psychiatric history* and *psychological history* refer respectively to specific psychiatric and psychological factors in the patient's life. *Family history* is information on the family life of the patient relevant to the case and usually includes information on any genetic relatives with similar symptoms (thus indicating a genetic link).

histrionic personality disorder *personality disorder* characterized by extreme and over-dramatic expressions of mood and reactions to events.

hit *true positive.*

HIT *Holtzman Inkblot Technique.*

HIV-associated dementia *AIDS dementia complex.*

Holborn Reading Scale Reading test for participants aged 5–13 years. Consists of sentences which increase in difficulty as the test progresses. The test terminates when the participant has made a set number of errors. The *Salford Sentence Reading Test* has a similar format.

hold tests See *deterioration quotient (DQ).*

holding Term sometimes used in therapy to denote the therapist's aid to the patient whilst the patient comes to terms with his/her problem.

holergasia An illness which affects all aspects of psychological functioning.

holistic research Research which attempts to measure all aspects of a phenomenon, rather than concentrating on isolated aspects.

holistic therapy General term for therapeutic techniques which consider the whole person rather than just one aspect of his/her psychological profile.

Holtzman Inkblot Technique (HIT) *projective personality test* in which participants (age 5 years and over) describe impressions formed by a series of inkblots. Has a tighter construction and constraints on administration than the *Rorschach Inkblot Test* (e.g. set number of answers permitted for each inkblot).

HOME *Home Observation for Measurement of the Environment.*

Home Observation for Measurement of the Environment (HOME) Measurement scale of influences likely to influence mental development. Uses a combination of tester observation and interviewing.

homeostasis The maintenance of an equilibrium (often used of physiological functions – e.g. regulating the body's temperature).

homogeneity of variance Identical or nearly identical patterns of *variance* in two or more sets of data.

homogeneous group Group of individuals with an attribute or attributes in common. See *heterogeneous group.*

homophobia A *phobia* of homosexuals and homosexuality.

homoscedacity See *scedacity.*

honesty test *integrity test.*

Hopelessness Scale *Beck Hopelessness Scale (BHS).*

hormone therapy Therapeutic method in which the patient is administered extra hormones (e.g. in older women to replace those lost during the menopause).

Hospital Anxiety and Depression Scale (HADS) A questionnaire providing a measure of levels of *anxiety* and *depression.*

hospitalism (1) *reactive attachment disorder of infancy.* (2) The term has been used (not entirely accurately) by some authors as a synonym for *institutionalization.*

hostility personality Personality type found in some older people – those possessing it (illogically) blame others for their present misfortunes.

hot-seat technique Therapeutic technique in which other members of a therapy group tell an individual patient exactly what they think of him/her.

Hotelling-Lawley trace Significance test for *multivariate analysis of variance.*

Hotelling's T² test A refinement of the *test*, in which two groups are compared on several *variables*, and assessed on whether there is a *significant* difference in the overall trend of scores, regardless of differences/similarities on individual variables.

House-Tree-Person Test (H-T-P) A *projective personality test* – the subject is asked to draw the three objects of the title and then talk about them.

'How I Feel' Test *Children's State-Trait Anxiety Inventory.*

Hoyt's analysis of variance Statistical assessment of *reliability*, utilizing the *analysis of variance* formulae.

HRNB *Halsted–Reitan Neuropsychological Battery.*

HRS *Hamilton Rating Scale.*

H-T-P *House-Tree-Person Test.*

human engineering (1) *ergonomics*, with particular emphasis on the design of machine controls. (2) Any method of attempting to manipulate learning and attitudes using psychological techniques.

human factors American term for *ergonomics.*

human potential movement General term for a wide range of theories (perhaps most notably *Roger's self theory of personality*) which have the growth of the self as a prime objective.

human relations training group (T group) *encounter group* whose primary aim is usually to increase awareness of the self and others in social interaction.

humanistic psychology General term for therapies (particularly *client-centred therapy* and *Gestalt psychology*) and theories of human development which recognize the growth of the individual, rather than seeking to make everyone develop in one 'correct' manner, as in some of the more rigid forms of *psychoanalysis*. Most popular manifestation is probably *Maslow's hierarchy of needs.*

Hunter-Grundin Literacy Profiles Reading test, which assesses several related reading and linguistic skills, including: *cloze procedure*; spelling; creative writing; ability verbally to describe a pictorial scene; and motivation to read. Consists of four 'Levels', commensurate with the age of the subjects: Level 1: 6–8 years; Level 2: 7–9 years; Level 3: 8–10 years; and Level 4: 10 years and over.

Huntington's Chorea Older term for *Huntington's Disease.*

Huntington's Disease An illness of neural decay with the principal characteristics of disturbed gait and movements. Some patients develop *demented* symptoms. Ultimately fatal, the illness can strike at any age, from childhood through to old age. Strong genetic component.

Hutchison-Gilford syndrome *progeria.*

Huynh-Feldt correction See *sphericity test.*

HVM Test *Haptic Visual Matching Test.*

Hy scale See *Minnesota Multiphasic Personality Inventory.*

hydrocephalus Accumulation of fluid in the skull, causing damaging pressure on the brain, which, if not treated, can lead to serious and permanent damage, or even death. Symptoms may include *dementia*-like behaviour.

hydrophobia A *phobia* of water.

hygiene factors In *occupational psychology*, the physical and contractual working conditions of an employee.

hyp- As a prefix, it conveys the same meanings as *hypo-*.

hypacusia Poor hearing – not to be confused with *hyperacusia*.

hypalgesia Abnormally high pain threshold. The reverse (an abnormally low pain threshold) is *hyperalgesia*.

hyper- As a prefix: good, above, or excessive. Compare with *hypo-*.

hyperactive delirium See *delirium*.

hyperactivity An inappropriately high level of activity, which cannot be voluntarily controlled. Many adults with the condition are better at covering up their problem than are children, who are the most conspicuous sufferers. The definition of hyperactivity is rather over-inclusive, and covers a variety of conditions from 'spoilt brat' through to individuals with genuinely serious problems. See *attentional deficit disorder*.

hyperacusia Abnormally good hearing. Not to be confused with *hypacusia*.

hyperaesthesia (1) extreme sensitivity to sensory stimulation (if it is one sense in particular, this is indicated in a prefix – e.g. visual hyperaesthesia). (2) *hyperparaesthesia*.

hyperalgesia See *hypalgesia*.

hyperalgia *hyperalgesia*.

hypergasia manic activity.

hypergeusia Abnormally good taste (re: eating and drinking).

hypergraphia Excessive writing.

hyperkinesia (1) *attentional deficit disorder*. (2) Generally, excessive activity and restlessness.

hyperkinesis Over-activity reaching *manic/hyperactive* levels.

hyperkinesthesia Abnormally high sensitivity to movement.

hyperkinetic syndrome *attentional deficit disorder*.

hyperlexia (1) Reading accurately but with no evidence of comprehension of what is being read. See *demented dyslexia*. (2) Reading at a precociously early age.

hyperlogia *hyperphasia*.

hypermania Abnormally high levels of activity.

hypermetamorphosis The compulsive urge to touch everything.

hypermnesia Abnormally good memory.

hypermotility *hyperkinesis*.

hyperorality The urge to put everything seen into the mouth.

hyperorexia over-eating.

hyperosmia An abnormally good sense of smell.

hyperparaesthesia Abnormally sensitive touch/sense of being touched on the skin.

hyperphagia over-eating.

hyperphasia Talking incoherently and quickly.

hyperphrasia *hyperphasia*.

hyperphrenia Excessive (and usually incoherent) thinking/mental activity.

hyperpiesia *hypertension*.

hyperprosessis *hyperprosexia*.

hyperprosexia *compulsively* paying attention to an item or train of thought, usually for an excessively long time.

hyperRESEARCH A commercial computer programme used for a variety of *qualitative research* techniques.

hypersomnia Sleeping for abnormally long periods.

hypertension See *blood pressure*.

hyperthymia Abnormally grandiose expressions of emotion.

hyperthyroidism (Graves' disease) *organic affective syndrome* caused by an over-active thyroid gland, and resulting in extremely energetic behaviour, bordering on *mania*. *Hallucinations* are sometimes present.

hyperventilation Very rapid breathing, usually triggered by an attack of *anxiety*. The condition can cause the subject to faint.

hypnagogic Pertaining to sleep.

hypnagogic hallucination *hypnagogic image*.

hypnagogic image A 'dream' had whilst drowsy, rather than when fully asleep. A phenomenon which seems only to be experienced by a fraction of the population. The experience can be a strange one, in that often one is simultaneously aware that one is dreaming.

hypnogenic sleep-inducing.

hypnosis The induction of a deeply relaxed state. This is usually done by encouraging the patient to relax, whilst aiding him/her in this process with e.g. a series of relaxing verbal images, asking him/her to concentrate on a repetitive and calming movement, etc. The state is unlike normal relaxation, in that the patient is willing to lower (but rarely completely abandon) normal levels of disbelief, and accept what the hypnotist suggests. In some cases, patients can be persuaded to 'shut out' feelings of pain, and major surgery has been successfully carried out on some hypnotized patients. Because of the lowering of reality control, some patients can be persuaded to accept commands to perform certain deeds when they are awoken from their trance *(post-hypnotic suggestion)* – commands which they would, if conscious, probably resist. This can be used as a therapy – e.g. to persuade people to stop smoking by implanting the idea that they will feel sick if they put a cigarette in their mouth. The technique is also open to potential abuse – e.g. by persuading a patient to do something ethically wrong. Hypnosis, by blocking out normally present 'filters', may also help a participant recall a memory more clearly – the technique has been used by e.g. police forces to see if it improves a witness's recall of an event. However, because a hypnotized person is prone to suggestion, the questions must be carefully posed by the therapist to avoid the danger of leading the witness. Another use of hypnosis is to enable patients with repressed memories and emotions to 'liberate' them under the loosened constraints of the hypnotic state. This is efficacious, because it enables the patient to confront the problem. An early example of this was the patient *Anna O*, treated by the nineteenth century physician Josef Breuer. It should be noted that all aspects of hypnosis have been criticized – the technique is open to abuse (although responsible therapists are at pains to avoid this, and have a self-imposed code of conduct). In addition, although the majority of people can be hypnotized, the depth of a hypnotic state varies considerably between individuals. See *mesmerism*.

hypnotic susceptibility The ease with which an individual succumbs to *hypnosis*.

hypo- As a prefix: below, lesser, smaller. Compare with *hyper-*.

hypoactive delirium See *delirium*.

hypoacusia hypacusia.

hypobulia *abulia*.

hypochondria A *somatoform disorder*, characterized by the erroneous and persistent belief that one is ill, and/or that mild symptoms are indicative of a serious illness. Note that the term in its lay use refers to a milder form which would probably not merit professional treatment.

hypochondriasis *hypochondria.*

hypoergasia An abnormally low level of activity, as found in many patients suffering from *depression.*

hypogeusia Impaired sense of taste (re: eating and drinking).

hypoglossal cranial nerve *cranial nerve* number XII. Concerned with muscular control of the tongue.

hypokinaesthesia An abnormally low awareness of/sensitivity to movement.

hypokinesis Abnormally low level of movement.

hypolexia *dyslexia.*

hypologia Abnormally poor linguistic ability. Usually the term refers to disability resulting from general mental impairment, rather than to specific brain damage. See *aphasia.*

hypomania See *mania.*

hypomnesia An abnormally poor memory.

hypophagia under-eating.

hypophrasia *bradylalia.*

hypophrenia *mental retardation.*

hypoprosessis *hypoprosexia.*

hypoprosexia Abnormally poor attention.

hyposmia Abnormally poor sense of smell.

hyposomnia Sleeping abnormally little.

hyposthenia physical weakness.

hypothalamus *sub-cortical* section of the brain, whose primary task is to control bodily drives (e.g. hunger and satiety, sex, anger).

hypothesis A model of a phenomenon from which predictions about it can be drawn, and tested. E.g. one might develop the hypothesis that all children called Alistair will prefer chocolate from a range of flavoured ice creams. The hypothesis can be easily tested by getting a group of Alistairs and giving them a choice of ice creams.

hypothesis testing The process of establishing whether the *null hypothesis* or the *alternative hypothesis* is to be accepted.

hypothetical construct *construct.*

hypothymia Abnormally low level of emotional expression.

hypothyroidism (myxoedema) Illness caused by an under-active thyroid gland, resulting in 'sluggish' thought and behaviour.

hypotrophy *atrophy.*

hypoxaemia Abnormally low levels of oxygen in the blood.

hysteria Older term for *conversion disorder.*

hysterical When the term prefixes the name of an illness, the term denotes that the illness is not due to physical causes, but to a *somatoform disorder.* See e.g. *hysterical blindness.*

hysterical ataxia *Somatoform disorder* in which the principal symptom is *ataxia.*

hysterical blindness *somatoform disorder* in which the patient claims to be blind, although there is no physical damage to the eyes or visual pathways.

hysterical deafness *somatoform disorder* in which the patient claims to be deaf, though there is no physical damage to the ears or auditory pathways.

hysterical neurosis Old term for *somatoform disorder.*

hysterical personality *histrionic personality disorder.*

hysteriform Pertaining to, or resembling, *hysteria.*

I

i *class interval width.*

I (1) *inductive reasoning. (2) Introversion.*

I-E measure *internal-external measure.*

IARS *Intellectual Achievement Responsibility Scale.*

iatrogenic Prescribed by a doctor.

iatrogenic poisoning Illness arising from an adverse reaction to legally-prescribed drugs.

Ibogaine A *hallucinogen.*

IBR *Infant Behaviour Record.*

ICC *item characteristic curve.*

ICD *WHO classification of diseases.*

ICL *Occupational Interest Checklist.*

ictal emotion A sudden feeling of emotion without apparent cause.

icthyophobia A *phobia* of fish.

ictus *stroke.*

id See *Freud's psychoanalytic theory.*

ideal self The self the patient would most like to be. See e.g. *Roger's self theory of personality.*

ideas of influence *delusion of control.*

ideas of reference *delusion of reference.*

ideation Formation of ideas.

ideational agnosia An *agnosia* for symbols.

ideational apraxia An inability to perform the correct functions associated with an object.

ideational fluency Fluency at producing names of items belonging to a given category (e.g. types of neurological disease, animals, etc.).

idée fixe A pathological obsession with an idea or concept.

identification The acquisition of personality and behavioural characteristics which are seen as 'copying' from other people (e.g. parents, teachers etc.).

identity crisis (1) *identity disorder.* (2) The process of deciding what one's adult *persona* will be.

identity disorder Profound distress and loss of function created by a feeling of a lack of personal identity, of having chosen the wrong lifestyle, career, etc. See *depersonalizdtion* and *dissociative disorders.*

identity foreclosure See *Erikson's theory of development.*

identity versus role confusion See *Erikson's theory of development.*

ideokinetic apraxia An inability to perform sequences of actions (although individual actions within a sequence can be adequately performed).

ideomotor apraxia Inability to perform a complex movement on command.

ideophobia A *phobia* of ideas.

ideoplasty Thought control by means of *hypnosis.*

idiographic That which is unique to the individual. See *nomothetic.*

idiographic research Research based upon individual *case studies.*

idiot See *mental retardation.*

idiots savants (from the French) Individuals with severe *mental retardation* who are surprisingly adept at an isolated intellectual skill (an *islet of intelligence*). E.g. there are some *autistic* children who are (by any standards) extraordinarily talented at a facet of arithmetic or drawing, yet who otherwise have a very low IQ.

IDPS *Irlen Differential Perceptual Scale.*

IDS *Inventory for Depressive Symptomatology.*

IIP *Inventory of Interpersonal Problems.*

illusion The misidentification of a stimulus. Compare with *delusion.*

imaginal exposure Imagining encountering a particular situation or stimulus. The technique is used in some forms of therapy to train patients to cope with situations which have produced maladaptive or abnormal responses. See *imaginal flooding.*

imaginal flooding *implosion.*

imbecile See *mental retardation.*

imipramine Form of *antidepressant.*

impermeable constructs See *personal construct theory.*

implicit personality An extrapolation of what a person's total personality 'must' be like, from a brief sample of it.

imploding *implosion.*

implosion See *flooding.*

implosive therapy Therapeutic technique using *implosion* as its principal tool.

impotence A man's inability to produce an erection in the appropriate circumstances. In ***primary impotence***, the patient has never produced an erection. In ***secondary impotence***, the patient has produced erections intermittently, or has produced them consistently in the past. Some commentators have replaced the terms with the general description of male *inhibited sexual excitement.*

impression management Shaping one's image to improve other people's perceptions of oneself.

impulse control disorder *impulse disorder.*

impulse disorder A failure to control an activity. The commonest examples are *kleptomania, pathological gambling, and pyromania.*

impulsivity *impulse disorder.*

in-basket exercise *situational exercise* in which the participant (a white collar worker) is presented with a workload (in the 'in basket') which s/he must work through. Typically, the prime areas of interest are in what and how much the participant delegates to others and how much time s/he allocates to each job.

in vitro study *laboratory study.*

in vivo desensitization (-isation) See *desensitization.*

in vivo study *naturalistic research* (definition 2).

inappropriate affect Having an inappropriate emotional reaction to a piece of information.

incomplete case Subject who has not been tested on all the measures which the rest of his/her group has received.

incomplete pictures test Any test which follows the same general procedure as the *Gollin Incomplete Figures Test.*

incomplete sentence test *sentence completion test.*

incremental validity The degree to which the predictive power of a test is improved by removing certain items from the test.

independent sample Sample, the selection of whose members does not influence the selection of members of other samples within the same study (e.g. as in the random allocation of subjects to two or more groups). Compare with *dependent sample.*

independent variable See *dependent variable.*

index case *proband.*

index of variability *measures of dispersion.*

indirect correlation *negative correlation.*

indirect scaling A measure of ability to detect changes in the intensity of a stimulus by ranking the size of stimulations necessary to produce *just noticeable differences*. See *direct scaling*.

individual coping strategies A therapeutic regime tailored to the needs of an individual person. Often produced to cope with stress. See *organizational coping strategy*.

individual differences The study of how and why people differ psychologically (particularly in intelligence and personality).

individual psychology Theory and resultant therapeutic method developed by Alfred Adler (1870–1937). At its heart is the theory of the *inferiority complex* – i.e. people usually feel inferior in some respect and so develop strategies and behaviour to compensate for this (*compensatory strivings*). E.g. at the most literal, a person with a weak voice may take vocal training and become a singer. The root of inferiority feelings lies in childhood, and the theory emphasized how upbringing can create feelings of being on the wrong end of a power relationship or of having weaknesses (Adler rejected the prevailing *Freudian* notion of sexual drive as the root cause of problems). The general *striving for superiority* can be healthy if properly channelled, but can become maladaptive if directed towards inappropriate goals (e.g. a too-great attempt to compensate, resulting in only superficial feelings of power and control is known as a *superiority complex*).

individual test Test which must be administered to one participant/patient at a time.

individual therapy Therapy which must be administered to one patient at a time.

induced psychotic disorder *folie a deux*.

induced schizophrenia Copying *schizophrenic* symptoms from a genuinely schizophrenic patient.

inductive reasoning (I) See *deductive reasoning*.

inductive statistics *inferential statistics*.

industrial psychology *occupational psychology*.

industry versus inferiority See *Erikson's theory of development*.

Infant Behaviour Record (IBR) Scale within the *Bayley Scales of Infant Development*, which measures the infant's temperament.

infant intelligence tests Misleading shorthand for tests assessing mental development in babies. Such tests can only detect fairly gross levels of functioning, and beyond very broad generalizations (e.g. there is evidence of *mental retardation* or there is not), it is impossible to give a precise indication of future *IQ*. Indeed, many authors of these measures explicitly reject the idea that they have produced intelligence tests.

infantile autism *autism* (definition 2).

infantile neurosis The theory (principally in *psychoanalysis*) that adult *neuroses* are attributable to maladaptive practices in infancy.

infantile perversion The theory (principally in *psychoanalysis*) that oddities in adult sexual behaviour are attributable to maladaptive practices in infancy.

infantilism Using behaviours more appropriate for someone far younger.

infarct A 'miniature *stroke*', causing the death of a tiny proportion of brain tissue. Infarcts occur in most older people's brains, but on too small a scale to cause serious damage. However, in *multi-infarct dementia*, the number of infarcts is considerably greater than normal. See *stroke*.

inferential statistics Calculations of how representative a sample is of the *population* from which it is drawn (e.g. gauging the likely efficacy of a 'flu vaccine from how it affects a group of volunteers). Typically, assesses the statistical *significance* of differences and relationships. See *descriptive statistics*.

inferior In anatomy, a body section is inferior if it is located below another section (which is termed the *superior*). There is no implication that the inferior section has a less important function.

inferiority complex (1) See *individual psychology*. (2) *Dependent personality disorder*.

inferred number right (INR) score Traditional scoring system for a multiple choice test, in which the first answer given is the only one accepted. See *answer until correct (AUC) score*.

infinite population See *population*.

informal reading inventory Reading measure in which the child reads from a variety of books (rather than taking a more formal reading test).

informed consent Ethical principle that a participant/patient is aware of the purpose of all tests/therapies s/he takes part in, and has given his/her consent to their administration. See *blind study* and *placebo study*.

Inglis Paired Associate Learning (IPAL) Test Test assessing paired associate learning (and hence mnemonic /cognitive efficiency) in older psychiatric patients.

inherited Characteristics which are the result of genetic transmission. Compare with *congenital*.

inhibited orgasm Condition in which the person feels sexual excitement and can produce all appropriate responses except orgasm itself.

inhibited sexual excitement Inability to produce a physical sexual response.

inhibition deficit A failure to inhibit unwanted thoughts or items from memory.

inhibitory (neurons) An inhibitory neuron (in combination with many other inhibitory neurons) which (i) stops a previously active neuron from transmitting signals and/or (ii) slows the rate of transmission. Compare with *excitatory (neurons)*.

initial factoring procedure See *factor analysis*.

initial letter priming Providing participants with the initial letters of words in a list the participant is trying to *recall*.

initiative versus guilt See *Erikson's theory of development*.

injunction In some therapeutic theories, a commandment (usually following the general command 'do not do x because x is wrong') acquired in childhood which may cause subsequent maladaptive behaviour.

innate *inherited*.

inner dialogue A conversation 'in the head' which most individuals can subjectively report.

inner speech The inner thoughts – e.g. internal monologues, or the 'voice in the head' which most people experience when reading. This contrasts with **external speech**, which is speech for communicating with other people.

INR score *inferred number right (INR) score*.

insectophobia *entomophobia*.

insight therapy Any therapeutic technique in which the patient is encouraged to attain insights about him/herself.

insomnia A profound inability to sleep. Types of insomnia include *sleep onset insomnia* (problems with falling asleep), *sleep maintenance insomnia* (being incapable of staying asleep for satisfactorily lengthy periods) and *terminal insomnia* (waking up too soon).

instantia crucis *crucial experiment.*

instigation therapy Any therapeutic technique in which the patient is encouraged to adopt certain behaviours/attitudes at the behest of the therapist.

institutionalized behaviour *institutionalization.*

institutionalization (-isation) The general intellectual and emotional degradation experienced by many long-term patients in institutions such as hospitals, retirement homes, etc. See *deinstitutionalization.*

instrumental learning *operant conditioning.*

instrumental value See *terminal value.*

instrumentation errors Errors in measurement due to faults in the test equipment (NB in this instance, some commentators classify human experimenters as 'equipment').

insulin therapy See *convulsion therapy.*

insult *injury.*

integer A whole number.

integrity test Measure of honesty/trustworthiness.

intellect See *five factor model of personality.*

Intellectual Achievement Responsibility Scale (IARS) Questionnaire examining the degree to which a pupil attributes his/her academic achievements to him/herself, and how much s/he attributes to parents, teachers, etc.

intellectualization (-isation) (1) Talking about a problem as a means of avoiding tackling it. (2) Treating a problem in a detached manner as an intellectual puzzle.

intelligence The level of ease with which a subject can accurately respond to intellectual tasks. Since the range of tasks which have an intellectual component is vast, it is unlikely that precisely the same skill underlies all of them. Equally, it is unlikely that a different type of skill is required for each and every different task. However, researchers have made claims for both these extremes and practically every permutation in between. See *fluid intelligence* and *crystallized intelligence.*

intelligence quotient (IQ) Often (erroneously) used as a synonym for 'intelligence'. The intelligence quotient is used to denote how intelligent a person is, in comparison with the rest of his or her *age cohort* (also known as the *deviation IQ*). Traditionally, a score of 100 has denoted a person of average intelligence for his/her age cohort – i.e. 50% of the group are cleverer, 50% are less clever then this person. A score of more than 130 indicates someone who is exceptionally bright for the group (i.e. there are few people in the age group with better scores) and a score of 70 or below indicates someone who is unusually intellectually disadvantaged. The older method of measuring IQ in children was by the formula of *mental age* divided by *chronological age*, multiplied by 100. (The problem with this method is that it is useless for participants aged over 18 years, because mental age is relatively stable in adulthood up to about 60 years of age. This means that the formula will cause their IQs to decrease as they age.) See *educational quotient.*

intelligence test Any test which claims to measure *intelligence*. Typically, the test will yield a single measure of *general intelligence*, which is usually expressed in terms of an IQ score.

intention tremor A trembling of the muscles, which occurs when the subject is making a movement s/he intends, but not during involuntary movements. Generally, the trembling worsens the closer the patient is to his/her goal (e.g. reaching for and picking up an object). It is often associated with damage to the *cerebellum*.

inter-rater reliability The degree to which two or more observers agree in their ratings of a subject or event (often expressed as a *correlation* between their scores).

inter-stimulus interval (ISI) The time interval between one test item appearing and the next one appearing (or, between the first disappearing and the next appearing – other definitions are also possible).

interaction (ANOVA) In an *analysis of variance*, a measure of how different groups may perform in a qualitatively different manner on the same measures. The analysis indicates only whether an interaction is *significant* or not – the pattern of the interaction has to be gleaned by looking at the data themselves. The interaction is normally prefixed with the phrase 'x-way', where x is the number of measures involved. E.g., a two-way interaction might describe how two groups perform qualitatively differently on a measure with two levels (e.g. group A may be comparatively better on test X than on test Y, whilst the reverse pattern may hold for group B). Note that the interaction does not state which group has the higher scores (e.g. in the previous example, group A might be significantly better at test Y than group

B), only what is relatively harder within a group. Interactions larger than two-way are hard to interpret. E.g. a three-way interaction might be found between measures of time of day when tested, membership of group A or B, and a test with two formats X and Y. It might show that for group A, scores are higher in the morning for format X, and higher in the afternoon for format Y, but overall, group A performs better in the afternoon; whilst group B find Y easier in the morning and X easier in the afternoon, but overall, group B performs better in the morning. Four-way interactions and beyond are virtually impossible to understand in one conceptual unit. An absence of an interaction (also called an *additive interaction*) indicates that all groups are responding in a qualitatively identical fashion. A significant interaction is sometimes called a *non-additive interaction*. A two-way interaction, in which group A is better than group B on measure x, but is worse on measure y, is called a *cross-over interaction* (because the graph of the results looks like cross).

interaction variance The proportion of the total *variance* attributable to *interactions*.

interactional psychology *interactionism*.

interactionism The view that psychological growth is attained through the interaction between the environment and an individual's innate characteristics.

interbrain *diencephalon*.

intercept of the regression line See *regression*.

interest inventory A catalogue of a participant's hobbies, likings, etc. The measure has obvious uses in careers guidance, therapy, etc., but may also be used as a general measure of lifestyle.

interference task Task which is designed to interfere with the processing/memory of information (e.g. as in the *Brown–Peterson task*). Performance on the interference task itself is usually not of central importance.

interictal Between seizures.

internal consistency See *reliability*.

internal control (1) The degree to which a participant's own behaviour can shape events. (2) The participant's perception of the same. See *external control*.

internal-external measure (I-E measure) Any measure of the degree to which a person feels s/he is controlled by external circumstances, versus internal motivations and wishes. For a more specific definition, see *internal-external scale*.

internal-external scale See *causal attribution theory*.

internal locus of control *internal control*.

internal reward *intrinsic reward*.

internal validity The degree to which findings from a study have been subjected to unplanned contamination by external factors.

internalization (-isation) The assimilation of ideas and opinions into one's own set of values. See *introjection*.

International Classification of Diseases *WHO classification of diseases (ICD)*.

interpersonal Between people – see *intrapersonal*.

Interpersonal Styles Inventory (ISI) A measure of how well a participant interacts with others. The test consists of a set of statements with which the participant indicates agreement/disagreement.

interpolated task *interference task*.

interpretative phenomenological analysis (IPA) A *qualitative research* method concerned with the analysis of people's understanding and response to events or states, rather than an objective account of the events or states themselves. A key consideration is the input of the researcher in their interpretation of the data.

interquartile range (IQR) See *range*.

interrupted time series study See *time series study*.

interval censoring See *left censoring*.

interval estimate Given the *mean* or other measure of a sample, the range of values within which the *population* mean or other measure is likely to lie.

interval of uncertainty See *threshold*.

interval recording Recording a participant's behaviour at set time intervals. This is usually done because recording all of the participant's behaviour would create an unmanageably large amount of data. See *continuous recording* and *time sampling*.

interval scale Scale in which units of measurement are spaced apart equally, and in which the value of zero is arbitrary (e.g. temperature measured on the Fahrenheit scale – the value of zero degrees does not mean that there is no temperature). See *nominal scale*, *ordinal scale* and, especially, the *ratio scale*.

interval schedule The timing schedule of rewards/punishments to be administered in a *conditioning* study.

intervening variable An experimental *variable* which is not directly measured, but which is presumed to intervene between an *independent variable* and a *dependent variable*. E.g. if the independent variable is number of hours of food deprivation, and the dependent variable is the amount eaten when food is presented, then the intervening variable is hunger.

intimacy versus isolation See *Erikson's theory of development.*

intraclass correlation The strength of relationship between two variables.

intrapersonal Within a person. See *endogenous,* and *interpersonal.*

intrapsychic Within the mind.

intrapsychic ataxia *mental ataxia.*

intrapsychic conflict A hypothesized conflict between different parts or aspects of the mind.

intrapsychic disease model Any model which concentrates upon a mental illness as an endogenous process, largely to the exclusion of exogenous factors.

intrauterine experience The experience of the foetus. Some *psychoanalytic* theories argue that this shapes subsequent personality.

intrinsic drive Being impelled to do something for its own sake.

intrinsic motivation A *drive* to perform an act because of an internal need, without any material reward. This contrasts with *extrinsic motivation,* where there is a tangible goal.

intrinsic reward see *extrinsic reward.*

intrinsic test bias *test bias:* see *extrinsic test bias.*

intrinsic validity *a priori validity.*

introjection Term used in *psychoanalysis* to denote *internalization,* particularly of deeply-held moral values (e.g. those of parents).

introversion (I) See *extraversion.*

intrusion error (1) In memory tasks, 're-calling' an item which was not present.

(2) In reading, inserting a word which is not in the to-be-read material.

Intuition (N) See *Myers-Brings Type Indicator.*

intuitive personality see *Jung's psychoanalytic theory.*

inventory In the context of psychological testing, a 'checklist' of attributes against which the participant is measured (e.g. how often they cry, how often they lose their car keys, etc.). The inventory is either completed by the experimenter interviewing the participant, by people who know the participant well, or by the participant filling in the inventory him/herself (often known as the *self-report questionnaire*).

Inventory for Depressive Symptomatology (IDS) A measure of the severity of depressive symptoms.

Inventory of Interpersonal Problems (IIP) Measure of the degree to which a patient can (or cannot) interact with other people (e.g. form friendships, assert him/herself, etc.).

Inventory of Suicide Orientation-30 (ISO-30) Thirty item questionnaire designed for teenagers assessing their level of suicidal behaviour.

inverse correlation *negative correlation.*

inverse factor analysis *Q factor analysis.*

inverse J curve See *J curve.*

inverse J distribution *inverse J curve.*

inverted-U curve A curve which looks like an upside-down 'U'. Such curves are often found when e.g. plotting performance ability on the *Y axis* against arousal level of the *X axis*. As arousal increases, performance at first improves, but above a certain level of arousal, performance declines.

involutional depression *involutional psychotic reaction.*

involutional melancholia *involutional psychotic reaction.*

involutional psychotic reaction A profoundly negative reaction to the onset of middle age. See *mid-life crisis.*

I/O Psychology Industrial/occupational psychology –s synonym of *occupational psychology.*

iophobia A *phobia* of poisoning.

IPA *interpretative phenomenological analysis.*

IPAL Test *Inglis Paired Associate Learning (IPAL) Test.*

ipsative Measured against the self.

ipsative behaviour Behaviour judged against the participant's normal standards.

ipsative questionnaire Any questionnaire in which the participant makes judgements gauged against his/her own values.

ipsative scale (1) Any scale of measurement in which the participant bases his/her judgements against his/her own values. (2) A scale on which items must be put in order and no items may share a 'joint equal' ranking.

ipsative score Score relative to the participant's own *mean.*

ipsative test Measure of an individual's abilities in which their strengths and weaknesses are compared with each other (i.e. as opposed to being compared with other people's).

ipsatization (-isation) The creation of *ipsative scores.*

ipsilateral On the same side of the body (see *midline*) as the section of the body in question. Compare with *contralateral.*

IQ *intelligence quotient.*

IQR *interquartile range.*

Irlen Differential Perceptual Scale (IDPS) Measure of various visual perceptual abilities designed to identify the presence or absence of scotopic sensitivity, a perceptual problem resulting from an unbalanced perception of the spectrum. It is argued by some that this is a cause of *developmental dyslexia*, and that dyslexic readers should wear tinted spectacles to redress the spectral balance and so remove scotopic sensitivity. Some also advocate their use in managing autistic sensory problems. The efficacy of these *Irlen lenses* has been disputed.

Irlen lenses See *Irlen Differential Perceptual Scale.*

irregular spelling A word whose logical pronunciation differs from the way it is supposed to be pronounced. Examples of irregular spelling abound in English – 'quay', 'misled', etc.

irrelevant variable See *relevant variable.*

irresistible impulse criterion The (now largely outmoded) American legal principal that a person cannot be judged guilty of an offence committed because of an irresistible impulse forced on him/her through mental illness.

IRT *item response theory.*

IS *Hachinski Ischaemic Score.*

ischaemic cascade Series of events leading to cell death after cessation of blood supply (e.g. in a *stroke*).

Ischaemic Rating Scale *Hachinski Ischaemic Score.*

ISI (1) *Interpersonal Styles Inventory.* (2) *inter-stimulus interval.*

islets of intelligence See *idiots savants.*

ISO-30 *Inventory of Suicide Orientation.*

isocarboxazid Type of *monoamine oxidase inhibitor.*

isokurtic lacking *skew.*

isolation The removal or suppression of the association of a negative emotion with a particular memory or action.

isolation syndrome *transcortical sensory aphasia.*

It Scale for Children Test in which child expresses preferences for toys and objects with a strong 'sex bias' (e.g. dolls, prams, etc.). Designed to test strength and direction of stereotypical sex roles in children.

item (tests) a question.

item analysis Assessing whether individual *items* in a test are worthy of inclusion. There are a number of methods of assessing this, the best known of which are the *Kuder-Richardson formulae.*

item bias Test *item* which favours some groups of subjects more than others (e.g. in the UK, a question requiring calculations in pre-decimal money would be unfair to any participant aged under 30).

item characteristic curve (ICC) A mathematical function describing how the probability of answering a test question in a particular manner is related to the strength with which a participant possesses a particular trait. E.g. the probability of correctly answering an easy question on an intelligence test might be 70% for a not very bright participant. This probability figure might gradually increase, the brighter the participant being considered, until a top value of 99% might be reached for a very bright participant. If a curve was drawn of this, it would appear relatively flat. However, suppose we consider a very difficult question from the same test. Here, there might be only a 5% probability that a dull participant will get it right, and this figure might rise to e.g. 80% for the very brightest participant. A curve drawn of

this would appear much steeper. See *Rasch scaling.*

item difficulty The proportion of participants correctly answering a question on a test.

item discrimination *item reliability.*

item facility The proportion of participants who get a particular test *item* wrong (a score of 1 = everyone gets it wrong, and 0 = everyone gets it right).

item reliability The *correlation* between scores on items within a test and the total test score.

item-remainder reliability *item reliability.*

item response theory (IRT) Theory of test performance based on the *item characteristic curve.*

item universe All the questions devised for a test or series of tests.

item validity The degree to which performance on *items* from a test predicts performance on another measure.

iterated principal axis see *factor analysis.*

iterative Repeating.

IV *independent variable.*

J

J *Judging.*

J coefficient The *correlation* between a test predicting ability at a particular task or job, and actual performance of the job.

J curve A curve shaped approximately like a 'J'. Low values on the *X* axis are met with low values on the *Y* axis, but a slight further increase in the value of x is met with a meteoric increase in the value of y. The *inverse J curve* has the inverted shape – low values of x are matched by high values of y, but a further increase in x creates a drastic fall in the value of y.

J distribution *J curve.*

jacksonian epilepsy See *epilepsy.*

jamais vu A feeling that a familiar place or event is entirely novel.

JAQ *Job Analysis Questionnaire.*

jargon aphasia Syntactically garbled speech (often containing *paraphasias* and *neologisms*) which is characteristic of many *aphasias.*

JAS *Jenkins Activity Survey.*

Jenkins Activity Survey (JAS) Questionnaire which assesses the degree to which a subject has a *Type A personality.*

Jesness Behaviour Checklist Test for adolescents, measuring 14 *bipolar dimensions* of personality. Assessment can be by self-report or by the participants' teachers.

JIIG-CAL A computerized career guidance package. The acronym stands for Job Ideas and Information Generator-Computer Assisted Learning.

JND *just noticeable difference.*

JNND *just not noticeable difference.*

job analysis The analysis of a job or task into the component skills required to execute it effectively, the equipment used, etc.

Job Analysis Questionnaire (JAQ) Questionnaire designed to perform *job analysis* by asking participants how often they perform a range of activities as part of their work routine.

job characteristics The tasks and responsibilities required of the holder of a particular job.

job evaluation The calculation of the financial worth of a job to the organization.

job families Occupations and tasks which demand similar skills and tasks.

job satisfaction The degree to which a job is found to be emotionally rewarding.

John Henry effect In some experimental designs, an *experimental group* may receive treatment which the *control group* may see as being preferential. Accordingly, the control group members may work 'artificially' harder at the tasks set them to demonstrate that they can do just as well without receiving beneficial treatment. This mars the accuracy of the study.

joint probability *probability* of two or more events occurring simultaneously.

Judging (J) See *Myers-Briggs Type Indicator.*

Jungian archetype See *Jung's psychoanalytic theory.*

Jungian theory See *Jung's psychoanalytic theory.*

Jung's psychoanalytic theory Carl Jung (1875–1961), initially a disciple of Freud, who later founded his own, highly influential theory (*Jungian theory*) of *psychoanalysis.* Although based on *Freud's psychoanalytic theory,* Jung believed that several drives for self-fulfilment motivated people, and de-emphasized the role of *psychosexual development.* Also, Jung argued that in addition to the unconscious as conceived by Freud, there is a **collective unconscious.** This is a set of inherited images (**archetypes**) of God, of heroes, etc., which have the power to shape development, but of which the person is not consciously aware (although they may appear in the guise of art, folk tales, etc.). Jung identified four methods of perceiving the world: the *feeling personality* (the emotional impact is of principal importance); the *intuitive personality* (the world is judged on hunches and intuitions); the *sensing personality* (the direct perception of the world as it appears through the senses); and the *thinking personality* (the primary emphasis is on abstract thought). Jung also conceived of individuals being primarily *extraverted* or *introverted*, and being a mixture of active and 'masculine' elements (*animus*), and passive and 'feminine' elements (*anima*). Jung's theory appear gentler and more spiritual than Freud's, and his concept of the collective unconscious attracted the attention of a wide audience. However, the general criticisms which can be levelled against Freud's theories can just as heavily be laid against Jung's. See *neo-Freudian movement*.

just noticeable difference (JND) See *threshold*.

just not noticeable difference (JNND) See *threshold*.

juvenile delinquency *delinquency*.

K

k (1) See *grouped frequency distribution*. (2) In some theories, *spatial ability*.

K *coefficient of alienation*.

K-ABC *Kaufman Assessment Battery for Children*.

K-BIT *Kaufman Brief Intelligence Test*.

K-FAST *Kaufman Functional Academic Skills Test*.

K-R formula See *reliability*.

K-R 20 See *reliability*.

K-R 21 See *reliability*.

K-SADS-P See *Schedule of Affective Disorders and Schizophrenia*.

K scale See *Minnesota Multiphasic Personality Inventory*.

K-SNAP *Kaufman Short Neuropsychological Assessment Procedure*.

K-TEA *Kaufman Test of Educational Achievement*.

K-W test *Kruskal-Wallis one-way ANOVA by ranks*.

KAI *Kirton Adaptation-Innovation Inventory*.

Kaiser criterion *factor analysis*.

Kaiser image analysis See *factor analysis*.

Kaiser–Meyer–Olkin value (KMO value) In conducting a *factor analysis*, variables being considered for entry into the equation can be assessed for suitability and given a KMO value. A value of < 0.50 is deemed unacceptable (i.e. the variable should not be entered). KMO values > 0.50 are graded into increasingly more 'acceptable' groups up to a top group with values > 0.90.

Kaiser's normalization (-isation) See *factor analysis*.

KAIT *Kaufman Adolescent and Adult Intelligence Test*.

Kanner's syndrome *autism* – some commentators particularly apply the phrase to cases of the illness in which the symptoms clearly display themselves early in infancy.

kappa *Cohen's kappa*.

Kaufman Adolescent and Adult Intelligence Test (KAIT) Intelligence test based on measures of *fluid* and *crystallized intelligence*.

Kaufman Assessment Battery for Children (K-ABC) *test battery* for children aged 2–12 years. The battery is heavily influenced by the theories of the Russian neuropsychologist Luria, and, under his categorization scheme, measures the ability to perform sequential tasks and successive tasks. The measures are heavily biased towards non-verbal skills.

Kaufman Brief Intelligence Test (K-BIT) Intelligence test measuring both *fluid intelligence* and *crystallized intelligence*.

Kaufman Functional Academic Skills Test (K-FAST) Measure of reading and mathematical skills in adults.

Kaufman Short Neuropsychological Assessment Procedure (K-SNAP) Measure of basic memory, perceptual and intellectual skills in older children and adults.

Kaufman Test of Educational Achievement (K-TEA) A battery of *achievement tests*, assessing mathematical, reading and spelling skills.

KDCT *Kendrick Digit Copying Test.*

Kelly's personal construct theory *personal construct theory.*

Kendall coefficient of concordance (W) A *non-parametric* measure of the degree to which two or more sets of ranks are in agreement. Scores vary between 1 (full agreement) and 0 (no agreement).

Kendall partial rank correlation coefficient (TXYS) See *Kendall rank correlation coefficient.*

Kendall rank correlation coefficient (t) Like the *Spearman rank order correlation coefficient*, a measure of *correlation* between two *variables* measured on *ordinal scales*. Unlike the Spearman measure, however, the Kendall method can calculate a *partial correlations*, in the form of the *Kendall partial rank correlation coefficient*. See *Kendall coefficient of concordance.*

Kendall's tau *Kendall rank correlation coefficient.*

Kendall's I *Kendall rank correlation coefficient.*

Kendrick Battery for the Detection of Dementia in the Elderly Early

version (1972) of the *Kendrick Cognitive Tests for the Elderly.*

Kendrick Cognitive Tests for the Elderly *test battery* for identifying *dementia* in participants aged 55 years and over. Consists of two tests. The *Kendrick Object Learning Test (KOLT)* is a memory test for arrays of pictures in varying numbers, and the time over which the memories must be retained. The *Kendrick Digit Copying Test (KDCT)* measures the speed at which the participant copies a set of 100 numbers.

Kendrick Digit Copying Test (KDCT) See *Kendrick Cognitive Tests for the Elderly.*

Kendrick Object Learning Test (KOLT) See *Kendrick Cognitive Tests for the Elderly.*

keraunophobia A *phobia* of lightning.

Kernicterus Brain damage induced by excessive jaundice.

key informant In interview studies, an interviewee who provides information of a significantly higher than average calibre.

KeyMath test *achievement test* of mathematical skills.

KFD *Kinetic Family Drawing.*

KGIS *Kuder General Interest Survey.*

khat Fibrous tropical plant – chewing it induces (relatively mild) feelings of euphoria. At the time of writing, it is still legal in Britain.

kindling The increased susceptibility of *neurons* to activation resulting from repeated stimulation. The phenomenon is often linked to *epilepsy*-like attacks.

Kinetic Family Drawing (KFD) *projective test* in which the participant draws a picture of his/her family 'doing something'.

Kinetic School Drawing (KSD) *projective test* in which the child participant draws a picture of him/herself performing an act at school.

kinetic tremor *action tremor.*

Kirton Adaptation-Innovation Inventory (KAI) Measure of *creativity* and problem-solving, which also assesses the style in which these skills are executed.

Kleinian theory *neo-Freudian* model devised by Melanie Klein, which emphasizes the importance of early infancy. The theory is complex, but an often cited tenet of the theory is the internal conflict the infant has to resolve between perceived good and bad attributes of the same object. E.g. the breast can be seen separately as *good breast-bad breast* because it provides sustenance but is not always available immediately on demand. The infant has to learn that these attributes belong to the same object. Resolving the conflict leads into a more mature state in which hostile feelings towards the bad aspects of things are restrained. Failure adequately to resolve these stages is alleged to lead to problems in later life. As with other *psychoanalytic* models, it is ingenious but untestable.

kleptolagnia Pleasure from theft.

kleptomania An *impulse disorder* – the patient has an irresistible urge to steal, even though the stolen items may be of no value to him/her.

kleptophobia A *phobia* of crime (either suffering it or of being accused of being a criminal).

Klinefelter's syndrome Possession of two X chromosomes and one Y, resulting in incomplete sexual development and *mental retardation.*

Kluver-Bucy syndrome A collection of abnormal behaviours, including *hyperorality, bulimia, visual agnosia, hypermetamorphosis,* and loss of *affect.* There may also be a grossly heightened sexual appetite, particularly in younger patients.

KMO value See *Kaiser–Meyer–Olkin value.*

knowledge-based test Measure of how much a participant knows or what s/he has an aptitude for. By contrast, a *person-based test* is a measure of the participant him/herself (e.g. their personality, emotional state, etc.).

Knox Cubes Test A measure of visuo-spatial memory – the subject is required to tap cubes in a pattern provided by the experimenter.

Kohn Problem Checklist (KPC) Measure of social and emotional functioning/dysfunctioning in children aged 3–5 years.

Kohn Social Competence Scale (KSC) Measure of social skills and emotional expression in children aged 3–6 years.

Kohs block design test *block design test.*

KOIS *Kuder Occupational Interest Survey.*

Kolmogrov-Smirnov one sample test A *non-parametric measure* of whether the *cumulative frequency distribution* of a sample significantly differs from a hypothesized population distribution (i.e. whether the distribution might be expected by chance). Thus it is a *goodness of fit test.* The test has greater *power* than the *chi squared one sample test.*

Kolmogrov-Smirnov two sample test *non-parametric measure* of whether two groups are derived from *populations* with the same *cumulative frequency distribution* (and hence, it is assumed, the same population). Cumulative frequency distributions of the two groups are compared to see if they have the same pattern. Sufficiently similar patterns indicate a *non-significant* difference. Different formulae are employed for small and large samples, and also depending upon whether a *one-tailed test* or a *two-tailed test* is desired.

KOLT *Kendrick Object Learning Test.*

koro A mental illness peculiar to those raised in a Chinese culture – the belief (particularly among males) that one's genitals will be absorbed into the body, leading to death.

Korsakoff's amnestic syndrome *Korsakoff's syndrome.*

Korsakoff's psychosis *Korsakoff's syndrome.*

Korsakoff's syndrome Profound *anterograde amnesia*, usually coupled with *confabulation*. Results from long-term vitamin deficiency, and is most often encountered in alcoholic patients. The condition is often found in patients with *Wernicke's dementia (Wernicke–Korsakoff syndrome)*.

KPC *Kohn Problem Checklist.*

Krathwohl's chain of reasoning model Model of reasoning/research design by Krathwohl. The model emphasizes that the design and execution of research or other forms of enquiry is essentially linear, and that any stage in its execution is only as sound as the stages which preceded it.

Kreutzfeldt-Jakob Disease *Creutzfeldt-Jakob Disease.*

Kruskal-Shepard scaling test A *multidimensional scaling* technique for use on subjects' ratings of similarities between items.

Kruskal-Wallis one-way ANOVA by ranks (K-W test) *non-parametric test* for comparing three or more groups of subjects on the same measure. Scores for all groups are pooled and ranked, and whether different groups tend to possess different ranks (e.g. group A has most of the high ranked scores,

group B the middle ranks and group C the low ranks) is calculated. The K-W test is thus the non-parametric equivalent of the one-way between groups *analysis of variance.*

Kruskal-Wallis test *Kruskal-Wallis one-way ANOVA by ranks.*

KSC *Kohn Social Competence Scale.*

KSD *Kinetic School Drawing.*

Kucera and Francis word list *Teachers' Word Book of 30,000 Words.*

Kuder General Interest Survey (KGIS) American test of general areas of interest (e.g. outdoor, scientific, etc.) for use in preliminary careers counselling in children in grades 6–12.

Kuder Occupational Interest Survey (KOIS) American measure of careers interests for use in careers counselling for pupils and participants in grades 10 to adult.

Kuder-Richardson formula See *reliability.*

Kuhlman-Anderson Tests *test battery of scholastic aptitude tests.*

kurtosis The 'pointedness' of the shape of a *frequency distribution*. Gives an indication of how widely spread the results are around the *mean.*

kymograph Any mechanical method of recording performance as a graph.

L

L data Data from *naturalistic research* (definition 2).

LAC *Lindamood Auditory Conceptualization Test.*

L scale (1) See *Minnesota Multiphasic Personality Inventory.* (2) See *Eysenck Personality Questionnaire (EPQ).*

L1 first language.

L2 second language.

la belle indifference See *conversion disorder.*

labile variable.

laboratory study See *ecological validity.*

labyrinth Pertaining to the structure of the inner ear.

lack of emotional continuity See *Allport's theory of personality development.*

lacunar amnesia *episodic amnesia.*

lacunar deficits The phenomenon, sometimes encountered in brain-damaged patients, whereby some intellectual functions are almost completely destroyed, whilst others remain relatively intact.

lacunar dementia (LD) Some (although not all) commentators argue that patients suffering from *multi-infarct dementia*, and who exhibit *lacunar deficits*, should be reclassified as suffering from lacunar dementia.

laddering In *personal construct therapy*, a technique of getting the patient to provide basic *constructs* which are explored to encourage the patient to produce more general constructs, etc, until the *superordinate constructs* underlying the other constructs are produced. In **pyramiding**, the opposite technique is used – the patient begins with a superordinate construct, and then 'works down' until s/he has identified the basic constructs s/he uses in everyday life.

lalling *infantilism* of speech.

lalopathy Any disorder of speech.

lalophobia A *phobia* of speaking.

laloplegia Paralysis of the vocal chords.

lalorrhea *hyperphasia.*

lambda Measure of *correlation* between *dichotomous* and/or *nominal variables.*

Landolt C A measure *of acuity* – the participant is shown upper case 'C's in which the 'arms' of the letter are very close together (i.e. nearly forming an 'O'). The participant must judge if he/she can see a gap.

language centres Areas of the brain responsible for language comprehension and production.

language delay In children, a delay in acquiring language or in progressing to an age-appropriate stage of linguistic development.

large n design A study with many participants (usually this means thousands). There is also the implication that some of the more complex statistical tests will be used to analyse the data.

LARR Test *Linguistic Awareness in Reading Readiness Test.*

latah Mental illness, principally found in the Far East, characterized by *echolalia* and complete subservience.

late adult transition The period around retirement.

late life psychosis Any psychosis (any mental illness characterized by a severe loss of contact with reality in the absence of *dementia* or *delirium*; principally the term describes *schizophrenia*) which manifests itself in later life. The condition can appear in tandem with dementing symptoms, but need not do.

late onset schizophrenia (LOS) *schizophrenia* arising in middle age or later life. Whether the illness spontaneously develops at this age is debatable. LOS patients may have atypical behaviours/lifestyles prior to onset, typically protected either consciously or tacitly by parents or friends. Often, death/incapacitation of a caregiver precipitates more pronounced schizophrenic symptoms.

late paraphrenia Mental disorder of later life, characterized by symptoms of feelings of persecution and elaborate fantasies of the same. Commoner in women. Can have a variety of causes, including cardiovascular problems and previous episodes of mental illness.

latency period See *Freud's psychoanalytic theory.*

latent See *manifest.*

latent schizophrenia *schizotypal personality disorder.*

latent trait modelling *item response theory.*

latent variable See *structural equation modelling.*

latent variable structural modelling *structural equation modelling.*

lateral Anatomical term. Further away from the *midline* than another section of the body under consideration. Compare with *medial.*

lateral fissure A *fissure* which marks the boundary between the *frontal lobe* and the *temporal lobe.*

lateral hypothalamic syndrome Combined *adipsia* and *aphagia*, caused by damage to the *lateral* area of the *hypothalamus.*

laterality The degree to which one side of the body/brain is favoured over the other in performing a task.

lateralization (-isation) In *neuropsychology*, the term is used to describe the extent to which the left and right *hemispheres* share control of certain skills. Typically, the left controls most verbal skills, and the right, most visuo-spatial skills.

Latin square design A method of *counterbalancing* the presentation of treat-

ments. A y x y matrix is drawn (where y is the number of treatments) and where each treatment appears once in each column. For example, in the case of three treatments, the Latin square might look like:

1st	2nd	3rd
A	B	C
C	A	B
B	C	A

Some experimenters elect to give the first participant the treatments in the order specified in row 1, subject 2 row 2, subject 3 row 3, subject 4 row 1, subject 5, row 2, etc. Others would devise a new set of permutations for the each block of three subjects. In a **balanced Latin square**, each treatment equally often precedes and follows the other treatments.

law of averages The belief that unusually extreme measures will tend to cancel each other out in an analysis, because unusually large measures will be compensated for by unusually small measures.

law of filial regression *filial regression.*

law of large numbers (1) See *significance.* (2) The larger the sample, the more likely it is to be an accurate representation of the *population* from which it is derived.

LAWSEQ Questionnaire measuring self-esteem.

LCU *life change unit.*

LD (1) *learning disabilities.* (2) *lacunar dementia.*

learned helplessness Theory that some mental illnesses (e.g. *anxiety disorders, depression*) result from the patient's erroneous belief that s/he cannot control his/her own fate.

learning curve The rate at which information about a topic is learnt. Typically (although not universally), this is a case of diminishing returns – a lot is learnt early in the study period, but progressively less new information is acquired the longer the person studies.

learning disabilities (LD) *specific learning difficulties.*

Learning Potential Assessment Device (LPAD) Intelligence test in which the child performs a *culture-fair test*, followed by training on problem-solving methods relevant to the test, followed by retesting.

Learning Process Questionnaire (LPQ) Questionnaire measuring study skills and motivation in secondary school pupils. See *Study Process Questionnaire.*

learning theory General term for any theory which argues that people are best taught by *conditioning* or which assesses learning in terms of conditioning. See *behaviourism.*

least significant difference test *Fisher's PLSD test.*

least squares regression A common method of calculating *regression*. The *regression line* is constructed so that the squares of the distances between the points of the graph and the line are minimized.

left (anatomy) The 'left' refers to what the patient would describe as the left hand side of their body.

left brain skills Loose term for skills associated with the left *hemisphere* – chiefly linguistic and logical skills. This contrasts with *right brain skills*, which are said to be concerned with artistic and creative matters.

left censoring Lack of information about a feature of interest to an experimenter that occurred before the study began. E.g. in cases of *dementia*, although the date a patient first pre-

sented for treatment by a doctor can be easily determined, it is notoriously difficult to determine when the first symptoms of the illness began, since they may have been too subtle to be noticed. *Right censoring* refers to lack of information about a feature of interest after the study has ended. E.g. a study of recurrence of symptoms of mental illness over the period of a study is uninformative about what happened in the years following the study's end. *Interval censoring* refers to a lack of information before and after a period of observation (i.e. both left and right censoring). See *censored observations.*

left dominant thinking *left brain skills.*

legasthenia A profound inability to join letters into words (reading and writing).

leisure counselling Advising people on how to spend their free time.

Leiter International Performance Scale Non-verbal intelligence measure for children.

leniency error *leniency set.*

leniency set See *evaluative set.*

leptokurtic distribution *frequency distribution* with a very peaked shape. See *mesokurtic distribution*, and *platykurtic distribution.*

lesion Damage to a defined area of the body (as opposed to widespread general decay).

letter strings Groups of letters which may or may not form real words.

leucotomy *lobotomy.*

leukotomy *leucotomy.*

level of measurement The level of information contained in the measurement scale (i.e. whether *interval scale, nominal scale, ordinal scale,* or *ratio scale*).

level of significance *significance level.*

level (of spinal cord) See *spinal cord*.

levelling *cognitive style* in which there is a tendency to assimilate new information into existing patterns of knowledge. This contrasts with **sharpening**, in which there is a tendency to see new information as being distinct from the old.

levels (of variable) The number of values the *variable* has in a particular experiment (e.g. if the variable is a drug, it might have three levels, corresponding to three intensities of dosages, such as one, three, or 10 mgs). Typically, the experimenter chooses how many levels a variable can have.

leverage statistic (h) A measure of in effect the distorting effect of individual cases in a *regression* equation. Generally, a case with a leverage > 0.5 is removed from the calculation.

levophobia A *phobia* of anything on one's left hand side.

Lewis Counselling Inventory Test assessing the kind of therapy/counselling the (adolescent) participant requires.

Lewy body A form of damage found in the brain cells of some *demented* patients (particularly those suffering from *Parkinson's disease*). Under a microscope, the Lewy body is a round body comprised of a dense packet surrounded by looser filaments.

lewy body disease A proposed (but not as yet universally accepted) category of *dementia* attributable to the presence of *Lewy bodies*.

lexical decision task A very heavily used *cognitive* psychological experimental method. Subjects are shown *letter strings* and asked to judge as quickly as possible whether or not the strings form real words. Note that the subjects do not have to judge what a discovered real word 'says'.

lexical dysgraphia *surface dysgraphia*.

Leyton Obsessional Inventory Measure of *obsessional* behaviour and *obsessive-compulsive disorder*.

libido In *Freudian* theory, the energy fuelling sexual drive. See *Eros*.

lie scale A set of questions interspersed within some forms of personality test, which measure the degree to which a subject is lying, or is 'guilty' of *social desirability responding*. Questions on a lie scale typically ask the subject if s/he is impossibly virtuous (e.g. 'have you never told a lie?'). The lie scale score can be used to reject extreme subjects, or to *weight* their scores appropriately. In some tests, the lie scale score can in itself form part of the personality assessment.

life change unit (LCU) A measure of the extent to which *life events* affect a person's lifestyle.

life event Any event which is likely to have long-term influences on a person's behaviour and lifestyle (e.g. getting married, death of a parent, etc.). The term is often used purely to refer to negative influences.

life review Process of reviewing one's past. Usually the term refers to planned part of a therapeutic process.

life space Concept invented by Kurt Lewin (1890-1947), that a person's behaviour is determined by a combination of environmental and internal factors which are immediately 'at hand' and noticed by the person, and are known collectively as the life space.

likelihood ratio (LR) (1) The ratio of the probability of something occurring under one condition against the probability of the same thing occurring under another condition. (2) Hence, by extension from (1), in *signal detection analysis*, the ratio of *hits* to *false alarms*. (3) Hence, also by extension from (1), a concept used in statistics when deciding whether a sample is derived from a particular *population*.

likelihood ratio chi square Alternative method of calculating the *chi squared test*.

Likert scale *attitude scale* in which subjects respond on a five point scale (strongly agree, agree, neutral, disagree, strongly disagree). See *Thurstone scale*.

limbic lobe Section of brain at the junction of the *hemispheres* and the *brain stem*. Involved in sexual behaviour, emotion and memory.

limited response question Question where the participant provides his/her own answer, within limitations provided by the experimenter. See *free response question*.

Lindamood Auditory Conceptualization Test (LAC) Measure of ability of children and adolescents to conceptualize word sounds in a visual format. The measure assessed the development of linguistic skills.

line graph A graph in which the *X axis* represents an *independent variable* and the *Y axis* the *dependent variable*. The data plotted by a line drawn between the points. The line graph should not be confused with the *frequency polygon* (which is a measure of frequency occurrence of a single variable).

linear combination Creating a new variable by adding together several other variables. The variables being added up can be weighted.

linear correlation *correlation* whose graphical expression is a straight line (this is the 'conventional' correlation). In contrast, a *non-linear correlation* assumes a shape other than a straight line.

linear regression *regression* calculation which produces a straight *regression line*. See *non-linear regression*.

linear relationship A relationship between two or more *variables*, in which, if the scores on one variable are plotted on a graph against the scores on the other variable(s), a straight line is found (or at least, a straight line will fit the data best). In a *non-linear relationship*, the line is anything other than straight (e.g. a curve). A special version of this is the *step function*. Here, a variable does not change gradually, but in 'jumps' with little or no change between them (e.g. when y = any value between 0 and 10, x=1; y=11–20, x=2; y=21–30, x=3, etc.). The relationship, if shown on a graph, looks like a side view of some steps.

linear systematic sampling Selecting every nth member of a larger sample to act as an experimental subject.

linear transformation Mathematically adjusting data so that, when the original and the transformed data are plotted against each other as a graph, they take the form of a straight line. The transformation also retains the features of the original distribution, barring a change in the values of the *mean* and the *standard deviation*. By extension, a *non-linear transformation* alters the data so that an old-transformed data plot forms a curved line.

linguistic awareness The conscious awareness of one's linguistic skills, and of how language is structured.

Linguistic Awareness in Reading Readiness Test (LARR Test) Test of *linguistic awareness*, for beginning readers (i.e. tests ability to recognize what reading looks like, what it is used for, and awareness of the structure of language). Held by the test's authors to be a crucial determinant of whether the participant is ready to be taught to read.

linguistic bias *test bias* in which some participants are unfairly discriminated against because of linguistic problems rather than through substance of the test itself (e.g. participants from immigrant groups, culturally deprived backgrounds, etc., may fail test questions not because of the problem itself, but because they cannot understand the instructions).

Liquid Ecstasy *GHB.*

LISREL Form of *structural equation modelling.* The name is a rather contrived acronym of 'Analysis Of Linear Structural Relationships'.

lithium carbonate Drug used in the treatment of *bipolar disorders.*

Little Albert John Watson (1878–1958), psychologist, applied *classical conditioning* techniques to a child – 'Little Albert' – who was conditioned into fearing a white rat by a loud frightening noise being sounded every time he was shown the rat. Albert subsequently feared not only the rat but many other white furry things. Albert was an orphan, and was adopted and moved away before *deconditioning* could take place. Not one of *behaviour therapy's* greater achievements.

Little Jiffy see *factor analysis.*

living will Signed and witnessed declaration by a person that in the event of their becoming severely mentally and/or physically incapacitated, no effort will be made to prolong survival artificially.

lobe A segment of the *cortex.* The four lobes are the *frontal lobe, occipital lobe, parietal lobe* and *temporal lobe.*

lobectomy Removal of a *lobe* (note that the term may refer to removal of a section of lung, also called a lobe).

lobotomy Severance of (some or all) neural connections to a *lobe.* Often used as shorthand for *frontal lobotomy.*

localization (-isation) See *neuropsychology.*

Locke-Wallace Marital Adjustment Scale Measure of the state of the relationship between a married or cohabiting couple.

locomotor ataxia *tabes dorsalis.*

locomotor map following task *Weinstein maps.*

locus of control The degree to which a participant feels in control of his/her own life.

locus of evaluation The point(s) of reference an individual uses in making a judgement.

log-linear analysis Method of comparing three or more *categorical variables.* In essence, it is the multivariate version of the *chi squared test.*

log(arithm) transformation See *normalization.*

logistic regression *regression* calculation where the *predicted variable* is a *dichotomous variable.*

logoclonia Persistent repetition of a syllable or other word segment.

logorrhea *hyperphasia.*

logotherapy form of *existential therapy* devised by Viktor Frankl. A central feature of the method is the use of *paradoxical intention.* Like other existential therapies, it encourages the patient to come to terms with the demands and choices placed on him/her by their existence.

London Reading Test Reading test for participants aged 10–12 years. Consists of *cloze procedure* and comprehension tests.

long-term psychotherapy See *short-term psychotherapy.*

long-term span See *span.*

longitudinal fissure The *fissure* running between the left and right *hemispheres.*

longitudinal research/samples/ study The experimental method of testing the same group of people at different ages. Contrast with *cross-sectional research/samples/study.* See *overlapping longitudinal study, sequential research design* and *time-lag comparison.*

loose association In communicating, veering off the point and starting another topic, either tangentially associated with the previous one, or recalling a completely different earlier topic. The phenomenon can be indicative of a *thought disorder.*

LOS *late onset schizophrenia.*

loudness recruitment A physical complaint in which sounds in a particular frequency band (usually high) are (mis)interpreted as being louder than usual, sometimes to the point of being painful.

low frequency words Words which occur very rarely in common usage.

low functioning See *high functioning.*

lower apparent limit See *class intervals.*

lower real limit (LRL) See *class intervals.*

loxapine Form of *antipsychotic drug.*

LPAD *Learning Potential Assessment Device.*

LPQ *Learning Process Questionnaire.*

LR *likelihood ratio.*

LRL *lower real limit.*

LSD *d-lysergic acid diethylamide.*

LSD test *Fisher's PLSD test.*

lumbar level (spinal cord) *level* of the *spinal cord,* below the *cervical level* and *thoracic level.* Has five *segments,* labelled LI to L5 (LI being the highest).

Luria-Nebraska test battery Battery of *neuropsychological tests,* assessing 11 major aspects of functioning (e.g. linguistic skills, motor skills, etc.). Discoveries of dysfunction can help identify which part of the patient's brain is damaged.

Luscher colour test Personality test based upon the person's order of preference for a group of colours.

lying (L) scale *lie scale.*

M

M-MAC *McDermott Multidimensional Assessment of Children.*

MA *mental age.*

Ma scale See *Minnesota Multiphasic Personality Inventory.*

machiavellianism The degree to which an individual feels that the end justifies the means (regardless of the moral worth of the latter). Named after Niccolo di Bernardo dei Machiavelli (1469–1527), statesman and author, who advocated an often extreme version of such an approach, and set the tone for the British stereotype of continental politics.

machismo The stereotypical masculine attributes of being tough, resourceful, etc. With changing attitudes to gender roles, the term has become somewhat derogatory, denoting the stereotypical accompaniments of lack of sensitivity, pig-headedness, etc.

macho The adjective derived from *machismo.*

MACI *Millon Adolescent Clinical Inventory.*

macro (research) Pertaining to the whole or the combined effects of several smaller systems. Hence, the study of a whole system. By contrast, *micro* refers to the study of parts of the system in greater detail.

macropsia A disorder of visual perception, in which items are seen as too large.

mad cow disease *bovine spongiform encephalopathy.*

magical thinking Mistaken belief that one's thoughts alone can have a physical effect.

magnetic resonance imaging (MRI) A method of scanning an organ (e.g. the brain) to produce three-dimensional images. It involves placing the body in a strong magnetic field, then switching the field off. This causes the cells to release radio waves which can be read and interpreted by the MRI scanner.

magnification In therapeutic situations, the patient's maladaptive exaggeration of what they perceive to be the significance of events (e.g. claiming that non-threatening events are dangerous or that dangerous events are harmless or even beneficial).

magnitude estimation A form of *direct scaling*. A stimulus is given an arbitrary value (typically, 100), and the participant is asked to grade other stimuli relative to this value (e.g. if the participant perceives a light to be half as bright as the reference stimulus, then s/he grades it as '50'). See *method of halving.*

Mahalanobis D *Mahalanobis distance.*

Mahalanobis distance A measure of the degree to which an individual value in a *regression* calculation is aberrant and should thus be excluded from the calculation because, in effect, it is distorting results.

maieusiphobia A *phobia* of childbirth.

main effects (ANOVA) See *analysis of variance.*

mainstreaming (1) American term for placement of children with physical handicaps and/or *mental retardation* in normal schools. (2) Generally, the placing of patients from institutions or with appreciable psychological or physical problems in the community.

maintainance variables Behaviours and aspects of the person's environment which help maintain him/her in a particular state.

maintaining cause An item, event, person, etc., which causes one to maintain a particular form of behaviour.

major affective disorder A nebulous term describing any disorder of *affect* which is severely incapacitating.

major depression *unipolar disorder.*

major depressive episode Period of *depression* which lasts for an appreciable, uninterrupted period.

major tranquillizer Drug which removes or reduces the severity of many symptoms in *psychotic* and particularly *schizophrenic* patients. It effectively calms the patient, without inducing feelings of drowsiness. There are often unpleasant physical side-effects, however (e.g. see *lardive dyskinesia*).

Make A Picture Story Test (MAPS test) *projective personality test*, in which the participant creates a story from a set of pictures.

maladaptive schema A maladaptive pattern of thought habitually (and erroneously) applied in a situation so that the patient gains an inaccurate and damaging self-perception. E.g. a person may seek proof that another person s/he meets finds him or her boring. An *early maladaptive schema* is one which has been present since childhood.

mandrax Type of *barbiturate*.

mania *affective disorder* in which the patient experiences an extremely elated mood, usually coupled with extreme levels of activity and energy. The patient often has unrealistically optimistic thoughts and grandiose schemes. The condition can be found in isolation, but is more often encountered as a symptom of *bipolar disorder*. The same symptoms, in a relatively mild form, are classified as *hypomania*.

manic-depression *bipolar disorder*.

manic-depressive psychosis *bipolar disorder*.

Manic State Scale (MSS) *observer scale* of level of *manic* behaviour in patients.

manifest That which is presented, as opposed to *latent* (that which is hidden). The terms are used in many therapies to denote what the patient says, as opposed to the underlying motives for saying it, which are held to be consciously or unconsciously suppressed.

Manifest Anxiety Scale (MAS) Measure of *anxiety*, formed from test items from the *Minnesota Multiphasic Personality Inventory*.

manifest variable See *structural equation modelling*.

manifestation A way in which a particular psychological characteristic can make itself apparent through behaviour.

manikin test Any test in which the participant must fit together the pieces of a model of a human body.

manipulated variable *independent variable*.

Mann-Whitney U test *non-parametric* test of two *unmatched* groups' differences on the same *dependent variable* (which must be on an *ordinal scale*). The test can be regarded as the non-parametric equivalent of the *unpaired t test*.

MANOVA *multivariate analysis of variance*.

MAOI *monoamine oxidase inhibitor*.

MAP test *Miller Assessment for Preschoolers*.

MAPI *Millon Adolescent Personality Inventory*.

MAPS test *Make A Picture Story Test*.

marathon therapy Intensive therapeutic session (usually group *therapy*) lasting for 24 hours or more (usually, therapeutic sessions last 1-2 hours).

marche a petit pas 'Walking with little steps' – a rapid shuffling movement, sometimes encountered in patients with damage to the *motor area*.

Marfan syndrome Genetic disorder characterized by atypical tallness and thin, 'spidery' build. In some instances, *hyperactivity* is reported.

marginal mean Where there are two *factors* in an analysis, the *mean* of one factor averaged across all levels of the other factor.

marginal significance *borderline significance*.

Marianne Frostig Developmental Test of Visual Perception Test of perceptual skills presumed to underlie reading (e.g. hand-eye coordination, geometric figure identification, etc.). Designed for participants aged 3–10 years. Can be used as part of *reading readiness* measures or as a diagnostic tool in assessing poor readers.

marijuana See *cannabis*.

Marital Interaction Coding System Measure (by therapist or other observer) of the quality of interaction between married or cohabiting couples as they discuss a problem set for them.

Marital Satisfaction Inventory (MSI) A measure of marital satisfaction, and causes of dissatisfaction. The scale can be used to identify potential problems for either spouse separately.

marital therapy Any therapeutic method in which partners (usually married, or otherwise long-term cohabiters) are aided in resolving problems in their relationship.

Markov chain A representation of a sequence of events in which there are alternative pathways at each stage of the sequence, and the probability of taking each pathway is calculated. The key feature is that the probability of a particular choice being taken is held to be dependent only upon the preceding event – how that event was reached will not influence the subsequent choice. E.g., in a chain of 99 events, the choice of event number 99 is only dependent upon what choice number 98 was – choices 0–97 have no influence.

marriage guidance *marital therapy.*

MAS *Manifest Anxiety Scale.*

masculine identity The degree to which an individual identifies with *masculinity* traits.

masculinity Nebulous term for a collection of traits epitomizing aggression, forthrightness, etc., and everything which belongs to the stereotypical man. More generally, a collection of assertive and competitive attributes. This is contrasted with *femininity*, a collection of more passive, nurturing (traditional 'motherly') qualities. Often the traits are presented together as a *bipolar dimension* (i.e. *masculinity-femininity scale*) as if they are opposites. Although the descriptions might be descriptive rather than prescriptive, the issue can very easily slide into a debate about sexist stereotyping. See *androgynous personality.*

masculinity-femininity scale See *masculinity.*

MASI *Multilevel Academic Skills Inventory.*

masked epilepsy See *epilepsy.*

Maslach Burnout Inventory (MBI) A measure of the degree of actual or potential *burnout* experienced by individuals.

Maslow's hierarchy of needs Theory by Maslow that humans have a hierarchy of needs, which can be symbolically represented as a pyramid. At the 'base' are physiological needs for food, shelter, etc. Above these are safety needs, followed by social needs (e.g. to form friendships, to fit into the social world, etc.). Above these are *self-esteem*, and at the top of the pyramid lies *self-actualization* (i.e. searching for and achieving 'higher' goals and fulfilling one's potential). Maslow argues that these stages are acquired through development, and the complete structure will take 30 years or more to complete. Therapies based on the theory attempt to lead participants through the various stages, and to put them back 'on course' if they have strayed. Commonly this occurs when a participant attempts to follow other people's self-actualization plans rather than his/her own. See *humanistic psychology.*

masochism *paraphilia* in which the patient's principal source of sexual gratification is in being physically hurt or otherwise punished. See *sadism.*

mass behaviour *mass contagion.*

mass contagion The spread of an idea, behaviour, etc., through a group or community.

mass hysteria Form of *mass contagion*, in which an irrational belief or behaviour grips a group or community (e.g. *tarantism*).

massed practice Training session in which repetitions of the same act are placed closely together. This contrasts with *distributed practice*, in which the repetitions are relatively further apart.

MAST *Multilevel Academic Survey Tests.*

MAT *Motivation Analysis Test.*

matched subjects See *matching.*

matching Experimental procedure by which participants in one group are chosen so that they share the same characteristic(s) as participants in other groups (e.g. they have all had the same level of education). Such participants are called *matched subjects*. In this manner, any differences found between the groups cannot be attributed to the matching factors (e.g. the superiority of group A over group B on a maths test cannot be due to superior education levels if the two groups are matched for educational levels). A further refinement of this is the *paired samples* technique.

Matching Familiar Figures Test (MFF Test) Assesses children's visual skills and the degree of their impulsiveness in making responses. The child has to find the drawing identical to the target from a range of very similar alternatives. The accuracy and speed of response are both recorded.

matching questions Questions in which the participant is required to identify which items in one list match up with items in other lists.

maternal deprivation Lack of adequate care by the mother or other caregiver. Can be considered in terms of 'separation' and 'deprivation of maternal care'. The former is any separation of mother/caregiver and child whether on a regular basis (e.g. the mother/ caregiver goes to work) or occasional (e.g. hospital visits). If adequate substitute care is given, it is not usually serious. The latter is where the mother/caregiver is present all the time, but inadequately looks after the child.

mathematics anxiety (Irrational) *anxiety* created by fear of studying or working on mathematical or arithmetical topics.

matrilineal Inherited through females.

Matrix Analogies Test A measure of non-verbal intelligence for 5–17-year-olds.

maturation Physical ageing changes, coupled with acquisition of knowledge, experiences, etc.

maturational crisis Severe negative sensations produced by 'moving' from one developmental stage to another (e.g. *mid-life crisis*).

Mauchly's test of sphericity A commonly-used *sphericity test*. If the test results are not *significant* then the data are acceptable as they stand.

Maudsley Obsessional-Compulsive Inventory Measure of the level of *obsessive-compulsive* behaviour exhibited by a patient.

Maudsley Personality Questionnaire Older version of the *Eysenck Personality Questionnaire.*

maximum likelihood analysis See *factor analysis.*

MBD *minimal brain dysfunction.*

MBI *Maslach Burnout Inventory.*

MBMD *Millon Behavioral Medicine Diagnostic.*

MBTI *Myers-Briggs Type Indicator.*

McCall-Crabbs Standard Test Lessons in Reading *Standard Test Lessons in Reading.*

McCarthy Scales of Children's Abilities (MSCA) *test battery* of motor and intellectual development in children aged 3 years 6 months – 8 years 6 months. Comprises 18 subtests, yielding five scales of verbal, perceptual-performance, quantitative, memory, and motor skills.

McCarthy Screening Test Measures of potential learning difficulties, drawn from *McCarthy Scales of Children's Abilities*.

McDermott Multidimensional Assessment of Children (M-MAC) Computerized assessment programme. Comprises: Classification (interpretation of intellectual and academic abilities, and social skills and milieu); and Programme Design (creation of appropriate remedial regimes/goal setting).

McGill Pain Questionnaire (MPQ) Measure of perception of pain resulting from illness – its location, nature, severity, etc.

McGill Picture Anomalies Test A measure of ability to attend carefully to a visual stimulus/basic visual perception. The participant is shown a picture in which a detail is wrong. The participant's task is to identify the anomaly.

MCI *mild cognitive impairment.*

MCMI *Millon Clinical Multiaxial Inventory.*

McNaghten rule Nineteenth century UK legal ruling that a person was insane at the time of the illegal act, if they did not know what they were doing, or they did not know that it was wrong.

McNemar test *non-parametric* measure of the extent to which two groups change category membership after treatment. The test might be applied to a problem such as the following. After attending a political debate, a proportion of those who said they would vote for party X before the debate, now say they will vote for party Y. Similarly, a proportion of erstwhile party Y supporters now back party X. Is this change significant? The **Cochran Q test** is essentially the McNemar test applied to three or more groups.

MCT *Minnesota Clerical Test.*

MDI (1) *Multiscore Depression Inventory.* (2) *Mental Development Index.*

MDMA Acronym of the chemical combination of *Ecstasy*. Stands for methylenedioxymethamphetamine.

Mdn *median.*

MDQ *Menstrual Distress Questionnaire.*

MDS *multi-dimensional scaling.*

mean Arithmetical average – a *measure of central tendency*. See *geometric mean* and *harmonic mean*.

mean deviation *average deviation.*

mean square (1) See *ANOVA table*. (2) *variance*.

measurement error Errors in measurement created by chance variability.

measures of central tendency *summary statistics* which divide the data into two halves (i.e. half of the data fall below the figure produced, half above). This is an exact division in the case of the *median*, but can be more approximate for the *mean* and *mode*.

measures of dispersion *summary statistics* which measure how spread out the distribution of the *variable* in question is. Measures include *range* and *variance*.

Mechanical Ability Test *aptitude test* used in *personnel screening* for mechanical/engineering jobs.

mechanophobia A *phobia* of anything mechanical.

medial Anatomical term. Closer to the *midline* than another section of the body under consideration. Compare with *lateral*.

median A *measure of central tendency* – half the values in the distribution are greater than the median, half are less.

median test *non-parametric* measure of whether two groups are derived from a *population* with the same *median*. If the test demonstrates that they are, then it is assumed that the samples are from the same population, and hence, there is no significant *difference*, between them. The **extension of the median test** is a similar measure for comparing three or more groups.

mediating variable *intervening variable*.

Medicaid American health care scheme for the poor.

medical model of mental illness *disease model of mental illness*.

medical psychology The study of any psychological aspect of medicine, although the term is usually restricted to the study of psychological changes produced by illness, and the doctor – patient relationship.

Medicare American health care scheme for older people.

meditation A prolonged and deliberate period of relaxation, aided and abetted by concentration on a specific thought or mind exercise (i.e. not simply day dreaming). The technique is an integral part of some types of religious worship (and is central to *transcendental meditation*) and is also used in several forms of therapy. *Relaxation therapy* produces similar results, but requires the participant to concentrate on the responses of the body, rather than those of the mind.

medulla oblongata Area of *brain stem* – the junction of the brain and the *spinal cord*.

megavitamin therapy *orthomolecular psychiatry*.

melodic intonation therapy Many patients suffering from *aphasia* retain the ability to sing. It is therefore possible to train them to 'sing' (intone) words, and hence allow a modicum of communicative skill.

memoing The process of working through the possible structures a theoretical model might assume.

memory span *span*.

meningitis Inflammation of the meninges (the tissue surrounding the brain and spinal cord). The illness can cause permanent brain damage.

Menstrual Distress Questionnaire (MDQ) Self-report questionnaire of negative symptoms attributable to the menstrual cycle.

mental age (MA) The level of mental skills which is average for a particular age group. The measure is only revealing when other age measures are taken into consideration (e.g. a 12–year-old with a mental age of 12 is average, whereas one with a mental age of 16 is advanced). See *dyslexia* and *intelligence quotient*.

mental ataxia An incongruity between expressed emotions and genuine internal state.

mental deficiency *mental retardation*.

Mental Development Index (MDI) Measure of mental development derived from the *Bayley Scales of Infant Development*. *Mental age* can be extrapolated from it, if so desired.

Mental Measurement Yearbook (MMY) Publication listing details of the principal psychological tests currently available.

mental retardation Intelligence level well below normal, which is *congenital*, or becomes apparent in childhood/ adolescence. Definitions vary, but most refer to IQs of 80 or less at maximum. The DSM classifies it as occurring when IQ is less than 70 (i.e. more than two *standard deviations* below average on most IQ tests). According to the *AAMD* classification, there are several grades of retardation – *profound mental retardation* (IQ 25 or less), *severe mental retardation* (25–39), *moderate mental retardation* (40–54), and *mild mental retardation* (55–69). The DSM has the same terms, and similar IQ values (less than 20, 20–34, 35–49, and 50–70 respectively). An earlier (and now offensive) terminology classified retarded people into *idiots* (less than 30), *imbeciles* (30–50), and *morons* (American) *or feeble-minded* (UK) persons (50–70).

mental rotation task Any task in which the participant must judge whether a figure shown in an unusual orientation represents a particular target (e.g. whether an 'A' printed upside down is really an 'A'). To do this, the participant must mentally rotate the image.

Mental Status Examination (MSE) A *test battery* assessing the patient's general mental and physical state upon first presentation.

Mental Status Questionnaire (MSQ) A simple assessment of a (usually *demented*) patient's intellectual status and degree of functional independence. See *Blessed Dementia Scale*.

mentally gifted Nebulous definition, but typically refers to individuals with IQs of at least 125 (many commentators would place a higher figure of 140 and over).

mentally handicapped Nebulous term denoting appreciably lowered psychological abilities in some or many fields, resulting from brain damage. The term

is most often used synonymously with *mental retardation*.

Merrill Palmer Test Intelligence *test battery* for pre-school children.

mescaline A *psychedelic drug.*

mesmerism/Mesmerism Old-fashioned term for *hypnosis*. The term derives from one of its early practitioners – the eighteenth century physician, Anton Mesmer. Mesmer used the technique as part of a general therapy deriving from the belief that mental illness was due to an imbalance in the body's magnetic field (hence the term 'animal magnetism').

mesokurtic distribution A *frequency distribution* with moderate shape, between the extremes of the *leptokurtic distribution* and the *platykurtic distribution*. Accordingly, sometimes used to describe the shape of the *normal distribution*.

mesomorph See *Sheldon's personality types.*

meta-analysis (1) Method of assessing a trend in a corpus of studies. The mean *effect size* of the studies in question is calculated. (2) More generally, any overview of a body of research.

metamorphosia A disorder of visual perception, in which items are seen as undulating in shape.

metathesis The transposition of phonemes or syllables within a word.

methadone A *heroin substitute.*

methadyl acetate A *heroin substitute.*

methedrine Type of *amphetamine.*

method of bisection See *method of halving.*

method of halving Experimental method used in perception studies. The participant is told to alter a stimulus so that it appears half as intense. This yields a measure of perception of magnitude. This contrasts with the *method of bisection*, in which the participant must adjust the intensity so that it falls half-way between two other stimuli. See *magnitude estimation*.

method of limits Technique for discovering a participant's perceptual *threshold*. A stimulus or difference is presented at increasingly strong or weak intensities until the participant perceives it/can no longer perceive it. A variant of this is *the staircase method*, in which the participant is presented with a weaker intensity if s/he can perceive the stimulus or difference, and a stronger one if s/he cannot. This is a faster method.

method of minimal change *method of limits*.

metonymy Using a word which is incorrect, but which is related to the word which should have been used (e.g. 'biro' instead of 'pencil').

Metropolitan Diagnostic Tests Series of tests of scholastic attainment. See *Diagnostic Language Tests, Diagnostic Mathematics* and *Diagnostic Reading Tests*.

Mf scale See *Minnesota Multiphasic Personality Inventory*.

MFF Test *Matching Familiar Figures Test*.

MHV Test *Mill Hill Vocabulary Test*.

Michigan Picture Test – Revised (MPT-R) *projective personality test* for participants aged 7–15 years.

micro (research) See *macro*.

microanalytic research (1) Research which concentrates on specific incidents, rather than generalizations of sets of occurrences. (2) In *Bandura's theory of social learning*, the term refers to participants' ratings of how well they think they can perform in specific situations.

microcephaly Atypically small head and brain. People with the condition can have a wide range of symptoms, ranging from relatively mild learning difficulties to severe intellectual retardation and impairment of movement.

Microcog – Assessment of Cognitive Functioning (ACF) Computerized adult *test battery* assessing severity of cases of relatively mild cognitive impairment. Test include measures of reactivity, memory, perception, attention, abstract reasoning and mental calculation.

microphobia A *phobia* of small things.

micropsia A disorder of visual perception, in which items are seen as too small.

microsomatognosia The misperception that all or part of one's body is abnormally small.

microtome A device for producing thin slices from a tissue sample (e.g. a brain). The slices are so thin that they are semi-transparent, enabling them to be examined under a microscope.

M.I.D. *multi-infarct dementia.*

middle category responding Habitually choosing a moderate opinion ('sitting on the fence').

mid-life crisis Loose term for a set of negative feelings in some middle-aged people, stemming from the realization that they are at the peak of their careers and affluence, and that ageing will result (in their eyes) in a decline. See *involutional psychotic reaction*.

mid-life transitions Changes occurring in middle age (e.g. children leaving home, preparing for retirement, etc.). Negative changes can in some instances create a *mid-life crisis*. See *empty nest syndrome*.

midline Anatomical term. An imaginary vertical line which runs through the body, dividing it in half.

midpoint See *class intervals*.

midrange The value which is halfway between the lowest and highest values for the *variable* in question.

Mignon delusion A version of the *foster child fantasy*, in which the child is also convinced that his/her 'real' parents are wealthy, famous, etc.

migraine An extremely severe headache, which begins on one side of the head (and may remain solely on one side). It is accompanied by other complaints. The commonest are: a severe lowering of *cognitive* and/or linguistic functioning, a sensation of flashing lights or other forms of visual disturbance, and nausea (see *aura*). Migraine attacks in which there are disturbances of vision are sometimes called *classical migraine*, and attacks without these are termed *common migraine*.

mild cognitive impairment (MCI) Currently rather nebulous term for intellectual impairment associated with ageing, less than that experienced in *dementia*, though of greater severity than the relatively gentle intellectual loss normally found in old age (*normal cognitive ageing (NCA)*). Some commentators include impairment which others would classify as early stages of dementia.

mild learning difficulty (MLD) Nebulous term for a condition whose possessors usually have an IQ level commensurate with mild *mental retardation*, who are unlikely to thrive by conventional academic standards, but who are at the same time not completely ineducable.

mild mental retardation See *mental retardation*.

milieu therapy A deliberate alteration of the patient's environment (e.g. surroundings, lifestyle, etc.) for therapeutic reasons.

Mill Hill Vocabulary Test (MHV Test) A measure of vocabulary, the test requires participants to provide definitions of words, whose obscurity increases as the test progresses (there is no time limit). Commonly used *crystallized intelligence* measure. Available in 2 formats: Junior (for children over 6 years and adults) and Senior (for children over 14 years and adults; especially individuals and groups likely to be of above-average ability).

Miller Analogies Test Intelligence test using *analogy test* measures.

Miller Assessment for Preschoolers (MAP) *test battery* for children aged 2–6 years. Primarily intended to identify handicap.

Miller Behavioral Style Scale Test of personality, in which participants are measured on which of a range of options they would adopt in stressful situations.

Millon Adolescent Clinical Inventory (MACI) Measure of psychological dysfunction in adolescents.

Millon Adolescent Personality Inventory (MAPI) Measure of personality and behaviour patterns in adolescents.

Millon Behavioral Medicine Diagnostic (MBMD) Measure of psychological factors impinging on a chronically ill patient's treatment.

Millon Clinical Multiaxial Inventory (MCMI) Measure of *personality disorders*.

Millon Pre-Adolescent Clinical Inventory (MPACI) Measure of psychological dysfunction in children aged 9–12 years.

Mind Prober Computerized personality assessment programme.

mind, theory of (autism) Theory that the principal deficit of *autistic* patients is a lack of a concept of mind. This in turn leads to a failure to perceive the independence of other people's minds and thoughts. See *autism*.

mindblindness Failure to perceive that others may think differently from oneself. The term is often used to describe one of the principal cognitive dysfunctions in *autism* and *Asperger's syndrome*.

Mini Mental State Examination (MMS) Quickly-administered test of intellectual abilities of older subjects (particularly those suspected of being in the early stages of *dementia*). Measures basic competence at everyday skills, level of wakefulness, ability to follow and remember simple instructions, perform elementary calculations, etc.

minimal brain damage Old term for *minimal brain dysfunction*.

minimal brain dysfunction (MBD) Old term for *attentional deficit disorder*.

minimal competence *criterion*.

minimization (-isation) Unrealistically playing down the implications of (usually) positive information.

Minnesota Clerical Test (MCT) Measure of skill associated with clerical work (checking that word and number pairs are identical).

Minnesota method Therapeutic method for treating *alcoholism*.

Minnesota Multiphasic Personality Inventory (MMPI) Personality test, yielding scores on ten scales, which are indices of: *depression (D), hypochondriasis (Hd), hypomania (Ma), hysteria (Hy), masculinity-femininity (Mf),*

paranoia (Pa), psychasthenia (Pt), psychopathic deviate (Pd), schizophrenia (Sc), and *social introversion (Si).* The test also has three further scales. The *F scale* checks against *social desirability responding.* The *K scale* checks against subjects responding sloppily and carelessly (i.e. not bothering to give an accurate picture of themselves). The *L scale* is a *lie scale.* The test is primarily aimed at a clinical population, though it is applicable to normal subjects. See *California Personality Inventory* and *Fake Bad Scale (FBS).*

Minnesota Satisfaction Questionnaire (MSQ) A measure of *job satisfaction*.

Minnesota Test for the Differential Diagnosis of Aphasia (MTDDA) Test of major aspects of *aphasia* (includes disorders of writing and reading as well as speech and speech comprehension).

minor tranquillizer Drug with a mildly sedating effect. Most often used in treating *anxiety*.

mirror drawing task Task in which a participant must draw a design whilst only able to see the results of his/her efforts through a mirror.

miscue An error (particularly applied to children's reading errors).

misologia Avoiding speaking.

missing data The term can simply mean data of any description that are missing. However, it often specifically means where only some data are missing resulting in an incomplete record (e.g. a participant answers some but not all questions).

mixed ANOVA *analysis of variance* in which the measures are a mixture of *within groups* and *between groups measures*.

mixed delirium See *delirium*.

mixed design An experiment in which both *between-subjects* and *within subjects measures* have been used.

mixed hearing loss See *conductive hearing loss.*

mixed schizophrenia *undifferentiated schizophrenia.*

mixed transcortical aphasia *aphasia* in which virtually all linguistic abilities have been lost, barring the ability to repeat single words.

MLD *mild learning difficulty.*

MMPI *Minnesota Multiphasic Personality Inventory.*

MMR vaccine A single-shot vaccine given to young children to inoculate against measles, mumps and rubella. Its use was linked to an increase in cases of *autistic spectrum disorder* but subsequent research has largely rejected this theory.

MMS *Mini Mental State Examination.*

MMTIC *Murphy-Meisgeier Type Indicator for Children.*

MMY *Mental Measurements Yearbook.*

Mobility Inventory for Agoraphobia Measure of the degree to which patients suffering from agoraphobia are able to move about, and their strategies for avoiding open spaces.

modal Pertaining to the *mode.*

mode A *measure of central tendency.* The mode is the value within a sample for which there are the highest number of observations (i.e. it is the most popular score within the sample). In a *multimodal distribution*, there are two or more modes (i.e. there is no one score which is the most popular).

model A representation of a thought process and/or behaviour, usually in symbolic terms.

modelling (1) Training a patient to change an aspect of their behaviour by copying the desired behaviour from someone else (e.g. in the case of a *arachnophobic* patient, making them watch a film of someone handling a spider). In *covert modelling*, the patient imagines someone performing the behaviour. (2) The learning of behaviour by copying others – see *Bandura's theory of social learning.*

moderate mental retardation See *mental retardation.*

moderator variable *variable* which exerts a greater influence in some sections (e.g. sub-groups) of a sample than in others. If the moderator variable is statistically controlled for, then this may create a more accurate picture of the situation under review.

Modern Occupational Skills Test (MOST) Battery of tests of basic administrative and clerical skills.

molar (research) *macro.*

molecular (research) *micro.*

molysmophobia A *phobia* of infection.

Mongolism Outmoded and racist term for *Down's Syndrome* (Down felt that European Down's Syndrome patients were 'arrested' at a 'Mongolic' stage of development because of a supposed physical resemblance).

monitoring See *blunting.*

monoamine oxidase inhibitors (MAOI) General term for a group of *antidepressant* drugs.

monoideism An abnormal preoccupation with an idea.

monophobia *autophobia.*

monotonic Always going in the same direction. Hence, a *monotonic relationship* is one between two *variables* in which an increase in one is always met by an increase OR a decrease in the other (i.e. the direction of the change must be constant).

monotonic relationship See *monotonic*.

monozygotic (MZ) Of one egg. Hence, *monozygotic twins* are twins from the same egg (i.e. identical twins). See *dizygotic*.

monozygotic twins See *monozygotic*.

Monte Carlo method (1) Any statistical method which employs the generation of random numbers. E.g. in considering a set of data, it may be desirable to generate random numbers to see how often a more extreme set of data is produced by chance. (2) Method of simulating a model based on a *stochastic sequence*.

Montgomery-Asberg Scale Measure of the effectiveness of treatment for *depression*.

mood measure A measure of impermanent but appreciable feeling (e.g. grief upon bereavement). See *state measure*.

mood stabilizer Drug which attempts to remove extremes of mood (as in e.g. *bipolar disorder*).

Mooney Problem Check List Test for participants aged 12 years and over (there are different forms for different age groups). Presents participants with a list of problems, and asks them to identify which they suffer from. Measures problems with social life, relationship formation, etc.

Moray House Tests Battery of tests assessing English, mathematical and verbal reasoning skills (for age ranges 10–12 years, 10–12 years and 8–18 years respectively).

morbid Pertaining to disease.

morbidity (1) The presence of an illness. (2) Preoccupation with thoughts of illness and/or death.

morbidity risk The probability that a person will develop an illness.

Morgan Russell Assessment Schedule (MRAS) Measure of the symptoms of *anorexia nervosa*.

moron See *mental retardation*.

morphine See *opiates*.

Morrisby Profile (MP) A test which assesses a person's personality and work-related abilities within the same overall profile.

Mosaic Test A *projective personality test* – the participant is required to make patterns out of wooden shapes.

Moses test of extreme reactions *non-parametric measure* which measures whether one group has more extreme scores than another. This contrasts with most other tests of differences, which simply examine if there is a difference between groups.

MOST *Modern Occupational Skills Test.*

motherese Term for the language used by a parent in talking to pre-talking infants. Characterized by its simple structure, high pitched delivery, repetition, and exaggerated intonation.

motivated forgetting Depending upon which commentator one is reading – either *suppression or repression*.

motivation A drive to sustain a particular behaviour and/or aim for a particular goal.

Motivation Analysis Test (MAT) Measure of *motivation*: the participant is given a variety of measures (e.g. *forced choice test*) to select the more preferable of two actions.

motor (neurons) Carrying signals from the *central nervous system* to skeletal muscle, and hence movement-related. Sometimes inaccurately used to denote all signals emanating from the *central* *nervous system* (however, see *autonomic nervous system*).

motor amusia A profound inability to play even the simplest tune, beat the simplest rhythms, etc.

motor aphasia (1) *ataxic aphasia*. (2) *Broca's aphasia*.

motor apraxia Inability to perform planned actions (as opposed to spontaneous ones).

motor area An area of the *frontal lobe* (lying in a thin strip immediately adjacent to the *central sulcus*) involved in movement control.

motor cortex *motor area*.

motor neurosis Any mental illness in which the principal (or at least, most noticeable) symptom is an abnormal pattern of movement, ranging from *mania* through to a nervous tic.

motor skills General term for any skills which involve movement and muscular action. Often divided into *fine motor skills* (relatively delicate movements, such as finger movements, writing, etc.) and *gross motor skills* (relatively 'big' movements such as walking, jumping, etc.).

Movement ABC *Movement Assessment Battery for Children.*

Movement Assessment Battery for Children (ABC) *test battery* assessing movement problems in children. Incorporates a revised version of the *Test of Motor Impairment*.

movement therapy Often a synonym for *dance therapy* – may refer more generally to *disjunctive therapy*.

MP *Morrisby Profile.*

MPACI *Millon Pre-Adolescent Clinical Inventory.*

MPQ *McGill Pain Questionnaire.*

MPT-R *Michigan Picture Test – Revised.*

MRAS *Morgan Russell Assessment Schedule.*

MRI *magnetic resonance imaging.*

M.S. *mean square.*

MSCA *McCarthy Scales of Children's Abilities.*

MSE *Mental Status Examination.*

MSI *Marital Satisfactory Inventory.*

MSQ (1) *Mental Status Questionnaire.* (2) *Minnesota Satisfaction Questionnaire.*

MSS *Manic State Scale.*

MTDDA *Minnesota Test for the Differential Diagnosis of Aphasia.*

multi-axial classification Classification of an item, illness, etc., on the basis of several distinct scales of measurement. The *Cattell Sixteen Personality Factor Questionnaire* and the DSM are examples of this.

multi-dimensional scaling (MDS) (1) Name for a range of statistical techniques for converting a large quantity of data (often ratings) into a small set of scales. (2) In graphical representations, using the physical space between points to denote the strength of the statistical relationship between the *variables* represented.

multi-infarct dementia (MID) A form of *dementia*, caused by the brain suffering a large number of *infants* ('miniature strokes'). Patients typically suffer a step-wise rather than gradual pattern of decline, and often have a history of cardiovascular problems.

multicollinearity *collinearity*.

multidimensional Consisting of many dimensions. The term is sometimes applied to complex statistical analyses (e.g. *factor analysis*) and to psychological tests (e.g. personality measures) where the results are expressed as a pattern of scores on several subtests, rather than a single test score (the latter being referred to as *unidimensional*).

Multidimensional Personality Evaluation Test of personality, consisting of 200 multiple choice question, yielding measures on 18 scales. Primarily intended for the layperson.

multidimensional scale See *unidimensional scale*.

Multilevel Academic Skills Inventory (MASI) Measure of performance.

Multilevel Academic Survey Tests (MAST) Measure of the performance of pupils with specific educational needs.

multimodal distribution See *mode*.

multimodal therapy Therapeutic technique in which the different problems of the patient are treated with different methods (following the argument that different techniques may be optimal in solving different problems). Compare with *eclectic therapy*.

multiple act criterion Combination of behaviours related to a single *trait*.

multiple baseline technique Experimental method in which participants; are measured on two or more *variables*. before treatment, where the variables: are known to be closely linked to a common cause (e.g. swearing and muscular tics in *Tourette's syndrome*). One or more variables are treated, but it is the effect on the untreated variables which is of primary interest.

multiple censoring See *single censoring*.

multiple correlation coefficient See *multiple regression*.

multiple cutoff model Method of *personnel screening* in which applicants are scored on a variety of scales pertaining to different aspects of the job. In order to be accepted, the candidate must score above a minimum criterion on all the scales. In a similar technique – the *multiple hurdle model* – the candidates are evaluated on a sequence of measures, with those failing to reach criterion at each 'hurdle' being eliminated.

multiple discriminant analysis *multiple regression* technique in which the *criterion variable* is a *categorical variable* with more than two categories.

multiple hurdle model See *multiple cutoff model*.

multiple personality Very rare *dissociative disorder* in which the patient can assume several, often radically different, personalities and identities, and may only be aware of whichever persona s/he is at the particular time (i.e. when s/he thinks s/he is person X, s/he has no memory of being person Y, etc.). Where there are only two personalities, then the term *alternating personality* is also used. Often confused (particularly by the popular media) with *schizophrenia*.

multiple regression A *regression* technique which calculates how much of the performance of one *variable* (the *criterion variable*) is predicted by performance on other variables (the *predictor variables*). The technique can be used to gain a better prediction of the criterion variable than is afforded by a 'conventional' regression, where only one predictor variable is used. The technique is also used to compare the relative predictive powers of the predictor variables in question. In a *free entry multiple regression (step-wise regression)* the analysis calculates which predictor variable has the strongest relationship with the criterion variable. The 'second best' predictor is selected because it, in tandem with the first-entered variable, increases the ability to predict the criterion variable by the greatest amount. This procedure is repeated for all the other predictor variables being considered. The purpose of the analysis is to see not only how well the predictor variables acting together can predict the criterion variable, but also if some of the predictor variables are significantly better predictors than others, once mutually shared *variance* has been taken into consideration. Usually, the analysis is stopped when the entry of the next predictor variable does not significantly improve the predictive power of the regression equation (this is measured using the **F-to-enter test**). In some versions of the procedure, predictor variables are entered into the equation, and then later removed, if other combinations of predictor variables prove to be better predictors, and make the contribution of the variable-to-be-removed unnecessary (removal is determined by the **F-to-remove test**). In an **ordered multiple regression (forced multiple regression)** a predictor variable is deliberately entered at a particular-position into the equation. Usually it is entered last, to see if it is still significantly related to the criterion variable, even after all the shared variance from the other predictor variables has been taken care of. This seems a rather odd technique, but it can be impressive if a predictor variable can still uniquely account for some of the variance even after other predictor variables have taken their share. The degree to which two predictor variables correlate with each other is known as **collinearity**. The correlation of the predictor variable(s) with the criterion variable is called the **multiple correlation coefficient (R)**. By squaring the value of R, the proportion of the criterion variable's variance which has been accounted for can be calculated. This is known as the **coefficient of determination (R^2)**. The increase in R^2 created by adding

another predictor variable into the equation is called the **R^2 increment**. The total variance accounted for by all of the predictor variables is known as the **coefficient of total determination**. The relationship between the predictor variables and the criterion variable can be expressed as an equation: $Y = a + b1x1 + b2x2.-.b_nxn$; where Y is the criterion variable, x the predictor variables, a is a *constant*, and b is known as the **regression weight**. The formula is essentially the same as the *regression equation*, but with more values of x. Regression weights are sometimes converted to **beta weights**, which are the weights expressed as *standard scores*. The multiple regression technique shares a lot in common with the *analysis of variance* (including the measure of *significance*). See *canonical regression*, *discriminant function analysis*, *polynomial regression*, and *residuals*.

Multiscore Depression Inventory (MDI) A measure of level of *depression*. The 'score' can be divided into 10 sub-scales.

multistage cluster sampling See *cluster sampling*.

multivariate analysis of variance (MA-NOVA) *analysis of variance* for which there are two or more *dependent variables*. Several *significance* tests are available – the *Hotelling-Lawley trace*, the *Pillai-Bartlett trace* and *Wilk's lambda*. Which test is best depends heavily upon very specific requirements (consultation with an advanced textbook is strongly advised), although with large samples, there is probably little difference between them.

multivariate correlation *correlation* between more than two *variables*.

multivariate normality A situation in which all the variables and all combinations of variables are normally distributed.

multivariate statistics Analysis of more than two *dependent variables*. Often the term is confined to mathematically complex analyses, such as *factor analysis, structural equation modelling*, etc. See *univariate statistics*.

Munchausen syndrome The feigning of medical illnesses in order to gain the attention of medical personnel.

Munchausen syndrome by proxy A rare permutation of *Munchausen syndrome*, in which the patient feigns illnesses in another person (or even inflicts injury to the extent of murdering his/her victim) in order to gain the attention of medical personnel. Usually the patient and victim are a mother and her young child, although in one notorious case in Britain, the patient (a nurse) murdered and permanently maimed babies in her care.

Murphy-Meisgeier Type Indicator for Children (MMTIC) Version of the *Myers-Bnggs Type Indicator* for children.

music therapy Any therapeutic technique in which listening to music forms part of the treatment. The term has been particularly applied to the use of music to stimulate people suffering from severe *mental retardation*, who may be incapable of comprehending conventional language.

mutation analysis *targeted mutation analysis*.

mutually exclusive event Event whose outcome excludes the occurrence of another event (e.g. if a coin lands 'heads', then this excludes 'tails' – hence 'heads' and 'tails' are mutually exclusive events).

mutually independent event *mutually exclusive event*.

Myers-Briggs Type Indicator (MBTI) A personality measure, based on *Jung's*

psychoanalytic theory. Participants are classified on four 'either/or' scales. E.g. in the first of these, a participant is classified as possessing either *extraversion (E)* or *introversion* (I). The second measure is of **Sensing (S)** versus **Intuition (N)**. The former is characterized by a predominant interest in the present situation, the latter by a predominant interest in more abstract concepts and the potential of the situation. The third measure is of **Thinking (T)** versus **Feeling (F)**, which measures the relative reliance on objective, logical thought versus a more subjective, emotional approach. The final distinction is between **Judging (J)** and **Perception (P)**. This is essentially a contrast between a wish to organize and a wish to observe events. Participants can be classified into 16 types according to their predominant scores on each scale (e.g. 1STJ, ENTJ, etc.), and each grouping is provided with a description of likely strengths and weaknesses.

myotatic reflex *spinal reflex* – if a tendon is briefly stretched, the muscles connected to it briefly contract. The most familiar demonstration of this is the knee jerk reflex. The purpose of the reflex in everyday life is to maintain balance. Usually sudden tendon stretching indicates that there is a potential imbalance, and the muscle contraction rectifies this.

mysophobia A *phobia* of dirt.

myxedema *myxoedema*.

myxoedema *bypothyroidism*.

MZ *monozygotic*.

MZ twins *monozygotic twins*.

MZa twins *monozygotic twins* who were brought up independently of each other.

MZt twins *monozygotic twins* who were brought up in the same household.

N

n Number of members of a sample.

N (1) *neuroticism.* (2) *Intuition.*

n-Ach *need for achievement.*

NA *negative affectivity.*

NABC *Normative Adaptive Behaviour Checklist.*

nAff *affiliation need.*

naive subject Test participant who has no knowledge of the devices used by an experimenter. Compare with *test wise subject.*

naloxone A *heroin antagonist.*

NAPI test *Neurobehavioural Assessment of the Preterm Infant.*

narcissistic personality disorder *personality disorder* characterized by extreme levels of self-interest and self-preoccupation.

narcissistic rage *aggression* directed at factors affecting self-esteem.

narcoanalysis Any therapeutic method in which the patient is sedated prior to treatment.

narrative recording Noting events of apparent importance (e.g. in an interview or therapeutic session).

narratophilia A *paraphilia* characterized by an abnormal reliance on pornographic stories for sexual gratification.

narremic substitution Misreading a word but maintaining the narrative thread of the text.

narrow categorizing See *broad categorizing.*

NART *National Adult Reading Test.*

National Adult Reading Test (NART) A list of words, most with very *irregular spellings*, which the participant is required to read out loud (i.e. to pronounce). The more words correctly pronounced, the higher the test score.

national competency tests Tests (usually government-run) used to assess academic achievement across the country.

natural category See *category.*

natural dichotomy See *dichotomous variable.*

natural experiment An event or series of events which occur in 'the real world' (as opposed to a contrived laboratory environment) without the experimenter's actions, but which in effect act as an experiment which can be studied and analysed. E.g. the classic study of people's reactions in the USA to Orson Welle's famous radio dramatization of 'War of the Worlds'.

naturalistic research (1) A rather nebulous term, describing research which emphasizes the study of the individual as a whole. This is in contrast to the 'traditional' scientific viewpoint of analysing a group of individuals to extract a common formula usually concerning a specific attribute. (2) More generally and usually, a study of participants in their natural surroundings. See *participant observation.*

NBAS *Neonatal Behavioural Assessment Scale.*

NBAS-K *Neonatal Behavioural Assessment Scale with Kansas Supplements.*

NCA *normal cognitive ageing.*

Neale Analysis of Reading Ability Reading test for participants aged 7–11 years. Consists of passages of text which the participant reads aloud. S/he is marked for number of mistakes, reading speed and comprehension of the passage. Additional diagnostic tests can be used to assess knowledge of grapheme-to-phoneme correspondence rules, ability to distinguish different word sounds, etc.

necessary condition A factor which must be present for a particular state to exist. This contrasts with a *sufficient condition*, which is in itself enough for a particular state to exist, but is not necessarily the only condition which can cause the state. E.g. a necessary condition for ice to form is that the temperature must be low enough. However this is not a sufficient condition – water must also be present. Shooting someone in the heart is a sufficient condition to kill them, but it is not a necessary condition (e.g. strangling, poisoning, etc., would be just as effective). It is possible to have permutations of the two conditions (e.g. necessary but not sufficient, sufficient but not necessary, etc.).

necraudia The sound of death.

necromania An abnormal interest in death.

necrophilia *atypical paraphilia* in which the patient gains principal sexual gratification from sexual activity with a corpse.

necrophobia A *phobia* of death or dying.

necrosmia The smell of death.

need A drive to fulfil a particular want, because the participant perceives that s/he has a lack of the desired object in question.

need for achievement (n-Ach) A *need* to succeed.

need for affiliation A *need* to be accepted and liked by others.

need for positive regard According to *Roger's self theory of personality*, a person's drive for *unconditional positive regard*.

need for power A *need* for power, and to attain control over others.

negative affectivity (NA) An emotional state in which one's perceptions and thoughts (often unrealistically) take a gloomy/negative view of events.

negative correlation See *correlation*.

negative goal gradient The phenomenon whereby the further one is from an aversive stimulus, the weaker the drive to increase the distance still further.

negative reinforcement Learning to perform an action because it removes an aversive stimulus.

negative relationship A relationship in which the rise in size of one variable is met with a decrease in size of another variable.

negative result Result which fails to find evidence for the hypothesis in question. Depending upon the circumstances, this can be good (e.g. negative results of a test for a deadly disease) or bad (a lengthy and expensive experiment not finding any *statistically significant results*). A *positive result* indicates the opposite – namely, evidence that the hypothesis is correct.

negative symptom A profound lack of a normal behaviour (e.g. *flat affect*). This contrasts with a *positive symptom*, which is an over-exaggerated behaviour (e.g. a *delusion*).

negatively skewed distribution *distribution curve* in which there is a long 'tail' on the left (i.e. nearer to the junction of the *X axis* and *Y axis*), rising to a pronounced 'hump' to the right. A *positively skewed distribution* is the opposite (i.e. the 'hump' is on the left, the 'tail' on the right).

neglect (1) Failure to attend. (2) The abnegation of care (e.g. *child neglect* etc.). (3) A literal inability to detect what would be very obvious to a normal individual, usually resulting from brain damage (e.g. *sensory neglect*, *spatial neglect*).

neo-Freudian movement Psychoanalysts, who, whilst accepting some of *Freud's psychoanalytic theory*, have amended it in significant areas. One of the principal characteristics has been a lessening of the emphasis on the *id*, and a greater concentration on the ego (hence the movement is often known as *ego psychology*). The most often cited examples of *psychoanalysis* after Freud are *Erikson's theory of development and Jung's psychoanalytic theory.*

NEO Personality Inventory Personality measure yielding five principal scales of measurement (*agreeableness*, 'conscientiousness', *extroversion*, *neuroticism*, and 'openness to experience'), and a further 23 sub-scales.

neobehaviourism Revision of *behaviourism* which acknowledges the need to include considerations of mental processes.

neolalia Language containing an abnormally high proportion of *neologisms*.

neologism A made-up word. Characteristic of some children learning to speak, some mentally ill patients (particularly *schizophrenics*) and most *cognitive* psychologists.

Neonatal Behavioural Assessment Scale (NBAS) *Brazelton Scale.*

Neonatal Behavioural Assessment Scale with Kansas Supplements (NBAS-K) See *Brazelton Scale.*

neonate Infant aged between 0 and 1 month.

neophasia A language composed of words and even grammar invented by the speaker. The phenomenon is encountered (in a pronounced form, very rarely) in some children learning to speak, and in some types of *schizophrenia*.

neophobia A *phobia* of new things.

neoplasm A new growth/tumour.

neopsychoanalytic *neo-Freudian movement.*

nerve Strictly speaking, a pathway and collection of *neurons* in the *peripheral nervous system*, all with the same function, and bonded together by connective tissue. However, the terms 'neuron' and 'nerve' are often used synonymously by psychologists. Compare with *tract*.

nervous breakdown A nebulous, layperson's term for any mental illness severe enough to incapacitate. Usually it is reserved for cases of *neurosis*.

nested design See *crossed design*.

neural Adjective derived from *neuron*, hence a term describing anything pertaining to the nervous system.

neuritic plaques *senile plaques.*

Neurobehavioural Assessment of the Preterm Infant (NAPI) *test battery* measuring the developmental maturity of preterm (premature) infants.

neurodermatitis *psychophysiological disorder* – the physical symptom is a skin rash.

neurofibrillary tangles (NFT) Clumps of dead central nervous system *neurons* which (under a microscope) look like knotted string. Caused by abnormal protein metabolism.

neurofibromatosis (Nf) Genetic disorder causing growths or tumours on nerves. Symptoms are variable, but in some instances may result in short attention span and *hyperactivity*.

neuroglia *glial cells.*

neuroimaging Any method of providing information on the structure and/or functions of the nervous system. *structual imaging* provides information on the physical structure of the nervous system (particularly the brain) and *functional imaging* provides information on its activities.

neuroleptic drug *major tranquillizer.*

neurolinguistic programming (NLP) Therapeutic method which is a combination of several disparate strands of thought, including linguistic research, information processing and mainstream therapeutic techniques. In essence, NLP seeks to train people to 'reprogramme' their brains to remove maladaptive behaviours. NLP has been heavily criticized by some researchers and therapists for what they claim is a lack of verifiable support and vague theoretical stance, whilst it is supported vociferously by others.

neurolinguistics The study of the relationship between neural functioning and linguistic skills.

neurological correlation A link between damage to a specific area of the brain and a specific change in behaviour.

Neurological Impairment Scale (NIS) A measure of symptoms of neurological dysfunction.

neurology The study of the structure, function and diseases of the nervous system.

neuron/neurone An individual component of a *nerve* or (very loosely) 'nerve cell'. Used by many psychologists as a synonym for 'nerve'. The basic unit of transmission in the nervous system.

neuronal *neural.*

neuropathology The study of disorders of structure and functioning of the nervous system.

neurophysiology The study of the physiology of the nervous system. The term is often used synonymously with *neurology.*

neuropsychiatry Branch of medicine concerned with the effects of nervous system (dys)function and structure on mental health.

neuropsychological testing Testing brain-damaged patients to assess the degree to which the physical damage has affected psychological functioning. Also, calculating from measures of psychological dysfunction which areas of the brain have been damaged.

neuropsychology The study of psychological processes in direct relationship to the workings of the nervous system (e.g. how physical brain damage affects psychological performance). This is sometimes expressed in the concept of *localization* – the theory that psychological functions can be attributed to specific areas of the brain.

neurosciences General term for any branch of study concerned with the scientific examination of the structure and function of the nervous system.

neurosis Nebulous term for any mental illness in which the patient still has a grasp of all or most of reality (unlike *psychosis*), but whose behaviour/beliefs are sufficiently abnormal to merit treatment. In addition, the complaint cannot be attributed solely to *mental retardation*, and probably causes serious negative emotions, in the patient and/or people who come into contact with him/her. A large collection of fairly disparate illnesses (i.e. practically all, the major exceptions being *mental retardation*, *schizophrenia*, and *bipolar disorder*) have been classified as 'neuroses' (principally for the historical reason that *psychoanalysis* classified them all as stemming from *anxiety*, although note that this theory is now largely discredited). It should be noted that some classification systems (e.g. some earlier versions of the DSM) do not recognize 'neurosis' as a valid categorization. In the DSM-HI the majority of what used to be termed 'neuroses' were re-classified as types of *anxiety disorder*.

neurosurgery Any surgical procedure intended to treat a dysfunction of the nervous system (including the brain).

neurosyphilis A degeneration of the nervous system due to the syphilis virus. Syphilis is a venereal disease which passes through two relatively innocuous phases, before lying apparently dormant for several months or (more usually) years. The disease then enters a third and final stage (*tertiary syphilis*), in which there is damage to the cardiovascular system and/or the nervous system (neurosyphilis). The symptoms include blindness, *syphilitic dementia*, and *tabes dosalis*.

neurotic The adjective derived from *neurosis*.

neurotic disorder *neurosis*.

neurotic process (1) In some theories, the conflict between the (impossibly perfect) *self-image* and the real self, which is held to cause *neurosis*. (2) *neurosis*.

neurotic solution Removing a *neurosis* by suppressing it from one's consciousness.

neuroticism (N) See *Eysenck's model of personality*.

neuroticism-emotional stability scale See *Eysenck's model of personality*.

neurotoxin Any substance or infection which is capable of damaging nerves and/or their functioning.

neurotransmitters Chemicals transmitted between *neurons* – the method by which neurons communicate with each other. The chemicals can also be released from neurons onto muscles or glands, affecting their functioning.

neutral stimulus Any stimulus which is intrinsically unlikely to either attract or repel the subject.

New Adult Reading Test Name given to an early version of the *National Adult Reading Test*.

new learning deficit Relative difficulty in learning new information, in comparison with older information and/or another group of people. Used by some commentators to describe the relative weakness of older people in learning a new piece of information and/or task.

New Sucher-Allred Reading Placement Inventory Reading test for 4–15-year-olds.

New Technology Tests (NTT) *aptitude test* of ability to work with computers.

Newman-Keuls test A *t test for multiple comparisons and post hoc test* for the *analysis of variance*.

Nf *neurofibromatosis*.

NFER Reading Tests A, AD and BD Reading tests which require participants to complete unfinished sentences. 'A' is designed for participants aged 6–8 years, 'AD', 8–10 years, 'BD', 7–10 years.

NFER Reading Tests EH A battery of three reading tests for participants aged 11–16: EH 1 measures *sentence completion*, EH2 comprehension and EH3 reading rate.

NFER Reading Tests SR-A and SR-B Reading tests, designed for participants aged 7–12. Both consist of *sentence completion* problems.

NFT, *neurofibrillary tangles*.

nicotine The active constituent in tobacco. Produces feelings of relaxation and mild euphoria, and is addictive.

nictophilia An abnormal preference for night.

nictophobia *achluophobia.*

Niemann-Pick disease Inherited failure to metabolize fat. Symptoms include *mental retardation.*

nihilism The belief that there is no meaning to life. This can be either a philosophical creed or a symptom of mental illness. In more severe manifestations of the latter, the patient believes that s/he and/or others have no real existence.

NINCDS-ADRDA criteria A set of criteria for evaluating the probability that a patient is suffering from *dementia of the Alzheimer type.* The initials refer to the 'National Institute of Neurological and Communicative Disorders and Stroke' and the 'Alzheimer's Disease and Related Disorders Association of America', the two bodies who jointly devised the scheme. It provides a diagnosis of 'probable', 'possible' or 'definite'.

NIS *Neurological Impairment Scale.*

NLP *neurolinguistic programming.*

NMR *nuclear magnetic resonance.*

no-trial learning See *Bandura's theory of social learning.*

nocebo A *placebo* which, the recipient is informed, has negative effects or side-effects. This can result in the recipient reporting unpleasant sensations.

nocturnal enuresis bed-wetting. See *enuresis.*

noise (1) Unwanted sound. (2) Random neural activity which can be confused with a genuine signal (see *signal detection analysis*).

nominal aphasia *anomic aphasia.*

nominal scale Scale in which each value represents a category, rather than a progression of values changing in size (e.g. an arbitrary grading in which 1 = male,

2 = female). See *interval scale, ordinal scale,* and *ratio scale.*

nominal variable *Variable* measured on a *nominal scale.*

nomological validity *construct validity,* although note that some commentators use the phrase to denote how well the test corresponds to wider theoretical considerations, rather than those purely assessed within the test.

nomothetic That which individuals have in common. Compare with *idiographic.*

non-additive interaction See *interaction.*

non-directional hypothesis Any hypothesis in which a difference is predicted, but not the direction in which it will fall. See *two-tailed test.*

non-directional significance A *significant* effect where its direction is unimportant (e.g. group A can have an average score which is significantly lower or higher than group B, provided that the difference is significant).

non-directive therapy *client-centred therapy.*

non-equivalent control group *control group* of participants who are selected completely separately from the *experimental group.* Because the two groups were not assigned randomly from the same population, this makes inferences about their performance difficult to make (e.g. differences between them could be due to factors beyond the experimenter's control, such as differences in upbringing).

non-fluent aphasia *Broca's aphasia,* or more generally, any *expressive aphasia.*

non-linear correlation See *linear correlation.*

non-linear regression *regression* in which there is a non-linear relationship between two variables. Calculations usually assume that the relationship will instead be a curved one. See *polynomial regression*.

non-linear relationship See *linear relationship*.

non-linear transformation See *linear transformation*.

non-parametric statistics Statistical techniques which make no presumptions about the nature of the distributions of the *populations* from which the data are derived. Contrast with *parametric statistics*.

non-projective personality test Measure of personality in which the participant answers a set of *limited response questions* which are scored using a *standardized scale*. Compare with *projective personality test*.

nonrandom measurement error See *random measurement error*.

non-reactive measure See *reactive measure*.

Non-Reading Intelligence Tests (NRIT) Set of three standardized tests (Level 1 for ages 6:4 months–8:3 months, Level 2, 7:4–9:3; Level 3, 8:4–10.11) presented orally, and assessing linguistic and cognitive abilities.

non-recursive mode See *path analysis*.

non-response (NR) Simply, not responding to a stimulus. The term is sometimes used of an (allegedly) characteristic phase of children's reading skills, in which the majority of errors take the form of non-responses, rather than misreadings of words, etc.

non-verbal behaviour *non-verbal communication*.

non-verbal communication (NVC) Information conveyed by means other than language. The term includes *body language*, but extends further to deliberate acts of communication (e.g. physical gestures).

non-verbal intelligence Any aspect of intelligence that does not overtly require linguistic skills in its performance.

non-zero sum game A game in which the gains of one player are not necessarily reflected in a loss by the other player (e.g. golfers can play together and get the same score). This contrasts with a *zero sum game*, in which the gain of one player means a loss for the other.

nonsense syllable Any syllable which does not form a real word. Memorizing lists of nonsense syllables is sometimes (somewhat erroneously) used as a test of 'pure' memory, because the syllables supposedly have no associations which could be used as 'aides memoires'.

nonsense words Words which either are not recognizably part of the language when spoken or written, or are not recognizable when written, but when spoken aloud, sound like a real word (e.g. 'phrock'). Such words can only be read by 'sounding them out'.

Noonan syndrome Genetic disorder characterized by stunted stature, widely spaced, sloping eyes, and atypically low ears. There may be numerous other atypical physical features. Individuals with the syndrome typically have relatively mild intellectual impairments and problems with hearing and speech.

noradrenergic system Network of *neurons* using noradrenaline as their *neurotransmitter*. Primarily used in the control of smooth muscle.

norm The typical standard(s) of a group or *population*.

norm group *standardization sample*.

norm referenced test Test for which the average scores for the *population* are known (and hence which may serve as a guide to the quality of the participants' performance). See *domain referenced test*.

normal (1) State of being considered unexceptional on any attribute when compared with the standard of the population. (2) Not possessing the problem faced by a patient group being cited as a comparison (e.g. in observing patients with *schizophrenia*, a *control group* may be a collection of individuals who are not diagnosed as mentally ill). The term is a convenient shorthand, but should not be taken as a value judgement.

normal cognitive ageing (NCA) See *mild cognitive impairment*.

normal curve The shape of the *normal distribution* when plotted as a graph.

normal curve equivalent Expression of a test score in terms of its position on a distribution curve of *standardized test* scores (i.e. where the scorer is placed relative to the rest of the population).

normal distribution A *frequency distribution* with the following characteristics: (1) it is symmetrical and bell-shaped, with its 'peak' pointing away from the *X axis*; (2) the *mean, median*, and *mode* are equal. Because the frequency distribution of a great many *continuous variables* (e.g. height, weight, IQ, etc.) assume this pattern, it has been accepted as the norm (hence its name). However, this does not mean that other shapes of distributions are somehow 'aberrant'. See *standard deviation*.

normal pressure hydrocephalus Caused by the failure of *cerebrospinal fluid* to drain away, leading to a destructive pressure on brain tissue. The complaint can lead to *demented* symptoms.

normalization (-isation) In statistics, mathematically manipulating a set of data so that it assumes a *normal distribution* (and hence can be analysed by parametric tests). Common methods include taking the logarithms of the data (*log transformation*), the reciprocals (*reciprocal transformation*), the square (*square transformation*) and the square roots (*square roots transformation*). Which procedure is adopted very much depends on the nature of the individual data set. E.g. severe *positive skew* is corrected using a negative reciprocal root, a moderate positive skew using a log transformation or the square root, moderate *negative skew* by squaring the values and severe negative skew by cubing the values.

normative (1) That which defines what is *normal*. E.g. 'normative data' describe the types of data readings one would normally expect to find. (2) That which determines the correct or appropriate standards.

Normative Adaptive Behaviour Checklist (NABC) Measure of adaptive skills, both intellectual and housekeeping, for subjects aged 0–21 years.

normative test Any measure that enables the scores of different individuals to be compared.

NOS *not otherwise specified*.

nosological Pertaining to the classification of disease.

nosology The classification of diseases.

nosophobia *pathophobia*.

not otherwise specified (NOS) As a suffix to a description of a disorder or an illness – a condition in which the patient's symptoms identify his/her illness as belonging within a general category but not as matching named diseases within that category.

Nowicki-Strickland Locus of Control Scale Measure of concept of self-assurance, designed for children and young adults.

NR *non-response.*

NRIT *Non-Reading Intelligence Tests.*

NTT *New Technology Tests.*

nuchal rigidity Unnaturally tense neck muscles. It can be a symptom of *meningitis.*

nuclear conflict See *Erikson's theory of development.*

nuclear magnetic resonance (NMR) A method of scanning an organ (e.g. the brain), producing three-dimensional images. The section of the body in question is stimulated with a magnetic field, and the resultant changes in the magnetic orientation of the cells are recorded.

nuclear schizophrenia *process schizophrenia.*

null hypothesis (Ho) The assumption that there will be no difference and/or relationship discovered in the statistical test which is to be conducted. See *alternative hypothesis* and *significance.*

number completion test A *completion test* in which the subject must supply the number missing from a numerical sequence. The test is a measure of numerical and logical abilities, and more generally, *fluid intelligence.*

numerator In a fraction, the numerator is the number above the line, and the denominator is the one below it. E.g. in the fraction 1/2 – '1' is the numerator, and '2' the denominator.

NVC *non-verbal communication.*

nymphomania A grossly excessive desire by a woman for sexual activity. Despite the sexist jokes on the subject, the condition is not a happy one, not least because, by implication, the patient is never fulfilled by her encounters. See *satyriasis.*

O *openness.*

object assembly test A sub-test of the *Wechsler* intelligence tests, and a generic name for similar measures. The participant is given 'jigsaw'-like pieces which have to be assembled to form a picture.

object blindness *agnosia.*

Object Memory Evaluation (OME) Measure of memory for objects. The participant is presented with a set of everyday objects, and is asked to recall them at short (30 or 60 seconds) and long (5 minutes) intervals. Five learning trials are given, and measures are taken of which items are recalled on which trial (and which are not).

object relations The relationship between the internal mental world and external reality, how *significant others* have shaped the formation of this internal world, and how this in turn affects relationships with the real (external) world. The theory has been developed particularly in *psychoanalysis.*

Object Relations Technique (ORT) *protective* test in which the participant interprets a series of ambiguous pictures.

objective test (1) Test whose questions have definite right and wrong answers. (2) Test which, in its marking, is not reliant on subjective interpretation. Some commentators add the additional caveat that the participants must not be able to discern the purpose of the test (hence preventing biased responses, in an attempt to create a favourable impression). See *open-ended test.*

objectivity (of test) The degree to which a test is immune to the subjective biases of the person administering it.

oblique factor analysis See *factor analysis.*

oblique solution The solution derived from an *oblique factor analysis*.

observational learning *modelling*.

observational research Research in which participants or items are observed without any attempt to interact with and/or alter the behaviour of the participants/items.

observed score *raw score*.

observed variable *dependent variable*.

observer bias The tendency of observers to make judgements (usually unconsciously) in favour of a preferred outcome.

observer drift The tendency of two or more observers to become more in agreement in subjective judgements the longer they work together.

observer scale Any measure which is formed from observations by a person of someone else (e.g. by a doctor of a patient). The term often carries the implication that a *behaviour checklist* is involved.

observing ego In some *psychoanalytic* theories, the aspect of the ego involved in rationally interpreting the therapeutic process, whilst the *experiencing ego* is the 'part' of the ego which undergoes the therapeutic transformation.

Observing Pupils and Teachers in Classrooms (OPTIC) An observation schedule for assessing the positivity and/or negativity of teachers' responses to pupils (Section A), and the degree to which pupils are attending to the lesson's set tasks (Section B).

obsession A recurrent set of ideas which the patient cannot 'get out of his/her head', and which are often irrational.

obsessional personality A rather nebulous term for a character type prone to *obsessions*, and pedantry. In a severe form, the term is synonymous with *obsessive-compulsive disorder*.

obsessive-compulsive disorder One of the *anxiety states*. The patient is 'captured' by recurrent thoughts s/he cannot 'get out of his/her head' and/or feels compelled constantly to repeat the same act (e.g. repeatedly washing one's hands, having to go through a set routine before going out of the house).

obtained score *raw score*.

obtrusive observation Study in which the participants are aware that they are being observed. This contrasts with **unobtrusive observation**, in which they are unaware.

O'Connor Finger Dexterity Test See *pegboard task*.

Occam's razor *parsimony principle*.

occipital lobes The region of the *cerebral cortex* roughly in the region of the 'back of the head'. Their principal function is in visual perception.

occupational drinking The 'requirement' to drink large quantities of alcoholic beverages as part of one's job (e.g. a business person entertaining clients).

Occupational Interest Checklist (ICL) Questionnaire used in careers guidance. The participants list their interests and general ambitions, which are matched against the typical profiles of members of various occupational groups.

occupational neurosis *neurosis* induced by the patient's occupation (e.g. because it is stressful, or because the person is not suited to the job, etc.).

Occupational Personality Questionnaires (OPQ). Measure of a person's skills and personality used to assess suitability for a variety of occupations.

occupational psychology The study of psychology of the workplace, and the use of psychological methods to change the workplace (e.g. selection of personnel through psychological tests, and the use of *ergonomics* to improve working practices). The related discipline of the examination and improvements of relationships within a working environment (e.g. methods of communication between management and workers) is sometimes called 'occupational psychology', but is better classified as **organizational psychology**.

Occupational Stress Indicator (OSI) Measure of level of stress being experienced by an employee, and its likely effects on the employee and the organization.

occupational therapy The use of practical or creative tasks for a therapeutic purpose. E.g. to provide long-term patients with tangible goals (thereby providing a sense of purpose and counteracting boredom) and to help injured patients learn to recover function in injured limbs, etc.

OCEAN *five factor model of personality.*

ochlophobia *demophobia.*

Ockham's razor *Occam's razor.*

oculomotor cranial nerve cranial nerve number III. Concerned, along with the *abducens cranial nerve* and the *trochlear cranial nerve* with the muscular movements of the eye (compare with *optic cranial nerve*).

ODD *oppositional defiant disorder.*

odd-even technique *split-half correlation*, in which the odd-numbered items on a test are correlated with the even-numbered items.

odd man out question Common question in intelligence (particularly *fluid intelligence*) tests. Participants must select an item which does not belong to the same category as the rest of the items displayed.

odd man out test See *Assessing Reading Difficulties.*

oddity task *odd man out question.*

oedema The excessive accumulation of fluid in tissues. Following a *stroke*, such accumulation in the brain can occur, causing death of brain cells in the afflicted area with a concomitant loss of psychological functioning.

Oedipus complex See *Freud's psychoanalytic theory.*

offloading (Mis)using therapeutic situations as an excuse simply to talk to relieve tension.

olfactory cranial nerve *cranial nerve* number I, primarily concerned with smell.

olfactory evoked potential *evoked potential* created by administering a smell to the subject.

oligoencephaly *mental retardation* resulting from an abnormally small brain.

ombrophobia A *phobia* of rain.

OME *Object Memory Evaluation.*

omission training The removal of a reward if an undesirable behaviour is exhibited (i.e. the participant does not have to do anything to get the reward, other than simply not do a particular act).

ondansetron Drug whose effects include the enhanced release of acetylcholine (see *cholinergic hypothesis*) and thus a potentially beneficial treatment of some forms of *dementia*. See *ganglioside* and *tacrine*.

one sample runs test *non-parametric* measure of whether a sequence of events with only two possible outcomes significantly deviates from chance. The test is used on *mutually exclusive events* with only two possible outcomes (e.g. coin tosses, possession or lack of a particular attribute, etc.). Different formulae and tables are used depending on whether the size of the run is greater or lower than 20 events.

one sample t statistic *parametric* test estimating the *mean* and parameters of the *population* from which a sample is drawn.

one sample t test A measure to determine if a sample of *normally distributed* data is drawn from a particular population.

one sample test Statistical measure to determine whether a sample is derived from a particular *population*.

one-tailed test See *two-tailed test*.

onomatomania Disorder in which the patient is unable to stop thinking about a particular word or set of words.

onomatophobia A *phobia* of a particular word or phrase.

onset The time or time period when an illness first manifested itself.

ontogenesis Can be synonym for *ontogeny*, but can also refer to growth of a particular aspect or part of the individual.

ontogeny The growth of the individual. See *ontogenesis* and *phylogeny*.

open coding Coding data without restricting coding to a limited set (e.g. not just paying attention to data that are instances of a specific concept).

open-ended test Test whose answers cannot be totally objectively classified as definitely right, or definitely wrong. E.g. a question such as 'what is the capital of the United Kingdom?' has only one correct answer. However, a question such as 'how can one solve the ills of the British economy?' is open-ended, because there is a practically infinite range of answers. Contrast with *objective test*.

open question See *closed question*.

open system Any system which is affected by external forces.

openness (O) Personality *trait* (one of the 'Big Five') measuring the degree to which the participant is prepared to seek out and cope with the unfamiliar.

operant behaviour (1) Voluntary behaviour performed in order to attain a reward. (2) *emitted behaviour*.

operant conditioning Broadly, the training of a participant to perform a particular act by rewarding him/her for doing it or to stop an act by punishing him/her. The basis of much of *behaviour therapy*.

operational definition A description of a process, providing details of materials and how they must be used (i.e. a 'recipe').

operator-machine system Any working process in which a human operator uses a machine.

opiate receptors See *opiates*.

opiates Group of drugs derived from or similar in structure to opium. Principal amongst these are **opium** (extracted from the juice of the opium poppy); **morphine** (synthesized from opium), **codeine** and **heroin** (both synthesized from morphine). All are taken up by **opiate receptors** in the brain. The drugs have excellent pain-killing properties and induce euphoria (hence their legal use for patients in extremes of pain), but they are also addictive. The body also produces its own opiates (though their effects are milder) called **opioid peptides**.

opioid peptides See *opiates*.

opium See *opiates*.

opportunistic sampling Gathering a sample of participants from a particular *population* by taking whoever is available at the time. This does not necessarily result in a *biased sample*, but in most student reports, the term is a euphemism for 'I got my friends to act as subjects'.

opposites test Any measure in which the participant must either supply the opposite of a word presented by the experimenter, or must identify pairs of opposites from a list of alternatives.

oppositional defiant disorder (ODD) Atypically pronounced defiant and aggressive behaviour.

OPQ *Occupational Personality Questionnaires.*

OPTIC *Observing Pupils and Teachers in Classrooms.*

optic aphasia A profound difficulty in naming objects which have only been seen.

optic cranial nerve *cranial nerve* number II. Concerned with vision, particularly information from the retina.

oral fluency The ability to speak fluently on a given topic.

oral personality According to *Freud's psychoanalytic theory*, personality type caused by a *fixation* at the *oral stage*.

oral reading Reading aloud (e.g. pupil reading to the teacher, experimenter, etc.).

oral stage See *Freud's psychoanalytic theory*.

orbital cortex Area of *frontal lobe* responsible for controlling social behaviour, observing proprieties, etc.

order (of regression) See *first order regression, second order regression* etc.

order effect (1) A biasing of results resulting from a particular order of presentation of test items. See *counterbalancing* and *fixed order presentation*. (2) The phenomenon whereby in a long test session performance of later tests

may be lowered because of fatigue. (3) *Practice effect*.

order of magnitude (1) An arrangement of values in order of their size. (2) Ten times bigger or smaller.

order statistics Any statistical method which analyses data arranged on an *ordinal scale*.

ordered multiple regression See *multiple regression*.

ordered recall A memory task in which items have to be recalled in exactly the order in which they were originally presented. Compare with *free recall*.

ordinal interaction Form of *interaction* in which a graph of the results displays lines which do not cross over. In a *disordinal interaction*, the lines cross over.

ordinal scale Scale in which items are ranked according to a characteristic (e.g. order of finishing in a race), but in which the magnitude of the difference between the items is not recorded (e.g. the gap between first and second place could just as easily be two seconds as two hours). See *interval scale, nominal scale,* and *ratio scale*.

ordinal variable *Variable* measured on an *ordinal scale*.

ordinate *Y axis*.

orectic Pertaining to emotion.

organic affective syndrome *organic mental disorder* (or, by the DSM's criteria, an *organic brain syndrome*) characterized by a profound alteration of mood.

organic brain syndrome See *organic mental disorder*.

organic delusional state *Organic mental disorder* (or, by the DSM's criteria, an *organic brain syndrome*) characterized by *delusions* resulting from brain damage.

organic hallucinosis *Organic mental disorder* (or, by the DSM's criteria, an *organic brain syndrome*) characterized by *hallucinations* resulting from brain damage.

organic mental disorders (1) General term for a group of mental illnesses whose cause can be linked to physical damage or impairment to the brain (see *functional mental disorder*). The damage can be of any nature – common sources are physical blows to the head, tumours, and poisoning by an excess of hormones or drugs. (2) The DSM system uses a rather tighter definition of organic mental disorders (NB in DSM-IV they are given the unwieldy title of ***Delirium, Dementia, Amnesia and other Cognitive Disorders***), reserving the term for illnesses which can be linked to a specific cause, and contrasts this with ***organic brain syndrome***, where the illness can be linked to brain damage, although using existing technology, measures record, at the most, only slight physical damage. By the DSM-III's criteria, organic mental disorders include most of the *dementias* (notably *dementia of the Alzheimer type* and *multi-infarct dementia*), and disorders resulting from *substance abuse*; whilst organic brain syndrome encompasses e.g. *acute confusional state, Addison's disease, amnestic syndrome, Cushing's syndrome, hyperthyroidism, hypothyroidism, Korsakoff's syndrome, organic affective syndrome, organic delusional syndrome, organic hallucinosis, organic personality syndrome,* and *Wernicke's dementia*.

organic personality syndrome *organic mental disorder* (or, by the DSM's criteria, an *organic brain syndrome*) characterized by a severe personality change, resulting from brain damage.

organic therapy Any physical method of treatment.

organism In some therapies, the word has a special meaning. See *Roger's self theory of personality*.

organismic *endogenous*.

organizational coping strategy A therapeutic regime designed to reduce *stress* or other deleterious psychological effects in groups (usually of employees). See *individual coping strategy*.

organizational psychology See *occupational psychology*.

orgone therapy Therapeutic technique devised by Wilhelm Reich (psychotherapist). The methodology revolved around the theory of the 'orgone', a particle of 'life force', which was accumulated and then released through sex. Mental health problems were held to occur because not enough orgones were accumulated, and/or they weren't released properly. The therapy consisted of various rituals of massage, etc., and of the 'orgone accumulator' – a metal lined box which supposedly accumulated orgones, and in which the orgone-deprived patient sat. The therapy is reminiscent of some of the wilder excesses of the South Sea Bubble (although in fairness, some successes were claimed for the technique) and since Reich's death in the 1950s, has been largely abandoned.

orgonomy *orgone therapy*.

Orleans-Hanna test Test of potential ability at algebra – the test measures ability to process symbolic representations.

ORT *Object Relations Technique*.

orthogonal Unrelated.

orthogonal factor analysis See *factor analysis*.

orthogonal solution The solution derived from an *orthogonal factor analysis*.

orthomolecular psychiatry The school of thought, founded by Linus Pauling, that mental illness can be attributed to problems in the chemical balance of the body and the brain. Therapy includes taking enormous quantities of vitamins (hence its other, less serious, name of *megavitamin therapy*). In spite of the late Professor Pauling's undoubted abilities (he was twice a Nobel Prize-winner), the theory has not met with universal acceptance.

orthopsychiatry The study of prevention of mental illness.

OSI *Occupational Stress Indicator.*

osmophobia A *phobia* of smells.

Othello syndrome *delusional jealousy.*

outcome research Assessing the effectiveness of a treatment.

outlier Participant whose scores differ appreciably from those of the rest of his/her group. This may indicate that something went wrong with his/her testing and/or the scoring procedure. Accordingly, there may be grounds for excluding the participant from the analysis. However, exclusion of outliers should not take place solely because they mar an otherwise conveniently neat set of findings.

outlying case *outlier.*

outplacement counselling The provision of *counselling* to individuals or groups faced with redundancy. It is usually a combination of helping to cope with the emotional blow and assisting with finding a new job.

overachievement Performing appreciably better at a (usually scholastic) task than would be predicted from *aptitude tests*. In contrast, *underachievement* is performing far worse than would be predicted.

overanxious disorder An *anxiety disorder* restricted to children. Principal symptoms include *generalized anxiety* (the DSM-IV classifies overanxious disorder as a sub-set of generalized anxiety), and an abnormal concern about scholastic performance and the future in general.

Overcoming Depression Computerized programme designed to help lower *depression* levels in patients using it.

overcontrolled behaviour Behavioural problem (particularly in children), in which apprehension about an event, person, etc., controls their lives to the point of creating *anxiety* and/or *depression*.

overcorrection Therapeutic method of counteracting the wrong behaviour pattern by following it with intensive practice of the correct method.

overinclusive language Using too wide a range of references in speech, rather than sticking to the main point. The disorder is found in *schizophrenia*.

overlapping longitudinal study An attempt to overcome the pitfalls of the *cross-sectional research* and *longitudinal research* methods. Different age groups of participants are tested and compared, and then retested some time (usually years) later. At each testing, the different age groups can be compared, as in a *cross-sectional study* (e.g. a group of 40-year-old participants can be compared with a group of 60-year-old participants). Also, however, the same age cohort's scores can be compared across test periods (e.g. and the scores of a group of participants who were 40 on the first test session and 60 on the next can be compared). This enables researchers to keep a check on possible *cohort effects*. E.g. suppose that on retesting, the 40-year-old participants have scores 20% higher than the 60-year-old participants. This might seem to indicate an age decline. However, suppose it is found that the scores of the 60-year-old group, when they were 40, were only 5% higher. This indicates that a principal cause of the difference is not ageing per se, but rather that the two age groups have been reared differently. Finally, a *time-lag comparison* is possible (i.e. each age cohort's scores can be compared as they reach the same age).

overt behaviour Aspects of behaviour which can be measured; the way the participant presents him/herself to the rest of the world.

overt compulsion See *compulsion*.

OWLS tests Set of measures of various aspects of linguistic skills in younger children.

own-control research *ABA design*.

P

p (1) *probability*. (2) *significance/significance level*.

P (1) Psychotism. (2) Perception.

P-3 *Pain Patient Profile*.

P technique A *factor analysis* method for examining how consistently a participant's pattern of behaviour is maintained across different testing conditions.

Pa scale See *Minnesota Multiphasic Personality Inventory*.

Padua Inventory Measure of *obsessive-compulsive* behaviour.

paedolalia infantile speech.

paedophilia *paraphilia* in which the (adult) patient has a desire to have sex

with children or teenagers under the age of consent (most often the desired individuals are pre-pubertal).

Pain Assessment Questionnaire (PAQ) Questionnaire measuring the degree to which chronic pain sufferers experience subjective discomfort.

Pain Patient Profile (P-3) Measure of factors relevant to a patient's experience of chronic pain.

paired associate learning Remembering which item was previously presented with which (e.g. the participant sees the words 'cat' and 'briefcase' presented together, and later when shown 'cat' must recall 'briefcase').

paired comparison (1) Statistical test examining differences between members of *paired samples*. (2) Psychological measure, in which the participant compares every item in a set of stimuli with every other item in the set (e.g. for brightness, aesthetic value, etc.).

paired comparison ranking See *ranking*.

paired sample Form of *matching*, in which participants are matched, so that the scores of one participant are directly compared with those of the other. Participants matched in this way must be very similar indeed to justify this one-to-one comparison. A common use of the method is in comparing the same participant at two different times (e.g. before and after treatment).

paired t test See *t test*.

palilalia Disordered speech characterized by the persistent repetition of the same information.

palinopsia A disorder of visual perception, in which items are seen as remaining after they have actually disappeared from view.

palsy (1) Now largely superseded term for paralysis. (2) Paralysis accompanied by hand tremors.

panel study (1) Study of a group (a panel) of participants, usually over a period of time. Participants may share a particular characteristic (in which case it is more accurately called a *cohort study*), but more usually, they are selected simply because they are able and willing to come to the test sessions. (2) Not necessarily at odds with definition (1), the term is also often applied to a body of participants who are willing to experience fairly aversive test procedures (e.g. injections, drug treatments, etc.).

panic attack See *panic disorder.*

panic disorder One of the *anxiety states.* Characterized by frequent *panic attacks* – in addition to feelings of severe apprehension, there are sensations of not being in control, and physical symptoms of shallowness of breath, dizziness, chest pains, etc.

panophobia A *phobia* of everything.

pantophobia *panophobia.*

PAQ (1) *Pain Assessment Questionnaire.* (2) *Position Analysis Questionnaire.*

paradigm (1) An experimental method usually employed to demonstrate or investigate a particular concept or phenomenon. (2) A theoretical model.

paradoxical injunction *paradoxical intention.*

paradoxical intention Therapeutic technique employed most notably in *logotherapy.* The patient is placed in a (usually exaggerated form of a) situation of which s/he is afraid or embarrassed, and by going through with it, comes to terms with the fact that

choices can be made and acted upon. E.g. a (probably apocryphal) story concerns a man shy of looking people in the eye who was instructed to enter a pharmacy, look the assistant in the eye, and ask if the shop stocked smaller condoms because the normal ones were too big for him.

paraesthesia Subjective impression of sensations on the skin (e.g. burning, tickling, etc.) although no physical alteration of the skin has occurred. The sensation has several causes, including drug side-effects, and *conversion disorder.* When the condition is coupled with *epilepsy*, it is known as *sensory epilepsy.*

parageusia An illusory or abnormally distorted sense of taste.

paragnosia clairvoyance.

paralalia The persistent substitution of sounds within a word.

paralexia (1) A misreading of words. (2) A form of *dyslexia* where there is a high frequency of such errors.

parallel forms (of a test) Different versions of the same test, with equal predictive powers (see *alternate form reliability*). They are employed because, if a participant needs to be repeatedly tested on the same skill, using different versions of the same measure minimizes the *practice effect.*

parallel forms reliability *alternate form reliability.*

Parallel Spelling Tests (PST) Spelling test for children aged 6–13 years. The test uses blocks of sentences drawn from a large set, and by using different combinations, a wide variety of test blocks can be created.

paralog A *nonsense word* of two syllables.

paralogia Illogical language.

paralysis agitans *Parkinson's disease.*

paralytic dementia *paresis.*

parametric statistics Statistical methods which presume that the data being analysed come from *populations* with particular sets of characteristics (parameters). Typically (but not invariably), it is assumed that the data are *continuous variables*, and come from populations with a *normal distribution*. Examining data which are derived from populations with the 'wrong' characteristics for the test in question will produce spurious *significance* values, because, inter alia, the *sampling distributions* will be inappropriate. See *non-parametric statistics.*

paramimia An impaired ability to perform gestures.

paramnesia An incorrect or entirely false memory. Sometimes applied to a déjà vu experience.

paranoia Irrational feelings of persecution and/or of self-importance.

paranoid disorder Irrational suspicion of persecution or of being deceived by others.

paranoid personality disorder *personality disorder* characterized by an irrational suspicion of other people's motives, leading to a secretive and unemotional personality.

paranoid pseudocommunity A group of people who believe the arguments of a patient suffering from *paranoia.*

paranoid schizophrenia See *schizophrenia.*

paranosic gain A direct benefit from being ill (e.g. avoiding work). See *epinosic gain.*

paranosis *paranosic gain.*

paraparesis Weakness in the legs, resulting from neural damage.

paraphasia A profound misuse of words.

paraphemia Habitual misuse of words and/or phonemes.

paraphilia A group of *psychosexual disorders,* in which the patient solely or principally gains sexual gratification from activities and items either forbidden by societal conventions, or which would not elicit such extreme responses in an average person. See *atypical paraphilia, ecoutism, exhibitionism, fetishism, masochism, paedophilia, sadism, transvestism,* and *voyeurism.*

paraphobia See *phobia.*

paraphonia Abnormal voice production.

paraphrasia *paraphasia.*

paraphrenia *paranoid schizophrenia.*

paraphrenic schizophrenia *paranoid schizophrenia.*

paraphresia *parosmia.*

paraplegia See *hemiplegia.*

parapraxis A minor slip of the tongue or pen, or moment of absent-mindedness.

parapsychology The study of psychological phenomena falling outside the confines of conventional scientific theory and experience (e.g. *extrasensory perception, psychokinesis*). There is a body of respectable and rigorously executed research in this area, but, unfortunately, it is overshadowed by a mass of 'pop psychology' with little or no experimental rigour. Perhaps because of this, in the popular imagination the field is often (unfairly) associated with people who also have interesting ideas about the Loch Ness Monster and the whereabouts of Elvis Presley.

parasexuality Any form of sexual activity or predilection considered abnormal by the society in which it is practised.

parasomnia A disorder of sleep, or disorder which occurs during sleep.

parasuicide Attempted (but unsuccessful) suicide; self-inflicted but not fatal harm.

parataxis Lack of integration of thoughts and/or emotions.

parathymia *inappropriate affect.*

paratypic Caused by the environment.

parent distribution The *population* distribution.

parent ego state See *transactional analysis.*

Parenting Stress Index (PSI) Measure of parenting abilities of parents with children aged under 10 years. The test identifies aspects of parenting which are under stress, and of potential problems which might result.

paresis Neurological disorder, characterized by partial paralysis or complete paralysis (**general paresis**) and *dementia.*

paresthesia *paraesthesia.*

parietal lobes The region of the *cerebral cortex* which occupies an area contiguous with a hairband across the head. Their role is hard to concisely define, but they can be said to be involved in maintaining an awareness of the body's state and location, and in interpreting symbols (e.g. object recognition and some aspects of reading).

Parkinsonism (1) A set of symptoms strongly akin to those of *Parkinson's disease*, although they are present in other disorders of psychological and/or neurological functioning. (2) *Parkinson's disease.*

Parkinson's disease (PD) *organic mental disorder*, characterized by severe muscular trembling in resting muscles, and *akinesia*. In later stages walking is reduced to a characteristic shuffle. Patients are often depressed, and a sizeable proportion are also intellectually impaired. Symptoms of Parkinson's disease are found in patients suf-

fering from many of the *dementias*. Causes of the illness are several, but a lack of dopamine in the *substantia nigra* within the brain has been cited as a key factor.

parmia Cattell's term for a personality *trait* corresponding to degree of adventurousness.

parosmia Impaired sense of smell.

parosphresia *parosmia.*

paroxetine Type of *selective serotonin re-uptake inhibitor* drug.

parsimony principle The general principle that in explaining an experimental finding, the simplest explanation should be preferred.

part correlation *semi-partial correlation.*

partial correlation A technique for assessing how much of the *correlation* between two *variables* is due to the coincidental effect of a third variable. E.g. suppose that a high correlation is found between children's feet sizes and their maths ability. This could be taken to mean that being good at maths makes your feet grow (or vice versa). However, a more plausible explanation is that the relationship is due to a coincidental factor – namely, that older children tend both to have bigger feet and to be better at maths tests than younger children. In order to demonstrate this, a partial correlation would calculate how much of the correlation between feet size and maths score was due to this third variable of age, and demonstrate the extent to which feet and maths were still related once the coincidental effect of age had been accounted for. The technique has certain similarities with *analysis of covariance*. The difference lies in the fact that analysis of covariance assesses whether differences between groups remain after allowing for a third variable, whilst partial correlation assesses whether any relationship between them is still present. See *correlation* and *semi-partial correlation*.

partialled out The process whereby the coincidental effect of a third variable is mathematically removed from the *correlation* between two variables. See *partial correlation* and *correlation*.

participant A person who participates in an experiment. In many statistical texts and older psychological writings, the term **subject** is used instead. Generally, psychology journal and book editors now prefer 'participant' because it is thought to be more neutral sounding and thus less offensive, but often 'subject' is still used when referring to statistical analyses.

participant observation Experimental method in which the experimenter 'disguises' him/herself as one of the group of participants to be studied in order to gain greater insight, closer observations, etc. See *action research* and *naturalistic research* (definition 2).

partile A division of a sample into equal sizes (e.g. *quartiles*).

parturiphobia A *phobia* of childbirth.

passing stranger effect The phenomenon whereby some people are willing to talk about their problems with complete strangers whom they meet for a brief while, and know they will never meet again, whilst they would never do this with closer associates, therapists, etc.

passive-aggressive personality disorder *personality disorder* characterized by avoiding obeying other people's requests (the avoidance is felt by some theorists to be a substitute for being aggressive and refusing altogether). Note that the DSM-IV has removed the definition from its list.

passive-dependent personality disorder *dependent personality disorder*.

passive therapy See *active therapy*.

Patau's syndrome Genetic disorder characterized by intellectual dysfunction (may vary from relatively mild to severe in individual cases).

path analysis Complex technique for analysing causal links from *correlations* between *variables*, both directly, and indirectly through other variables. The variables can be single measures, or several measures grouped together (e.g. a 'mathematical skills' variable could simply be a score on a single mental arithmetic test, or alternatively, a battery of tests of different maths skills). The experimental hypothesizes is that links between variables fall in particular directions – in a **recursive model**, all influences fall in one direction only (e.g. A can affect B, but B cannot affect A). In a **non-recursive model**, the influences can be mutual (though not necessarily equally strong in both directions). The relationships between variables are traditionally expressed with a diagram, in which the names of the variables are linked by arrows, and the strength of the relationship is expressed as a **path coefficient** (expressed as a *correlation coefficient*, or as the number of *standard deviations* by which one variable alters when the other variable changes by 1 standard deviation) printed above the arrow. The direction of the arrow indicates the direction of the relationship (e.g. A→B indicates that A influences B, but not vice versa). A straight arrow means that the experimenter has identified the nature of the causal link. A curved double-headed arrow indicates that a link has been identified, but the direction of its causality is as yet uncertain. It should also be noted that the technique requires a degree of subjective judgement in deciding which measures should be grouped together as variables.

path coefficient See *path analysis.*

pathognomonic symptoms Symptoms which are typical of a particular disease.

pathological gambling An *impulse disorder* – the patient has an irresistible urge to gamble.

pathomimicry Imitation of illness (either deliberately malingering or unconsciously through mental illness such as *factitious disorder*).

pathoneurosis Excessive reaction to illness.

pathophobia A *phobia* of illness.

Pathways to Independence A *behavioural checklist* measuring the degree to which a patient is capable of independent living.

patient cohort A group of people with not only illness in common, but also a set of attitudes (e.g. feeling 'unhealthy'). Compare with *cohort* and *disease cohort.*

patient history See *history.*

patrilineal Inherited through males.

pattern variable A value on a *nominal scale* where each score on the scale represents a unique combination of attributes (e.g. 1 = males who like ice cream; 2 = males who hate ice cream; 3 = females who like ice cream; 4 = females who hate ice cream).

PC (1) *politically correct.* (2) personal computer. (3) percentage correct.

PCA *principal components analysis.*

PCC *Portage Classroom Curriculum.*

PCL *Hare Psychopathy Test.*

PCP *phencyclidine* – the initials are an acronym for the drug's chemical formula.

PD *Parkinson's disease.*

PDD *pervasive developmental disorder.*

PDDNOS *pervasive developmental disorder not otherwise specified.*

PDS *Post-traumatic Stress Diagnostic Scale.*

Pd scale See *Minnesota Multiphasic-Personality Inventory.*

p.d.f. *probability density function.*

PDI *Psychiatric Diagnostic Interview.*

PE *probable error.*

Peabody Individual Achievement Test (PIAT) *achievement test* principally assessing mathematics, reading and spelling skills.

Peabody Picture Vocabulary Scale See *British Picture Vocabulary Scale.*

peak experience A highly emotionally-charged experience.

Pearson correlation coefficient (r) A measure of *correlation* when both *variables* are measured on *interval scales* or *ratio scales.*

PEC scale A measure of level of conservatism of political and economic attitudes.

peccatophobia A *phobia* of being sinful.

pedophilia *paedophilia.*

pegboard task There are several variants of this test of psychomotor skills, but the central feature of all of them is that the participant is required to put pegs into holes as quickly as possible. One commercial version of the test is the ***O'Connor Finger Dexterity Test.***

penetrance The proportion of people with a genetic makeup known to cause a particular condition who actually have the condition. Complete penetrance occurs when all affected individuals have the condition, and incomplete penetrance occurs when only some have it. Incomplete penetrance indicates that another factor is required (typically an environmental one) before the condition will manifest itself.

penile plesthymograph Device measuring the size of the male sexual organ, and accordingly, changes in the level of sexual arousal.

penis envy See *Freud's psychoanalytic theory*.

People Pieces Test *analogy test* using schematic figures, rather than words.

per-comparison error rate See *familywise error rate*.

Perceived Competence Scale for Children Measure of children's assessment of their own abilities at intellectual, social and physical skills, plus a measure of general self-esteem.

percentage cumulative frequency curve Graphical representation of a *percentage cumulative frequency distribution*.

percentage cumulative frequency distribution *frequency distribution* in which each observation is given a 'score' indicating the percentage of total observations which have values equal to or below the observation in question. E.g. the highest recorded mark on a test might be 40. Therefore, in a cumulative frequency distribution, 40 would be given a score of 100 (since 100% of scores are equal to or below 40). Similarly, a score of 50 would indicate that half of the sample scores are at or below this point. These points are often called *percentiles*. E.g. '90th percentile' indicates that 90% of the sample have lower scores. (Note, however, that some commentators apply the reverse of this – i.e. '90th percentile' would mean that 90% of the sample have better scores.) The *50th percentile* is also referred to as the *median*. See *cumulative frequency distribution*.

percentile See *percentage cumulative frequency distribution*. Also, see *quartiles*.

percentile norm A *norm* expressed in terms of the *percentile* of the group recording certain scores.

percentile rank *percentile*.

Perception (P) See *Myers-Briggs Type Indicator*.

Perception of Relationships Test (PORT) Measure of the degree of emotional closeness a child feels towards their parents and the ways in which these relationships are expressed.

perceptual defence Raising the *threshold* for recognizing items which are emotionally disturbing/embarrassing, etc.

perfect correlation See *correlation*.

performance anxiety *anxiety* induced by fear of performing an act which others will judge. The term has been applied not only to performing before a large audience (**public performance anxiety**), but to worries about how one will 'perform' (e.g. sexually) with a partner, in an examination (**test anxiety**), etc. See *performance neurosis*.

performance asymmetry Consistently preferring to perform an act in a particular way (e.g. opening a boiled egg at the peaked rather than the rounded end).

performance neurosis A *neurosis* induced by fear of performing an act which others will judge. See *performance anxiety*.

Performance scales (WAIS) See *Wechsler Adult Intelligence Scale*.

performance test A non-verbal test (usually of non-verbal intelligence).

period effect *cohort effect*.

periodicity Pertaining to something which occurs at periodic intervals.

peripheral construct See *personal construct theory*.

peripheral nervous system (PNS) Collective term for neurons not of the *central nervous system*.

permeable constructs See *personal construct theory*.

perseveration A failure to stop repeating an action or statements. The phenomenon is characteristic of patients with damage to their *frontal lobes*, and certain types of *schizophrenia*.

persistent vegetative state (PVS) See *vegetative state*.

person-based test See *knowledge-based test*.

person-centred therapy *client-centred therapy*.

person-situation debate The debate over whether the state of the individual or the effect of the environment upon him/her should be the central concern of research.

persona A mode of behaviour adopted to fulfil a particular societal role. Note that an individual's personal needs and feelings need not concur with this. Too large a disparity between the personal and public role is held by many theorists to result in behavioural and other problems.

personal construct See *personal construct theory*.

personal construct theory George Kelly (1905–1967) argued that people view the world through *constructs*, which are collections of ideas and opinions, and that in order to perceive a person's personality, his/her personal constructs have to be determined, rather than measuring how s/he scores on *common traits* (i.e. seeing how their *traits* compare with the rest of the population). The theory has a certain intuitive appeal: it is a commonplace observation that everyone views the same situation dif-ferently, based upon their own unique set of knowledge and beliefs (*constructive alternativism*). Several types of constructs are proposed: many are basic building blocks (*subordinate constructs*), which can be combined in a variety of ways to form *superordinate constructs*. Others (e.g. a strong stance on a particular issue) can only exist by themselves (*preemptive constructs*). *constellatory constructs* are prejudices which shape how other constructs are designed. *Permeable constructs* will permit additions to their structure, whilst *impermeable constructs* will not. The process of expanding a construct is known as *dilation*, whilst narrowing it is known as *constriction*. *Core constructs* cannot be removed without altering a fundamental feature of personality (in contrast, *peripheral constructs* can). The therapeutic regime derived from the theory essentially seeks to get patients to change inaccurate or inappropriate constructs for ones which are more suitable: why the person formed the constructs in the first place, or why s/he is motivated to do so are not of central importance. A method often employed is *role play therapy*. A person may not be able verbally to explain all his/her constructs, since many are not stored in a verbal form. To allow a person to identify many of their constructs, Kelly developed two major measures – the *Role Construct Repertory Test (REP Test)* and the *repertory grid test*. See *laddering*.

personal construct therapy Therapeutic method based *on personal construct theory*.

personal equation Adjustment to scores to allow for individual differences in ratings of an item, when attempting to gain an accurate rating of the item (e.g. one might wish to adjust for individual differences in *reaction times* in attempts to time exactly when an event occurred).

personal growth group *encounter group* aimed at promoting personal growth.

personal-universal scale *internal-external scale.*

personality A person's set of behaviours, attitudes and experiences which define his/her responses to others and to the environment.

personality dimension A *dimension* which measures a personality *trait.*

personality disorders General term for a group of illnesses whose principal symptom is a personality *trait* which is sufficiently extreme and at odds with societal norms to cause distress, either to the patient or to those whom s/he comes into contact with. These include: *antisocial personality disorder, avoidant personality disorder, borderline personality disorder, compulsive personality disorder, dependent personality disorder, histrionic personality disorder, narcissistic personality disorder, paranoid personality disorder, passive-aggressive personality disorder, schizoid personality disorder,* and *schizotypal personality disorder.*

personality inventory Questionnaire test of personality.

personality test Any test which seeks to codify a person's *personality* (see e.g. *Eysenck Personality Questionnaire*).

personality type See *type.*

personalization (-isation) The misperception that remarks and events are directed against oneself.

personnel screening Assessing the information about job applicants.

personology A *biosocial* movement, centred around Henry Murray, and most active in the 1940s and 1950s. Concentrated on personality, princi-

pally using in-depth analyses of relatively small numbers of subjects.

persuasive therapy Any therapeutic technique in which the therapist gives direct advice to the patient.

PERT *Programme Evaluation and Review Technique.*

pervasive developmental disorder (PDD) Group term for a set of conditions originating before three years of age, and characterized by profound problems with communication and interacting with others. PDD comprises five separate conditions: *autism, Rett's disorder, childhood disintegrative disorder (CDD), Asperger's syndrome,* and *pervasive developmental disorder not otherwise specified (PDDNOS).*

pervasive developmental disorder not otherwise specified (PDDNOS) A severe impairment, originating in early childhood, of communication and/or social skills, stereotyped patterns of behaviour and/or interests. The symptoms of the condition resemble, but are not adequately similar to those of other *pervasive developmental disorders (PDD).* The degree to which PDDNOS is a separate entity or a failure to diagnose other forms of PDD is debated.

PET scan *positron emission tomography.*

pet therapy See *animal assisted therapy.*

petit mal epilepsy See *epilepsy.*

PFQ *Positive Feelings Questionnaire.*

PGR *psychogalvanic skin response.*

phagophobia A *phobia* of eating/swallowing.

phallic stage See *Freud's psychoanalytic theory.*

phantom limb Phenomenon experienced by some amputees that the missing limb(s) feels as if it is still there.

pharmacodynamic tolerance The lessening of the effectiveness of a drug through repeated dosages.

pharmacokinetic tolerance The lessening of the effectiveness of a drug because less of it reaches the target (e.g. because it is metabolized increasingly slowly).

pharmacophobia A *phobia* of drugs.

phencyclidine (PCP) *psychedelic drug* – in relatively low doses, it creates a feeling of euphoria.

phenomenal Pertaining to that which is perceived.

phenomenological experience The participants' awareness of his/her own perceptions, thoughts and feelings.

phenomenological therapies Group term for therapies which emphasize the patient's own experiences and interpretations. Best-known examples are *client-centred therapy* and therapies derived from *personal construct theory*.

phenomenology The doctrine that the principal focus of interest is the contents of the mind and/or experience, rather than behaviour.

phenothiazines A group of *antipsychotic drugs*.

phenylketonuria (PKU) Genetically inherited metabolic disorder, resulting in failure to process phenylalanine, a chemical found in many foodstuffs – unless given a diet which omits this substance, *mental retardation* results.

phi correlation coefficient *(rŞ)* See *tetrachoric correlation coefficient*.

Phillips scale Questionnaire assessing the *premorbid adjustment* of a *schizophrenic patient*.

phinothiazines Group of *major tranquillizers*.

phobia (phobic disorder) A type of *anxiety disorder* – an irrational and extreme fear of an item or event which cannot be reasonably considered to be denoted by a prefix (usually Greek in the case of a single source of anxiety, and English if it is a set of things or a general situation). Among the better known are fear of enclosed spaces (*claustrophobia*), fear of open spaces (*agoraphobia*), fear of spiders (*arachnophobia*) and fear of heights (*acrophobia*). Other phobias can be more general, such as *social phobia* (fear of mixing and dealing with people). A phobia held in a mild (i.e. not incapacitating) form is known as a *paraphobia*. Treatments for phobia have included *systematic desensitization* and *flooding*.

phobic disorder *phobia*.

phobic object The object producing the *phobia* (e.g. a spider in the case of an *arachnophobic* patient).

phobophobia A *phobia* of fear.

phonemic dyslexia *phonological dyslexia*

phonological dysgraphia An inability to spell words using phonological skills. E.g. patients can spell real words, but cannot spell *nonsense words* dictated to them. See *phonological dyslexia*.

phonological dyslexia An *acquired dyslexia* – the patient is incapable of reading nonsense words, indicating a failure to translate letters into their oral representations.

phonophobia A *phobia* of sound.

photophobia An extreme physical sensitivity to light (i.e. so that 'normal' lighting levels may be painful). The term bears no connotations normally associated with the suffix of *phobia*.

phrenaesthesia *mental retardation*.

phrenology The inference of personality type from the contours of the skull (i.e. reading 'bumps on the head'). Popular in the nineteenth century, but now discredited.

phylogenesis *phylogeny.*

phylogeny The growth and development (in evolutionary terms) of the species. Contrast with *ontogeny.*

physical therapy *organic therapy.*

physiological addiction See *addiction.*

physiological age *biological age.*

physiological correlates The physiological processes which are linked with a particular psychological act.

PIAT *Peabody Individual Achievement Test.*

piblokto A mental illness restricted to Eskimo people. The principal symptoms are running uncontrollably, screaming and crying.

pica A mental illness characterized by the habitual eating of non-food substances.

PICA *Porch Index of Communicative Abilities.*

Pick's bodies Damaged *neurons,* found in the brains of *Pick's Disease* patients, which under a microscope have a characteristic swollen appearance.

Pick's Disease Named after its discoverer, a form of *dementia* characterized by a progressive deterioration of brain tissue commencing in the 'front' of the brain (more accurately, the *frontal lobes*) and progressing backwards. Psychologically, there are often disturbances in personality before any intellectual changes manifest themselves (unlike other dementias, memory loss is usually one of the last symptoms to appear).

picture anomalies test Any test in which the participant must identify what is 'wrong' with a series of pictures (e.g. a dog with chicken's legs, a car with square wheels, etc.).

Picture Arrangement Task Sub-test on the *Weschler* intelligence tests. The participant is shown a set of pictures which must be placed in a sequence so that a cartoon-like story is told.

picture completion task A measure of intelligence. The participant is shown a picture from which something is missing (e.g. a door without a handle). The participant's task is to identify the missing piece. The test can be prone to *cultural bias* (e.g. showing a picture of a Porsche's dashboard might not be readily accessible to most of the population).

picture frustration test A *projective test,* in which the participant is required to judge how s/he would behave in the frustrating scenes shown on a series of pictures.

Piers-Harris Children's Self-Concept Scale Measure of children's *self-esteem.*

Pillai-Bartlett trace *significance* test for *multivariate analysis of variance.*

pilot study Small scale study which is a 'dress rehearsal' for a proposed larger, but identically structured study. It is used to practise running tests and ironing out problems which could not be foreseen at the planning stage. Also it can be used to evaluate whether a larger (and costlier) study is worth running at all.

pineal gland Located adjacent to the *thalamus.* Involved in regulation of the 'body clock'.

PIP Developmental Charts *behaviour checklist* assessing the key developmental 'milestone' of pre-school children.

PIPS *Preschool Interpersonal Problem Solving Test.*

pituitary gland Located adjacent to (and principally controlled by) the *hypothalamus.* Secretes hormones into the blood stream.

Pk The *percentile*. The value assumed by k indicates its value. E.g. P20 = 20th percentile, etc.

PKU *phenylketonuria.*

placebo A treatment which whilst appearing to be real, in fact contains nothing of real value. However, the recipient of the treatment is convinced that s/he is receiving the genuine thing. Usually the treatment consists of a 'drug', but the term can also be applied to e.g. types of therapy. See *nocebo.*

placebo effect Improvement resulting from administration of a *placebo*. Since the placebo does not contain anything of real worth, the improvement must be from purely psychological factors (e.g. feeling better because of the attention being received). It follows from this that even when given a genuine treatment, part of the improvement in the participant must be due purely to the placebo effect. One way of assessing whether an improvement following a treatment is due to expectation or to a real effect is to run a *placebo study*, in which one group receives a placebo and another the real treatment. One would expect both groups to display some improvement, but to be of any value, the treatment must score significantly higher marks than the placebo. The placebo study can be criticized for providing a bad service to those receiving the placebo, if the genuine treatment yields appreciably better results. See *nocebo.*

placebo study See *placebo effect.*

planned comparison Experimental design in which the experimenter intended to perform the comparison performed. See *unplanned comparison.*

platykurtic distribution *frequency distribution* with a very flattened shape. See *leptokurttc distribution* and *mesokurtic distribution.*

play therapy Therapeutic technique in which the patient (usually a child) is allowed to play with various toys and materials. The manner in which s/he plays forms part of the diagnosis, and amending some of the ways in which s/he plays forms part or all of the treatment (e.g. by treating the toys as substitutes for real-life people and situations).

pleasure principle See *Freud's psychoanalytic theory.*

PLSD test *Fisher's PLSD test.*

pluralism (1) Belief that things can have many causes. (2) The belief that there is more than one 'ultimate principle' (moral, logical, etc.). (3) The belief that more than one belief system or theory can co-exist within the same society/field of study.

PMAS *primary mental abilities.*

PMA Test *Primary Mental Abilities (PMA) Test.*

PMPQ *Professional and Managerial Position Questionnaire.*

PMS (1) *premenstrual syndrome.* (2) *Profile of Mood States.*

PMT (1) *premenstrual tension.* (2) *Porteus mazes* test.

PN Test *projective personality test*, akin to the *Blacky Test.* 'PN' is a pig, shown in pictures of a variety of situations designed to assess aspects of development according to *Freudian* theory.

pneumoencephalograph X-ray image of the brain after air has been injected into it via the spinal cord. The technique reveals distortions in the brain's shape.

PNS *peripheral nervous system.*

pogonophobia A *phobia* of beards.

point biserial correlation coefficient (rpb) A measure of *correlation* between a *dichotomous variable* and a *variable* measured on an *interval scale* or a *ratio* *scale*. The dichotomous variable must have 'natural' categories (e.g. male and female) – if it is an *artificial dichotomy*, then the analysis required is a **biserial correlation coefficient**. If the groups being compared score at opposite extremes of a measurement scale, then a *widespread biserial correlation coefficient* is used.

point estimate A figure that is an estimate of the value for the *population*. The degree to which it is accurate may be gauged by including the *confidence interval* as well.

pointedness of distribution *kurtosis*.

Poisson distribution Special form of the *binomial distribution* in which one of the *mutually exclusive events* has a lower probability of occurrence than the other.

politically correct (PC) The degree to which an item conforms to currently acceptable moral standards. The term is in principle useful, but has become a contentious one because of the debate (largely media-fuelled) over who decides what is acceptable.

polydipsia Over-drinking (any fluids).

polydrug abuse See *substance abuse*.

polygraph A machine measuring heart and breathing rates, *galvanic skin response*, *blood pressure*, etc., to monitor a participant's physical responses to questions. The most familiar use for the machine is as a 'lie detector'.

polynomial regression *non-linear regression* in which a curved, rather than straight *regression line* is calculated. The line is calculated by predicting y from x plus x to any number of powers specified by the experimenter. For example, a line calculated by predicting y from values of x and x (a *second order regression line*) yields a curved line with one 'bend'. A line calculated from x, x , and

x (a *third order regression line*) yields a curved line with two 'bends'. (A *first order regression line* simply predicts y from x, and is the procedure used in *linear regression*).

polyopsia A disorder of visual perception, in which items are seen as multiple.

polyphagia over-eating.

ponophobia (1) A *phobia* of pain. (2) A *phobia* of being over-worked.

pons Part of *brain stem*. Functions include relaying information between the *spinal cord* and the brain.

Pool Reflections Test A measure of visuo-spatial skills. The participant is required to identify (from a multiple choice) a figure which is the mirror-image of a given figure.

pop psychology (1) Derogatory term for over-simplified (often to the point of being inaccurate) works on a psychological theme devised for the popular media. (2) Everyday explanations of psychological processes offered by non-psychologists, usually based on an interpretation (and often further simplification) of media interpretations of psychology.

Popper's theory of science See *falsifiability*.

population The total set of subjects, items, or data possessing a particular characteristic (e.g. one could consider populations of students, crested newts, humans, coal scuttles, etc.). A *finite population* has a limited number of members (e.g. cars made in 1968), whilst an *infinite population* has no size constraints (e.g. numbers). It is often obviously impossible to measure every member of a population, and therefore, its characteristics have to be inferred from a sample from it (*inferential statistics*).

population mean The *mean* of the *population*. Unless the values of every single member of the population are taken into account (which is usually impractical) then this has to be estimated from the *sample mean*.

population validity The degree to which a sample represents the *population* from which it is drawn.

population variance The *mean* of the sum of the squared *raw score deviations* of the sample.

Porch Index of Communicative Abilities (PICA) *test battery* used in the assessment and classification of aphasia.

poriomania A compulsion to walk around aimlessly.

PORT *Perception of Relationships Test.*

Portage Classroom Curriculum (PCC) *Behaviour checklist* for assessing the psychological and motor development of children aged 2–6 years.

Porteus mazes A set of paper and pencil mazes, designed to assess visuo-spatial intelligence. They are also used to assess patients with some forms of brain damage.

Position Analysis Questionnaire (PAQ) A *job analysis* questionnaire yielding ratings on six categories appropriate to commonly sought-after jobs (e.g. extent to which job requires use of machinery, physical skills, etc.).

positive asset search See *asset search.*

positive correlation See *correlation.*

Positive Feelings Questionnaire Measure of level of a person's positive feelings for his/her partner.

positive psychology The study of leading a happy and fulfilling existence.

positive reinforcement Rewarding a participant for performing the behaviour which s/he is being taught.

positive result See *negative result.*

positive symptom See *negative symptom.*

positively skewed distribution See *negatively skewed distribution.*

positivism Philosophical doctrine that only that which can be observed and objectively measured is fit for study.

positron emission tomography (PET scan) Body scan in which the patient is given a mildly radioactive tracer (e.g. injection of radioactive glucose) whose passage in the blood stream is then charted. The PET scan can thus measure, inter alia: abnormal metabolism, thereby indicating *atrophy* or abnormally functioning cells (e.g. in a tumour); blood flow; energy use by different areas of the brain (and hence how areas change activity levels depending on the nature of the psychological task being prevented).

post hoc comparison *post hoc test.*

post hoc reasoning Explaining events with the gift of hindsight.

post hoc test Any method of investigating an *unplanned comparison* (contrast with *a priori test*).

post-hypnotic suggestion See *hypnosis.*

post-natal depression State of *depression* which occurs in some mothers shortly after giving birth. Symptoms include feelings of inadequacy and hopelessness.

post-test Assessing the effect of a treatment – this is usually compared with the results of a *pre-test*, which measured the state prior to treatment.

Post-traumatic Stress Diagnostic Scale (PDS) Diagnostic test of *post-traumatic stress.*

post-traumatic stress disorder (PTSD) Feelings of anxiety, *depression*, and an emotional numbing and distancing from once-liked events and people, resulting from being subjected to a catastrophic experience (e.g. hijacking, war, etc.) which have lasted for 1–3 months (*acute post-traumatic stress disorder*) or over 3 months (*chronic post-traumatic stress disorder*). *Acute stress disorder* has similar symptoms but is shorter-lasting (the DSM-IV specifies that it must arise within 4 weeks of the event and last less than 4 weeks).

posterior Anatomical term. In a quadruped, it denotes the rear/tail section of the animal. In bipedal animals, it denotes the back section (i.e. the back rather than the belly side). See *ventral*.

postural echo (Consciously or otherwise) mimicking the posture of someone else. In normal interaction, this usually indicates that the people concerned are in accord with each other.

postural tremor Trembling that occurs when the affected body part is being held in a posture against gravity.

potency dimension See *semantic differential technique*.

power (of a statistical test) Calculated as 1 − *beta*. The higher the score, the less likely the test is to make a *Type II error*. Typically, a value of circa 0.8 is considered acceptable. Generally, *parametric tests* have greater power than *non-parametric tests*. Also, power increases with the sample size being considered (see *power-efficiency*).

power curve Graphical representation of the *power* calculation. The curve becomes narrower with increasing sample size.

power-efficiency The increase in sample size required to make a statistically weak test have the same *power* as a stronger one. This is calculated as 100 x (sample size of test A yielding power size p / sample size of test B yielding power size p), where B is the weaker test. E.g. if test B has power p when it has 20 participants, whilst test A attains the same power with 10 participants, then B has 50% of A's power. The power-efficiency measure is used to compare the relative powers of statistical tests, especially comparisons of *non-parametric* and *parametric* tests (usually the former are weaker).

power test Any measure in which the accuracy of the answers, rather than the time taken to complete, is of prime importance. This contrasts with the *speed test*, in which the speed at which correct answers can be produced is the principal consideration.

practice effect The phenomenon whereby the more a participant is tested on a particular test, the better s/he gets (through practice). This can distort findings (e.g. if the participant has to be repeatedly tested as in a *longitudinal study*). More generally, repeated testing, even on different tests, can produce *test wise participants*. See *parallel forms (of a test)* and *Solomon four-group design*.

Prader–Willi syndrome (PWS) Genetic disorder characterized by excessive appetite, poor muscle tone and immature physical development. There is usually emotional instability and a degree of intellectual impairment.

praxernia Cattell's term for a personality *trait* corresponding to degree of realism and practicality.

pre-delinquent Child whose behaviour pattern indicates a danger of him or her becoming a *delinquent*.

pre-morbid Before the illness.

pre-morbid adjustment The degree to which the patient 'fitted in' with 'normal' life prior to falling ill. With certain mental illnesses (e.g. many forms of schizophrenia), the patient may be reported as e.g. being 'eccentric' or a 'loner' (see *Phillips scale*).

pre-morbid IQ The IQ level (usually estimated) of a person before the onset of an illness (usually one which has affected the intellect – e.g. *dementia*).

pre-morbid state State before the onset of illness.

Pre-School Behaviour Checklist *behaviour checklist* for assessing the development of children aged 2–5 years.

pre-senile dementia *dementia* whose onset occurs before the patient's 60th birthday was once felt to be qualitatively distinct from *senile dementia*, but this division is now disputed.

pre-test See *post-test.*

precision (h) A measure of the narrowness of the *frequency distribution* (i.e. how closely the values fall around the *mean*). Calculated as the reciprocal of the *variance.*

preconscious Term denoting those thoughts which are subjectively perceived as not in consciousness but which can be almost instantly 'brought to mind'.

predictability The degree to which a statistical formula can predict the value of a *predicted variable* given the values of the *predictor variables.*

predicted variable A *variable* whose value is predicted from the values of other variables (e.g. in a *regression* equation). In *multiple regression*, a synonym of the *criterion variable.*

predictive research See *explanatory research.*

Predictive Screening Test of Articulation (PSTA) Test which assesses a child's articulation defect and also predicts whether the child will automatically 'grow out of it'.

predictive validity The degree to which a test score predicts the future behaviour or performance of the participant. *Concurrent validity* measures the degree to which the test predicts behaviour/performance at or near the same time as the test. Both measures are expressed as *correlations* between the test and the behaviour/performance in question. Sometimes predictive and concurrent validity are subsumed under the title of *criterion-related validity.* See *validity.*

predictor variable A *variable* whose value is held to predict another variable (the *predicted variable*).

preemptive constructs See *personal construct theory.*

premature ejaculation Achievement of orgasm by the male before he or his partner wishes. The term is usually specifically applied to an habitual 'hair trigger' level of responsiveness.

premenstrual syndrome (PMS) Extreme feelings of bloatedness, *depression* and irritability felt by many women for several days prior to their period. Some commentators treat PMS and *premenstrual tension (PMT)* as synonyms, whilst some reserve the label of PMS for more severe cases of the symptoms.

premenstrual tension (PMT) See *premenstrual syndrome.*

premsia Cattell's term for a personality *trait* corresponding to degree of tender-mindedness.

preparedness The degree to which a participant is predisposed to acquire a particular habit, mental illness, etc.

presbycusis Hearing loss characterized by a relatively greater difficulty in perceiving high frequency sounds.

presbyopia An inability to focus on near objects.

Preschool Interpersonal Problem Solving Test (PIPS) Presents participants with pictures of various social problems, to which the participants must provide as many solutions as possible.

prescriptive Providing guidance or instructions.

presenilin-1 Gene located on chromosome 14 associated with a variant of early onset *dementia of the Alzheimer type.*

presenilin-2 Gene located on chromosome 1 associated with a variant of early onset *dementia of the Alzheimer type.*

Present State Examination (PSE) Standardized measure of a patient's current mental state.

presenting symptoms (1) The symptoms which a patient possesses when first presenting for treatment. (2) The symptoms which first cause the patient to seek or be sent for treatment (this is different from definition 1, because the patient may have other symptoms of which s/he is unaware).

pressure of speech Habitually garbled and rapid speech.

preventative ritual A *compulsive* and irrational behaviour in which the patient repeatedly performs an act to avoid a negative event (e.g. repeatedly checking that the gas taps are turned off before going to bed). In contrast, a *restorative ritual* is a compulsive act performed to remove the perceived negative effects of an event (e.g. compulsively washing after meeting someone of the opposite sex).

prevention (of disease) Classified by some commentators into three types. *Primary prevention* corresponds to *prophylactic treatment. Secondary prevention* is identifying cases in the early stages before they can become established. *Tertiary prevention* is simply the treatment of the disease.

preventive counselling *counselling* intended to dissuade individuals from commencing or maintaining potential or actual dangerous behaviours (e.g. providing guidance on 'safe sex').

Prevue assessment system Measure of a person's skills and personality used to assess suitability for a variety of occupations.

primacy effect The phenomenon whereby items at the beginning of a list are remembered better than those in the middle of a list. See *recency effect.*

primal scream See *primal therapy.*

primal therapy Therapeutic technique devised by Arthur Janov, who held that underlying the patient's problems were unresolved problems and conflicts in childhood (the *primal trauma*). The therapy encouraged patients to emit a *primal scream* – a wholehearted yell – to vent pent-up feelings about the primal trauma. This was held to be therapeutic.

primal trauma See *primal therapy.*

primary amenorrhoea See *amenorrhoea.*

primary auditory cortex Area of *temporal lobe*, responsible for receiving auditory signals. The *secondary auditory cortex* and the *tertiary auditory cortex* are adjacent to the primary area, and are responsible for the interpretation and identification of sounds.

primary cortex Collective name for areas of cortex directly receiving sensory and motor information. The *secondary cortex* refers to areas adjacent to the primary cortex, which integrate and interpret this information. The ***tertiary cortex (association cortex)*** refers to the remaining cortical areas, which are involved in *cognitive* processes, but which do not appear to have a specific function. Note that some commentators group the secondary and tertiary cortices together, and label them the *association cortex*.

primary drive See *drive*.

primary factor See *factor analysis*.

primary impotence See *impotence*.

primary memory *short-term span*.

primary mental abilities (PMAs) The most basic mental skills, held to underlie all mental processes. Often classified as verbal, numerical, and visuo-spatial, but many researchers cite Thurstone's wider calculation of seven primary mental abilities (memory, numerical, perceptual, reasoning, space, verbal, and *word fluency*). See *Primary Mental Abilities (PMA) Test*.

Primary Mental Abilities (PMA) Test Intelligence *test battery* assessing ability at Thurstone's seven *primary mental abilities*.

primary prevention See *prevention (of disease)*.

primary process thought See *Freud's psychoanalytic theory*.

Primary Reading Test (PRT) Reading test for participants aged 6–12. There are two 'Levels': Level 1, for 6–10-year- olds, and Level 2, for 7–12-year-olds. Both consist of word-picture matching and *sentence completion* tasks.

primary sensory area An area of the *parietal lobe* (located in a strip adjacent to the central sulcus) involved in touch, pain and temperature perception.

primary source The original report of an experiment, observation, etc. (e.g. a journal article). See *secondary source*.

primary symptoms Symptoms which are presumed to be a core feature of an illness (most commonly the term is used in *schizophrenia*). Symptoms which are thought to be the results of primary symptoms are called ***secondary symptoms***.

primary visual cortex Area of the *occipital lobe* which receives the direct input from the eyes. The ***secondary visual cortex*** is principally responsible for interpreting the information received by the primary cortex.

primitive conflict According to some commentators, an anxiety formed in early childhood, which underlies later fears.

primitive reflex *reflexes* found only in babies, which normally disappear by the first birthday (best known is the *Babinski reflex*). If present in adults, then they are indicative of neurological problems.

principal components analysis Statistical method for summarizing a large number of *variables* in terms of a smaller number of indices, which are uncorrelated with each other (akin to the factors in an *orthogonal factor analysis*). The indices are also ordered, so that the first index accounts for the largest amount of variance, the second index the second largest amount, etc. See *factor analysis*.

principal components factor analysis See *factor analysis*.

principal factor analysis See *factor analysis*.

prion disease (Speculative) group term for a range of degenerative brain diseases such as *bovine spongiform encephalopathy* and *Creutzfeldt-Jakob*

Disease, which some commentators believe are due to an abnormal protein metabolism. 'Prion' is an abbreviation of 'proteinaceous infectious particle'.

privation See *deprivation.*

probability (p) The fraction of occasions upon which a particular event is likely to occur. Probability can be represented as a fraction, a percentage, or a decimal fraction (with a maximum value of 1.0). For example, $1/2$, 50% and 0.5, all mean that the event is predicted to occur on half the occasions in question. The decimal fraction is the most commonly used. See *classical probability.*

probability curve Graph displaying the *probability* of different values of the same variable occurring.

probability density The *probability* of an event occurring between two specified values.

probability density function (p.d.f.) *frequency distribution.*

probability level *significance level.*

probability ratio The *probability* of an event occurring expressed as a fraction of the probability of all possible alternatives occurring.

probability sampling Choosing different participants for a sample in proportion to their representativeness in the general population (e.g. if 40% of a population is working class, choosing 40% of one's sample from people with a working class background). The criteria chosen can vary according to the needs of the study. E.g. in examining the attitudes of the public to political issues, getting the correct mix of classes would be an important factor, and e.g. quality of eyesight would be unimportant. However, in examining ability to perceive road signs, class may be relatively unimportant, but eyesight would be of crucial interest.

probable error (PE) A *measure of dispersion,* which can be calculated as 0.6745 of the *standard error.* In a *normal distribution,* 50% of the observations fall within the *mean* plus or minus the probable error.

proband Individual who possesses a particular trait, disease, etc., who is chosen as the starting point of a study of genetic inheritance. The proband's blood relatives are examined to see if they also possess the trait/disease in question.

process schizophrenia See *schizophrenia.*

Procrustes rotation See *factor analysis.*

product-moment correlation coefficient See *correlation.*

product variable *variable* produced by multiplying other variables.

Professional and Managerial Position Questionnaire (PMPQ) *job analysis* questionnaire aimed at white collar workers.

profile The psychological composition of a participant as defined by his/her scores on a set of tests of psychological attributes.

Profile of Mood States (PMS) A measure of the current mood of the participant. Has two formats: 'monopolar', measuring a set of single moods (e.g. tension/anxiety); and 'bipolar', measuring a set of moods each presented as a continuum between extremes (e.g. composed-anxious).

profile matching (1) Any process of matching a participant to the psychological characteristics of known 'good' exponents of the skill in question. The phrase is most commonly used for comparing job applicants' scores to those of a person known to be good at the job in question. (2) Identifying the characteristics of the person being sought, and then searching for an individual who fits the description. E.g. in searching for a criminal, identifying what s/he is likely to be like may reduce the police search time.

profound mental retardation See *mental retardation*.

progeria A congenital condition characterized by stunted physical growth, rapid physical ageing, and onset of *dementia* whilst still in childhood.

prognosis Anticipated result (of treatment etc.). Contrast with *diagnosis*.

Programme Evaluation and Review Technique (PERT) System of planning a research programme. The problem is identified and itemized into a series of smaller problems. Problem-solving methods and their logistics (including time taken to execute them) are calculated using a series of formulae.

progressive When referring to an injury – an injury which is getting worse.

Progressive Matrices Test *Raven's Progressive Matrices*.

progressive relaxation *relaxation therapy*.

progressive supranuclear palsy (PSP) An illness characterized by disturbances of motor function and mild to moderate *dementia*.

projection In *psychoanalysis*, transferring one's own faults onto other people – e.g. a man who is a compulsive liar decides that everyone tells lies except him.

projective hypothesis See *protective personality test*.

projective personality test Personality measure in which the participant is required to make up stories or other descriptive passages based upon a picture or other object. The technique supposedly reveals details of the participant's personality (the ***projective hypothesis***). It is favoured most strongly by some branches of *psychoanalysis* – the opinions of mainstream experimental psychology have generally been less complimentary. Compare with *non-projective personality test*.

projective test *projective personality test*.

pronoun reversal Language disorder in which the patient refers to him/herself in the third person.

prophylactic treatment Taking precautionary measures to avoid catching a disease or to prevent other undesired outcomes (e.g. barrier contraception, inoculation, etc.). See *prevention (of disease)* and *preventive counselling*.

proportional stratified sampling See *stratified sampling*.

propositus *proband*.

proprioception Awareness of the position of one's body and parts of one's body.

proprioceptor Any sensory process involved in *proprioception*.

proprium See *Allport's theory of personality development*.

prosopagnosia A profound failure to recognize faces.

prospective memory task Memory measure in which the participant is required to remember to do something in the future.

prospective study Experimental method in which a group of participants is studied, and then followed over a period of time to see if some of the group develop a particular condition (e.g. a mental illness). The participants who do are compared with those who do not, to see if they differed on any of the measures they were originally assessed on. The method avoids the biasing problems of the *retrospective study*, but is logistically difficult to run. Since many conditions are relatively rare, a very large number of people must be tested and kept track of, in order to yield a reasonable sample of participants with the condition in question.

protected t test *Fisher's PLSD test.*

protocol (1) A set of instructions. (2) Records of an experiment, observations, etc.

protriptyline A *tricyclic drug.*

proverb test Any test in which participants are asked to provide explanations for proverbs.

proximal Anatomical term. Closer to a reference point on the body than another section of the body under consideration. Compare with *distal.*

proximal effects Changes directly attributable to changes in another process (e.g. a *stroke*, due to a defect in the cardiovascular system). See *distal effects.*

proximate cause The immediate cause of an event. This is contrasted with the **ultimate cause**, which may be a more general factor underlying the proximate cause. E.g. the immediate cause of a blow on the head might be that a bottle was thrown by a person. The ultimate cause may be that the said person suffered the results of faulty parenting.

proximo-distal growth Growth progressing from the *midline* outwards.

Prozac Brand name of *fluoxetine.*

PRT *Primary Reading Test.*

PSE *Present State Examination.*

pseudo- The prefix denotes that the suffix is a 'fake', in that its causes are not the ones normally associated with the condition (see e.g. *pseudodementia*).

pseudoconvulsion A convulsion or fit, attributable to a *somatoform disorder.*

pseudodementia A side-effect of *depression* in some older people – a lowering in intellectual abilities, which in turn masquerades as *dementia.*

pseudodepression A lack of activity and conversation exhibited by some patients with damaged *frontal lobes*, who from their behaviour appear *depressed*, although they are not.

pseudolalia Emitting meaningless speech sounds.

pseudologia fantastica A syndrome characterized by the compulsive telling of tall stories, which the patient briefly believes, and then discards.

pseudomania A compulsive urge to confess to crimes (of which the patient is innocent).

pseudomemory *paramnesia.*

pseudoneurotic schizophrenia *schizotypal personality disorder.*

pseudoparkinsonism *Parkinsonism* induced by long-term use of certain drugs.

pseudopsychosis *factitious disorder* in which the 'faked' illness is a mental one, particularly a *psychosis.*

pseudoretardation Mental abilities commensurate with *mental retardation*, which are attributable to poor upbringing rather than a congenital problem.

PSI *Parenting Stress Index.*

psilocybin See *psychedelic drugs.*

psopholalia meaningless language.

PSP *progressive supranuclear palsy.*

PST *Parallel Spelling Tests.*

PSTA *Predictive Screening Test of Articulation.*

psychalgia A physical disorder not attributable to physical causes.

psychasthenia *psychoasthenia.*

psychedelic drug (Illegal) drug which produces *hallucinations*, and feelings of an altered reality. The sensations are often reported as being profoundly beautiful and calming, but equally, nightmarish 'trips' are not uncommon. The most common of these drugs are *d-lysergic acid diethylamide (LSD)*, *mescaline*, *phencyclidine*, and *psilocybin* (synthetically manufactured, derived from the peyote cactus, and derived from the psilocybe mushroom). In the 1960s and 1970s in particular, the experience of such drug-taking attracted various artists, pop groups, etc., as well as more serious research on whether the effects of psychedelic drugs mimicked those of psychoses (particularly *schizophrenia*). Users of psychedelic drugs may also be prone to *flashbacks* – these are recurrences of images from a 'trip' which occur months or even years after the last dose has been taken.

Psychiatric Diagnostic Interview (PDI) A diagnostic test, conducted by interview, which identifies the principal mental illnesses from which the patient might be suffering.

psychiatric history See *history.*

psychiatry The treatment of mental illness by qualified medical practitioners with appropriate specialist training. Treatment usually involves conventional medical treatments, such as drug therapies, but psychiatrists may also provide non-drug therapies as well (e.g. *counselling*).

psychic ataxia *mental ataxia.*

psychic determinism The belief that behaviour is controlled by the unconscious.

psychic energy See *Freud's psychoanalytic theory.*

psychoactive Having an effect on psychological functioning.

psychoanalysis The treatment of mental illness by means of analysing the patient's subconscious, which is argued to be the cause of aberrant conscious behaviour and/or negative feelings. Psychoanalysis is usually confined to the treatment of relatively mild complaints. See *ego analysis, Freud's psychoanalytic theory.*

psychoanalytic Adjective *of psychoanalysis.*

psychoanalytically-oriented psychotherapy General term for any method of *psychotherapy* which has adopted *psychoanalytic techniques* and theories as an appreciable component of its therapeutic content, although without an adherence to all its principles.

psychoasthenia *mental retardation.*

psychodiagnosis Diagnosis of (mental) illness through assessment of psychological symptoms.

psychodrama A therapeutic technique in which the patient must act out the role of him/herself or another key person in his/her life in a dramatic enactment of an event. The main therapeutic focus is on one group member, and it is his/her issue that is worked on by the group throughout one session. Members of the group act as witness to their drama, and as auxilliary egos in role as the protagonist's *significant others*. The experience supposedly enables the patient objectively to view his/her situation, in so far as it allows the presentation of personal truth in the protected world of make-believe as a way to master and cope vicariously with stressful life events in a creative and adaptive manner. *Dramatherapy* is incorrectly used by some commentators as a synonym, but the term actually refers to therapy in which the role playing concentrates upon the group participating and its perceptions. Fictional, metaphorical, story-based material is used, and through this individual and group issues can be explored indirectly. Rolls are often self-assigned.

psychodynamic Pertaining to *dynamic psychology*.

psychogalvanic skin response (PGR) *galvanic skin response*.

psychogenesis (1) The belief that mental faculties originate in the mind (rather than in physiological mechanisms). Hence, (2), the belief that mental illness originates in the mind. (3) The growth of psychological mechanisms. See *somatogenesis*.

psychogenetic (1) *psychogenic*. (2) Pertaining to the genetic inheritance of psychological factors.

psychogenic Produced by the mind.

psychogenic amnesia *dissociative disorder* in which the patient cannot remember information about a particular period or aspect of his/her life. The information which cannot be recalled often pertains to a particularly stressful or otherwise distressing aspect of the patient's life.

psychogenic pain A *somatoform disorder*, characterized by a feeling of persistent pain for which no physical cause can be found.

psychogeriatrics The study of mental illness in older people.

psychokinesis The (as yet unproven) ability to cause physical actions by thought alone. See *parapsychology*.

psycholepsy A sudden drop in mood and/or alertness.

psychological addiction See *addiction*.

psychological age A person's psychological state compared to that of an average person of the same *chronological age*.

psychological autopsy Reviewing the case of a patient who has (usually successfully) attempted suicide, or who has otherwise died, to attempt to determine the causes.

psychological deficit An aspect of psychological functioning which is appreciably below par on a *criterion-referenced test*, and/or below the participant's level of performance on other psychological tasks.

psychological dependency See *addiction*.

psychological history See *history*.

psychological moratorium See *Erikson's theory of development*.

psychological profile *profile*.

Psychological/Psychiatric Status Interview Diagnostic test (conducted by interview) which identifies the patient's general mental and social state upon first presenting for treatment.

psychological reactance *reactance*.

psychological zero A perception that a stimulus is neutral.

psychologically shaken Nebulous term for a mental state which has been temporarily disturbed by a stressful event (e.g. bereavement).

psycholytic drug *psychedelic drug*.

psychometrics Strictly speaking, the measurement of psychological traits and skills. Generally used as a synonym of *individual differences*.

psychometry *psychometrics*.

psychomotor Pertaining to the mental control of movement.

psychomotor agitation Extreme restlessness and generally excessive (and usually pointless) mental and physical activity.

psychomotor epilepsy See *epilepsy.*

psychomotor hallucination An illusion of movement of parts of the body.

psychomotor retardation A gross slowing of movement and thought processes.

psychoneurosis *neurosis.*

psychonosology The classification of mental illness.

psychopathic deviate (Pd) See *Minnesota Multiphasic Personality Inventory.*

psychopathology (1) The study of the causes and nature of mental illness. (2) mental illness.

psychopathy *antisocial personality disorder.*

psychopharmacology The study of the effect of drugs on psychological processes.

psychophysiological disease Physical illness in which psychological factors play a causal or strong contributory role (e.g. cardiovascular problems resulting from *stress*).

psychophysiological measurement The inference of physiological state from physical indicators (e.g. *galvanic skin response*).

psychose passionnelle *de Clerembault's syndrome.*

psychosexual arousal dysfunction A failure to produce the physical responses necessary for sexual intercourse or other forms of sexual activity to take place, due to psychological factors.

psychosexual development The process of acquiring one's adult sexual preferences (the topic is of central importance in many branches of *psychoanalysis*).

psychosexual disorders General term for a group of illnesses whose principal symptom is a 'failure' to have a contented sexual life because of psychological factors. The DSM identifies the principal categories as: *gender identity disorder, paraphilia,* and *psychosexual dysfunction.* It must be stressed that the classification is not evaluative – a person's sexual preferences are only classified as a disorder if they cause him/her or other people distress, or place them or others in danger.

psychosexual dysfunction *psychosexual arousal dysfunction.*

psychosis A nebulous term for any mental illness in which the patient, although not *mentally retarded,* has a poor grasp of reality with accompanying negative effects. The commonest example is *schizophrenia.* Compare with *neurosis.*

psychosis with cerebral arteriosclerosis *multi-infarct dementia.*

psychosomatic complaint A complaint of physical dysfunction for which no physical explanation can be found, and which therefore must be produced by the patient's imagination. The term, though popular in lay use, is not used by all classificatory systems (e.g. the DSM).

psychosurgery Operations on the brain and (less commonly) other parts of the nervous system, to control or cure psychological problems.

psychotherapy Any therapeutic method of treating illness by psychological means (as opposed to by purely drug treatments, surgery, etc.).

psychotic depression Condition in which there is *depression,* with *delusions* (of failure, unworthiness, etc.).

psychoticism (P) See *Eysenck's model of personality.*

psychotomimetic illness Condition in which the symptoms of a *psychosis* are evident, although the underlying cause is different (a common cause is taking *psychedelic drugs*).

psychotrauma The psychological effects of *trauma*.

psychotropic drug Any drug which alters psychological functioning.

Pt scale See *Minnesota Multiphasic Personality Inventory*.

PTSD *post-traumatic stress disorder.*

public performance anxiety See *performance anxiety*.

puerperal Pertaining to birth.

puerperal psychosis *psychosis* induced in the mother by giving birth.

pugilistic dementia *dementia*-type symptoms resulting from blows to the head. The precise symptoms vary, but usually include disturbances of movement as well as intellectual impairment. The symptoms are permanent, unlike the colloquial notion of being 'punch drunk', which can be relatively shortlived. Most often encountered in boxers (hence the name), but also can occur as a result of other violent activities or accidents.

Pupil Rating Scale – Revised Measure of pupils who appear 'normal' but who have learning difficulties.

Purdue Pegboard Test A commercial version of the *pegboard test*.

pure erotomania *de Clerembault's syndrome.*

pure word blindness *agnosic alexia.*

pursuit rotor An apparatus consisting of a rotating cylinder on which is printed a target (e.g. a wavy line). The cylinder rotates, and the participant, viewing the cylinder from a fixed position (and often through a slit), perceives the target as moving (e.g. as a continuously undulating line). The participant is required to track the target (e.g. with a pen, stylus, etc.). See *pursuitmeter*.

pursuitmeter Any device for assessing how well a participant can track a moving target. The traditional device for this is the *pursuit rotor*, but more modern devices, using computer-generated displays, are likely to eclipse it.

PVS *persistent vegetative state.*

PWS *Prader–Willi syndrome.*

Pygmalion Effect The phenomenon whereby in some (particularly training) studies, participants whom the experimenters expect to do well, do perform well.

pyramidal tract *tract* composed of *neurons* (which have a characteristic pyramidal shaped cell body) running directly from the *cortex* to the *spinal cord* (i.e. without involving the *brain stem*). Involved in the control of movement.

pyramiding See *laddering*.

pyromania An *impulse disorder* – the patient has an irresistible urge to set fire to things (particularly buildings).

pyrophobia A *phobia* of fire.

Q

Q data Data from a questionnaire.

Q1 data Data from an item within a questionnaire.

Q factor analysis *factor analysis* in which the *correlations* between participants, rather than the *variables*, are used as the basis for the analysis. This identifies groups of similar subjects. See *R technique*.

Q sort Method of assessing personality, in which the participant arranges a selection of attributes in order of how well they describe him/herself.

Q technique (1) *Q factor analysis.* (2) *Q sort.*

Q1 Q2 Q3 See *quartiles.*

QOLI *Quality of Life Inventory.*

quaalude Type of *barbiturate.*

quadriplegia See *hemiplegia.*

qualitative prediction Predicting an outcome in terms of *qualitative variables.*

qualitative research (1) Research that emphasizes the subjective experience and understanding of events. Such research is usually based heavily (or exclusively) upon the researcher's subjective understanding and interpretation of the event. Research methods generally eschew statistical or other 'objective' numerical measures, and are usually heavily reliant on the analysis of narratives. (2) A statistical method concerned with producing objective categories. See *quantitative research.*

qualitative variable *variable* which describes a set of categories which cannot be automatically expressed as a mathematical scale of measurement (e.g. gender, living or inanimate, etc.). See *quantitative variable.*

quality of life Precise definitions vary between commentators, but generally the term refers to the degree a person feels they have a contented existence. The issue is important in some therapeutic situations where what is in theory the best option may result in an unacceptable lowering of quality of life, leading to adoption of a less 'effective' treatment that impinges less on quality of life. More generally, quality of life measures can measure changes in satisfaction with daily life following treatment.

Quality of Life Inventory (QOLI) Measure of *quality of life* across a variety of everyday activities.

quality ratio In studies of *creativity*, the ratio of good to indifferent works produced by a person during a particular period.

quantifiable Can be converted to a numerical value.

quantitative prediction Predicting an outcome in terms of *quantitative variables.*

quantitative research Research which emphasizes objective analysis, with a minimizing of the influence of the experimenter's subjective opinions. See *qualitative research.*

quantitative variable *variable* which is expressed on a mathematical scale. See *continuous variable, discrete variable,* and *qualitative variable.*

quartamax See *factor analysis.*

quartile deviation *semi-interquartile range.*

quartiles The 25th, 50th and 75th *percentiles*, known as the first quartile (Q1), the second quartile (Q2), and the third quartile (Q3) respectively.

quasi-experiment Study in which the experimenter cannot control some or all of the *independent variables* (e.g. as in *naturalistic research*).

questionnaire Strictly speaking, a set of questions. The term is usually restricted to a set of questions designed to analyse the degree to which a participant possesses a particular attitude or personality *trait*. In well-designed questionnaires, 'pilot versions' have been subjected to *item analysis* or similar methods to ensure that they have adequate levels of *reliability* and *validity.*

Quick Test *receptive vocabulary test*, for subjects aged 2 years and over.

quota sampling *block sampling.*

R

r (1) *Pearson correlation coefficient.* The symbol is often used as a symbol for other measures of *correlation*. (2) *regression.*

r^2 *coefficient of determination.*

r_{adj} *adjusted correlation.*

R (1) *multiple correlation coefficient.* (2) When following the name of a test, indicates a revised version (NB 'revised' is not necessarily a synonym of 'new', since the revision may have been e.g. 20 years ago).

R correlation A *correlation* between test scores.

R technique A *factor analysis* on similarities between tests rather than participants. See *Q factor analysis.*

R-Z scales *Reynell-Zinkin Scales.*

R^2 *coefficient of determination.*

R^2 increment. See *multiple regression.*

RA *reading age.*

radical therapy General term for any therapeutic method which as a central tenet holds that mental illness is principally attributable to faults in society.

RAGS *Relatives' Assessment of Global Symptomatology.*

random groups design Experiment in which participants have been randomly assigned to different groups (i.e. no *matching* takes place).

random measurement error Errors of measurement which are unsystematic. This contrasts with ***nonrandom measurement error***, in which the error is systematic and hence may be attributed to a consistent source of bias in the measurement.

random variance *variance* within a measure which cannot be explained by the analyses performed.

random walk A process whereby an item can move freely from point to point within an array of points. The direction and/or magnitude with which the item moves when it moves away from a point is random. In some permutations of this model, barriers are introduced – *absorbing barriers* absorb the item and stop further movement, while ***reflecting barriers*** 'bounce' the item away, allowing it to continue its journey.

randomization (-isation) In experimental design, presenting the treatments, stimuli, etc., in random order. See *counterbalancing.*

randomization (-isation) test *non-parametric* measure of the probability of finding more extreme differences than the ones actually found between two groups (different formulae are used for *paired samples* and *independent samples*). The test is only of practical use for small group sizes (if n > 12, then the calculations become impractically large). For large sample sizes, the randomization test assumes that the sample is derived from a population with a 'standard' *sampling distribution*. If the groups are paired samples, then some commentators recommend using the *Wilcoxin matched pairs signed ranks test* instead.

randomized block design Experimental design in which participants are classified into groups (*blocks*), and then randomly assigned to different treatments. The design is sometimes represented by the symbol ***RB-k***, where k is the number of groups the participants are divided into. See *completely randomized design* and *repeated measures design.*

range (of sample) A *measure of dispersion.* The term can have several finely shaded meanings depending on the commentator, but generally refers to the size of the difference between the smallest and biggest members of a sample (obviously, the bigger the difference, the bigger the range). The *interquartile range* is the difference between the 25th and 75th *percentiles*. The interquartile range divided by 2 is the *semi-interquartile range*. See *truncated range*.

range, correction for restriction of See *correction for range restriction*.

rank correlation *Spearman rank order correlation coefficient*.

rank difference correlation coefficient *Spearman rank order correlation coefficient (rs)*

rank order correlation coefficient *Spearman rank order correlation coefficient (rs)*.

rank score Score expressing a participant's position relative to the rest of his/her group.

rank sum test A *non-parametric* measure of differences in the *median* scores of two groups.

Rankian therapy *will therapy*.

ranking Placing in order of size. Where this is based on a single measure, and participants are simply placed in order of their scores, it is known as *straight ranking*. In some instances, participants, having been put in order, are then grouped into broader, but still ordered categories (e.g. 'well below average, below average, average, above average, well above average'). This is known as a *forced distribution ranking*. Another method requires each participant to be compared with every other participant in turn, and rated as first or second in each case. The final ranking of participants is based on how many times the participants were ranked first.

This is known as *paired comparison ranking*.

ranking scale *ordinal scale*.

Ranschburg effect The phenomenon that lists of *to-be-remembered* items are less well remembered if some of the items are repeated within the list.

rapid smoking technique Therapy to cure a smoking addiction. Patients are required to smoke cigarettes at a rapid rate in an enclosed space. This induces feelings of nausea, which then come to be associated with smoking, thereby making it an aversive activity.

RAS *Rathus Assertiveness Schedule*.

Rasch scaling A method of calculating (using information derived from the *item characteristic curve*) which items from a large test can be used to form a smaller sub-test with equivalent, or near-equivalent predictive value. Similarly, the procedure enables one to calculate how a participant would probably perform on a large test, when, for logistical reasons, there has only been time to administer a small section of the test.

Rasch simple logistic response model *Rasch scaling*.

ratee-based rater bias A biased classification of a participant or item based upon a bias for or against the participant or item. See *halo error*, and *task-based rater bias*.

rater bias *experimenter bias*, usually where the experimenter is observing and rating a performance or other activity.

Rathus Assertiveness Schedule (RAS) Measure of degree to which an individual asserts him/herself.

ratings recording Recording the strength of an impression of an event (e.g. how strongly the observer felt a participant was displaying aggression).

ratio estimation A perception experiment – the participant is presented with two stimuli, and is required to judge how intense one of them is relative to the other.

ratio scale Scale in which units of measurement are spaced equally apart, and in which a value of zero indicates a complete absence of the quantity being measured (e.g. weight). This is also known as *true zero*. See *nominal scale, ordinal scale*, and, especially, the *interval scale*.

rational-emotive therapy (RET) Therapeutic method (founder, Albert Ellis) in which the therapist explicitly directs the patient in *cognitive restructuring* of 'faulty' thoughts and concepts held to underlie problem behaviours and attitudes.

rational psychotherapy *rational- emotive therapy.*

rationalization (-isation) Analysing one's behaviour to explain an aspect of one's behaviour or beliefs. In *psychoanalysis*, there is the added meaning that the behaviour or belief is basically irrational.

Raven's Progressive Matrices *IQ* test in which participants have to find from a multiple choice the item (a figure or pattern) which follows the same rules as some given examples. The test items, whilst maintaining the same format, get progressively harder (hence the name). The test is available in three forms: *Coloured Progressive Matrices (CPM)* for children and intellectually compromised adults; *Standard Progressive Matrices (SPM)* for children over 6 years and adults; and *Advanced Progressive Matrices (APM)* for children over 11 years and adults (and particularly intended for assessing groups likely to be of above-average ability).

raw score A *dependent measure* as it is first recorded. In some instances, the raw score is the one which is subsequently analysed, but in others, the raw score has to be manipulated before it is of use to the experimenter. E.g. given the same test, a 7-year-old might get 10 answers correct, compared with a 16-year-old's 20. In terms of raw score, the 16-year-old is obviously better. However, there is also a great disparity in their ages. To allow for this, it would be more sensible to see how the two participants fare compared to their age peers. When this is done, it might transpire that a score of 10 is better than 95% of other 7-year-olds can manage, whilst a score of 20 might be below average for a 16-year-old. Accordingly, raw scores are often treated with caution. A raw score, after it has been adjusted, becomes a *derived score*.

raw score deviation The difference between a *raw score* and the *mean* for the *variable* in question. See *average deviation*.

RB-k *randomized blocks design.*

RBD *recurrent brief depression.*

rbis *biserial correlation coefficient.*

RBMT *Rivermead Behavioural Memory Test.*

rCBF *regional cerebral blood flow.*

RCRT *Role Construct Repertory Test.*

RDC *Research Diagnostic Criteria.*

RDLS *Reynell Developmental Language Scale.*

re-attribution See *distancing.*

re-educative therapy Any therapeutic technique in which there is a deliberate attempt to teach the patient to adopt a new method of behaviour/thought, hence 'weaning' him/her away from maladaptive practices.

reactance The tendency to dislike an activity or belief one has been forced to undertake or swear allegiance to, and conversely, to find more attractive an activity or belief one has been barred from.

reaction formation In *psychoanalysis*, converting a belief or emotion to its opposite (e.g. feeling happy rather than depressed), even though this may be an illogical response.

reaction time (RT) The time taken for a person to respond to the appearance of a stimulus. A *simple reaction time (SRT)* is the time taken for a participant to respond when there is only one type of stimulus and one type of response. A *choice reaction time (CRT)* is the time taken for a participant to make the correct response to a stimulus, when there is more than one stimulus, and each stimulus requires a different response. The *speed-error-tradeoff function* measures the degree to which an individual is prepared to 'trade' speed at performing a choice reaction time task (i.e. slow down) in order to reduce the number of errors made. Reaction time measures are used frequently in experimental psychology, because they give a measure of the efficiency with which a mental process occurs, and by manipulating the information being processed, and comparing the speed with which they are processed, an indication of how the underlying mental models operate can be gleaned. In addition, the reaction time is very well *correlated* with *fluid intelligence*, indicating that both are measures of neural processing efficiency. For these reasons, the technique is also used in *individual differences* research, and sometimes in diagnosis and therapy.

reactive attachment disorder of infancy Retardation of motor, intellectual and emotional development in some children who spend long periods in hospital. The effect is attributable to lack of normal contact/stimulation.

reactive depression See *depression*.

reactive fluency How well a person responds to demands for a change in the type of response required (e.g. during the *Wisconsin Card Sorting Task*).

reactive measure A measure which the participant may respond to less than honestly because s/he wishes to create a different impression. In contrast, a *non-reactive measure* does not engender false responses, either because of the phrasing of the question, or because the participant is unaware of the import of its underlying meaning.

reactive schizophrenia See *schizophrenia*.

reactivity See *subject role*.

readability Any measure of the ease with which a passage of text can be read. Typically, a mathematical formula (for the mathematically minded, a *regression* equation) derived from characteristics of a sample of the text in question is used. Usually, readability is expressed in terms of the minimum age at which an average person could read the text. The measures produced can be reasonably accurate, though they can make erroneous judgements about non-standard texts (e.g. selected sections of James Joyce often cause errors). Readability is usually used to assess if instructional and recreational texts can be comprehended by the target audience (usually schoolchildren), but researchers have also used it as an objective measure of text difficulty.

reading age (RA) The level of reading attainment which is average for a particular age group. A person's reading age is often only revealing of his/her abilities when compared with other 'age' measures (e.g. a 12-year-old with a reading age of 12 is average, whilst a 7-year-old with a reading age of 12 is very advanced for his/her years). See *dyslexia*.

Reading Miscues Inventory Test for assessing 'miscues' (reading errors).

reading quotient (RQ) Calculated as for *intelligence quotient*, except that reading development, rather than general intellectual development, is calculated. Thus, a child's reading ability relative to his/her peers can be assessed.

reading readiness Measure of how cognitively and linguistically prepared a child is for learning to read.

reading therapy Therapeutic technique in which the patient comes to terms with his/her problems through reading and analysing texts dealing with issues similar to those facing him/herself.

Reading Vocabulary Tests Reading test for participants aged 6–12 years. Consists of *sentence completion* problems.

real limit The limit to the accuracy of a measurement, usually expressed as half the smallest measure the measuring instrument is capable of recording (e.g. if a reaction timer can only measure to an accuracy of one hundredth of a second, then measures must be assumed to have a real limit (or leeway for error) of plus or minus 0.005 secs).

reality principle See *Freud's psychoanalytic theory*.

reality testing Accurately interpreting the real world and distinguishing between true memories from false memories, and thereby recognizing what is real.

reality therapy Therapeutic technique which emphasizes that the patient, through a warm and friendly relationship with the therapist and others (usually members of a therapy group), must come to realize that not all problems centre on the patient, and that his/her problems, like others, can be quantified and evaluated (i.e. they can be controlled). The patient is expected to commit him/herself to a regime of improvement. This process is sometimes known by the acronym **WDEP** (the wants of the patient, the direction s/he is heading in, the evaluation of this, and how improvements can be planned). The theoretical rationale for the regime is called *control theory*.

rebirthing therapy Therapeutic technique in which the patient, through breathing and other exercises, is placed in a state of imagining the experience of being newly born, and of feeling the sensation of new opportunities, etc.

recall task Memory measure in which the participant must attempt to remember a set of items purely from memory (contrast with *recognition task*). In a *cued recall task*, the experimenter provides the participant with a prompt (e.g. the first letter of a to-be-remembered word).

receiver operating characteristic (ROC) A graph plotting a participant's *hits* against his/her *false alarms*. A formative part of *signal detection analysis*.

recency effect (1) The phenomenon whereby items at the end of a list are remembered better than those in the middle. See *primacy effect*. (2) The tendency to judge people by their recent, rather than long-term behaviour.

receptive aphasia See *aphasia*.

receptive dysphasia *receptive aphasia*, sometimes with the implication of less severe manifestations of the symptoms.

Receptive-Expressive Emergent Language Test (REEL) Measure of linguistic dysfunction in infants and young children.

receptive vocabulary test Measure of comprehension.

recessive trait A genetically-transmitted factor which is only passed on to offspring if both parents have the recessive gene in question.

recidivism A habitual relapsing into criminal activity.

reciprocal determinism In *Bandura's theory of social learning*, the interaction between the participant's personality, behaviour, and environment.

reciprocal inhibition therapy *behaviour therapy* in which the patient is trained to respond in the opposite manner to their usual reaction to a problematic stimulus. See *reconditioning therapy*. Can also be synonymous with *systematic desensitization*.

reciprocal transformation See *normalization*.

Recognition Memory Test Standardized test of ability to recognize verbal and visual materials. The pattern of scoring is used to identify certain forms of brain damage.

recognition task Memory measure in which the participant is required to decide if a presented item has been encountered before. In a *forced choice recognition task*, the participant is presented with an item s/he has encountered before, together with others which have not previously been encountered – the task is to choose between them. Contrast with *recall task*.

reconditioning therapy Any therapeutic technique in which the patient is conditioned to react in a different, and 'better' manner to a stimulus which has previously elicited disadvantageous reactions.

recovered memory Recovery of a suppressed memory by means of hypnosis, drugs, or other therapeutic methods. Has gained media notoriety because it has been alleged that many recovered memories of e.g. being the victim of *child abuse* may be *false memories* triggered by suggestions (unwitting or otherwise) of therapists anxious to prove child abuse as the root of all or most ills – the *false memory syndrome*.

recreational drugs Drugs whose primary function is to provide pleasure rather than the alleviation of symptoms of an illness. Commentators usually divide these into legal substances such as coffee and tobacco and illegal ones, such as *cannabis* and *heroin*.

recurrent brief depression (RED) A mental illness in which the patient suffers brief periods (i.e. no more than a few days) of *depression*, interspersed with periods of normality.

recurring items test Any test of memory in which a participant is presented with a series of items, and must indicate when s/he detects a repetition.

recursive model See *path analysis*.

Reductionism Describing an event in terms of its most basic components. Sometimes used (not always politely) of attempts to explain behaviour in terms of the physical processes of the nervous system.

redundant predictor A *predictor variable* which adds little or no new information beyond that provided by other predictor variables already considered.

reduplicative paramnesia A condition in which the patient, who otherwise has a relatively normal memory, and has no other *delusions* or *hallucinations*, believes him/herself to be in another geographical location.

REEL *Receptive-Expressive Emergent Language Test.*

REEL test *Bzoch-League Receptive-Expressive Emergent Language (REEL) test.*

reference group (1) A group which is used as a standard by which others are judged. (2) A group whose attributes are used as a reference point.

referred pain Sensing a pain in a part of the body other than the one which is actually afflicted (e.g. heart trouble can manifest itself as a pain in the left arm). The effect is due to different parts of the body sharing the same sensory pathways.

reflecting barrier See *random walk.*

reflex An involuntary response, controlled usually only by the *spinal cord*, and certainly without any 'higher' brain functions such as those controlled by the *cerebral cortex*. Reflexes can be categorized according to the site of the stimulation causing them. Hence, *deep reflexes* are responses to stimulation of tendons (e.g. the famous knee jerk reflex). *Superficial reflexes* are responses to skin stimulation. *Special reflexes* are other, usually complex responses (e.g. the pupil contracting in bright light).

reflex arc The *neurons* involved in a *reflex.*

reflex epilepsy *epileptic* attack triggered by a particular type of stimulation. The most often-cited example is a flickering light or rapidly altering visual images.

refrigerator parent Parent with a 'cold' unemotional personality who may also be ambitious for his/her children. This parenting style had sometimes been held responsible for the onset of *autism* in children. This seems unlikely, but the cold personality may indicate a mild form of the illness in the parents, pointing to genetic transmission.

regional cerebral blood flow (rCBF) technique A study of brain functioning. A radioactive tracer is placed in the blood, and its course around the brain is observed. More active areas of the brain have a greater demand for blood, and accordingly, the technique can be used to observe which areas of the brain are used during different tasks.

regression (psychoanalysis) Assuming the behaviours of younger days (usually childhood), usually as a reaction to a threatening situation.

regression (statistics) Any statistical method for predicting the value of one variable from another. In its simplest form, the regression has the following *regression equation*: $y = ax + b$. This is the formula for predicting the value of y from x, where b is a *constant*, and the 'ax' expresses the *slope of the regression line*. This at first seems daunting to non-mathematicians, but is easier to understand if we imagine plotting a graph of participants' scores on two variables. Almost inevitably, the plot will not form a neat straight line of points, but they may appear to form a pattern. The regression equation calculates if the points represent a trend which can in turn be represented as an 'idealized' line on the graph (the *regression line*). In order to plot this line, we need to know two things. The first is where the line starts – in other words, when x = 0, what does y equal? Referring back to the equation $y = ax + b$, we can see that when x = 0, y = b. Therefore, b marks the point on *Y axis* where the line starts. Because this point 'cuts through' the Y axis, it is known as the *intercept of the regression line*. The second thing to be ascertained is the steepness of the line. Referring back to the equation $y = ax + b$, it is the term 'ax' which determines this. The bigger the value of a, the bigger the values of y. The bigger the value of y, the steeper the slope. (Readers can test the validity of these arguments by plotting graphs when x = 1,2,3,4, and 5, a = 2 or 6, and b = 3 or 0.) There are more complicated versions of the regression equation, but most take this relatively simple form, and assume that the relationship between x and y is best described by a straight line (e.g. rather than a curve). The strength of the relationship between x and y is expressed as a *correlation*, and called *r*. This has the same meaning as the *correlation coefficient* (i.e. it expresses the percentage of variance of x accounted for by y, but unlike the correlation, it also enables one to predict the actual values of x given values of y, and vice versa). Also, as with the correlation, the regression does not indicate the direction of the causation, or even if a third factor might underlie the relationship (see *partial correlation*). See *least squares regression, linear regression, multiple regression, non-linear regression, polynomial regression, regression towards the mean*, and *residuals*.

regression artifacts See *regression towards the mean*.

regression equation See *regression (statistics)*.

regression line Graphical representation of a *regression equation*.

regression towards the mean (1) The phenomenon whereby very high or low scores are likely to be followed by more moderate scores (i.e. lower or higher scores respectively) on a subsequent test session. This is because freakishly extreme scores are often the result of a certain amount of (good or bad) luck, and do not reflect a participant's true ability. (2) The phenomenon also holds true for offspring of parents with 'extreme' measurements (e.g. height, IQ, etc.) – the child will usually have less extreme measurements than the parents' (although not inevitably, and also, the child may still be unusual relative to the rest of the population).

This is also known as *filial regression*. (3) The statistical explanation is that in a *regression equation*, the value of x is further away from the mean of its sample, than the value of y is from its sample's mean. A variety of factors (called *regression artifacts*) can cause regression towards the mean to become a problem – the principal culprits are poor measurement and badly designed tests.

regression weight See *multiple regression*.

Reichian therapy *orgone therapy*.

reification Treating an abstract concept as if it is a tangible object.

related measures design *repeated measures design*.

related sample *dependent sample*.

relative frequency distribution *frequency distribution* in which the frequency of an observation is expressed as a percentage of the total number of observations. E.g. if a score of x points is recorded by 50 people out of a total sample of 500, then x's 'score' on a relative frequency distribution would be 10.

relative risk See *absolute risk*.

Relatives' Assessment of Global Symptomatology (RAGS) Questionnaire measure of symptoms of the patient observed by his/her *caregivers*.

relaxation therapy Therapeutic technique in which the patient learns to relax, usually for a set period each day. Usually this involves sitting or lying down, breathing deeply, and (sometimes in addition) concentrating on gently relaxing and tensing a part of the body. The resultant relaxed state is akin to that found in *meditation*.

release therapy Any therapeutic technique which emphasizes the release of pent-up emotions as *catharsis*.

relevant variable A *variable* which it is appropriate to examine in the context of the analysis. This contrasts with an *irrelevant variable* which has nothing to do with the situation in question, and should not be in the analysis.

reliability The degree to which a test will yield the same findings if given to the same group of participants: (1) at different times (*test-retest reliability*); or (2) in different formats (*alternate form reliability* – see *parallel forms (of a test)*). The former is measured with the *coefficient of stability*, and the latter with the *coefficient of equivalence*. In addition, the degree to which the items within a test measure the same thing (known as *internal consistency*) can be assessed. The most common method is the *split-half correlation*, or *coefficient of internal consistency*, in which scores on the first half of the test are correlated with scores on the second half. Another method is the *Kuder-Richardson formula (K-R formula)*. Several versions of this exist, of which the most frequently used are **K-R 20** and **K-R 21**. K-R 20 is also known as *Cronbach's Alpha*, and is used in analysing multiple choice tests. See *item reliability* and *validity*.

reliability coefficient Any *correlation co-efficient* created in a *reliability* calculation.

remission The disappearance or reduction in the severity of symptoms.

remote memory Memory for non-autobiographical events which have occurred during a participant's lifetime. A frequent proviso is that these events must not include very famous ones, which are seen as part of common general knowledge.

renifleur A *paraphilia* characterized by an abnormal interest in smells (particularly some of the less pleasant bodily odours of others).

rep grid *repertory grid test.*

REP Test *Role Construct Repertory Test.*

repeated measures analysis of variance *Analysis of variance* in which the *within groups measure* is administered on more than one occasion. The principal aim of such an analysis is to study the *interaction* (i.e. to find out if there is a qualitative group difference in the pattern of changing scores on the within groups measure across time).

repeated measures design An experimental design in which the same group of subjects receives all treatments. Sometimes represented by the symbol **RM-k**, where k is the number of treatments. See *completely randomized design*, and *randomized blocks design*.

repertory grid test Refinement of the *Role Construct Repertory Test*, devised by Kelly (see *personal construct theory*). Participants cite two *significant others* who are alike on a given attribute, and a third significant other who is not (the difference is known as the *contrast pole*). The process is repeated for other attributes. A grid is drawn, in which significant others are plotted against attributes which they do, or do not, represent. Using a mathematical procedure, it is possible to identify the participant's *constructs* connected with these attributes. The technique has been used not only in therapeutic settings, but also to determine patterns of attitudes more generally.

replication Strictly speaking, repeating the same experimental procedure on a new set of participants (often also known as *direct replication*). More loosely (and more often), examining the same phenomenon on a new set of participants, with an amended (*systematic replication*) or even a completely new procedure (*conceptual replication*).

Reporter's Test Measure of linguistic skills (and particularly used in the assessment of *acquired aphasia*) in which the patient observes the experimenter performing a sequence of actions, and has to describe them. See *Token Test.*

representative design The degree to which a study's design has *ecological validity.*

representative scores *measures of central tendency.*

repression See *Freud's psychoanalytic theory.* Contrast with *suppression.*

repression sensitization The degree to which an individual confronts an aversive stimulus or situation by repressing or denying its existence.

research design The plan of an experiment.

Research Diagnostic Criteria (RDC) Compendium of mental illnesses indentified by sets of symptoms. The RDC was intended to provide a 'benchmark' measure, so that different research establishments would select groups of patients on the same criteria, thereby making comparisons between research programmes easier.

research hypothesis *alternative hypothesis.*

research question The issue examined by the research in question.

researcher bias *experimenter bias.*

reserpine A *major tranquilliser,* now no longer used because the size of dose required had dangerous side-effects. In much smaller doses, is used to treat certain heart conditions.

residual learning ability Skills which are retained by neurological patients.

residual schizophrenia See *schizophrenia.*

residuals In statistics, the difference between the predicted and the actual values of a *variable* (e.g. between predicted and actual values of y in *regression* equations). **Standardized residuals** express the size of the residuals in terms of a *standard* score (usually a z score).

response acquiescence *response style* in which the participant has a tendency to say 'yes', even though his/her true opinion may be more negative. See *response negation.*

response bias *response style.*

response criterion See *signal detection analysis.*

response effect The difference between a participant's statement about him/herself and his/her true opinion.

response magnitude *response strength.*

response negation *response style* in which the participant has a tendency to say 'no', even though his/her true opinion may be more positive. See *response acquiescence.*

response prevention Preventing a patient from making a response or performing an action which is to be discouraged (e.g. preventing a patient with *obsessive-compulsive* disorder from performing a ritualized act).

response set *response style.*

response shift bias The phenomenon whereby if participants are asked to rate their abilities before and after training, the 'baseline' they use to judge themselves will have shifted (in the light of what they have learnt during training) and accordingly, a straight comparison of 'before' and 'after' judgements is likely to be inaccurate.

response strength The vigour with which a participant responds (e.g. speed, strength of button pressing, etc.).

response style The habitual manner in which a participant responds to questions (e.g. if a participant is habitually self-effacing in front of strangers, then this might seriously distort his/her performance on psychological tests). See *response acquiescence*.

response variable Any *dependent variable* which is a measure of how a participant responds to a stimulus.

rest tremor *static tremor*.

restorative ritual See *preventative ritual*.

RET *rational-emotive therapy*.

retarded depression *depression* accompanied by extreme lethargy.

retrograde amnesia See *amnesia*.

retrospective falsification See *retrospective study*.

retrospective study Experimental method in which participants are required to recall past events, in which the events themselves are the topic of interest, and not the participant's memory per se. The technique is used in psychology to identify unusual aspects of a participant's behaviour which in later life made him/her 'unusual' (e.g. mentally ill or unusually intelligent). Data are collected from the participant and/or his/her relatives, friends, etc. There are obviously interpretive problems, because recollections with hindsight tend to be biased (*retrospective falsification*), but the method may provide the only available record of the early stages of the condition. See *prospective study*.

Rett's disorder A type of *pervasive developmental disorder* characterized by normal development up to circa 18 months, then regression, characterized by poor speech/communication/gait and abnormal hand wringing/'washing' movements.

reversal design *ABA design*.

reversal error Perceiving or reporting an item as the reverse of its true image (e.g. reading or remembering a 'b' as 'd').

reverse coding (1) Putting some response items in a questionnaire such as a *Likert scale* in the 'reverse direction' to prevent participants responding out of habit or gaining too much insight into the purpose of the test. E.g. in a scale measuring attitudes towards ethnic minorities, some items may express support for minorities and thus a person who is supportive of minorities will agree with these. Other items may express hostility towards minorities and thus a person supportive of minorities will disagree with these. Which items are said to be reverse coded is arbitrary (i.e. in the above example, either the set of pro- or anti-minority statements could be said to be). (2) The process of encoding the scores on a Likert scale or similar according to the 'direction' of the view stated in the question. E.g. in the example in (1), agreeing strongly with pro-minority statements and disagreeing strongly with anti-minority statements would both count as high scores on a pro-minority measure.

reverse J curve *inverse J curve*.

reversibility Assumption that identical characteristics in different species have the same basic cause.

reversion The presence of an inherited condition which was absent in the parents of the participant, but present in other, more distant, relatives.

Revised Token Test See *Token Test*.

Rey-Osterreith figure A complex geometric drawing which participants are required to copy from sight, and then later to copy from memory. Used for testing visuo-spatial skills and memory.

Reynell Developmental Language Scale (RDLS) *test battery* measuring development of a variety of linguistic skills (comprehension, expression, etc.).

Reynell-Zinkin Scales (R-Z scales) Set of scales of a variety of psychological skills intended for children aged 0–5 years with a visual handicap.

RFT *rod and frame test.*

Rhett's disorder A decline in head size and psychological, motor and/or social skills after normal development of 5 months–4 years.

rho *Spearman rank order correlation coefficient (r_s).*

Richmond Test of Basic Skills Reading and study skills *test battery* for participants aged 8–14 years. Includes measures of vocabulary, comprehension, spelling, punctuation, as well as maths and map and chart reading.

right (anatomy) The 'right' refers to what the patient would describe as the right hand side of their body.

right brain skills See *left brain skills.*

right censoring See *left censoring.*

right dominant thinking *right brain skills.*

Right Wing Authoritarian Scale (RWA) Measure of the degree to which a participant subscribes to the views of the test's title.

RISC *Rust Inventory of Schizotypal Cognitions.*

Ritalin Drug used in the treatment of *hyperactivity.*

Rivermead Behavioural Memory Test (RBMT) A set of memory tasks analogous to everyday situations where memory is required (e.g. face recognition, *prospective memory tasks*, remembering a route set out by the experimenter, etc.).

Rivermead Perceptual Assessment Battery (RPAB) A set of tests of visual perception. Used in the diagnosis of certain forms of brain damage.

RM-k *repeated measures design.*

robust test Statistical test which will yield a meaningful analysis even though the data being analysed are not entirely in a format/distribution which the test is designed to assess (e.g. many *parametric tests* will meaningfully analyse data which are not quite from a *normal distribution*).

ROC *receiver operating characteristic.*

rocking chair personality *dependent personality.*

rod and frame test (RFT) See *field dependence.*

Rogerian therapy *client-centred therapy.*

Rogers' self theory of personality Carl Rogers (1902–) argues that the basic drive in personality development is *self-actualization* – the full realization of one's (positive) attributes and potential (also see *Maslow's hierarchy of needs*). Central to this is that the person should receive **unconditional positive regard** – an uncritical acceptance and feeling of warmth towards the person, which enables him or her to be true to his/her feelings (other goals include *congruence* – the harmony of self with experience, and **empathic understanding** – the ability to perceive the needs and feelings of others). However, during development, authority figures (parents, teachers, etc.) place value judgements on acts, which may not coincide with the child's true motivations and beliefs. This is known as **conditional positive regard** (i.e. positive responses will only be given for certain acts). This creates a conflict (e.g. the girl likes to eat earthworms, a parent tells her this is wrong; she accepts the value that it is wrong, and stops eating the hapless creatures, but retains a feeling of conflicting ideas). Such conflicts mean that the person behaves in one manner because that is the one which will be rewarded (the **condition of worth**), although s/he may really want to do something different. Such conflicts, Rogers argues, retard personality development. In time this leads to problems, because the person's *self-image*, which has been built on inconsistencies, does not match up with reality (the *organism*), and in order to protect the self-image, the person experiences anxiety, and has to create defences. The therapeutic solution to this is *client-centred therapy*, which is largely based upon Rogers' theory. See *need for positive regard*.

Rokeach Dogmatism Scale Measure of dogmatism/authoritarianism.

role The others-perceived personality and general status of oneself or other individuals. See *role concept*.

role concept The self-perceived personality and general status of oneself or other individuals. See *role*.

Role Construct Repertory Test (RCRT) Personality test devised by Kelly (see *personal construct theory*). The participant describes people and events of importance (*significant others*) in connection with various key concepts (e.g. industriousness, happiness, etc.). The descriptions are analysed to extract a core statement from them, and this indicates the *personal constructs* of the participant. The methodology of the RCRT was refined into the *repertory grid test*.

role play testing *situational testing*.

role play therapy Therapeutic technique in which the patient acts out a role in a miniature 'play' which replicates a situation the patient has difficulty dealing with in real life (e.g. being assertive with bossy people). The therapist suggests a way in which the role might be played, which is more effective than the patient's own strategy and which accordingly teaches him/her a way of coping with the situation. It is anticipated that such learning will help the patient to re-evaluate other aspects of their lifestyle. See *situational testing*.

Romberg's sign A pronounced bodily swaying initiated in a patient standing upright with feet together, when s/he closes his/her eyes. The sign is indicative of brain damage.

Rorschach Inkblot Test A *projective personality test* – the participant is shown a series of inkblots (rather like the paint 'butterflies' formed by painting on one half of a piece of paper and then folding it in two, so beloved of kindergarten art classes), and s/he is required to say what pictures s/he sees in sections of the picture or in the picture as a whole. In the hands of a skilled administrator, the test can be revealing, but the highly subjective nature of the test has left it open to severe criticism.

Rosenberg SES *Self-Esteem Scale*.

Rosenthal effect *experimenter effect*.

Rosenzweig Picture Frustration Study *picture frustration test*.

rostral *anterior*.

rotary pursuit motor *pursuit motor*.

rotating room test (RRT) A measure of *field dependence*. An entire room is tilted, and the participant must adjust his/her chair (on a pivot, held above the floor of the room) so that it is truly level with the 'real' ground. *Field dependent* participants tend to set the chair to align with the floor of the room.

rotation The process of moving the factor axes in a *factor analysis*.

rounding-up error *approximation error*.

row marginal The sum of all values contained in a row in a table. Similarly, a *column marginal* is the sum of all the values contained in a column in a table.

RPAB *Rivermead Perceptual Assessment Battery.*

r_{pb} *point biserial correlation coefficient.*

RQ *reading quotient.*

RRT *rotating room test.*

r_s *Spearman rank order correlation coefficient.*

r_t *tetrachoric correlation coefficient.*

RT *reaction time.*

rumination disorder Eating disorder characterized by regurgitating partly-digested food and then either re-swallowing it or spitting it out.

runs test *Wald-Wolfowitz runs test.*

Rust Inventory of Schizotypal Cognitions (RISC) Inventory which measures the degree to which a patient possesses thought disorders characteristic of *schizophrenia* and *schizotypal personality disorder.*

rust out Lack of drive and motivation resulting from an undemanding occupation.

Rustrak record Print-out from a particular commercial event-recorder which records several different actions simultaneously.

RWA *Right Wing Authoritarian Scale.*

r_w**bis** *widespread biserial correlation coefficient.*

S

s *standard deviation.*

S (1) *spatial ability. (2) Sensing.*

S-B scale *Stanford-Binet Scale.*

S-R learning *stimulus-response learning.*

S^2 *sample variance.*

SA *spelling age.*

SAAST *Self-Administered Alcoholism Screening Test.*

sacral level (spinal cord) *level of spinal cord*/located between the *lumbar level* and the *coccygeal level.* Has five *segments,* labelled SI (the topmost) to S5.

SAD (1) *seasonal affective disorder.* (2) *Social Avoidance and Distress.*

SADD *Short Alcohol Dependence Data.*

sadism *paraphilia* in which the patient's principal form of sexual gratification is in inflicting pain or other forms of punishment. See *masochism.*

sado-masochism Term for sexual activity (usually consensual) in which sadists punish and/or hurt *masochistic* partners for their mutual sexual gratification.

SADS (1) *Schedule of Affective Disorders and Schizophrenia.* (2) *Social Activities and Distress Scale.*

SADS-L See *Schedule of Affective Disorders and Schizophrenia.*

SAI *Social Anxiety Inventory.*

Saint Vitus's dance *chorea.*

Salford Sentence Reading Test Reading test for participants aged 6–11 years. Similar in format to the *Holborn Reading Scale.* Participants are given a series of sentences to read, which increase in difficulty. The test ends when a set number of errors has been made.

same-different experiment Any experimental method in which the participant is presented with pairs of items and must judge if they are the same or different. One of the most frequent uses of this method is in assessing the degree of difference which must exist between objects for the difference to be noted (e.g. two very slightly different shades of the same colour).

same-opposite test *synonym-antonym test.*

SAMI *Sequential Assessment of Mathematics Inventories.*

sample mean The *mean* of the scores from a sample.

sample variance (s^2) The total of all the squares of all *raw score deviations*, divided by the number of *degrees of freedom* (in this instance, *n-1*). The measure is an *unbiased estimate* of the *variance* of the *population*. See *standard deviation*.

sampling bias (Accidental or deliberate) selection of participants which makes them unrepresentative of the *population* it is claimed they represent.

sampling distribution The *frequency distribution* of a statistic as it would appear if it was derived from an infinite number of measures taken from perfectly identical *populations*. E.g. if the sampling distribution was of differences between two groups' scores on the same test, and the two groups are from the same population, then the probability of finding a big group difference is low. By chance, large differences will occur, but these should be infrequent. The probability of any particular difference occurring can be calculated. Sampling distributions are computed differently according to the statistical measure employed. They are essential in deciding if an experimental finding is statistically *significant*. E.g. suppose that a difference is found between two groups' scores. By consulting the sampling distribution, one can see the probability of a particular difference being found if the two groups are from the same population. This is the *significance level*, and if it is

lower than the level set by the ***decision rule***, then the group difference will be judged to be significant (i.e. the difference is judged to occur too infrequently in the same population for the explanation that the two groups are from the same population to be considered plausible). Typically, the significance level is set at < 0.05. The *mean* of the sampling distribution is called the ***expected value***, and its standard deviation is called the ***standard error***. It should be noted that the sampling distributions vary according to the sizes of the samples used. Small samples tend to produce low and wide distributions, whilst large samples produce comparatively tall and thin ones. This makes intuitive sense. If one were to compare the average heights of pairs of people, then the chances are that one would find quite a range of differences. However, if one was comparing the average heights of groups of 1000 people, then the chances of there being big group differences are very remote. Hence, large samples tend to produce little variation in differences, small samples tend to produce a lot. It follows from this that finding a large difference is more likely to be within the bounds of normal variation for small groups, whilst being highly unlikely for a large group. It is tempting to conclude from this that it is easier to find a significant difference from a large sample (however, see *significance*). It should also be noted that the ***central limit theorem*** states that the larger the samples taken, the more the shape of the sampling distribution resembles that of a *normal distribution*.

sampling distribution of the mean *sampling distribution* of *mean* values of an infinite number of equally sized samples of the same *variable*.

sampling error The degree to which the *sample mean* differs from the *population mean*.

sampling fraction The fraction of the population that is sampled. Accordingly, the probability that a member of the population will be selected for testing. E.g. a sampling fraction of 1/10,000 means that there is a 1 in 10,000 chance of being selected.

sampling frame The method of selecting the sample.

sampling population The *population* from which the sample in question has been taken.

sampling procedure The process of selecting a sample of a *population*.

sampling stability The probability that another sample drawn from the *population* would yield the same results.

sampling validity The degree to which a test measures the traits it claims to measure.

sampling with replacement Sampling a member of a *population*, who is not barred from being tested again if another sample of the population is taken. This compares with *sampling without replacement*, in which a participant can be tested on one occasion only.

sampling without replacement See *sampling with replacement*.

SAT *Scholastic Aptitude Test.*

satanophobia A *phobia* of the Devil.

satiation *habituation.*

satyriasis A grossly exaggerated sexual drive in a man. The condition is an unhappy one, because by implication, the patient is left unsatisfied by his encounters (compare with *nymphomania*).

Satz-Mogel method Adaptation of *Wechsler Adult Intelligence Scale*, in which for most tests, only every third item is administered, and the participant's final score is multiplied by three to create parity with the full test score. The method greatly reduces the time to administer the test – a problem with the full version (although of course the accuracy of the test is somewhat compromised). A similar method – the *Yudin method* – has been applied to the *Wechsler Intelligence Scale for Children.*

savings method Any experimental technique in which learning/memory is assessed by how much faster a participant performs a task/learns a set of items when s/he does it for the second or subsequent time.

Sc scale See *Minnesota Multiphasic Personality Inventory.*

scale attenuation effects Collective term for *floor effects* and *ceiling effects.*

Scales of Independent Behaviour Measure of adaptive behaviour (i.e. how well participants can adapt to their surroundings).

scaling Any method of assigning a set of values to a scale of measurement.

SCAT *School and College Ability Tests.*

scatophobia A *phobia* of excrement.

scatter *variability.*

scatter plot (1) Loosely, any graph in which *variables* on the X axis and Y axis are plotted against each other, and expressed purely as points on the graph, with no lines or bars being added. (2) More accurately, the plotting of two *dependent variables*, expressed purely by intersection points on the graph. Also, unlike other occasions (see entry for X axis), the X and Y axes must be equal in length.

scattergram *scatter plot.*

scattering Highly disordered thought.

scedacity The level of concordance between different samples' levels of *variability*. **Heteroscedacity** denotes that the variability is different, and **homoscedacity** that it is the same.

Schedule of Affective Disorders and Schizophrenia (SADS) Measure of the illnesses of the test's title, assessed using a *semi-structured interview*. Variants include **SADS-L** which measures the lifetime symptoms of the patient, and **K-SADS-P**, which is for child patients.

Schedule of Growing Skills (SGS) Measure of skills and behaviours which assesses the development of children aged 0–5 years and assesses their growth relative to age *norms*.

Scheffé test A *t test for multiple comparisons* and *post hoc test* for the *analysis of variance*.

schema A collection of memories about an event or item which enable one to plan responses and to interpret information surrounding the said event or item. For example, if one is asked to dinner at an expensive restaurant, one's schema for expensive restaurants will indicate that turning up in jeans and a t-shirt would not be a good idea.

schizoaffective disorder Disorder in which there are symptoms of both *schizophrenia* and an *affective disorder*.

schizoid (1) *schizoid personality disorder.* (2) Possessing some of the 'milder' symptoms of *schizophrenia*. (3) *schizophrenic*. Because of this contradictory usage, the term is usually best avoided.

schizoid disorder of childhood or adolescence An abnormal lack of drive to form social contacts, and absence of pleasure in social interaction. However, there is not a loss of reality as in full-blown *schizophrenia*. The illness is reclassified as *schizoid personality disorder* if it continues into adulthood.

schizoid personality disorder *personality disorder* characterized by an insensitivity to emotions, and lack of social contacts.

schizophrenia A *psychosis* characterized by profound disorders of thought and language (but without signs of *mental retardation*), loss of perception of reality, and concomitant changes in emotions and behaviour. The DSM requires that the symptoms must be present for a minimum of six months to be classified as schizophrenia (see *schizophreniform disorder* and *brief reactive psychosis*). The symptoms of the illness have been extensively categorized, and a full listing is impossible within the confines of this book. However, the principal characteristics are as follows. In most cases, the patients are unaware that they are suffering from a mental illness, and/or that their behaviour and beliefs are seriously unusual. The said beliefs range enormously in type, although a common element in many is a feeling of persecution. Others include the belief that other beings (either human, spiritual, or extraterrestrial) are controlling the patient's thoughts and deeds, that the patient's thoughts are being read by other people, and *ideas of reference*. These *thought disorders* are often accompanied by *delusions* and *hallucinations* (including the famous 'voices in the head'). It follows from the above that the language and conversational style of a schizophrenic patient are characteristically unusual. When interviewed, his/her responses can often best be described as 'surreal', either because they appear at best to be only tangentially connected with the question, or because the answers, whilst obeying the rules of conversation, are magnificently false (e.g. 'where are we?' – 'the planet Zog'). There may be a tendency to produce *neologisms*. Another reasonably frequent phenomenon is the clang association. Alternatively, language may be severely impoverished, with a limited vocabulary, or statements which 'tail off' before they are completed. Emotional expression is often either virtually non-existent, or otherwise may be inappropriate for the situation. The DSM divides schizophrenia into several sub-categories, based upon the most prevalent symptoms. *Catatonic schizophrenia* is characterized by extremes of motor activity – the patient alternates between high activity and periods of extraordinary immobility, 'freezing' into postures which are maintained for several hours (see *catatonic state*). The symptoms are found in some other schizophrenics, but not to the same extent. *Disorganized schizophrenia* is characterized by a disorganization of thought, inconsistent and extreme moods, and a general lack of control (e.g. of personal hygiene). In cases of *paranoid schizophrenia*, the patient has delusions of persecution and/or of self-importance, and/or has *delusional jealousy*. Ideas of reference are also often present. *Residual schizophrenia* describes a state in which a patient who has suffered from schizophrenia in the past, whilst not now suffering from the illness in its full-blown form, nonetheless continues to exhibit some symptoms. *Undifferentiated schizophrenia*, is a rather nebulously defined condition, in which the patient possesses symptoms characteristic of more than one of the other types of schizophrenia. The illness can also be sub-categorized according to rate of onset. *Process schizophrenia*, has a very slow and gradual onset, whilst *reactive schizophrenia*, has a sudden and dramatic onset (and may be triggered by a stressful or otherwise distressing event). Recovery is often less good from the former condition. See *schizoaffective disorder*, and *schizotypal personality disorder*.

schizophrenic Pertaining to *schizophrenia*.

schizophreniform disorder *psychosis* in which the patient exhibits some of the symptoms of *schizophrenia*, but which lasts over a fortnight and under six months. See *brief reactive psychosis*.

schizophrenogenic Causing, or helping to cause, *schizophrenia*.

schizophrenogenic parent Parent whose emotionally cold and harsh parenting style is supposed, according to some theorists, to induce *schizophrenia* in his/her offspring.

schizotypal personality disorder *personality disorder* characterized by an insensitivity to emotions, lack of social contacts, and some eccentricity of thought reminiscent of full-blown *schizophrenia*, such as odd language, *illusions*, etc.

scholastic aptitude test Any test which measures skills taught in the classroom, or skills which are felt to impinge directly on scholastic abilities. Often used to predict a pupil's likely scholastic performance. When the term has capital letters – i.e. the *Scholastic Aptitude Test* – then a specific test is implied.

Scholastic Aptitude Test (SAT) Test used by the College Entrance Examination Board in the USA, which tests basic scholastic aptitude in university/college entrants. Not to be confused with *scholastic aptitude test*, which is a generic term for any test of scholastic skills.

Schonell Graded Word Reading Test Reading test for participants aged 6–12. Consists of a list of words (most with irregular spellings) which the participant has to pronounce. Words increase in difficulty as the test progresses. Testing ceases when the participant has incorrectly pronounced a set number of words.

Schonell Graded Word Spelling Test Spelling test for participants aged 5–15 years. Participants spell words which increase in difficulty as the test progresses. Testing ceases when the participant has made a set number of errors.

School and College Ability Tests (SCAT) American *test battery* assessing intellectual abilities in terms of the school grades in which the abilities usually manifest themselves.

school phobia A *phobia* of school, and not simply of leaving home to go to school. See *school refusal*.

school psychology *educational psychology*.

school refusal A refusal to go to school. The term may be synonymous with *school phobia*, but can also describe a reluctance to leave home per se.

Schuell Short Examination for Aphasia (SSEA) *test battery* used in the assessment and classification of *aphasia*.

Science Lesson Analysis System (SLAS) Score sheet of activities and objectives in school science classes. Includes measures of both verbal interaction between pupil and teacher, and non-verbal interaction with the lesson materials.

scientific method A rather nebulous term. Several commentators define it as the examination of a phenomenon by observation, inference, and verification. In addition, there is an implication that an objective measure is being taken, not based upon subjective opinions. However, philosophers of science would dispute whether there can ever be true objectivity in observation, and, inter alia, arguments that science has taken an essentially 'masculine' approach have been advanced. For

the interested reader, there is a large and increasingly tedious literature on the subject.

SCII *Strong-Campbell Interest Inventory*.

SCL-90-R *Symptom Check-List-90-Revised*.

scopophilia A *paraphilia* in which the patient needs to see erotic material (e.g. pornographic magazines, books, etc.) to attain sexual satisfaction.

scopophobia A *phobia* of being watched.

scoptophilia *scopophilia*.

scotophilia (1) *scopophilia*. (2) *nictophilia*.

scotophobia *achluophobia*.

SCR *skin conductance response*.

scrapie Degenerative brain disease in sheep, akin to *bovine spongiform encephalopathy* in cattle.

scream therapy *primal therapy*.

scree analysis See *factor analysis*.

screening A check of a group or an individual to determine if a more detailed examination of all or some of those screened is necessary. The term often denotes a search for negative attributes (e.g. drug taking).

sculpting Therapeutic technique in which the patients adopt postures representing their attitudes towards other people and situations. A variety of props such as small objects or animals may also be used.

s.d. *standard deviation*.

SD *standard deviation*.

SDMT *Stanford Diagnostic Mathematics Test*.

SDRT *Stanford Diagnostic Reading Test*.

SDS *Zung Self-Rating Depression Scale*.

SDT *signal detection theory*.

SE *standard error*.

Seashore Test A measure of basic musical skills (e.g. ability to spot similarities and differences in pieces of music).

seasonal affective disorder (SAD) An unusually pronounced reaction to seasonal changes, characterized by a deep *depression* during the winter months.

second-order factor See *factor analysis.*

second order regression line See *polynomial regression.*

second rank symptoms *secondary symptoms.*

secondary amenorrhoea See *amenorrhoea.*

secondary auditory cortex See *primary auditory cortex.*

secondary cortex See *primary cortex.*

secondary drive See *drive.*

secondary factor See *factor analysis.*

secondary gain *epinosic gain.*

secondary impotence See *impotence.*

secondary language delay Atypical development of linguistic skills that can be attributed to an underlying problem (typically, an intellectual deficit) rather than being an isolated problem.

secondary memory *long-term span.*

secondary prevention See *prevention (of disease).*

secondary process thought See *Freud's psychoanalytic theory.*

secondary source A report of a finding originally reported in another publication (e.g. a review article). See *primary source.*

secondary symptoms See *primary symptoms.*

secondary visual cortex See *primary visual cortex.*

segment (of spinal cord) See *spinal cord.*

Seguin-Goddard formboard A measure of visual and tactile skills. The participant (who in some versions of the test is blindfolded) must fit a set of shapes into their corresponding holes in a board as quickly as possible.

SEH *seriously emotionally handicapped.*

selected group Group of participants who are selected because they share a particular set of characteristics which the experimenter is interested in investigating.

selection index Any measure of the degree to which a test discriminates between members of a target group and the general population.

selection ratio The proportion of participants identified as meeting or passing a *criterion* as the result of a selection procedure/test.

selective abstraction (Incorrectly) inferring a general theme from a minor event, usually with the implication that the majority of evidence does not support this conclusion.

selective amnesia *psychogenic amnesia.*

selective attention The ability to concentrate on one aspect of a stimulus to the exclusion of other aspects of it and other inputs. See *attention.*

selective coding Coding data only in terms of a specific variable or concept, ignoring other potential coding possibilities.

selective mutism *elective mutism.*

selective serotonin re-uptake inhibitors (SSRIs) General term for a group of *antidepressant* drugs. The best known of these is *Prozac.*

self-actualization (-isation) See *Maslow's hierarchy of needs*, and *Roger's self theory of personality*.

Self-Administered Alcoholism Screening Test (SAAST) Measure of level of *alcoholism*, derived from a self-administered test.

self-attitude *self-concept*.

self-care skills The skills which an individual must possess if s/he is to look after him/herself in a normal community setting.

self-concept What one conceives one's own personality, status, etc., to be. This includes a value judgement of how one feels about this, also known as *self-esteem*.

self-conception (1) *self-concept*. (2) *virgin birth*.

self-congruence *congruence*.

self-construct *self-concept*.

self-control training The phrase can be used to indicate any training in which greater willpower is induced in the patient. However, the phrase is normally applied to a treatment of *anxiety*, in which the patient is instructed to mentally halt his/her thoughts when they become over-anxious.

self-correlation The *correlation* between scores on two forms of the same test (i.e. *equivalent forms reliability*), or on the same test taken and then re-taken (i.e. *test-retest reliability*) or between *items* on the same test.

self-defeating personality A concept, far from universally accepted, of a personality type whose possessor seems to 'invite' problems, and may have a streak of *masochism*. A problem with the concept is that it can easily (although erroneously) be taken as an argument that some people 'ask' to be put-upon,

beaten, etc., and hence deserve no better.

self-descriptive statement A statement describing an aspect of oneself. The phrase is sometimes used as shorthand in descriptions of psychological tests, to describe tests in which the participant is presented with a series of statements, against which s/he must indicate if they accurately describe him/her. E.g. in a measure of level of *depression*, the participant might be asked if the statement 'nothing excites me anymore' accurately describes him/her.

self-desensitization (-isation) *desensitization* which the patient has been trained to carry out on him/herself in the presence of an anxiety-provoking stimulus or situation.

self-disclosure Describing or admitting something about oneself to another person.

self-efficacy Belief in one's own ability to succeed or to cope.

self-esteem See *self-concept*.

Self-Esteem Scale (SES) A measure of *self-esteem*. Participants are given statements concerning self-worth to which they must indicate their level of agreement.

self-experience discrepancy The gap between the *self-concept* and feedback on one's worth from one's experience of the 'real world'. It is argued that discovery of the gap can be the cause of problems of varying degrees of severity (in part dependent upon the size of the gap). See *Roger's self theory of personality*.

self-focus Level of self-consciousness.

self-guides A set of standards which are used by an individual to determine the state of his/her *self-concept*.

self-image *self-concept*.

self-injurious behaviour (SIB) Behaviour in which a person inflicts injury on themselves. This most commonly consists of head banging, self-biting and similar, but some (though not all) commentators argue the term should be extended to include taking noxious substances, etc.

self-instructional training Therapeutic technique in which the patient learns a series of supportive statements about him/herself, which s/he is to repeat to him/herself at appropriate moments.

self-inventory *self-report questionnaire.*

self-management therapy See *contingency contracting.*

self-reinforcement The method by which an individual rewards and punishes him/herself by means of, or following, self-evaluation.

self-report questionnaire See *inventory.* Also see *structured self-report.*

self-schema *self-concept.*

self-selection bias Problem of accurately judging group differences when participants choose which group to belong to. E.g. arguing that classical music fans have greater musical skills than pop music fans because of the music they listen to may be true, but equally plausibly, people with greater intrinsic musical ability may select to listen to classical rather than pop music.

self-stimulatory behaviour Engaging in a behaviour that appears to bring pleasure to the individual but which otherwise serves no apparent purpose. The phrase is sometimes used of people with *autism* who may engage in repeated hand movements, bodily rocking and similar, which appear to offer some pleasure (or at least a calming influence).

self theory of personality See *Roger's self theory of personality.*

self-therapy Therapeutic regime which the patient undertakes by him/herself (usually following guidance from a trained therapist).

selves See *Allport's theory of personality development.*

SEM (1) *standard error of the mean* (2) *structural equation modelling.*

semantic Pertaining to meaning.

semantic differential scale Scale in which an item is evaluated by choosing one of a pair of contrasting terms (e.g. 'good/bad') to describe it. See *semantic differential technique.*

semantic differential technique Therapeutic method in which the patient rates him/herself, *significant others,* and relatively neutral items and people on a set of *bipolar scales.* E.g. the patient might be asked to rate him/herself on scales of tough – soft, stable-unstable, etc. The scales tend to produce three dimensions – **activity dimension** (literally, how active and reactive to events the person is); **evaluative dimension** (basically, how good or bad); and **potency dimension** (how powerful or weak).

semantic error Misperceiving a word for one of similar meaning (e.g. reading 'cabbage' as 'cauliflower').

semantic satiation The phenomenon that a rapidly repeated word or phrase is perceived as meaningless after several repetitions.

semantic therapy Any therapeutic technique in which the patient is corrected in his/her interpretation of words and phrases which have become emotionally loaded.

semi-interquartile range See *range.*

semi-partial correlation Statistical measure akin to the *partial correlation,* save that the effects of the third *variable* are removed from only one of the *variables* in the correlation.

semi-structured interview See *structured interview.*

Semmes maps *Weinstein maps.*

senescence *old age.*

senile chorea *chorea* occurring in the older people, but without any symptoms of *dementia.*

senile dementia *dementia* whose onset occurs after the patient's 60th birthday. Was once felt to be qualitatively distinct from *pre-senile dementia*, but this division is now disputed.

senile dementia of the Alzheimer type See *dementia of the Alzheimer type.*

senile plaques (SP) Amorphous clump: of dead *neurons*, found in the brains of all older people, but particularly prevalent in *demented* individuals.

senile psychosis Outmoded term for *senile dementia.*

senility Old age. Not a synonym for *dementia.*

sensate focus therapy Therapeutic technique used in *sex therapy.* The patients are given a regime, lasting days or weeks, for (re)discovering the sensual nature of their bodies. The exercises begin with bodily (but not sexual) contact through massage, etc., and gradually progress to full sexual activity.

sensation threshold *absolute threshold.*

Sensing (S) See *Myers–Briggs Type Indicator.*

sensing personality See *Jung's psychoanalytic theory.*

sensitivity (of a test) The degree to which a test can divide people by their scores (e.g. some tests may separate participants into a few groups, whilst other

may place individuals on a continuous scale).

sensitivity (signal detection theory) See *signal detection analysis.*

sensitivity training *encounter group* aimed at producing greater awareness of the needs of self and others.

sensorimotor aphasia *global aphasia.*

sensorineural hearing loss See *conductive hearing loss.*

sensory aphasia *Wernicke's aphasia.*

sensory apraxia *ideational apraxia.*

sensory ataxia *ataxia* resulting from impaired senses.

sensory awareness group *encounter group* designed to increase awareness all aspects of senses and emotions.

sensory epilepsy See *paraesthesia.*

sensory neglect The phenomenon observed in some brain-damaged patients, whereby they apparently are unaware of an area of space around them. Often this corresponds to their whole left or right side *(hemi-inattention).*

sentence completion test Any test in which the participant is required to complete unfinished sentences. The procedure can be used in a manner similar to the *cloze procedure*, to test linguistic skills, or can be used as e.g. a *protective personality test.*

separation anxiety *anxiety* felt upon being separated from a close friend/relative. Usually the term is reserved for the feelings of young children separated from their parent(s).

separation anxiety disorder Abnormally high levels of *anxiety* felt by a child upon separation from his/her parent(s).

sequela An abnormality caused by illness, which remains after the illness itself has been cured.

Sequenced Inventory of Communication Development (SICD) *test battery* of measures of linguistic skills in infants/young children.

sequential analysis Statistical analysis of results of an experiment to see if enough data have already been collected to produce a *significant* result.

Sequential Assessment of Mathematics Inventories (SAMI) *test battery* of mathematical skills.

sequential research design *longitudinal study* in which different *age cohorts* are tested at intervals over several years. In addition, age cross-sections of the population are also tested in tandem with the longitudinal test panel, to gain an insight into possible *cohort effects*.

sequential sums of squares *Type I sums of squares.*

seriously emotionally handicapped (SEH) General term (principally American) for children with severe emotional/mental health problems, who are not *mentally retarded*, nor are they inadequately socialized.

sertraline Type of *selective serotonin re-uptake inhibitor.*

SES (1) *socioeconomic status.* (2) *Self-Esteem Scale.*

SETOF *speed-error tradeoff function.*

setting representativeness *ecological validity.*

severe mental retardation See *mental retardation.*

severity error *strictness set.*

sex linkage Transmission of a characteristic through the sex chromosomes.

sex therapy Any therapeutic technique designed to treat sexual problems. Treatment often involves both sexual partners, but the term can also be applied to individual patients who have a more general problem with their sexuality.

sexual dysfunction Failure to have satisfactory sexual relations, for whatever cause (i.e. physical or psychological). See *psychosexual arousal dysfunction.*

sexual identity Which gender one considers oneself to be.

SGS *Schedule of Growing Skills.*

shadowing (1) *dichotic listening task* in which the participant is required to 'shadow' a piece of speech by repeating it as s/he is hearing it spoken. The technique is used in some measures of *selective attention.* (2) Following an employee around to gain greater insight into the demands of his/her job.

shaping Generally, refers to the modification of personality (e.g. by *conditioning*).

shared paranoid disorder *folie à deux.*

shared psychotic disorder *folie à deux.*

sharpening See *levelling.*

Sheldon's personality types Theory that personality type can be related to body shape. Sheldon (1940s) argued that there were three basic body shapes, with corresponding personalities. The *ectomorph* has a 'beanpole' body shape (tall and thin), and the corresponding personality (the *cerebrotonic personality*) is one of the 'shy academic' – reserved, and primarily cerebral in tastes. In contrast, the *endomorph* is fat, and has a *viscerotonic personality*, characterized by a rather 'laid back' attitude, and gregariousness. The final type – the *mesomorph* – is very muscular, and the corresponding *somatotonic personality* is one of seeking action and command. Sheldon argued that everyone can be categorized according to the degree to which they possess each of the three body types, and that their personality will similarly reflect this mixture. The theory has a specious attraction, but the appeal is built on societal stereotyping – fat people are expected to be jolly; muscular and physically fit people tend to be active, and are admired; and academics are popularly portrayed as beanpoles with no social life.

shell shock *combat stress.*

Shipley Institute of Living Scale (SILS) A self-administered IQ test, separately assessing vocabulary and abstract thinking.

SHL Decision Maker Measure of a person's skills and personality used to assess suitability for a variety of occupations.

shock treatment *electro-convulsive therapy (ECT).*

Short Alcohol Dependence Data (SADD) Measure of level of drinking and potential consequences.

Short Opiate Withdrawl Scale (SOWS) Brief test assessing the state of a patient addicted to *opiate* drugs in the *withdrawal* stage.

short-term memory (STM) A memory store which can hold a limited amount of information for a short period.

short-term psychotherapy Treatment which in total lasts a relatively short time (circa 3–6 months). This contrasts with *long-term psychotherapy*, which lasts a minimum of six months, and usually over a year.

short-term span See *span.*

Shortened Edinburgh Reading Test Truncated form of the *Edinburgh*

Reading Test. Three sub-scales measure vocabulary, syntax and comprehension.

shotgun research Study in which a large section of tests are administered, in the hope of finding something in the results. Usually not a recommended practice.

should statement Statement which indicates that a person has a rigid moral code (e.g. by explicit statement – 'I should do this in this situation' – or by implication).

Shprintzen syndrome *velocardiofacial syndrome.*

shrinkage correction The *multiple correlation coefficient* can sometimes be diminished in magnitude by the calculations used. The shrinkage correction is a statistical technique for restoring it to its correct size.

Si scale See *Minnesota Multiphasic Personality Inventory.*

SI units The standard units of measurement in scientific studies. All measures of length and weight are in 'metric measures' (metres, grams, etc). 'SI' stands for 'Systeme International'.

SIB *self-injurious behaviour.*

SICD *Sequenced Inventory of Communication Development.*

sight vocabulary The words which can be read by an individual without having to 'stop and think about them'/ sound them out loud etc. I.e., words which can be recognized on sight.

sigma (1) Z (2) a.

sign test *non-parametric measure of paired samples* which have been measured on a *continuous variable* (e.g. participants might be measured on a test score before and after a drug treatment).The test assesses whether the scores of one group are consistently higher than those of the other (note that the magnitude of the difference is immaterial).

signal detection analysis A method of determining how accurately a participant can discriminate between a signal and *noise*. The analysis has been principally applied to perception. The theory supposes that the participant, upon detecting any stimulus, will decide either that it is a signal, or that it is merely background noise (e.g. like listening for a faint morse code radio broadcast against a background of static hiss). Strong signals will be readily recognized as signals, but weaker signals may be less easily detected, and may be confused with noise. Conversely, strong noise may be erroneously identified as a signal. From this, it can be extrapolated that the participant can make four types of response: *true positive* (correctly identifying a signal as a signal, also known as a *hit*); *true negative* (*correctly* rejecting noise, because it is not a signal); *false positive* (incorrectly identifying noise as a signal, also known as a *false alarm*); and *false negative* (incorrectly rejecting a signal because it is misidentified as noise). A participant who only ever makes true positive and true negative responses has a perfectly operating system. However, if the participant makes an appreciable number of false responses, then his/her perceptions are faulty. The greater the accuracy, the greater the *sensitivity* of the participant. Sensitivity is usually represented by the symbol d *(d prime)*. When the participant makes mistakes, these tend to veer towards one of two kinds. Either s/he is over-cautious, and makes too many false negatives (i.e. anything s/he is unsure of, s/he rejects), or s/he is over-permissive, and makes too many false positives (i.e. s/he accepts very weak stimuli as signals, even though they could well be noise). The degree

of conservatism/liberalism shown by the participant is known as the *response criterion*, often identified by the symbol B (*beta*). The terms 'signal' and 'noise' can refer to realistic external stimuli, but may also refer to signals and noise within the neural pathways (e.g. in recalling faint memories from amongst competing 'half-memories'). In its most often-used form, the analysis assumes that the probabilities of a signal being a stimulus or noise can be plotted as separate *normal distributions*, which partly overlap (the distance between the peaks of the two distributions is d'). Other formats of the analysis are available for dealing with different distributions and more specialized data sets.

signal detection theory (SDT) *signal detection analysis.*

significance (a) In running an experiment, researchers (either consciously or unconsciously) make a *null hypothesis* – namely, that they will find no differences or relationships between *variables*, other than that which can be ascribed to chance variations in measurement (e.g. two groups will have virtually identical scores, a *correlation* between two groups is at or near 0, etc.). Significance is a measure of how confidently the null hypothesis can be rejected. All statistical tests produce a *significance level* for the data they have analysed. This is a statement of the probability that the null hypothesis is correct – i.e. that any difference or relationships are due to chance fluctuations, and that the data are derived from the same *population*. It is the convention within psychology that if the significance level is < 5%, then the null hypothesis is rejected. The setting of a level of significance is called the *decision rule* (see also *critical value*). Of course, much lower probabilities can be found, and the lower the probability, the more confidently the null hypothesis can be rejected. If a statistical test produces a probability that is just over 5%, then it is said to be have **borderline significance**. Given that the significance test only offers probabilities rather than certainties, errors can occur. For example, a test may find a significant result where no real difference actually exists. This is said to be a *Type I error*. Hence, another definition of the significance level is that it is the probability of making a Type I error. Conversely, a test may support the null hypothesis, where there is in fact a significant difference. This is an example of a *Type II error*. Significance levels are usually expressed as a fraction of 1, rather than a percentage. Thus, a 5% probability is written as 0.05. Although, strictly speaking, significance is represented by the symbol a, it is usual for it to be represented by the symbol p for *probability*. Thus, the finding that a measure is significant at the 5% level might be written as $p = 0.05$, rather than a = 0.05. A popularly held belief is that the chances of obtaining a significant result increase with the size of the test sample (the **law of large numbers**). E.g. it is 'easier' to find a significant difference between two groups of 100 participants than it is with two groups of five participants. This makes intuitive sense. Suppose that you measured two people from group A and found they had an average height of 5ft, whilst two people from group B had an average height of 5ft 6". One might be unwilling to assume that on average, people in group B were taller. However, if these figures were gathered from 1000 people in either group, one might be more willing to believe it. However, the 'rules' about sample size are not that clear-cut. Although increases in small sample sizes (e.g. moving from single to double figures) probably do improve the chances of getting a significant

finding, further increases may not yield the same return. In addition, it should be noted that some statistical techniques (e.g. *factor analysis*) require large samples as a matter of course. See *sampling distribution*.

significance level (p) See *significance*.

significant others People and events of central importance to an individual.

Significant Others Scale (SOS) Measure of the degree of social support a participant receives and his/her impression of its effectiveness.

silent stroke *stroke* which produces no symptoms, and is only discovered by either a brain scan or at autopsy. The term is sometimes used to describe a stroke which is unnoticed at the time of occurrence, but which subsequently causes a significant alteration in behaviour or functioning.

SILS *Shipley Institute of Living Scale*.

simple event In *probability theory*, a single outcome of an action (e.g. a coin toss). See *composite event*.

simple phobia A *phobia* of a single type of item, rather than of a general situation (e.g. being afraid of spiders is a simple phobia, being afraid of the dark is not). The term is replaced with the term **specific phobia** in DSM-IV, since 'simple' has connotations of a clear-cut problem, which often it is not.

simple reaction time (SRT) See *reaction time*.

simple regression *regression (statistics)*.

simple schizophrenia Form of *schizophrenia* whose most salient symptoms are an absence of normal emotional responses, and disordered thought.

simple structure See *factor analysis*.

simulated study Experimental design in which some or all of the participants are asked to 'fake' their performance, and to imagine how they would behave if they met certain imaginary criteria (e.g. they were mentally ill, were desperately trying to impress, were pathological liars, etc.). The design is generally used to test how well a measurement technique works (e.g. testing clinicians' abilities to detect the genuinely ill from the fakers).

simultanagnosia The inability to perceive more than one interpretation.

single blind study See *blind study*.

single case study Study in which there is only one participant. Typically, the participant is examined in very great depth. This may occur in e.g. unusual cases of brain damage where the patient's symptoms are unique.

single censoring Measuring the incidences of an event over a set period of time. This contrasts with *multiple censoring*, where the incidences over several time periods may be compared. See *censored observations*.

Single Photon Emission Computed Tomography (SPECT) Type of *neuroimaging* similar to a *PET scan*. SPECT measures uptake of blood glucose at a specific point in time (rather than over a period of time).

single session therapy (SST) Any therapeutic treatment in which the patient is only treated for one session.

single subject study *single case study*.

sitophobia A *phobia* of food.

situational When used before the name of an illness or condition, the term implies that the illness or condition is caused by the temporary situation the patient/participant finds him/herself in, rather than being attributable to an intrinsic aspect of him/herself.

situational exercise *organizational psychology* technique in which participants (often job applicants) are placed in a work situation, and asked to sort through a set of imaginary problems.

situational psychology *situationism*.

situational specific erectile dysfunction Failure by the male to produce an erection on a significant proportion of appropriate occasions.

situational specificity Argument that similarities in behaviour on different occasions are attributable to similarities in environment on these occasions (e.g. rather than to a *trait* possessed by the participant).

situational testing Experiment in which participants are assigned roles in an imaginary scenario, which they 'act out' whilst being observed. Sometimes used in personnel selection, etc., to see how well a participant or patient can cope with particular situations. See *role play therapy*.

situationalism *situationism*.

situationism Examining behaviours in terms of *exogenous* rather than *endogenous* factors.

SIV *Gordon's Survey of Interpersonal Values*.

16PF *Cattell Sixteen Personality Factor Questionnaire*.

skew (of distribution) The degree to which a *frequency distribution* has a disproportionate number of observations above or below the *mean*. See *negatively skewed distribution*.

skew correlation *non-linear correlation*.

skewed family Family in which one member dominates the rest.

skin conductance response (SCR) *galvanic skin response*.

SLAS *Science Lesson Analysis System*.

SLD (1) *specific learning difficulties* (alternative: *SPLD*). (2) Severe learning difficulty.

Slee 13+ Reading Test Reading test for participants aged 13–14 years. Tests comprehension of short passages of prose.

sleep maintenance insomnia See *insomnia*.

sleep onset insomnia See *insomnia*.

sleep therapy *narcoanalysis*.

sleeper effect Any effect of a treatment which takes some time to become apparent.

sleepwalking See *somnambulism*.

SLI *specific language impairment*.

Slingerland Screening Tests Set of measures for assessing children (5–12 years) with language difficulties.

slope The steepness with which a curve on a graph rise or falls.

slope of the regression line See *regression*.

Slosson Intelligence Test General intelligence test for participants aged 1 month –27 years.

slow learners Pupils who are just above the level of *mental retardation*, but who, relative to pupils of average intelligence, may be slow to attain new concepts. The term may also imply poor motivation/behaviour. See *slow starter*.

slow starter Rather nebulous term for pupil who at first makes slow academic progress, but who subsequently catches up to or exceeds his/her *age norm*. See *slow learner*.

small group In most psychological research, a group of under about 12 participants.

small n design Experiment in which there is a small number of participants.

Snellen chart The familiar eyesight test chart, in which the participant is required to read horizontal rows of letters, which become progressively smaller the further down the chart the participant progresses. The quality of eyesight is often expressed as a fraction of 20 (this being the distance in feet between the participant and the chart). The familiar phrase '20/20 vision' indicates that the participant can read from 20 feet what a normally sighted person should read from 20 feet (i.e. the participant's vision is normal). '10/20 vision', for example, would indicate that the participant has to be the equivalent of 10 feet away to read what a normal person reads at 20 feet (i.e. the participant has sub-standard eyesight).

snowball sampling Technique of sampling a group whose participants are hard to identify. The experimenter finds one member of the group, and asks him/her to identify other members whom s/he knows. These people in turn are asked to identify members they know, and so on.

SNST *Stroop Neuropsychological Screening Test*.

sociability The degree to which a person is sociable, gets along with others, etc.

sociability index Any measure of *sociability*.

Social Activities and Distress Scale (SADS) A measure of the degree to which a participant becomes anxious or upset when in social situations.

social age A set of behaviours and attitudes considered to be socially appropriate for the *chronological age* of the individual (i.e. what is colloquially known as 'acting one's age').

social anxiety The degree of *anxiety* provoked by social events.

Social Anxiety Inventory (SAI) Measure of *social anxiety* experienced by patients. The measure also assesses level of social skills.

Social Avoidance and Distress (SAD) Measure of the degree to which a person avoids social events and situations because of *social anxiety*.

social breakdown syndrome *institutionalization*.

social cognition The intellectual processes involved in understanding social situations. See *social cognitive theory*.

social cognitive skills The ability to analyse correctly and to respond appropriately to a social situation.

social cognitive theory Term for theories of *social learning* – the term stresses the cognitive processes at work in the hypothesized learning process. The term covers several theories, most notably *Bandura's theory of social learning*.

social comparison The assessment of one's own abilities by comparing them with other people's.

social competence The degree to which a person is able to cope adequately in social situations.

social decrement A decline in performance due to the presence of other people. This contrasts with ***social increment***, which is the improvement in performance due to the presence of others.

social desirability responding Giving a response which is socially proper/'politically correct', regardless of whether it expresses the respondent's true opinions. Can in part be counteracted by a *lie scale*.

social identity The placing of one's *self-image* within a social and/or cultural group.

social increment See *social decrement*.

social indicator A measure of a social group which indicates its usual behaviour in a particular situation (e.g. alcohol consumption, incidence of crime, etc.).

social introversion (Si) See *Minnesota Multiphasic Personality Inventory*.

social learning General term for models of personality and development based upon learning in a social context. See *Bandura's theory of social learning* and *social cognitive theory*.

social norm That which is regarded as normal and/or acceptable within a society.

social phobia See *phobia*.

social psychiatry The study of the effects of social interaction on mental illness.

Social Readjustment Rating Scale (SRRS) Measure of how recent events in a person's life have changed his/her lifestyle, and hence the degree of *stress* s/he might be expected to experience.

Social Situation Questionnaire (SSQ) A measure of *social cognitive skills*.

social skills training (SST) Therapeutic technique in which the patient is taught a greater range of social skills than s/he already possesses. The term is usually restricted to the training of the chronically shy/socially inept or the mentally ill in very basic social skills.

socialized conduct disorder See *conduct disorder*.

sociocentrism The blind acceptance of *social norms* as the definitive guide to appropriate behaviour.

socioeconomic status (SES) Classification of a person or group by their social class and/or economic worth.

sociogenic Caused by societal influences.

sociometric measurement Measures of an individual's social skills relative to the rest of his/her group, and/or his/her opinions about other members of the group.

sociopathy *antisocial personality disorder.*

sociotherapy Any therapeutic technique which emphasizes the role of social factors (e.g. interactions with other people) in mental illness.

Socratic dialogue Any conversation, interview or dialogue which moves towards an ultimate truth or solution by means of a series of questions and answers which progressively probe deeper and more tightly defined issues. Often the questioner is the prime mover of the dialogue, forcing (tacitly or openly) the respondent along a particular path. The term is derived from a favoured method of the Greek philosopher Socrates, but has been more recently applied to many forms of therapy which adopt this general approach.

Socratic method *Socratic dialogue.*

soft data Data which purely consist of subjective impressions.

soft sign Behaviour or abnormality which may be indicative of brain damage or mental illness, but which in itself is inconclusive.

Solomon four-group design Experimental paradigm designed to identify how much of the effect of a treatment on performance at a *dependent variable* is due to a *practice effect*. Participants are randomly assigned to four groups. One group is tested only once on the dependent variable (e.g. reading skill). Another is tested twice. A third receives the treatment (e.g. training in phonics), and is then tested on the dependent variable once. The fourth group is tested on the dependent variable, receives the treatment, and is then tested again. If the treatment is successful, then the two groups who received treatment should be better than the other two (i.e. they should have better reading scores) However, if there is an appreciable practice effect, then the groups who were tested twice on the dependent variable should show an appreciable improvement on the second test run (i.e. the treatment might be no more effective than simply having more practice at the skill in question; or in the example given, phonics training is no more effective than reading more often).

SOLSO Taxonomy *Structure of the Observed Learning Outcome (SOLSO) Taxonomy.*

solvent abuse Form of drug taking in which the (almost inevitably teenaged) participant inhales the fumes from glue, solvents, or similar substances. The effects are akin to intoxication from alcohol, and as with alcohol, carry considerable short- and long-term health risks.

somaesthesia Any sensory information about the body.

somasthenia Bodily weakness.

somatic Of the body.

somatization A physical illness which can be attributed to a mental illness (e.g. eczema caused by *stress*).

somatization disorder *Briquet's syndrome.*

somatize Verb from *somatization.*

somatoform disorders General term for a group of illnesses whose principal symptom is that there are physical symptoms but no physical cause (e.g. *Briquet's syndrome, conversion disorder, hypochondria,* and *psychogenic pain*).

somatogenesis (1) The belief that mental faculties originate in physiological mechanisms. Hence, (2), the belief that a disorder of the body causes mental illness. (3) The growth of physical mechanisms. See *psychogenesis*.

somatopsychosis A *psychosis* in which the principal symptom is a (false) conviction that part of the body is diseased, malformed, etc.

somatotonic personality See *Sheldon's personality types*.

somatotopic projection The phenomenon whereby the representation of the body on the *cortex* is topographically similar (i.e. parts of the body adjacent to each other are represented by adjacent sections of the cortex).

somatotype Body build – there is often the additional belief that personality types are associated with particular body builds (e.g. see *Sheldon's personality types*).

Somer's d Measure of *correlation* between *ordinal variables*.

somnambulism Sleep disorder in which the person is asleep according to many criteria, but nonetheless performs certain acts associated with a waking state (e.g. getting out of bed and walking around – hence the everyday term *sleepwalking*).

SOMPA *System of Multicultural Pluralistic Assessment.*

SORC Acronym denoting the principal factors of a (usually problematic) behaviour. 'S' stands for the stimulus evoking the behaviour (e.g. a cigarette). 'O' denotes the characteristic(s) of the organism pre-disposing him/her to respond (e.g. s/he is feeling anxious). 'R' is the response itself (e.g. smoking the cigarette), and 'C' denotes the *consequent variables* – the results of the action which reward it (e.g. smoking makes the participant feel relaxed).

sorting test Any test in which the participant is required to sort items (into categories, a set order, etc.).

SOS *Significant Others Scale.*

source trait *trait* held to underlie several other traits. The latter (**surface traits**) can be grouped into those with similar characteristics.

SOWS *Short Opiate Withdrawal Scale.*

SP *senile plaque.*

Spadafore Reading Scale American reading *test battery*, including measures of silent reading, reading aloud, comprehension, and *fluency*. The test is applicable for an age range up to (American) college level.

span Abbreviation of 'memory span' – simply, the number of items a person can remember. Strongly *correlated* with intelligence (particularly *fluid intelligence*). **Short-term span** is a measure of how many items can be remembered where recall is immediately after the list of to-be-remembered items has been presented. **Long-term span** is a measure of how many items can be remembered from a set presented some time ago (typically, at least 30 minutes, and often longer). Span can also be classified according to the nature of the to-be-remembered items. Hence, **verbal span** = words; **digit span** = numbers, etc.

SPAR *Spelling and Reading Tests.*

spasmophemia Spasms in the vocal tract leading to a speech abnormality (often stuttering).

spastic Pertaining to a spasm.

spastic paralysis Extreme muscular tension (due to brain damage), causing paralysis.

spasticity Extreme muscular tension (due to brain damage), causing an abnormal rigidity and grossly impaired movement.

spatial ability (S) The ability to judge and manipulate spatial information (i.e. the relative position of items in a space).

spatial disorder A loss or profound diminution of *spatial ability*.

spatial dysfunction A profound inability of the patient to identify the location of parts of his/her own body.

spatial neglect Failure to perceive anything within a certain specified region of the body. Caused by brain damage.

Spearman-Brown Prophecy formula (1) Formula for calculating *split-half correlation*. (2) Method for assessing the *reliability* of a test from its sub-tests.

Spearman rank order correlation coefficient (r^s) A measure of *correlation* between two *variables* measured on *ordinal scales*. See *Kendall's rank correlation coefficient*.

Spearman's rho *Spearman rank order correlation coefficient*.

special factor A specialized intellectual skill, hypothesized to operate on its own or in tandem with g. The factor is derived from *factor analysis* as a *specific factor*.

Special Needs Assessment Software Computerized package assessing the intellectual and verbal skills of *mentally retarded* and/or severely physically handicapped children and adults.

special reflex See *reflex*.

speciesism Criticism levelled against some animal researchers that they are upholding the good of humans above other species.

specific ability See *factor analysis*.

specific developmental disorder A specific problem arising in childhood and not attributable to general ill-health and/or general *mental retardation*.

specific developmental dyslexia *developmental dyslexia*.

specific factor See *factor analysis*.

specific-global scale See *causal attribution theory*.

specific hunger An appetitive drive for a particular edible substance (e.g. salt).

specific language delay *specific language impairment*.

specific language impairment (SLI) Intellectual deficit which is confined to a disorder of linguistic abilities.

specific learning difficulties (SLD) Problems with classroom learning which cannot be attributed to the pupil's intellect or motivation. Best known example is *developmental dyslexia*.

specific learning skill Ability to learn a specific skill, and by implication, the recognition that some skills can be learnt more easily than others. The concept can be used to compare between individuals or species. Compare with *general learning skill*.

specific mental abilities Intellectual skills felt to be relevant only to a narrow range of tasks (in contrast to g).

specific phobia See *simple phobia*.

specific reading difficulties (SRD) *developmental dyslexia*.

specific reading retardation (SRR) *developmental dyslexia*.

specific trait *trait* which occurs only in specific circumstances. See *general trait*.

specification error Statistical error in which the wrong model is examined (e.g. assuming in a *regression analysis* that the relationship between the *variables* is linear when it is not).

specious present What we subjectively think of as 'now', rather than the past or the future. Since time is a constant flow, this is clearly a false (specious) concept (doubly so, since what we perceive as 'now', given the delay in neural transmissions, actually happened a few milliseconds ago).

SPECT *Single Photon Emission Computed Tomography.*

spectator therapy Any therapeutic technique in which patients watch others receiving therapy as part of their own therapy.

speech area *Broca's area.*

speech block A momentary loss of speech.

speech therapy Any therapeutic technique designed to improve speech production. The therapy is usually undertaken by specially-trained speech therapists.

speed-accuracy tradeoff On any task in which both speed and accuracy of response are important (e.g. a *fluid intelligence* test, or a *choice reaction time* task), the degree to which the participant is prepared to go faster and risk making more errors. See *speed-error tradeoff function.*

speed-error tradeoff function (SETOF) Measure of the degree to which an individual is prepared to trade speed at performing a task (i.e. slow down) in order to reduce the number of errors made. A measure often used in *reaction time* experiments.

spelling age (SA) The level of spelling attainment which is average for a particular age group. A person's spelling age is only revealing of his/her abilities when compared with other 'age' mea-sures (e.g. a 12-year-old with a spelling age of 12 is average, whilst a 7-year-old with a spelling age of 12 is very advanced for his/her years). See *dysphasia.*

Spelling and Reading Tests (SPAR) Reading and spelling *test battery.* Reading test has same format as *Group Reading Test.* Spelling is to dictation from the experimenter.

sphericity test A measure of the degree to which variables are not *correlated* with each other and have equal *variance.* Violating these assumptions can distort tests such as *analysis of variance.* To compensate for lack of sphericity, the degrees of freedom should be adjusted. Two methods are in common use: the **Huynh-Feldt correction** and the **Greenhouse-Geisser correction.** The latter is more 'conservative' than the former.

sphygmomanometer See *blood pressure.*

spinal accessory cranial nerve *cranial nerve* number XI. Concerned with neck muscles.

spinal canal Cavity, containing *cerebrospinal fluid,* running the length of the *grey matter* of the *spinal cord.*

spinal cord The principal (although not exclusive – see *cranial nerves*) meeting point between *neurons* of the *peripheral nervous system* and *central nervous system.* The spinal cord is divided into five **levels** (see *cervical level, coccygeal level, lumbar level, sacral level,* and *thoracic level*), each of which in turn is divided into **segments.** The spinal cord is encased within the backbone.

spinal nerves Thirty-one *nerves* which enter and leave the brain through the *spinal cord.* Compare with *cranial nerves.*

spinal reflex Reflex controlled solely by the *spinal cord.*

SPLD (alternative: *SLD*) *specific learning difficulties.*

split brain patients See *commissurotomy.*

split-half correlation See *reliability.*

split half reliability *split half correlation.*

split litter technique In animal experimentation, taking animals from the same litters and putting them in separate groups, in an attempt to *match* on general genetic and environmental similarities.

split personality *multiple personality.*

SPM *Standard Progressive Matrices.*

spontaneity measurement Assessing participants by observing them behaving spontaneously in a naturalistic environment or in *dramatherapy.* The term is often applied to measurements of relationships.

spontaneity therapy A form of *psychodrama,* in which the issue at stake is acted out spontaneously, without preparation.

spontaneous fluency *divergent thinking.*

spontaneous recovery (1) *spontaneous remission.* (2) The return of a response which has supposedly been extinguished.

spontaneous regression The drop in strength with which a learned behaviour, skill, etc., is exhibited between therapy/training sessions.

spontaneous remission Recovery from illness which cannot be attributed to the treatment being received at the time.

sporadic Alzheimer's disease Form of *dementia of the Alzheimer type* in which the patient developing the disease has no 'obvious' genetic predisposition to develop the illness such as a parent who contracted the same disease at an early age. The term is slightly misleading since there may in fact be a genetic cause (hence why it is avoided in the main body of the book). It is used to distinguish the condition from *familial Alzheimer's disease.*

sports psychology The study of psychological aspects of sport (e.g. playing, training, etc.).

spouse abuse The physical and/or psychological mistreatment of a person by her/his partner.

SPQ *Study Process Questionnaire.*

SPS *Suicide Probability Scale.*

SPSS Statistical Package for the Social Sciences: a frequently used computerized statistical package.

spurious correlation A *correlation* which is statistically *significant,* but which does not indicate a causal link between the variables in question. See *partial correlation.*

SPV *Gordon's Survey of Personal Values.*

square root transformation *normalization* technique, in which the square roots of the scores are taken. Used to convert data with a *positively skewed distribution.*

square transformation *normalization* technique, in which the squares of the scores are taken. Used to convert data with a *negatively skewed distribution.*

S-R learning *stimulus-response learning.*

SRD *specific reading difficulties.*

SRR *specific reading retardation.*

SRRS *Social Readjustment Rating Scale.*

SRT *simple reaction time.*

S.S. *sum of squares.*

SSA *Survey of School Attitudes.*

SSEA *Schuell Short Examination for Aphasia.*

SSHA *Survey of Study Habits and Attitudes.*

SSQ *Social Situation Questionnaire.*

SSRIs *selective serotonin re-uptake inhibitors.*

SST (1) *single session therapy.* (1) social skills training.

stabilimeter A measure of the degree to which a participant can maintain a rigid posture, usually when deprived of visual feedback (i.e. s/he is blindfolded, and the degree to which s/he sways is measured).

stability under stress (SUS) The degree to which an individual can withstand *stress-inducing* experiences.

stable-unstable scale See *causal attribution theory.*

STAI *State-Trait Anxiety Inventory.*

staircase method See *method of limits.*

standard deviation (s, o) The square root of *sample variance.* In technical terms, the mean plus or minus the standard deviation represents the two points on the X axis of a graph of a *normal distribution* where the curve ceases to have a downward trend and begins a horizontal trend (i.e. where the curve begins to 'flatten out'). The standard deviation has an extremely useful feature which makes it indispensable to most researchers. The space between the *mean* −1.96 standard deviations and the mean + 1.96 standard deviations represents 95% of the curve's area. Accordingly, one can predict that approximately 95% of future observations of the same variable will fall within the sample mean ± 1.96 standard deviations. This is of use in calculating *significance* from *sampling distributions.* See *z score.*

standard difference The difference between two *means* divided by the *standard error* of the difference.

standard distance The difference between the mean and a particular value divided by the *standard deviation* (i.e. a measure of how many standard deviations from the mean a particular score is, and hence how unusual it is).

standard error See *sampling distribution.*

standard error of measurement The range of scores in which a participant's 'true' scores lies (i.e. allowing for testing error).

standard error of prediction (sy') The *standard deviation* of the differences between the actual values and the values predicted by a statistical test (e.g. a *regression*). The smaller the value of sy', the better the prediction.

standard error of the estimate In a *regression* calclulation, a measure of the level of differences between the actual scores and the regression line. This gives an estimate of the likely spread of all scores (plus or minus 2 standard errors of the estimate should cover circa 95%).

standard error of the estimate of the predicted scores See *expectancy table.*

standard error of the mean (1) Statistic measuring the likely difference between the *mean* of the *sample* and the mean of the *population.* (2) *standard error.*

standard multiple regression *multiple regression* in which all the *predictor variables* are entered at the same time.

standard observer Psychology's equivalent of 'the person in the street'. A hypothetical person of normal abilities, senses and emotions.

standard partial regression coefficient *beta weight,* definition (2).

Standard Progressive Matrices (SPM) See *Raven's Progressive Matrices.*

standard ratio *standard difference.*

Standard Reading Tests *test battery* of reading ability and potential reading problems. Ability is assessed by a sentence reading task. Possible problems are examined with a variety of measures assessing e.g. visual perceptual skills, phonological skills, etc.

standard score The scoring of test performance in terms of units of *standard deviation* away from the mean. Most commonly used method is the *z score* (the two terms are often used – erroneously – as synonyms), but also see *stanine scale* and *T score*.

Standard Test Lessons in Reading Collection of texts of various (standardized) levels of difficulty. A reading test, but has also been employed to assess accuracy of *readability* formulae.

standardised coefficient (beta) See *unstandardised coefficient*.

standardised test *standardized test*.

standardization (-isation) The creation of a *standardized test*.

standardization sample Sample of participants used in a *standardization*.

standardized regression coefficient *beta weight*, definition (2).

standardized residuals See *residuals*.

standardized test A test which is either *domain referenced* or *norm referenced*, and which is reliable, in that different testers should produce identical findings given the same set of participants. Such tests have well-established procedures for administration and scoring.

standardized variable *variable* mathematically altered to conform to a desired set of parameters. In practice, this nearly always means that the mean is 0 and the *standard deviation* is 1.

Stanford-Binet (S-B) Scale/Test *IQ test* – the first to be standardized. Based on original work by Binet, standardized by Terman at Stanford University. Revised several times, and still in common use. See *Cattell Infant Intelligence Scale*.

Stanford Diagnostic Mathematics Test (SDMT) Mathematics *test battery*.

Stanford Diagnostic Reading Test (SDRT) Reading *test battery*, concentrating on comprehension, decoding, vocabulary, and reading rate.

stanine scale A *standard score* in which the *mean* is converted to a nominal value of 5, and the *standard deviation* has a value of 2. E.g. a score 1.5 standard deviations below the mean would have a score on the stanine scale of 2. Extrapolating from this, a score of 5 will contain 20% of all scores; scores of 4 and 6 each account for 17%; 3 and 7 = 12%; 2 and 8 = 7%; and 1 and 9 = 4%.

stasiphobia A *phobia* of standing.

stat rat Prediction of a participant's behaviour by (computer) simulation.

stat subject *stat rat*.

state anxiety See *trait anxiety*.

state measure A measure of current psychological state. This can be a simple *mood measure*, but can also include more wide-ranging questions. Contrast with *trait*.

State-Trait Anger Expression Inventory (STAXI) Measure of the level of anger a participant feels, and the events likely to create the emotion.

State-Trait Anxiety Inventory (STAI) Self-report questionnaire recording levels of *state anxiety* and *trait anxiety*.

State-Trait Personality Inventory (STPI) Collective measure of anger, *anxiety* and curiosity.

static When referring to an injury – an injury which is neither getting better nor getting worse.

static tremor Trembling that occurs when the affected body part is at rest and is supported.

statistical artifact An incorrect conclusion resulting from a faulty use of statistics.

statistical association *correlation.*

statistical attenuation The reduction in the size of the *correlation* between two *variables* due to errors of measurement. There are methods of mathematically adjusting for this.

statistical contamination A lowering of the accuracy of a statistical analysis because of the unwanted effects of an extra *variable(s)* (e.g. see *partial correlation*).

statistical control Mathematically adjusting the values of data collected before they are analysed, to control for factors known to have had an unwanted biasing effect on the data.

statistical dependence *correlation.*

statistical hypothesis *null hypothesis.*

statistical power *power (of a statistical test).*

statistical rarity *outlier.*

statistical regression *regression towards the mean.*

statistical significance *significance.*

statistical validity *validity.*

statistical weighting *weighting.*

status validity *concurrent validity.*

STAXI *State-Trait Anger Expression Inventory.*

stem and leaf display A method of representing raw data and creating a histogram of its distribution. The first (i.e. the numbers furthest to the left) x numbers of each data entry are made into 'stems', and what are left become the 'leaves'. The size of x depends upon the data and the researcher's personal aims. However, suppose that the researcher decides to give x a value of 2. A number such as 1234 will have a leaf of 34, and a stem of 12. The number 1249 will have the same stem (12), but a different leaf (49). Traditionally in a stem and leaf display, the stems are arranged in a column on the left of the page, and any leaves found in conjunction with that stem are put in a row to the left of their associated stem. Not all the stems in a numerical sequence might be found (e.g. there might be a stem of 12 and one of 14, but not one of 13). Such 'empty stems' are nonetheless included in the final display. In the following example, the value of x is 1, and by this criterion, the following data set (10,11,11,12,17,21,23,26,45,46, 51) can be displayed as:

Stem	Leaf
1	0,1,1,2,7
2	1,3,6,3
4	5,6
5	1

By rotating the page by 90 degrees, such that the 'stem' is now at the bottom, it can be seen that a rudimentary *histogram* is created.

sten A *standard score* which creates a ten point scale.

step-down analysis Form of *multiple regression* in which the *criterion variables* are entered in a specific order.

step function See *linear relationship.*

step interval *class interval.*

stepping stone theory See *gateway drugs.*

stepwise regression *free entry multiple regression.*

stereognosis The ability to recognize an object by touch.

stereotaxic atlas See *stereotaxy.*

stereotaxic instrument See *stereotaxy.*

stereotaxy A method of brain surgery, whereby the operating site is calculated beforehand using a ***stereotaxic atlas*** (a set of three-dimensional 'maps' of the brain), and the position is mapped onto the patient's brain using a ***stereotaxic instrument***. The afflicted tissue is removed, by e.g. radioactive pellets, cauterization, etc. The method enables the surgeon to operate deep within the brain, whilst minimizing the amount of brain tissue which has to be removed.

stereotyped behaviour A behaviour which is repeated in identical fashion whatever the circumstances, and no matter how inappropriate it might be in the situation in question.

stereotypic movement disorder Repetitive and prolonged use of non-functional movements (that may be self-injurious). The disorder appears without symptoms that would be expected in conditions that manifest similar movements, such as some types of *autism.*

stereotypy The persistent repetition of a complex sequence of actions or speech.

Sternberg test A *recognition* test in which the participant is shown a small group of items, and must then indicate whether a presented item belongs to the set just seen.

sthenometer Any measure of muscular strength.

stick test A measure of visuo-spatial skills. The participant is required to copy a design made out of matchsticks, both directly, and as a mirror-image.

Stilling test Test of colour blindness.

stimulant General term for any drug or substance that increases activity, particularly activity in all or part of the nervous system. The psychological effect is typically of euphoria and increased alertness. Stimulants can in some instances be used for medically legitimate purposes and caffeine (a stimulant) is a commonly used everyday substance. However, the majority of stimulants are socially proscribed (e.g. amphetamines used as *recreational drugs*).

stimulus attenuation A reduction in the strength of the perceived signal produced by a stimulus.

stimulus continuum *stimulus dimension.*

stimulus control Therapeutic *conditioning* technique in which the patient learns to associate a stimulus with only appropriate reactions, rather than a range of appropriate and inappropriate reactions.

stimulus dimension The scale of measurement along which a stimulus can assume its values (e.g. temperature).

stimulus over-selectivity Attending to one aspect of something to the exclusion of its other attributes.

stimulus-response (S-R) learning Type of learning associated with *behaviourism* – the stimulus given to the participant and the response made to the stimulus are measured, but no assumption is made about the participant's thought processes in making the response.

STM *short-term memory.*

stochastic sequence A series of events in which each event is random. However, there is often the implication that although each event is random, overall the series can be predicted with some accuracy. An example commonly given is stock market prices – although on a day to day basis shares may fluctuate with some degree of unpredictability, over longer periods of time, there tend to be reliable upward or downward trends in prices.

Stockholm syndrome The emotional bond which sometimes is created between a jailor/kidnapper and his/her prisoner/victim.

stocking anaesthesia See *glove anaesthesia*.

stocktaking In therapy, cataloguing and evaluating the achievements attained so far (either in the patient's life or in the therapeutic process).

STPI *State-Trait Personality Inventory*.

straight ranking See *ranking*.

stranger reaction The reaction to a stranger – the term is particularly used of young children (where e.g. an extreme display of fright can be indicative of problems).

stratified random sampling *stratified sampling*.

stratified sampling Taking a sample of participants, so that all types present in the population are represented. In *proportional stratified sampling*, types are selected in proportion to their incidence in the population.

strephosymbolia A distortion of symbolic information. Found in e.g. many forms of *developmental dyslexia*.

stress Condition of coping with events beyond an individual's normal working capacity (in quantity and/or level of difficulty), and the negative psychological and physical ailments which can result from this.

stress counselling *counselling* designed to alleviate the effects of *stress* and to train patients to reduce the stressful content of their lives.

stress inoculation therapy Technique of introducing patients to a *stress-provoking* incident under controlled conditions, and demonstrating how they can cope with it (i.e. inoculating the situation against stress).

stress interview Interview in which the candidate is deliberately placed under stress to see how s/he performs under demanding conditions.

stress inventory General term for any measure of the level of *stress* experienced by the participant.

stress management Any therapeutic method designed to reduce *stress* and help control situations giving rise to stress.

Stress Management Computerized *stress management* programme.

stress test Any test in which the participant is placed under stress to see how s/he performs under pressure.

stressor Factor causing *stress*.

striate cortex *primary visual cortex*.

strictness set See *evaluative set*.

striving for superiority See *individual psychology*.

stroke Damage to brain tissue caused by the cessation of its blood supply. This can either be because a blood vessel bursts (**cerebral haemorrhage**) or it becomes blocked with a clot (**cerebral thrombosis**). The psychological and physical effect of the stroke very much depends upon the location of the injury. The term is often reserved for a relatively large-scale loss, to contrast with *infarct*.

Strong-Campbell Interest Inventory (SCII) Modernized version of *Strong Vocational Interest Blank*.

Strong Vocational Interest Blank (SVIB) Measure of range of interests and attitudes, which are matched against the patterns of interests found in particular occupational groups.

Stroop Neuropsychological Screening Test (SNST) A standardized form of the well-known cognitive psychology experiment. The Stroop task presents the participant with a printed list of names of colours printed in a variety of ink colours (one colour per word). The participant must read out the words, ignoring the colour of the ink (e.g. read the word 'blue' which is printed in red ink) or read out the colour of the ink, ignoring the word (e.g. in the aforementioned example, say 'red'). The test is a measure of the participant's ability to ignore conflicting signals. It can be used to diagnose certain forms of brain damage.

structural equation modelling *multivariate statistical* technique, which examines how a series of test measures, or *manifest variables*, can be expressed as a smaller number of 'factors', or *latent variables*. The latent variables in turn can be measured for their effects on a tangible measure (e.g. of a skill). The calculation of latent variables from manifest variables is done using *factor analysis*, whilst the influence of the latent variables on the skill in question involves similar techniques to those used in *path analysis*. The technique is very complex, and is open to a degree of subjectivity (e.g. in the choice of what constitutes a latent variable).

structural group Group of patients for a therapeutic regime who are felt likely to be supportive of each other.

structural imaging See *neuroimaging*.

structural therapy Any therapeutic technique in which the patients' lives have an order or structure placed upon them. The term is particularly used of such a treatment for *autistic* patients.

Structure of the Observed Learning Outcome (SOLSO) Taxonomy Method of classifying older pupils'/students' understanding of the structure and aims of a piece of instruction. Students are asked to describe 'what the course was about', and answers are classified according to how many aspects of the course are mentioned and the degree to which interrelationships between them are identified.

structured interview Interview technique in which the questions and their order of presentation are fixed. Participants' responses to questions are not followed up with further questions, although in the *semi-structured interview* they are. In an *unstructured interview*, there may be an initial plan of topics to be covered, but no set order is pre-arranged, and the interview is allowed to find its own course.

structured personality test *personality inventory*.

structured self-report *self-report questionnaire* in which the participant's responses are restricted to a limited set of answers (e.g. to 'yes' 'no' and 'maybe').

Student's t test *t test*. See *Student's test*.

Student's test *t test*. 'Student' was the pen-name of the inventor of the t test.

Study of Values Questionnaire assessing value judgements at a relatively abstract level and also in applied settings, such as religion, politics, etc.

Study Process Questionnaire (SPQ) Questionnaire measuring study skills and motivation in older pupils/students. See *Learning Process Questionnaire*.

sub-cortical Pertaining to areas of the brain other than the *cerebral cortex*.

sub-cortical dementias *dementias* whose principal focus of damage is not in the *cerebral cortex*. Compare with *cortical dementias*.

subdural haematoma A severe leakage of blood between the brain and the skull, usually arising from a heavy blow, and a source of potentially severe and widespread brain damage.

subject See *participant*.

subject attrition Loss of participants before the completion of testing, through illness, deliberate withdrawal of participation, etc. This can pose problems, because the experimenter cannot be sure that s/he is left with a representative sample. This can be demonstrated in *longitudinal studies*, where several researchers have reported that the 'drop out' participants are on average less intelligent.

subject mortality Sometimes used as a synonym for *subject attrition*, rather than its more literal meaning of proportion of subjects now dead.

subject representativeness *population validity.* See *variable representativeness.*

subject role The role the subject perceives s/he is 'playing' in an experiment. In some instances, this can be a major influence on performance (e.g. feelings of inadequacy can lead to *subject attrition*). A change in behaviour because of the presence of an experimenter is also known as *reactivity.* See *evaluation apprehension.*

subject variable Any experimental *variable* pertaining to the subject (e.g. age, IQ etc).

subjective test Any test which is marked by the subjective opinion of the examiner.

subjective unit of distress (SUD) On a numerical scale, the level of negative feelings a participant or patient feels they are suffering from.

sublimation Converting a response which the participant would like to make, but which would be frowned upon, into a more innocuous action.

subliminal A stimulus too weak to be consciously detected. However, subsequent behaviour may indicate that it was detected 'unconsciously' (e.g. an item presented subliminally may subsequently be selected from a set of items at a higher-than-chance level). By extension of this principle, **subliminal learning** is the acquisition and possession of knowledge which one is unaware of having been explicitly taught.

subliminal learning See *subliminal*.

subliminal psychodynamic activation Psychoanalytic technique in which the patient is presented with *subliminal* stimuli intended to stimulate subconscious thoughts.

subnormal intelligence *mental retardation.*

subordinate constructs See *personal construct theory.*

substance abuse The use of illegal drugs, or socially acceptable drugs (alcohol, etc.) in amounts considered excessive by societal norms, such that physical and/or mental functioning is impaired. The patient usually is incapable of voluntarily ceasing to use the drug. **Substance dependence** shares the same symptoms, with the additional problem that the patient's body is physically dependent on the drug (i.e. without further dosages, s/he is physically ill, as well as suffering a purely mental craving). **Polydrug abuse** is *addiction* to more than one substance. See *alcoholism*.

substance dependence See *substance abuse.*

substance-related disorder Any disorder created by use of a *psychoactive* substance (e.g. alcohol, illegal drugs, etc).

substantia nigra Area of the *pons* whose malfunction is associated with *Parkinson's disease.*

substitution error In reading, perception, memory, etc., replacing the target item with another item (often related).

subvocal speech (1) *inner speech.* (2) Minute movements of the muscles involved in speech exhibited when a participant is thinking/reading.

subvocalization *subvocal speech.*

success rate for hiring The proportion of employees hired on the basis of their selection test scores who turn out to be good at their job.

successive approximation The process whereby a behaviour which is being *shaped* becomes progressively more like the target state.

SUD *subjective unit of distress.*

sufficient condition See *necessary condition.*

Suicide Probability Scale (SPS) A measure of propensity to commit suicide.

suicidology The study of suicide.

sulci Plural of *sulcus.*

sulcus A fold or crease in the wrinkled surface of the *cortex.* The term is generally used for a relatively small crease and *fissure* for a relatively large crease.

sum of squares (S.S.) See *ANOVA table.*

summary statistic *descriptive statistic.*

summation curve *cumulative frequency distribution.*

sundown syndrome The phenomenon observed in some *demented* patients, who get up during the night and wander about, without apparent regard for the propriety of the time or place.

superego See *Freud's psychoanalytic theory.*

superficial reflex See *reflex.*

superficial symptom Symptom which is an expression of a more serious underlying cause, and whose treatment will not remove the root of the problem.

superior In anatomy, a body section is superior if it is located above another section (which is termed the *inferior*). There is no implication that the superior section has a more important function.

superiority complex See *individual psychology.*

superordinate constructs See *personal construct theory.*

superstitious behaviour (1) The lay meaning of 'being superstitious'. (2) A behaviour found in some participants – having been rewarded for performing an action, they continue to do so in the hope of further reward, even though it may be intermittent or not forthcoming.

supportive therapy Therapeutic aid to help a patient cope with a condition which is unlikely to respond to treatment.

suppression The conscious submerging of unpleasant ideas and memories. Contrast with *repression.*

suppressor variable *variable* whose actions distorts the perceived relationship between other variables.

surface dysgraphia A complex failure of writing – patients have most problems with *low frequency* words, which may be partially correctly spelt; or a similar-sounding word may be erroneously offered; or may be spelt as a nonsense word, but with the required pronunciation (e.g. 'kee' for 'quay').

surface dyslexia An *acquired dyslexia* – the patient shows a complex set of symptoms, which most closely resemble a child learning to read. Some words are immediately correctly read, but others have to be 'sounded out', or are pronounced as a word which looks like the to-be-read word.

surface traits See *source trait.*

surgency See *five factor model of personality.*

survey A study in which people are asked about a particular aspect of themselves (including their opinions on topics), their lifestyle, and/or their possessions. Surveys are almost invariably used to collect data on large samples, and attempt no experimental manipulation of the participants. They are for these reasons usually descriptive, and used to collect demographic data. Common uses include collecting information on consumer purchases and attitudes to products, and political attitudes and voting habits.

Survey of School Attitudes (SSA) Measure of pupils' attitudes to their education.

Survey of Study Habits and Attitudes (SSHA) Measure of study skills and pupils' attitudes to their education.

survival analysis Statistical analysis of the length of time a person or item survives (i.e. does not die or become inoperative). The analysis is often predicated on the **survival function**, a measure of the probability that at a particular time a particular person or item will still survive.

survival function See *survival analysis.*

survivor (1) A person in a particular age group who is still alive (e.g. there are relatively few survivors from the group of people born in 1900, whilst there are a lot from 1984). (2) An individual who has experienced traumatic events in the past.

survivor guilt Feelings of guilt engendered by being a *survivor* (definition 2) – i.e. of feeling guilty that s/he survived whilst others did not.

SUS *stability under stress.*

sustained attention The ability to concentrate on a task without being distracted. See *attention.*

SVIB *Strong Vocational Interest Blank.*

Swansea Test of Phonic Skills Test of phonological skills, for participants aged under 7 years.

Sydenham's chorea Childhood illness (associated with rheumatic fever) with symptoms of *chorea*, and occasionally *acute confusional state*, or (temporary) general intellectual impairment.

syllogism A statement consisting of three premises, of which the third is a conclusion drawn from the first two (e.g. 'all As are B; all Bs are C; therefore, As are C').

sy' *standard error of prediction.*

symbol-digit test *digit-symbol substitution task.*

symbolic loss Concept (particularly in *psychoanalysis*) that a patient (mis)interprets an act as representing a total loss of something or someone valued (e.g. total loss of affection).

symbolophobia A *phobia* of one's words being misinterpreted.

symmetric correlation *correlation* where the order in which the variables being correlated is entered into the equation is unimportant. In some more specialized forms of correlation (rarely encountered in psychological research), *asymmetric correlation* is used, in which some of the *variance* in the equation is held constant, and in these instances, order of entry is important.

symmetrical distribution *distribution curve* which can be split in half into left and right mirror-images, and in which the *mean* and *median* are equal.

Symonds' Picture Study Test A *projective personality test* for adolescents. The test materials are a series of pictures depicting personal relationships.

symptom bearer The member of a disharmonious family, who possesses a mental illness, largely as a result of shouldering the burdens of, or being sensitive to, the family's problems.

Symptom Check-List-90-Revised (SCL-90-R) A questionnaire designed to classify a patient on nine scales of broad categories of mental illness (e.g. *depression, psychoticism*). Patients are presented with a list of 90 symptoms and asked to identify the degree to which each applies to themselves.

symptom substitution The appearance of new symptoms upon the disappearance of old ones, usually indicating that the symptoms are merely expressions of a deeper-rooted problem.

symptom wearer *symptom bearer.*

symptomatic therapy Treating the symptoms rather than the underlying cause.

synaesthesia Detecting a stimulus in the wrong sensory modality (e.g. 'seeing' a sound as a colour, rather than hearing it).

synalgia *referred pain.*

synchronic See *diachronic.*

syncope A brief fainting spell.

syndrome A collection of symptoms indicative of a particular cause.

synergic See *synergism.*

synergic drug *synergist.*

synergism The joint action of several factors aiming at a common goal. There is often the implication that the joint action is greater than the sum of the individual components. The adjective, derived from synergism is **synergic**.

synergist A drug which, in combination with another drug, has a greater effect (for good or ill) than the sum effect of the two drugs taken separately.

synkinesis An unintentional movement made when another movement is being deliberately attempted.

synonym-antonym test Test in which the participant must decide if word pairs mean the same or are opposites.

synonym test Test in which the participant must supply a word meaning the same as one supplied by the experimenter.

syntactical aphasia *conduction aphasia.*

syntonia Gross over-reaction to the environment.

syphilitic dementia *dementia*-like symptoms found in the terminal stages of untreated syphilis (see *neurosyphilis*).

system effect The effect of a change in one part of a system on the system as a whole.

System of Multicultural Pluralistic Assessment (SOMPA) *test battery* designed to allow for advantages and disadvantages conferred by different cultural backgrounds.

systematic desensitization See *desensitization.*

systematic distortion The alteration of memories to conform to a *schema*.

systematic error Error in which there is a *constant error* or erroneous trend in test instruments or responses.

systematic replication See *replication*.

systematic sampling *linear systematic sampling*.

systemic Present throughout a system (most often the system in question is the body).

systemic therapy Therapeutic method akin to *holistic therapy*, with concepts derived from system theory or the interaction between the patients' beliefs and their situation.

systemizing The ability to analyse a problem systematically in terms of its components. The skill is believed by some commentators to be atypically good in people with *autism* and *Asperger's syndrome*.

systolic pressure See *blood pressure*.

T

T *Thinking*.

T data Data from a (*standardized*) test.

t distribution See *t test*.

T group *human relations training group*.

T maze A maze shaped like a 'T'. The participant (almost invariably a laboratory rat) starts at the base of the long arm, and must elect whether to finish its journey in the left or the right top cross-section.

T-scope *tachistoscope*.

T score A *standard score* in which the mean is converted to a nominal value of 50, and the *standard deviation* has a value of 10. E.g. a person with a score two standard deviations above the mean would have a T score of 70.

t test *parametric test* of differences between two groups' performance on the same measure (which must be a *continuous variable*). It tests the *null hypothesis* that the two groups are derived from the same *population*, and assumes that the population has a *normal distribution*. The *t test for a single mean* analyses whether the mean of a sample differs significantly from the population from which it is drawn. The t test has two other main forms – in the *paired t test*, participants in the two groups being compared are *dependent samples* (e.g. two groups matched on a certain set of criteria, the same participants before and after treatment, etc). In the *unpaired t test*, participants in the two groups are *independent samples*. The *sampling distribution* for the t test is the *t distribution*, which also forms the basis of several other statistical measures. The t test is only valid for comparing two groups on one measure. For comparisons of larger numbers of groups and/or measures, the *analysis of variance* is to be preferred, rather than running multiple t tests. For reasons too lengthy to elaborate, running multiple t tests on pairings of groups on the same set of data greatly increases the probability of making a *Type I error*, unless mathematical adjustments are made. Under certain circumstances, however, these are necessary (e.g. *post hoc tests* in an *analysis of variance*). Several of these *t tests for multiple comparisons* are available *(Duncan's multiple range test, Dunnett t-test, Fisher's PLSD test, Newman-Keuls test, Scheffe test, Tukey HSD test)*. See *Hotelling's T test, Mann-Whitney U test, one sample t statistic*, and *Wilcoxin matched pairs signed ranks test*.

t test for a single mean See *t test*.

t test with two random independent samples *unpaired t test*.

t tests for multiple comparisons See *t test*.

TA *transactional analysis.*

tabes dorsalis A manifestation of *neurosyphilis*, characterized by loss of coordination, unsteady walking and loss of bladder control.

tabo paresis The simultaneous presence of *syphilitic dementia* and *tabes dorsalis.*

TABP *Type A behaviour pattern.*

tachistoscope (T-scope) An instrument for presenting visual stimuli for very brief periods of time (*tachistoscopic presentation*).

tachistoscopic presentation See *tachistoscope.*

tachylalia Abnormally fast speech.

tachyphasia *tachylalia.*

tachyphrenia rapid thought.

tachyphylaxis The rapid development of *tolerance* to a drug.

tacrine Drug whose effects include the enhanced release of *acetylcholine* (see *cholinergic hypothesis*), and thus a possible treatment for some forms of *dementia.*

tailored test (1) Test which is devised to be especially appropriate for an individual participant's abilities. (2) *adaptive test.*

tails (of distribution) The extreme left and right of a *distribution curve.* They represent the extreme low and high scorers within a sample.

talking cure Largely derogatory term for any therapeutic method (particularly *psychoanalysis*) in which the treatment largely consists of the patient talking about his/her problems, without any training in coping with the said problems.

talking therapy Any therapeutic method which uses talking (e.g. through discussion) rather than physical treatment (e.g. drugs) as its principal method of treatment. Note that the term is uncomfortably similar to *talking cure*, and is perhaps best avoided.

tanyphonia A thin, 'weedy' voice.

TAP *Test of Academic Progress.*

taphophilia An abnormal liking for cemeteries.

taphophobia A *phobia* of graves and burials.

tapping test Test of *psychomotor* functioning, in which the patient must tap out a rhythm.

TAQ *Test Anxiety Questionnaire.*

tarantism A form of *mass hysteria* in which the victims are gripped with an urge to 'dance' (or at least, flail their limbs about uncreatively a la disco). The phenomenon has been rarely seen in modern times, but was apparently more prevalent in previous centuries.

Tarchanoff phenomenon *galvanic skin response.*

tardive late in appearing.

tardive dyskinesia *dyskinesia* resulting from long-term dosage of *major tranquillizers.*

target behaviour The behaviour which is the desired result of the therapeutic process.

target population The population to whom the findings of a study are applicable.

target response *target behaviour.*

targeted mutation analysis Genetic test which seeks out a specific type of genetic mutation (i.e. rather than looking at a larger unit of genetic material).

TAS *Test Anxiety Scale.*

task-based rater bias A biased classification of participants or items based upon a misuse of the test scale being used, rather than a bias for or against the participants or items themselves. See *ratee-based rater bias*.

task-specific tremor Trembling that occurs only during a specific activity.

TAT *Thematic Apperception Test.*

tau correlation coefficient *Kendall rank correlation coefficient.*

tautophone A device used in a *projective personality test*. It produces a garbled set of speech sounds, which the participant is asked to interpret.

taxonomy A classification system.

Tay-Sachs disease An *innate* lack of the enzyme hexoseaminidase-A, which results in a failure to process certain fats. This in turn leads to severe physical handicap and *mental retardation*. The patient usually dies before school age.

Taylor Manifest Anxiety Scale *Manifest Anxiety Scale.*

TBR *to-be-remembered.*

TEA *Test of Everyday Attention.*

Teacher Rating Scale B(2) 26 item questionnaire eliciting teacher's rating of a pupil's behaviour and aptitude.

Teachers' Word Book of 30,000 Words Book written by Thorndike and Lorge and usually known by their surnames. Comprises a list of the 30,000 most commonly used words in (American) English, which are assessed for frequency of occurrence. The ***Dale word lists*** (included in the Thorndike – Lorge book as Appendices A & B) give smaller lists – the Dale 3000 word list gives the 3000 most common words, and Dale 769 word list the 769 most common words.

teleology (1) The study of the purpose of things. (2) The erroneous belief that

because something is the way it is, that must be its cause (e.g. 'birds have wings because they have to fly').

teleopsia A disorder of visual perception, in which items are seen as too far away.

telephone scatologia *atypical paraphilia* in which the patient gains principal sexual gratification from making obscene telephone calls.

temazepam A sedative, legally prescribed as such or as a sleeping tablet. However, if dissolved and injected it can produce feelings of considerable euphoria (although at a price – several deaths have been reported), and accordingly it has found favour as an 'illegal drug'.

temporal lobe epilepsy See *epilepsy*.

temporal lobes Sections of the *cerebral cortex* occupying, roughly speaking, the area of the left and right temples. Their chief function is interpreting information – in most individuals the left temporal lobe is essential in comprehending and producing speech and writing. They are also strongly involved in the storage of memories.

temporal maze Maze in which there are no physical clues indicating the correct route (e.g. always follow the blue paths), and hence in which the correct route must be remembered as a sequence of turns.

Tennessee Self-Concept Scale (TSCS) Measure of *self-concept* in Participants aged 12 years and over. Participants express agreement/disagreement with a series of *self-descriptive statements*.

TEP *token economy programme.*

teratogen Any environmental factor that can cause damage to a developing foetus.

Terman-Merrill tests Revised versions of the original intelligence test by *Binet*.

terminal drop model A theory that older individuals maintain the same level of intellectual functioning until a sudden and precipitous decline a few months/years before their death.

terminal insomnia See *insomnia*.

terminal tremor *intention tremor*.

terminal value A goal or ambition. This contrasts with an **instrumental value**, which is the code of conduct by which a person operates in moving towards this goal.

tertiary auditory cortex See *primary auditory cortex*.

tertiary cortex See *primary cortex*.

tertiary factor See *factor analysis*.

tertiary prevention See *prevention (of disease)*.

tertiary syphilis See *neurosyphilis*.

test age *mental age*.

test anxiety See *performance anxiety*.

Test Anxiety Questionnaire (TAQ) Measure of *test anxiety*.

Test Anxiety Scale (TAS) Early version of the *Achievement Anxiety Test*.

test battery Collection of tests assessing the same skill or behaviour, or aspects of the same general skill or behaviour.

test bias Flaw in the construction of a psychological (usually IQ) test, which favours some groups of participants more than others. E.g. some researchers argue that many IQ tests unfairly favour participants from a white middle class background.

test ceiling Full or nearly full marks. See *ceiling effect*.

Test Critiques Large collection of critical surveys of psychological and educational tests.

Test of Academic Progress (TAP) *test battery* of scholastic attainment in maths, reading and spelling (plus sub-tests of writing speed and composition).

test of association Measure of the degree to which a measure of *association* is statistically *significant*. Not to be confused with *association* test.

Test of Everyday Attention (TEA) Measure of *attention* divided into eight sub-tests of realistic attention tasks (e.g. searching a telephone directory for specific target symbols).

Test of Motor Impairment – Henderson Revision (TOMI) Test for children 5–11 years, assessing motor skills (e.g. peg board, catching, hopping, etc.).

Test of Reception of Grammar (TROG) Test assessing comprehension of various grammatical forms. Participants are shown a set of four pictures, and are asked to point to the picture which best describes a sentence read out by the tester. The sentences increase in grammatical complexity as the test progresses. It is designed for use with children (particularly those with suspected language difficulties), but norms are also available for older and low IQ participants.

test reliability *reliability*.

test-retest coefficient The statistical measure of *test-retest reliability*.

test-retest reliability See *reliability*.

test savvy subjects *test wise subjects*.

test smart subjects *test wise subjects*.

test specifications The collection of factors which a test is intended to measure.

test statistics Any method of assessing the statistical properties of tests.

test utility The degree to which a test is useful (e.g. in terms of how much money it will save by correctly treating a patient, by choosing the best person for the job, etc.).

test validity *validity.*

test wise subjects Participants who have been given so many psychology tests that they score higher marks than would be predicted on any further tests, because they are used to the general procedures and wiles of psychologists and their testing procedures (the *carry-over effect*). Compare with *naive subject.*

testwiseness The attribute of a *test wise subject.*

tetrachoric correlation coefficient (r_t) *correlation* between two variables, both of which are *artificial dichotomous* variables, derived from *normal distributions*. If the two variables are both *natural dichotomies*, then a *phi correlation coefficient* is used. See *contingency coefficient*, and *point biserial correlation coefficient.*

TGA *transient global amnesia.*

thalamus Area of brain responsible, inter alia, for coordination and channelling of information and execution of motor movements. Damage to this area can lead to *Parkinsonism.*

thanatology The study of death and dying.

thanatomania The *compulsion* to kill (oneself or others).

thanatophobia A *phobia* of death or items pertaining to death.

Thanatos *death instinct.*

Thematic Apperception Test (TAT) *projective personality test* in which the participant is shown a series of pictures and is required to make up stories derived from them.

theomania A delusion that one is a deity or a deity's agent.

theophobia A *phobia* of a deity.

theoretical coding Integrating concepts and data into a model that explains the data in a parsimonious manner.

theory of mind The ability to comprehend that another person's mind may have emotions and thoughts different from one's own. E.g. theory of mind enables someone to comprehend another person's emotional state from their behaviour and statements. A poorly-developed theory of mind has been identified in people with *autism* and related disorders.

theory of true scores *true scores theory.*

therapeutic alliance General and rather vague term for those factors which enable the treatment of a patient by a therapist to work.

therapeutic window The range of strengths of treatment which can be applied for an effective cure to result.

therapy See *counselling.*

thermophobia A *phobia* of heat.

theta waves A pattern of electrical activity in the brain detected by *EEC* with a frequency between 4 and 8Hz.

Thinking (T) See *Myers-Briggs Type Indicator.*

thinking personality See *Jung's psychoanalytic theory.*

third force psychology *humanistic psychology.*

third-order factor See *factor analysis.*

third order regression line See *polynomial regression.*

third variable problem The presence of an unmeasured variable which may be the real cause of a *correlation* between two variables which are in reality not causally related. See *partial correlation.*

thoracic level (spinal cord) *level of spinal cord* located between the *cervical level* and the *lumbar level.* Composed of 12 *segments,* labelled T1 (the topmost) to T12.

Thorazine Trade name of *chlorpromazine.*

Thorndike-Lorge word list *Teachers' Word Book of 30,000 Words.*

thought control Therapeutic training in controlling unpleasant thoughts.

thought disorder An inability to think using conventional logic, which is not attributable to *mental retardation.* Is found in e.g. *schizophrenia.* See *loose association.*

thought experiment Thinking how a participant will respond to a set of experimental conditions.

thought stopping A therapeutic technique in which the patient is trained to think about something else when a train of thought becomes too unpleasant.

threshold In perception, the intensity of stimulation required to notice a difference in the stimulus. An *absolute threshold* is the lowest level of stimulation at which the stimulus can be detected (e.g. the dimmest light). The *difference threshold* is the smallest difference between two stimuli which can be reliably (not necessarily always) noticed (e.g. how much brighter one light has to be than another for the difference to be detected). The *interval of uncertainty* is the difference between the minimum intensity necessary always to notice a change, and the maximum intensity where the change is never noticed. In between these intensities, there is a probability that the difference will be detected, and this probability increases the stronger the inten-

sity. The difference threshold is calculated as the intensity where the difference is noticed on x% of occasions (the value of x varies between commentators – 50% and 75% are popular choices). The smallest change necessary to evoke a perception of change is known as the *just noticeable difference,* and the largest change which does not evoke a perception of change is known as the *just not noticeable difference.* See *method of limits,* and *Weber's law.*

threshold model The theory that individuals have a genetically fixed predisposition to develop a particular disease, but whether they actually do depends upon a trigger in the environment. In people with a low predisposition, a large environmental input is required, and vice versa.

threshold model of disease The conceptual model that exposure to disease-causing factors will only cause the disease to develop if the exposure exceeds a threshold. A modification of this theory argues that the threshold itself can be raised or lowered by various factors, including genetic inheritance, hence explaining why some conditions (e.g. some types of *dementia*) are commoner in some families but are rare (but crucially, not unknown) in others.

thrombosis Blood vessel blocked due to clotting.

Thurstone scale *attitude scale* in which participants are required to agree/disagree with a series of statements. The scale is created by having a group of participants grade the strength of intensity of opinion expressed by items in a collection of statements. Those items which are graded equally by the participants are used in the subsequent attitude scale. See *Likert scale.*

time and motion study A study of a task in terms of the time spent on each component of it, and the movements and operations involved. The aim is to find methods of increasing efficiency.

time and orientation measure A simple measure of whether the patient knows the time and date, and where s/he is.

time-lag comparison Comparing the performance of different *age cohorts* at the same age (e.g. scores on a maths test for school leavers over several years). The analysis can be complete in itself, or could be part of an *overlapping longitudinal study*. See *time series study*.

time-lag effect *cohort effect.*

time limited therapy Any therapeutic technique in which the total length of the therapy is specified and known at the start of treatment.

time on task (TOT) Time spent engaged in the target activity (e.g. in education, the amount of time the pupil spends attending to the lesson versus staring out of the window, etc.).

time sampling Observing behaviour for one or more periods of time out of the whole of the period when the behaviour could manifest itself. See *interval recording*.

time-sequential design An 'extended' *cross-sectional study design*. Two or more age groups are compared at one time period, and then several years later, different participants are tested, who are the same ages as the participants were in the first experiment when they were tested. E.g. a group of 30-year-olds and a group of 40-year-olds are tested in 1970, and then new groups of 30- and 40-year-olds are tested in 1985.

time series design *longitudinal study*, during which a treatment is administered to the participants, and differ-

ences in their behaviour and/or performance in the 'before' and 'after' periods are compared.

time series study A study employing the *time-lag comparison*. In an ***interrupted time series study***, an event occurs during the period of study which could potentially affect the performance of the later *cohorts* (e.g. the study might be of the state of 7-year-olds' teeth, and the provision of school milk might be halted half-way through the period of measurement).

tip of the tongue (TOT) Phenomenon whereby an item cannot be fully recovered from memory, but a lot of its features (e.g. number of syllables, words which sound like it, etc.) can be identified: i.e. the word is on the 'tip of the tongue'. The phenomenon illustrates how memories may be stored piecemeal rather than as whole chunks recovered in an 'all or nothing at all' fashion. The phenomenon, which can be generated by a number of experimental paradigms, has been used in comparisons of young and older adults' memory retrieval strategies.

TM *transcendental meditation.*

TMR *trainable mentally retarded.*

to-be-remembered (TBR) Items in a memory task which the participant is asked to remember.

Tocher's modification See *Fisher exact probability test.*

token economy Method of shaping behaviour/learning by means of reward (i.e. *conditioning*). Dismissed by many as too mechanistic for 'normal' people, the method has found greatest favour in the training of the mentally ill and retarded. Basically involves giving participants tokens as a reward for good behaviour/performance (e.g. not hitting other patients). When sufficient tokens have been earned, they can be exchanged for a reward (e.g. sweets). See *contingency contracting.*

token economy programme (TEP) *token economy.*

Token Test Assesses comprehension of verbal commands of varying levels of complexity, and short-term verbal memory. Used to measure *acquired aphasia* (in brain damaged and *demented* patients). Participants are shown a set of tokens of varying shapes, colours and sizes, and are asked to perform actions with them (e.g. 'put the yellow circle on the blue circle', etc.). The test has been updated (the **Revised Token Test**). See *Reporter's Test.*

tolerance (of a drug) *pharmacodynamic tolerance.*

tolerance test In *regression* measures, a test of *collinearity.* The closer the score to zero, the higher the probability of collinearity.

TOMI test *Test of Motor Impairment – Henderson Revision.*

tonic Describing a prolonged contraction of a muscle.

tonic convulsion See *convulsion.*

tonus The slight tension which exists in a resting muscle.

topagnosia A profound inability to recognize where on the body one has been touched.

top down data mining See *data mining.*

topography In a clinical diagnosis, the description of the patient's actions.

topophobia A phobia of a place.

Torrance Test of Creative thinking *test battery of creativity tests.*

TOT (1) *tip of the tongue.* (2) time on task.

Tourette's disorder *Tourette's syndrome.*

Tourette's syndrome Disorder characterized by muscular trembling, tics, and an uncontrollable need to use obscene language, and non-verbal sounds.

toxic psychosis *psychosis* caused by poisoning.

toxicosis Illness caused by poisoning.

toxophobia A *phobia* of poisoning.

tracking (1) The ability to follow a moving object. (2) The ability to detect the outline of a stationary object.

tract Group of *neurons* in the *central nervous system* carrying the same type of information. The distinction between a tract and a *nerve* is rarely observed in psychology, except in discussions of anatomy. See *nerve.*

Trail Making test Sub-test of the *Halstead – Reitan Neuropsychological Battery,* used to assess ability to follow sequences. The participant must make a pencil trail between particular numbers (or in another version, alternate between numbers and letters) printed on a sheet of paper.

trainable mentally retarded (TMR) American term – refers to person of very low IQ (less than 50), who can nonetheless be trained to perform very basic tasks. Compare with *educable mentally retarded (EMR).*

trait An enduring characteristic of personality and/or behaviour. Contrast with *state measure.*

trait anxiety The 'average' level of *anxiety* in everyday life. This contrasts with *state anxiety,* which is one's anxiety at a particular instant, in response to a particular situation, etc.

trait validity content validity for measures of a *trait.*

tranquillizer See *major tranquillizer* and *minor tranquillizer.*

transactional analysis (TA) Therapeutic technique devised by Eric Berne *et al.*, which assumes that in interactions, people tend to assume *ego states* or roles (hence the title of Berne's popular book on the subject – *'Games People Play'*). The ego roles consist of the *adult ego state*, *child ego state*, and *parent ego state*. These loosely correspond to the states of fulfilling the role of being a 'normal' adult, child and parent. The ego states can be subdivided – e.g. the child ego state can be subdivided into the *adapted child* (those aspects of childhood seen as involving obedience to others) and the *free child* (those aspects of childhood seen as being carefree). People move between the roles according to the situation (e.g. there may be times when a parent ego state is assumed in chastising a colleague for poor work). However, an excessive amount of time spent in an inappropriate ego state can cause problems, and the therapy shows patients when they are using the wrong role for the situation in question, and how to use the correct role.

transcendental meditation (TM) A spiritual movement (founder: the Mahesh Yogi), which stresses the spiritual grace to be attained through *meditation*. The meditative state is induced whilst concentrating on and repeating a word (a mantra). Various claims have been made for the efficacy of the process, but these have largely been either disputed, or been shown to occur equally often in other, less ritualistic forms of meditation and *relaxation therapy*.

transcortical aphasia An *aphasia* combining symptoms of both *transcortical motor aphasia* and *transcortical sensory aphasia*.

transcortical motor aphasia *aphasia* in which there is no spontaneous production of language, although the patient can accurately repeat what has been just been said by someone else.

transcortical sensory aphasia *aphasia* in which there is no comprehension of language, although the patient can repeat what is said to him/her, and speech is normally enunciated (although its meaning is usually unintelligible).

transfer The degree to which whatever is learnt in therapy is transferred to everyday life. The term is particularly used in the *behaviour therapies*.

transfer test A measure of how well something learnt in one test condition or situation is transferred to a different test or situation.

transference Stage in (usually *psychoanalytic*) therapy, where the patient responds to the therapist as if they were an authority figure from childhood (usually a parent). In *counter-transference*, the therapist experiences similar feelings about the patient (although often these are lesser in strength and subtler in effect).

transformation methods (factor analysis) See *factor analysis*.

transformed score *derived score*.

transient global amnesia (TGA) A temporary but severe loss of memory, caused by brain damage.

transmuted score *derived score*.

transorbital lobotomy Particularly gruesome method of performing a frontal lobotomy (through the eye socket).

transpersonal psychology General term for range of theories which emphasize mystic and spiritual factors beyond the needs and experiences of individuals.

transsexualism Type of *gender identity disorder*. The belief held by the patient that s/he is really of the opposite sex, and is 'trapped' in the wrong body. See *transvestism*.

transvestism A *paraphilia* in which the patient obtains sexual gratification from wearing clothes of the opposite sex. The majority of transvestites are content with their 'real' gender, and accordingly, the condition should not be confused with *transsexualism*.

tranylcypramine Type of *monoamine oxidase inhibitor*.

trauma A physical or psychological injury. Usually, the term additionally denotes a strongly negative event of sudden onset.

traumatophobia A *phobia* of injury.

treatment fidelity The degree to which a treatment goes as planned.

treatment variable *independent variable*.

trend analysis The statistical study of trends.

trend study A repeated sampling over time of the same *population*, but not necessarily the same members of it (e.g. an annual sampling of 13-year-olds' attitudes to smoking). This is to measure general trends in population behaviour.

triad of impairments Term used by Wing & Gould to describe characteristic *autistic* behaviour – impairment of social relationships, social communication and social understanding and imagination.

trial therapy Initial stage of therapeutic process in which the patient's suitability for the therapy in question is assessed.

trials to criterion The number of attempts at a task required before it is performed to a *criterion* set by the experimenter.

triarchic theory of intelligence Theory by Sternberg which argues that

intelligence is composed of three factors: ***componential intelligence*** (roughly akin to fluid intelligence); ***contextual intelligence*** (the ability to adapt to and live in one's environment); and ***experiential intelligence*** (intellectual skills derived from experience).

trichophagy A *compulsion* to eat or bite hair.

trichophobia A *phobia* of hair.

trichotillomania A disorder in which the patient has a *compulsion* to pull hair.

tricyclic drugs General term for a group of *antidepressant* drugs.

trigeminal cranial nerve *cranial nerve* number V. Concerned with the face and tongue.

trigger stimulus Stimulus which initiates a particular response (usually maladaptive).

trimmed mean *mean* after *outliers/ extreme scores* of the sample have been removed.

trimmed sample Sample of data from which the extreme scores have been removed.

triskaidekaphobia A *phobia* of the number thirteen.

trisomy Having three (rather than the usual two) copies of a cromosome. This causes the cromosome in question to malfunction.

trisomy 13 Having three (rather than the usual two) copies of a cromosome. This causes the cromosome in question to malfunction.

Trisomy 13 Genetic disorder characterized by numerous physical malformations, *microcephaly* and severe intellectual impairment.

trisomy 21 See *Down's Syndrome*.

trochlear cranial nerve *cranial nerve* number IV. Concerned, along with the *abducens cranial nerve* and *oculomotor cranial nerve* with the muscular movements of the eye (compare with *optic cranial nerve*).

TROG *Test of Reception of Grammar.*

true mean *population mean.*

true negative See *true positive.*

true positive Correctly identifying a signal or target as a signal or target, rather than rejecting it as an extraneous piece of information. Similarly, a *true negative* is the correct rejection of background noise or other extraneous information, because it is not a signal or target. The inaccurate rejection of a signal/target is a *false negative*, whilst the incorrect acceptance of an extraneous piece of information/noise as a signal/target is a *false positive*. See *signal detection theory.*

true score See *true scores theory.*

true scores theory The argument that a participant's test score is composed of his/her *true score* (reflecting his/her real worth), plus or minus a margin of error (the *absolute error*).

true variance The *variance* of the *population.*

true zero See *ratio scale.*

truncated range A narrow *range* of data, which can produce misleading results in some analyses which only work optimally with a wide range.

trypanophobia A *phobia* of needles (particularly hypodermic needles).

TSCS *Tennessee Self-Concept Scale.*

tuberous sclerosis Congenital disease characterized by skin, heart and kidney dysfunction, intellectual dysfunction and epilepsy.

tuinol Type of *barbiturate.*

Tukey HSD test A *t test for multiple comparisons* and *post hoc test* for the *analysis of variance.* The 'HSD' stands for 'honestly significant difference'.

Turner's syndrome Genetic disorder characterized by retarded growth and intelligence.

Twenty Statements Test Measure of adolescent self-perception. Participants are asked to make a series of statements about themselves. Generally, the older the participant, the fewer responses sound like replies to a census form (e.g. precise age, full name and address, etc.), and the more about aims, ideals, career hopes, etc.

two-tailed test Any statistical measure in which a difference in either direction is counted as *significant*, provided it is of sufficient magnitude (e.g., group A can have either higher or lower scores than group B). In a *one-tailed test*, the difference must lie in a particular, pre-ordained direction (e.g. group A must gain higher scores than group B). Whether a one- or two-tailed test is chosen depends upon the nature of the experiment (e.g. in examining whether one breed of rat learns faster than another, a difference in either direction is likely to be interesting; but in assessing the effects of a new 'learning drug', its effects must be demonstrably more efficacious than the old drug it is compared with, before it is of interest).

type (1) A *trait* which is either possessed, or it is completely absent. Contrast with *dimension*, and see *dimension versus type debate.* (2) More generally, an attribute which is either possessed or is absent.

Type A behaviour pattern *Type A personality.*

Type A personality Personality type in which the participant is fiercely competitive, and is always 'on the go' (what in the 1980s was termed typical 'yuppie' material). The condition has been linked to a higher than average incidence of *stress*-related illnesses, particularly cardiovascular disease. In contrast, the ***Type B personality*** type is very placid and easy-going, and possessors run significantly less risk of contracting a stress-related illness than Type A subjects.

Type B personality See *Type A personality*.

type I censoring Measuring the incidences of an event over a particular period of time. This contrasts with ***type II censoring***, where the time taken for a particular number of incidences to occur is measured. See *censored observations*.

type I conditioning *classical conditioning*.

Type I error Erroneously accepting a result as significant. See *significance*, and *Type II error*.

Type I sums of squares In *analysis of variance*, the variance shared by the first and second entered variables is 'given' to the first entered variable only. A similar method is also used in some forms of *multiple regression*. In ***Type III sums of squares***, all the variables are entered with only their unique variance being considered (this is the default option in many computer statistics programmes). Accordingly, the order in which they are entered into the equation is of no importance.

type II censoring See *type I censoring*.

type II conditioning *operant conditioning*.

Type II error Erroneously accepting a result as non-*significant*. See *significance*, and *Type I error*.

Type III sums of squares See *Type I sums of squares*.

type R conditioning *operant conditioning*.

type S conditioning *classical conditioning*.

type versus dimension debate *dimension versus type debate*.

typology System of classification.

U

U *Mann-Whitney U test*.

U curve A graph whose curve is shaped like a 'U'.

UCLSQ *University College London Study Questionnaire*.

ultimate cause See *proximate cause*.

unbalanced design Experimental design in which the groups being tested contain unequal numbers of participants or items.

unbiased estimate Any measure which gives an estimate of the characteristics of the *population* from which the test sample was drawn.

uncertain responding *middle category responding*.

unconditional positive regard See *Roger's self theory of personality*.

Unconventional Views Test A measure of *visual agnosia*. The patient must identify everyday objects, seen from unusual viewpoints.

underachievement Performing appreciably worse at a (usually scholastic) task that would be predicted from *aptitude* tests.

undersocialized conduct disorder See *conduct disorder*.

undifferentiated schizophrenia See *schizophrenia*.

undifferentiated sex role identity Personality type whose possessors have low scores on measures of both stereotypically 'masculine' and 'feminine' behaviours. Compare with *androgynous personality*.

unidimensional See *multidimensional*.

unidimensional scale A scale in which the particular item of interest is measured using a single measure. This contrasts with a *multidimensional scale*, in which the item is measured on a set of measures whose overall pattern must be interpreted. E.g. intellectual skills in children might be measured by number of exams passed (a unidimensional scale) or a package of measures including visuo-spatial, verbal, mathematical scales, etc (a multidimensional scale).

uniform distribution *frequency distribution* in which all values are represented equally.

unilateral couple counselling Segment of *couple counselling* in which only one partner is treated (e.g. for problems peculiar to him/her).

unilateral neglect *hemi-inattention*.

unimodal *frequency distribution* in which there is one *mode*.

uniovular *monozygotic*.

unipolar depression *unipolar disorder*.

unipolar dimension See *dimension*.

unipolar disorder See *depression*.

unique factor *specific factor*.

unique trait *trait* possessed only by one person.

unit character A genetically-transmitted factor which is either present or completely absent.

univariate statistics Statistical analyses in which there is only one *dependent variable*. See *multivariate statistics*.

universality Knowledge that one's problems are experienced by others, and hence that one is not alone, or a 'freak'.

University College London Study Questionnaire (UCLSQ) Measure generating eight sub-scales of personality attributes relevant to study skills (e.g. motivation, obsessionality, etc.).

unmatched subjects Participants from different groups upon whom no *matching* has taken place.

unobtrusive observation See *obtrusive observation*.

unpaired comparison Comparison using *unmatched subjects*.

unpaired t test See *t test*.

unplanned comparison An analysis of data which was not planned beforehand by the experimenter. E.g. an unexpected *interaction* in an *ANOVA* might require further investigation. See *planned comparison* and *post hoc test*.

unrotated factor matrix See *factor analysis*.

unspecified mental retardation *mental retardation* whose level cannot be judged because no test is capable of accurately assessing it.

unstandardised coefficient In *multiple regression*, a measure of the level of effect each *predictor variable* has on the *criterion variable* independent of any shared effects between predictor variables. A variant of this is the *standardised coefficient*, which is the unstandardised coefficient expressed as the number of *standard deviations* of the criterion variable. The analysis is structured so that the standardised coefficient ranges between -1 and +1. The closer the value to 1 (regardless of sign) the stronger the effect.

unstructured interview See *structured interview*.

unweighted means *equally weighted means.*

upper apparent limit See *class intervals.*

upper real limit (URL) See *class intervals.*

upper threshold The highest value of a stimulus which can be detected, because beyond that limit the senses cannot perceive (e.g. light or sound frequency), or physical damage would ensue (e.g. light or sound intensity).

URL *upper real limit.*

urolagnia Obtaining sexual gratification from urination.

urophilia *urolagnia.*

utility analysis Measure of the financial savings (or costs) created by selection procedures (e.g. giving a wide battery of tests to prospective part-time cleaners may guarantee the very best person is selected, but is it worth the extra cost?).

Uzgiris-Hunt Scale *test battery* of infant development, based on Piagetian theory of sensori-motor development. Measures include assessment of motor skills, object concept, etc.

V

v Symbol sometimes used to denote *degrees of freedom,* especially in *analysis of variance.*

V Sometimes used as a symbol for *verbal skills.*

VaD *vascular dementia.*

vaginismus An involuntary contraction of the vaginal muscles, making penetrative intercourse difficult or impossible, and very painful.

vagus cranial nerve *cranial nerve number* X. Concerned with viscera, heart and lungs, and voice production.

validity The degree to which a test measures what it claims. See *a priori validity, concurrent validity, congruent validity, construct validity, content validity, convergent validity, differential validity, discriminant validity, external validity, face validity, factorial validity, incremental validity, internal validity, item validity, nomological validity, predictive validity,* and *sampling validity. aetiological validity* is a related concept, although not part of the traditional idea of validity. See also *reliability.*

validity generalization (-isation) The degree to which a test designed for one group can be used for other, similar, groups. E.g. a selection test for a clerical assistant may be a valid assessment for bank clerks.

valium Trade name for *diazepam.*

variability The range of values which a *variable* typically assumes. For more precise measures, see *variance* et seq.

variable (1) In statistics, any item in an equation which can assume two or more values. See *continuous variable, dependent variable, discrete variable, independent variable, qualitative variable, quantitative variable,* and *constant.* (2) In experiments, strictly speaking, the same definition as (1) applies. However, more generally, the term refers to any items or persons being tested or measured or being used as tests. See *control variable, intervening variable, subject variable* and references for definition (1).

variable complexity See *factor analysis.*

variable error *chance error.*

variable inflation factor (VIF) Measure of *collinearity.* Generally, a score of 1 is taken as indicating potential collinearity, and the higher the score, the greater the chance.

variable representativeness The degree to which the *variable* used in an experiment is representative of the category from which it is drawn (e.g. whether using strawberry ice cream as a reward has the same effect as other flavours). See *subject representativeness*.

variance (1) The square of the standard deviation. (2) More generally, the term is used synonymously with *variability*. See e.g. *between-group variance, between-subject variance, population variance, random variance, sample variance, standard deviation, within-group variance,* and *within-subject variance*.

variance inflation factor *variable inflation factor.*

variant Creutzfeldt–Jakob Disease (vCJD) See *bovine spongiform encephalopathy (BSE)*.

variate *variable.*

variation ratio The proportion of the sample that does not have the *modal* value. The higher the value, the less representative the *mode* is of the sample.

varimax *See factor analysis.*

VAS *visual analogue scale.*

vascular accident *stroke.*

vascular dementia (VaD) *dementia* caused by damage to the blood vessels within the brain.

VCFS *velocardiofacial syndrome.*

vCJD *variant Creutzfeldt–Jakob Disease (vCJD).*

vegetative state A state of wakefulness though without discernible intellectual function. Typically seen in patients after a *coma* – if the patient remains in this state, then it is referred to as *persistent vegetative state (PVS)*.

VGA verbal comprehension age.

velocardiofacial syndrome See *DiGeorge syndrome.*

ventral An anatomical term denoting the front (belly) side of the body, anything near that side of the body, or the part of an organ nearest the belly side. In describing the *brain stem* and *spinal cord*, the term is used interchangeably with *posterior*.

ventricles In anatomical terms, chambers within the body. In the brain, there are several ventricles, filled with *cerebrospinal fluid*. Cerebrospinal fluid is produced by specialized blood vessels lining the surface of the ventricles. A change in size of the ventricles can indicate swelling or atrophy of the brain.

verbal alexia A profound failure of word recognition, although letter recognition remains intact.

verbal fluency measure Any measure which assesses the ease with which a participant can produce verbal information. A typical test might be to see how many words beginning with a particular letter can be produced within a time limit, or how many words can be formed out of the letters in another word (a type of *word fluency test*).

verbal skills with a heavy or sole emphasis on verbal materials.

verbal span See *span*.

verbatim record A transcript of the entire proceedings of an event, with no editing or summarizing.

verbomania *hyperphasia.*

verification time The time taken to decide on the validity of a statement or stimulus.

vertical group Group containing members of more than one social class or other hierarchical order.

vestibulocochlear cranial nerve *auditory-vestibular cranial nerve.*

vibrotactile perception The ability to detect vibration by touch.

vicarious conditioning *vicarious reinforcement.*

vicarious learning *vicarious reinforcement.*

vicarious reinforcement See *Bandura's theory of social learning.*

VIF *variable inflation factor.*

vigilance The ability to sustain attention or alertness over a (usually lengthy) period of time.

Vigotsky test *Vygotsky test.*

Vineland Adaptive Behavior Scales test battery measuring social and personal skills. The scales are primarily intended to assess children with atypical development.

Vineland Social Maturity Scale (VSMS) Measure of how capably a child can fend for him/herself. Consists of a checklist of skills (e.g. can button up coat, can use knife and fork, etc.).

visceral nervous system (VNS) *autonomic nervous system.*

viscerotonic personality See *Sheldon's personality types.*

visile *visual type.*

visual acuity Ability to focus clearly.

visual agnosia An inability to recognize by sight.

visual allaechesthesia Seeing objects in the wrong location.

visual analogue scale (VAS) Scale on which the intensity of a stimulus or opinion is represented by a position on a visual measure (typically, a straight line with extremes representing the extremes of the measure in question). E.g. the degree to which a person is *introverted* or *extraverted* might be repre-

sented by a line with ends representing 'extremely extraverted' and 'extremely introverted'. An average person will be roughly in the middle of the line, whilst a stereotypical 'shrinking violet' will be at the introverted end of the line.

visual aphasia *alexia.*

visual communication therapy Therapeutic technique employed with some patients with *aphasia.* They are taught to use visual symbols to signify basic pieces of information, requests, etc.

visual cortex *occipital lobe*-area of *cortex* responsible for visual perception.

visual evoked potential *evoked potential* created by showing a visual stimulus to the participant.

visual object agnosia A specific inability to recognize objects by sight.

visual reading error Misreading a word for one which looks similar (e.g. 'cabbage' for 'cribbage').

visual search task Task in which the participant must find a target item which is located in an array of distractor items.

visual-spatial agnosia A failure to perceive in three dimensions (i.e. the visual world is perceived as flat and two-dimensional). Compare with *visuo-spatial agnosia.*

visual type See *auditory type.*

visuo-spatial ability The ability to process all aspects of visual and spatial information. I.e., *spatial ability* coupled with an ability to judge and manipulate visual information (the visual appearance of an object in all aspects other than spatial information).

visuo-spatial agnosia A profound failure to identify spatial location. Compare with *visual—spatial agnosia.*

VMI Test *Developmental Test of Visual-Motor Integration.*

VNS *visceral nervous system.*

vocabulary test A measure of knowledge of word meanings.

vocational aptitude test Test assessing how well a participant's abilities match the demands of particular careers.

vocational evaluation The assessment of the most suitable career for an individual.

Vocational Interest Blank *Strong Vocational Interest Blank.*

vocational maturity The degree to which an individual's choice of career and related objectives is appropriate for his/her age.

Vocational Preference Inventory (VPI) Careers guidance test, which identifies 11 scales on which participants' interests pertaining to a career can be measured.

voice key Electronic switch activated by the voice. Can be used e.g. in *reaction time* experiments when conventional button-pressing is for some reason undesirable.

voice stress analyser Apparatus which gauges the degree of *stress* a person is experiencing by measuring the sound waveforms of his/her speech. A person under stress will be tense (including his/her vocal cords) and this produces a characteristic sound pattern.

voyeurism *paraphilia* in which the patient's principal sexual satisfaction is derived from watching unsuspecting people undressing, in the nude, and/or engaged in sexual activity.

VPI *Vocational Preference Inventory.*

VSMS *Vineland Social Maturity Scale.*

Vygotsky test *categorization test* in which participants must classify blocks of varying shapes sizes and colours.

W

W (1) *Kendall coefficient of concordance.* (2) *word fluency.*

Wada test Method of investigating brain hemispheric function. An anaesthetic is injected into the carotid artery serving the right or left *hemisphere.* This suppresses all activity in the hemisphere for several minutes, and the effects on behaviour can be observed.

WAIS *Wechsler Adult Intelligence Scale.*

WAIS-RNI *Wechsler Adult Intelligence Scale – Revised as a Neuropsychological Instrument.*

Wakefield Self-Assessment Depression Inventory A measure of *depression* – participants are judged to be depressed if their scores exceed a particular threshold.

Wald-Wolfowitz runs test *non-parametric* measure for groups in which some ordering of their scores in order of magnitude is possible. The test examines whether scores when ordered in this manner show large continuous 'runs' of either group's scores (i.e. scores from A and B look like e.g. AAAABBBB, rather than e.g. ABBAABABA). Lengthy runs indicate that the groups are *significantly* different.

Walker Problem Identification Checklist Checklist for teachers, assessing personality problems in their pupils.

WALMYR Assessment Scales Set of measures of aspects of state of well-being, relationships with others, etc., designed to assess the general state of a patient during treatment.

Walsh test *non-parametric* measure of differences between two samples, where both samples come from *populations* with *symmetrical distributions.*

wandering (dementia) Nebulous term describing any inappropriate walking behaviour. This can manifest itself as part of *hyperactivity*, but may also describe walking about apparently aimlessly or 'wandering off' on a walk for no apparently obvious reason (see also *sundown syndrome*).

Ward Atmosphere Scale (WAS) Measure of the general environment (social and physical) of a hospital ward or other therapeutic location.

WAS *Ward Atmosphere Scale.*

watchkeeping task A measure of *vigilance* – the participant must observe a display, and indicate when there is any change (which occurs rarely, hence testing vigilance).

water jar problem Test of intelligence/mathematical ability, in which, given a set of containers of known volumes, the participant must decide how they can measure a specified quantity. E.g. 'there are four jars which can hold 2, 2000, 40 and 20 litres – how can exactly 6 litres be measured?'.

Watts Vernon (WV) Test Reading test – comprises 35 *sentence completion* questions.

waxy flexibility See *catatonic state.*

WCST *Wisconsin Card Sorting Task.*

WDEP See *reality therapy.*

Weber's law The smallest change in intensity which will be noticed, divided by the original intensity of the stimulus, equals a constant. Symbolically represented as $AI/I = K$. It follows from this that the more intense the initial stimulus, the bigger the change needed to pass a *threshold*. Generally the law holds up for all but extreme intensities of stimulation.

Wechsler Adult Intelligence Scale (WAIS) An adult intelligence *test battery*

covering all commonly assessed areas of intelligence. The tests can be subdivided into those which test verbal skills, and those which have no strong verbal element (the *Performance scales*). See *WISC.*

Wechsler Adult Intelligence Scale – Revised as a Neuropsychological Instrument (WAIS-RNI) Adaptation of the *WAIS* with revised and new tests, designed for assessment of patients with compromised intellectual/linguistic abilities.

Wechsler-Bellevue Scale Early form of *Wechsler Adult Intelligence Scale.*

Wechsler Individual Achievement Test (WIAT) Manual giving *standardized* procedure for combining scores on *WOLD*, *WOND* and *WORD* tests to form a composite measure of individual academic achievement. A truncated and faster to administer version – *WIAT-Quicktest* – is also available.

Wechsler Intelligence Scale for Children (WISC) The *WAIS* adapted for older children (7–16 years). The tests can be subdivided into those which test verbal skills, and those which have no strong verbal element (the *Performance scales*). See *Bannatyne-WISC categories* and *Wechsler Preschool* and *Primary Scale of Intelligence.*

Wechsler Memory Scale (WMS) Memory *test battery* for adults.

Wechsler Objective Language Dimensions (WOLD) *test battery* of linguistic skills (listening comprehension, written and oral expression) for children aged 6 years–16 years 11 months.

Wechsler Objective Numerical Dimensions (WOND) *test battery* of numerical skills (mathematics reasoning and basic arithmetic skills) for children aged 6 years–16 years 11 months.

Wechsler Objective Reading Dimensions (WORD) Reading (word recognition and prose comprehension) and spelling *test battery* for children aged 6–16 years. Cross-linked with *WISC, WPPSI* and *WAIS*.

Wechsler Preschool and Primary Scale of Intelligence (WPPSI) Intelligence *test battery* for young children (3–7 years). See *Wechsler Intelligence Scale for Children*.

Wechsler test suffixes Often a Wechsler test (see e.g. preceding entries) carries a suffix, denoting the particular form or edition. A common suffix is 'R', denoting a 'revised' version (though this does not necessarily mean it is the most recent revised version). A number (in Roman numerals) denotes the edition. A suffix of initials denotes the country for which the test is *standardized* (e.g. 'UK' denotes United Kingdom). At the time of writing, the most current versions (for the UK) are: *WAIS*: WAIS-R (1986); *WAIS-RNL:* WAIS-RNI (1991); *WISC*: WISC-III (1992); *WMS*: WMS-R (1987); *WOLD*: WOLD (1995); *WOND*: WOND (1995); *WIAT*: WIAT (1995); *WORD*: WORD (1993).

weighted form A form (typically, a job application form) in which certain responses are given greater weight or prominence than others in making a decision about the respondent.

weighting Any method of adjusting scores to express their relative importance. This is done for numerous reasons. The most often encountered is in *test batteries*. Suppose that one is measuring ability to become a concert pianist. A number of measures might be taken – ability to play the right notes, speed of playing, quality of tone, knowledge of musical theory, dress sense, etc. Whilst all the measures will play some part, some are arguably more important than others. Suppose that

each measure is out of 10 – a score of 10 on dress sense is unlikely to mean as much as a score of 10 for accuracy of playing. Accordingly, the different measures might be weighted – in deriving an overall score, accuracy of playing might be weighted so that it has a greater role in determining the final mark (e.g. the accuracy mark might be multiplied by five).

Weinstein maps A set of tests of visuo-spatial ability. The participant is presented with nine dots drawn on the floor in a 3x3 square pattern. S/he is given a 'map' showing a route to be walked around the dots (the map cannot be turned to keep in the same orientation as the floor pattern). A variety of such routes (of increasing complexity) has to be taken.

Werner syndrome An illness akin to *progeria* in its effects, but whose onset is in the late teens, rather than at birth. Patients display signs of ageing at a faster rate than normal, and usually die in their forties.

Wernicke–Korsakoff syndrome See *Korsakoff syndrome*.

Wernicke's aphasia *aphasia* characterized by a failure to comprehend language, although speech may be relatively unimpaired. Contrast with *Broca's aphasia*.

Wernicke's area Area of *temporal lobe* (in most people, the left lobe) controlling various aspects of speech reception.

Wernicke's dementia *dementia* caused by vitamin deficiency (particularly Vitamin B1), and found most often in long-term alcoholics. Often there is an associated motor impairment, and drowsiness. Note that some authorities do not classify Wernicke's dementia as a dementia, preferring to refer to it as *Wernicke's disease* or *Wernicke's encephalopathy*. See *Korsakoff syndrome*.

Wernicke's disease *Wernicke's dementia.*

Wernicke's encephalopathy *Wernicke's dementia.*

WES *Work Environment Scale.*

Western Aphasia Battery *test battery* for assessing the type of *aphasia* a patient is suffering from.

Western Personnel Test (WPT) Brief and quickly-administered IQ test for basic screening of intelligence levels of personnel/job applicants.

white matter See *grey matter.*

WHO classification of diseases (ICD) The World Health Organisation's classification of diseases was first published in 1948 (full title: International Statistical Classification of Diseases, Injuries and Causes of Death – hence its initials). Although the sections of the early editions pertaining to mental illness were at odds with the *Diagnostic and Statistical Manual,* there is now a considerable degree of consensus between the two. The acronym 'ICD' is often followed by a number denoting the edition (i.e. ICD-1, ICD-2, etc.). ICD-10 was published in 1993.

WIAT *Wechsler Individual Achievement Test.*

WIAT-Quicktest See *Wechsler Individual Achievement Test.*

Wide Range Achievement Test (WRAT) *test battery* assessing basic reading, maths, and spelling skills.

Wide-span Reading Test Reading test for participants aged 7–15 years. Type of *cloze procedure* test – the required word is presented in the sentence preceding the test sentence.

widespread biserial correlation coefficient (r^wbis) See *point biserial correlation coefficient.*

Wilcoxin matched pairs signed ranks test *non-parametric* test of two *matched* groups' differences on the same *dependent variable.* The test analyses the differences between the scores of paired members of the groups, which are ranked by size. The test is the non-parametric equivalent of the *paired t test.*

wilderness experience Therapeutic method (often a *group therapy*) whereby the patients are placed in the countryside with suitably bucolic accommodation (e.g. tents, log cabins, etc.) and given a series of physical tasks. Those who agree with Sidney Smith's famous dictum that the countryside is 'a kind of healthy grave' may be less convinced of the method's efficacy than others.

Wilk's A *Wilk's lambda.*

Wilk's lambda Test of *significance* of overall group difference in a *multivariate analysis of variance.*

will therapy Therapeutic technique based on the idea that the patient must establish the will to be truly independent (and not symbolically tied to the mother).

Williams syndrome Genetic disorder that appears very rarely and spontaneously, caused by loss of part of chromosome 7. The symptoms include stunted growth, an 'elfin' like face, dental problems, cardiovascular problems, extreme sociability, and intellectual dysfunction. The symptoms possessed by individual patients vary widely.

Williams–Beuren syndrome *Williams syndrome.*

winter depression *seasonal affective disorder.*

WISC *Wechsler Intelligence Scale for Children.*

Wisconsin Card Sorting Task (WCST) Measure of hypothesis formation and the ability to reject or not persevere with an invalid one. Participants must discover the correct rule for matching up cards of differing patterns and colours (e.g. a yellow card must always be matched with a red card, etc.). Once they have discovered the correct rule, the experimenter changes the rule, and how quickly the participant stops using the old rule and searches for the new one is measured, as well as how quickly s/he solves the new problem. The test is used with normal participants and patients of all ages. However, the test was primarily designed to assess patients with brain damage (particularly to the *frontal lobes*).

wisdom Somewhat nebulous concept, with several separate though related definitions, depending upon the researcher in question. Most agree in essence that it refers to an ability to judge and resolve real-life problems which require a balance of logical and pragmatic factors, tempered by experience. However, within this broad remit, individual authors have used the term loosely, ranging from a synonym of *crystallized intelligence* to psychoanalytic theories.

withdrawal (1) Process of ceasing to use a drug or performing an activity to which the patient was *addicted*. Symptoms vary according to the nature of the addiction, but are always unpleasant. The best documented are those from the withdrawal of alcohol. In heavy abusers, *delirium tremens* (the *DTs*) – threatening *hallucinations*, and a feeling of terror – may be experienced. (2) Deliberately removing oneself from societal pressures. (3) Unconsciously becoming more 'distant' from people and society (can be symptomatic of mental illness).

within-group variance The degree to which members of the same group differ in their scores. See *between-group variance* and *within-subject variance*.

within groups ANOVA *analysis of variance* in which all measures are *within groups measures*, and only one group of participants is tested.

within groups measure See *analysis of variance*.

within-subject variance The degree to which an individual's scores differ between testing trials. See *between-subject variance* and *within-group variance*.

within-subjects design Experimental design in which each participant receives all treatments. This contrasts with a *between-subjects design*, in which each treatment is given to a different group of subjects.

within subjects measure *within groups measure*.

witzelsucht A puerile sense of humour and lack of fitting decorum. Symptom of certain types of mental illness and brain damage.

WMS *Wechsler Memory Scale*.

WOLD *Wechsler Objective Language Dimensions*.

WOND *Wechsler Objective Numerical Dimensions*.

Wonderlic Comprehensive Personality Profile (CPP) Measure of a person's skills and personality used to assess suitability for a variety of occupations.

Wonderlic Personnel Test A test of intellectual ability, primarily designed for *personnel screening*.

Woodcock-Johnson Psycho-Educational Battery *test battery* assessing intellectual skills in children. The battery broadly assesses intelligence, achievement, and general interests.

WORD *Wechsler Objective Reading Dimensions*.

word building test *word fluency test.*

word fluency (W) Efficiency with which words can be produced. See *word fluency test.*

word fluency test Any *verbal fluency measure* which requires participants to produce words. Often there are additional requirements – e.g. to produce words beginning with a certain sound, produce words formed out of the letters within a given word, usually against a time limit.

word fragment completion task A test of verbal ability in which the participant must identify a word from some of its component letters (e.g. 'f.gh..n').

Word Recognition Test *Carver Word Recognition Test.*

word salad Jumbled word and phrase order. Found in the speech of many *schizophrenics.*

Word Search Reading test using the *cloze procedure.* The test is in two forms – 1 (for ages 7–10 years) and 2 (for ages 9–12 years).

Work Environment Scale (WES) Measure of the general environment (social and physical) of a workplace.

work methods The actions required to perform a task or job.

Work Profiling System (WPS) A *job analysis* measure.

work sample test Assessment procedure for prospective employees, who are required to perform a sample of the work which they will be required to perform if they get the job.

work therapy *occupational therapy.*

workaholism *Type A personality.*

working space *workspace envelope.*

workspace envelope The physical space used by a worker in performing his/her job.

worried well A group of participants, who, whilst perfectly healthy, are still convinced that they must be ill. The term has been recently used to describe people who are convinced that they must have developed AIDS, simply because they belong to a higher risk group.

WPPSI *Wechsler Preschool and Primary Scale of Intelligence.*

WPS *Work Profiling System.*

WPT *Western Personnel Test.*

WRAT *Wide Range Achievement Test.*

wug test Test assessing children's knowledge of morphology (word structure). Named after an item on the test. The child sees a picture of an imaginary animal called a 'wug'. S/he is then shown a picture of two of these animals and is asked what they are called. A correct answer ('wugs') indicates that the child understands the principle of how to alter the structure of words, since s/he had never encountered the word 'wug' before, and thus cannot simply be answering from memory.

WV Test *Watts Vernon (WV) Test.*

X

X axis (abscissa) The horizontal line of a graph. The vertical line is called the *Y axis.*

xenophobia A *phobia* of strangers and/or foreigners (not hatred of the latter, as in the lay sense of the word).

X-linked disorder Any genetic disorder caused by a defective X chromosome. When a damaged X chromosome is paired with an intact X chromosome, then the intact chromosome is dominant and any potentially damaging actions of the damaged chromosome cannot be expressed. But when a damaged X chromosome is paired with a Y chromosome, then the X chromosome becomes dominant, thus allowing the atypical genes on the damaged chromosome to express themselves. Because women have two X chromosomes and men one X and one Y chromosome, X-linked disorders can be carried by women but usually only show themselves in some of their male offspring. Examples of X-linked disorder include haemophilia, *fragile X syndrome* and *Turner's syndrome*.

XYY syndrome In males, possession of an extra Y chromosome. Can result in *mental retardation* and/or an unusually high level of aggression.

Y

Y axis (ordinate) See *X axis*.

Yale-Brown Obsessive-Compulsive Scale Measure of the degree of *obsessive-compulsive* behaviour exhibited by a patient.

Yate's correction See *chi squared test*.

YAVIS patient Young, attractive, verbal, intelligent, and successful patient (i.e. an ideal participant for many psychotherapists). One of many examples of practitioners' acronyms, of varying degrees of politeness (e.g. 'FUR' – 'found under rock').

Yngve depth An analytical technique which gives a 'score' for the syntactic complexity of a sentence or phrase.

Yudin method See *Satz-Mogel method*.

Z

z score A form of *standard score*, in which the *standard deviation* assumes a nominal value of 1. E.g., if the standard deviation was 2, and the difference between the mean and the score was 2, then the z score would be 1. Similarly, if the difference had been 1, then the z score would have been 0.5. The z score gives a quick 'ready reckoner' of how an individual's score compares with the rest of the *population*.

z test *Fisher's z test*.

Zener cards Set of cards used in *extrasensory perception* studies, beloved of films of the paranormal (e.g. opening scene of 'Ghostbusters'). Each card carries a simple pattern of a star, square, cross, circle or wavy lines. One person looks at the card and the other person attempts to 'read his/her mind' to judge the identity of the card.

zero order correlation *correlation* in which possible effects of a *partial correlation* have not been accounted for.

zero sum game See *non-zero sum game*.

zoophilia Disorder in which the principal form of sexual gratification is with a non-human animal. See *bestiality*.

zoophobia A *phobia* of animals.

Zung SDS *Zung Self-Rating Depression Scale*.

Zung Self-Rating Depression Scale (Zung SDS) Measure of the level of *depression* experienced by a patient. Patients are required to indicate the extent to which various descriptions of depressed behaviour apply to them.